Amnesty for Crimes against Humanity under International Law

Amnesty for Crimes against Humanity under International Law

By

Faustin Z. Ntoubandi

LEIDEN • BOSTON
2007

This book is printed on acid-free paper.

A Cataloging-in-Publication record for this book is available from the Library of Congress.

ISBN 978 90 04 16231 0

PRINTED IN THE NETHERLANDS

CONTENTS

CHAPTER 1
GENERAL INTRODUCTION

CHAPTER 2
THE CONCEPT OF AMNESTY

CHAPTER 3
CRIMES AGAINST HUMANITY IN INTERNATIONAL LAW

CHAPTER 4
INDIVIDUAL CRIMINAL LIABILITY FOR CRIMES
AGAINST HUMANITY

CHAPTER 5
STATES OBLIGATIONS IN RESPECT OF CRIMES
AGAINST HUMANITY

CHAPTER 6
AMNESTY LAW IN SOUTH AFRICA: ASSERTION OF AN AMNESTY EXCEPTION TO THE GENERAL PROHIBITION OF CRIMES AGAINST HUMANITY

CHAPTER 7
INTERNATIONAL LAW AND THE REJECTION OF
THE AMNESTY EXCEPTION ARGUMENT

CHAPTER 8
GENERAL CONCLUDING ASSESSMENT AND SUGGESTIONS

PREFACE

In this book I have attempted to address the fundamental question of amnesty for certain types of conduct, which would otherwise amount to criminal offences under contemporary international law. This issue, as so many examples and scholarly writings of recent origin have demonstrated, still remains a thorny one from the perspective of public international law. In effect, whereas positive international law and *opinio juris* call for the criminal prosecution of serious crimes, States' practice on the matter tends to favour practical political solutions.

As many recent experiences have shown (e.g., Argentina, El Salvador, South Africa, Cambodia, etc.), almost all emerging democracies which have replaced dictatorial regimes in transitional societies have either manifested their unwillingness to deal with past criminal offences of the old political establishment, or have resorted to amnesty instead of criminal prosecution, as the best response to such offences. In the latter case, amnesties have been granted for all 'political crimes' the definition of which, in most cases, has included offences for which international law mandates criminal prosecution. The effects of such amnesty measures on the liability of the alleged perpetrators on the one hand, and on the rights of the victims or their relatives to have their case heard by a court of law on the other hand, have raised great concern about their legal validity. This question is even more complex from the perspective of international law whose stance on amnesty remains ambiguous. For example, whereas Article 6 (5) of Additional Protocol II of 1977 encourages grants of amnesty (without specifying the nature of the crimes concerned) at the end of non-international armed conflicts, the Rome Statute of 1998 insists on criminal prosecution for the core crimes under international law (without explicitly rejecting amnesty for the same crimes). This double and diverging requirement does nothing more than to deepen the confusion already existing as to the legal status of amnesty in international law.

This book attempts, therefore, through a coherent and theoretical analysis of the relatively few existing national and international legal documents as well as State practice, to clarify the legal status of amnesty with a particular focus on crimes against humanity. In so doing, it endeavours to find a compromise between the legal duty to prosecute core crimes under international law and national practical political considerations which could stand on the way of such a duty. I conclude the book by suggesting a possible legal framework within which any political decision to grant a valid amnesty has to be accommodated.

National and international case law and legal documents referred to throughout the book are those I consider relevant for the matter under discussion. Their choice was motivated only by the need to support the arguments developed, and the position adopted, in this book.

It is hoped that this volume will serve as a general guiding tool for practitioners, politicians, students and advanced scholars who are active in the field of international criminal law and transitional justice.

Faustin Z. Ntoubandi
Assistant Professor of International Law,
Giessen

ABBREVIATIONS

ACHPR	African Charter on Human and Peoples' Rights
ACHR	American Convention on Human Rights
ANC	African National Congress
AZAPO	Azanian Peoples Organisation
CODESA	Convention for a Democratic South Africa
ECHR	European Convention for the Protection of Human Rights and Fundamental Freedoms
ICC	International Criminal Court
ICCPR	International Covenant on Civil and Political Rights
ICJ	International Court of Justice
ICRC	International Committee of the Red Cross
ICTR	International Criminal Tribunal for Rwanda
ICTY	International Criminal Tribunal for the Former Yugoslavia
IFP	Inkhata Freedom Party
ILC	International Law Commission
IMT	International Military Tribunal
NP	National Party
SCSL	Special Court for Sierra Leone
SS	Schutzstaffel
UDHR	Universal Declaration of Human Rights
VCLT	Vienna Convention on the Law of Treaties

GENERAL INTRODUCTION

The common sense of mankind demands that law shall not stop with the punishment of petty crimes by little people. It must also reach men who possess themselves of great power and make deliberate and concerted use of it to set in motion evils, which leave no home in the world untouched.

Justice Robert H. Jackson[1]

This sharing of the international community's basic moral and legal position on apartheid [the recognition of apartheid as a crime against humanity] *should not be understood as a call for international criminal prosecution of those who formulated and implemented apartheid policies. Indeed, such a course would militate against the very principles on which this commission was established.*

The South African Truth and Reconciliation Commission[2]

Introduction

In the last three decades many nations in the world have witnessed a long and painful shift from dictatorial and tyrannical regimes to more democratic systems of government. This wave of change has hit both post-conflict and conflict-ridden societies as well as mature democracies. Countries such as Germany, Greece, Hungary, the former Soviet Republics, Yugoslavia, Cambodia, Thailand, South Korea,

---

1 United States Chief Prosecutor during the Nuremberg Trials in his opening statement before the Nuremberg Tribunal, 1945.
2 The South African Truth Commission rejecting criminal prosecution in favour of amnesty, in S de Villiers *Truth and Reconciliation Commission of South Africa Report* vol. 1 (1998) at 94 para. 2.

Faustin Z. Ntoubandi, Amnesty for Crimes against Humanity under International Law, pp. 1–8.
© 2007, *Koninklijke Brill NV. Printed in The Netherlands.*

Argentina, Chile, El Salvador, Guatemala, Honduras, Uruguay, Haiti, South Africa, Sierra Leone and Liberia[3] have undergone/are undergoing a process of political change in which they all had/have to deal with certain fundamental issues, proper to post-traumatic transitional societies. In fact, the newly elected government of each of these countries had/have to decide on the most appropriate way to deal with past atrocities and gross human rights violations while, at the same time, negotiating a peaceful transition from authoritarian regime to democratic rule.

In most cases, they had to face the dilemma of transitional justice, that is: either to prosecute the old political establishment and confront the danger of derailing the peace and reconciliation process, or to grant them amnesty and confront both the anger of the victims of past atrocities and other gross human rights violations, and the criticisms of the international community. In some cases, criminal prosecutions have been chosen as the most appropriate way of breaking with the past,[4] whereas in others, non-prosecutorial mechanisms have been adopted as the best way to address past atrocities. As a result of the latter choice, various nations have set up truth commissions whose functions were, among others, to investigate the circumstances of the commission of past crimes and, eventually, to grant amnesty to the perpetrators thereof.[5] However, the application of the amnesty provisions did not only cover domestic crimes, but they also extended to certain categories of crimes for which international law mandates criminal prosecution. Such categories of crimes, which include crimes against peace, war crimes, genocide, torture, and crimes against humanity are characterised as the most serious crimes of international concern.[6] Therefore, the contradiction between the imperative of criminal prosecution required for these offences and the foreseeable limitating effects of amnesty in respect of such prosecutions has sometimes led to question the international legal validity of such amnesties.

As far as the offence of crimes against humanity is concerned, various qualifications have been developed to describe its seriousness. The Nuremberg Charter of 1945 spoke of 'inhumane acts'[7] whereas Justice Jackson, the Chief Prosecutor for the United States of America during the Nuremberg Trials qualified inhumane acts as those that pass "in magnitude or savagery any limits of what is tolerable by modern civilisations", and which have 'repercussions reaching across international

---

3 For more details on the most significant transition processes see in general A Schlunck *Amnesty versus Accountability: Third Party Intervention Dealing with Gross Human Rights Violations* (2000); N.J. Kritz (ed.), *Transitional Justice: How Emerging Democracies Reckon with Former Regimes* Part III (1995).

4 In Greece for example.

5 Chile, Argentina, El Salvador and South Africa for example, have made use of this mechanism.

6 See Preamble and Article 1 of the Rome Statute for an International Criminal Court, UN Doc A/CONF. 183/9, 17 July 1998 (hereinafter Rome Statute).

7 Article 6 (c).

frontiers.'[8] Moreover, Jankelevitch, then Professor of moral philosophy at La Sorbonne, France, qualified crimes against humanity as 'imprescriptible', "something nameless and terrifying [...] something no human word can describe".[9] For Mansfield, acts of crimes against humanity are "so intrinsically evil that they represent a crime to the human race, to humanity as a whole".[10]

In addition, a multitude of international law instruments defining crimes against humanity prescribe criminal liability for the perpetrators thereof. These include the Charter of the International Military Tribunal for the Trial of the Major War Criminals of the European Axis of 1945,[11] the Statute of the International Criminal Tribunal for Rwanda,[12] the 1996 Draft Code of Crimes against the Peace and Security of Mankind,[13] and the Rome Statute for the International Criminal Court.[14] More specifically, the international Convention on the Suppression and Punishment of the Crime of Apartheid[15] imposes international criminal responsibility on apartheid perpetrators irrespective of the country in which the crime was committed,[16] whereas the Convention on the Non-applicability of Statutory Limitations to War Crimes and Crimes against Humanity[17] outlaws the application of any form of statutory limitations to war crimes and to crimes against humanity.[18] Moreover, certain international law instruments have been interpreted as imposing duties on States to either, prosecute and punish the perpetrators of the most serious criminal offences, or to extradite them to the requesting States or surrender them to a competent international court. These include, the 1948 Convention on the Prevention and Suppression of the

---

8 See E. Schwelb "Crimes against humanity" 23 *British Yearbook of International Law* (1946) at 195.

9 See "L'imprescriptible" *La Revue Administrative* No. 103 (January-February 1965) at 37.

10 See "Crimes against humanity: reflections on the Fiftieth Anniversary of Nuremberg and a forgotten legacy" 64 *Nordic Journal of International Law* (1995) at 293.

11 Signed on August 8 1945 by the Allied Powers composed of the Governments of France, Great Britain, the United States of America and the Soviet Union, for the purpose of punishing German officials who had committed atrocities during World War II (hereinafter, Nuremberg Charter or the IMT Charter), see especially Articles 6, 7 and 8.

12 Established in 1994 by Security Council Resolution 955, for the Prosecution of Persons Responsible for Genocide and Other Serious Violations of International Humanitarian Law Committed in the Territory of Rwanda and Neighbouring States Between 1 January and 31 December 1994; Statute adopted by Resolution S/RES/935 (1994) (hereinafter, the ICTR Statute), see particularly Article 3.

13 Adopted by the International Law Commission at its 51st Session, UN Doc A/51/10 (1996) (hereinafter, Draft Code of Crimes), Article 18.

14 See n. 6, Articles 7 and 25; hereinafter the ICC Statute or the Rome Statute.

15 Adopted on 30 November 1973 by UNGA Res. 3068 (XXVIII), UN GAOR, 28th Session, Supp. No. 30, UN Doc A/9030 (1974) (hereinafter, Apartheid Convention).

16 Article III.

17 Adopted on 26 November 1968 by UNGA Res. 2391 (XXIII), UN Doc A/RES/2391 (XXIII) of 9 December 1968.

18 Article 1.

Crime of Genocide,[19] which obligates State Parties to either prosecute and punish individual perpetrators of the crime of genocide, or to extradite them;[20] the Rome Statute, which entrusts State Parties with the primary duty to either prosecute and punish authors of genocide, crimes against humanity, war crimes, and the crime of aggression, or to surrender them to the International Criminal Court or extradite them to the State, which has jurisdiction over the case.[21]

Following the international prohibition of crimes against humanity, almost all national criminal law systems in the world contain provisions that criminalize acts constitutive of this offence; such acts include murder, torture, enslavement, persecution, rape and forced labour. Countries such as Israel and France[22] have introduced in their respective criminal law system the international law qualification of crimes against humanity as it evolved since Nuremberg.

The prohibition of crimes against humanity contained in the foregoing documents has sometimes been interpreted either as forming the basis for universal jurisdiction,[23] or as obligating States to prosecute their breach.[24] It is therefore the legal duty of sovereign States under international law to prosecute and punish offenders of such crimes.

On the other hand, amnesty is an act of clemency granted to persons who have committed a crime or a delict, in order to forgive them for their deeds. The effects of amnesty are, among others, to discharge the perpetrator from personal liability and to discontinue all proceedings in relation to the crime or delict allegedly committed. Therefore, amnesty has the potential to insulate a criminal act from the reach of law, thus resulting in shielding notorious criminals from criminal prosecution.

---

19 Adopted on 9 December 1948, GA Res. 260 A (II), 78 UNTS 277 (hereinafter, Genocide Convention).
20 See Articles I, IV, V, VI and VII respectively.
21 See Articles 1, 5, 89 and 90 respectively.
22 See the Israeli Nazi and Nazi Collaborators Act of 1950 and the French *Nouveau Code Pénal* of 1992, Articles 212–1 respectively.
23 See especially *The Attorney-General of the Government of Israel v. Eichmann* in 36 *International Law Reports* (1962) at 5; see also the Belgian laws of 16 June 1993 and 19 February 1999 recognising the jurisdiction of the Belgian courts over serious violations of international humanitarian law irrespective of the place of their commission, and irrespective of the nationality of the alleged perpetrator thereof.
24 See particularly, M.C. Bassiouni "Searching for peace and achieving justice" 59 *Law and Contemporary Problems* 9 (1996) at 17; N. Roht-Arriaza, Non-treaty sources of the obligation to investigate and prosecute, in N. Roht-Arriaza (ed.), 39 *Impunity and Human Rights in International Law and Practice* (1995) at 50–56; C. Edelenbos "Human Rights violations: a duty to prosecute?" 7 *Leiden Journal of International Law* 14 (1994) at 15.

The Setting of this Book

Granting amnesty is not a novel practice in international law. Early forms of modern amnesty, which were usually granted in situations of international armed conflicts, can be traced as far back as to the 1648 Treaty of Westphalia that ended the Thirty-Year War in Europe.[25] In this treaty, the parties granted general and unconditional amnesty to all persons who had committed criminal offences before and during the war. However, the practice of granting amnesties to perpetrators of crimes against humanity started soon after World War I, during which the term 'crimes against humanity' was first coined.[26] Soon after this war, the Treaty of Lausanne was signed in 1923 between the Allied Powers and Turkey, which granted amnesty to all Turk nationals responsible for the massacres of Armenians in 1915.[27]

Prosecution was also avoided after the Algerian war when, pursuant to the Evian Agreement of 18 March, 1962, France and Algeria decided not to prosecute persons who had committed grave violations of human rights during the war.[28]

Similarly, the Bangladesh war ended in 1971 with India and Bangladesh consenting not to prosecute Pakistanis charged with genocide and crimes against humanity, in exchange for political recognition of Bangladesh by Pakistan.[29]

State practice to grant amnesty to notorious criminals as a means of ending war between them would later be extended to cover internal conflicts such as civil war, insurrectional war and other domestic political disturbances. This was facilitated by the adoption in 1977 of Additional Protocol II to the Geneva Conventions of 12 August, 1949, and Relating to the Protection of Victims of Non-International Armed Conflicts, which encourages grants of amnesty at the end of hostilities.[30] However, the application of the amnesty provision of Additional Protocol II would later become problematic in that it does not indicate the nature of the acts for which amnesty shall be granted, nor does it specify the categories of persons who may be entitled to amnesty.

Nevertheless, many countries which have recently passed amnesty legislation as part of their political settlement to break away from past human rights abuses have heavily relied on Article 6 (5) of Additional Protocol II as an international legal basis for the recognition of their amnesty laws and decrees. However, the nature or seriousness of the crimes involved as well as the compelling nature of certain international law instruments criminalizing certain conduct have rarely been taken as a yardstick in determining the legality of amnesty decisions. This omission

---

25 A. Schlunck, n. 3 at 25.
26 G.J. Bass *Stay the Hands of Vengeance: The Politics of War Crimes Tribunals* (2000) at 116.
27 E. Schwelb, n. 8 at 182.
28 See Title I, clause k of the Accord, available at www.el-mouradia.dz/français/algerie/ histoire/accord%20evian.htm.
29 M.C. Bassiouni *Crimes against Humanity in International Criminal Law* (1992) at 228–230.
30 Article 6 (5).

has led to question the lawfulness of such amnesties under international law, and specifically, under Additional Protocol II. Moreover, in many cases, amnesty has been granted in violation of States' domestic laws requiring the punishment of the crimes involved. The lawfulness of amnesties in respect of serious human rights violations has been mostly challenged before domestic courts, both on domestic law and on international law grounds.[31] With respect to the latter grounds, the Salvadoran amnesty laws of 1992 and 1993 were declared invalid because they violated El Salvador's international obligations in many respects. Among the obligations disregarded were the Salvadoran obligations under Article 1 of the American Convention on Human Rights (ACHR) that requires that a State Party prosecute and punish human rights offenders. The Inter-American Commission on Human Rights found in this respect that the Salvadoran amnesty law was illegal in that it violated the Convention in part "because it applies to crimes against humanity."[32] Similarly, the South African amnesty law was challenged on the grounds, among others, that it disregarded international instruments calling for the application of international criminal liability on gross human rights offenders.[33] The claim was based on a provision of the South African amnesty law called the Promotion of National Unity and Reconciliation Act,[34] which stipulates that:

> No person who has been granted amnesty in respect of an act or omission shall be criminally or civilly liable in respect of such act or omission and no body or organisation or the State shall be liable, and no person shall be vicariously liable for any such act or omission.[35]

The question that comes to mind in respect of the South African amnesty provision is whether it has any legal effect as far as international law is concerned. This question is important in that most of the acts for which amnesty was granted were committed as part of the enforcement of the policy of apartheid, which is a crime against humanity under international law. Yet, dealing with apartheid as a crime against humanity has never been part of the amnesty agenda in South Africa. In these circumstances, one may wonder what credit international and foreign forums should give to such an amnesty.

The fundamental issue here is that the dichotomy between domestic amnesties the effect of which is to prevent prosecution of perpetrators of gross human rights violations, and international law which requires the prosecution and punishment of such perpetrators points to one fundamental question, which is the main issue discussed in this book: can such amnesties be legally valid and acceptable in respect

---

31 See e.g. *Azanian Peoples Organisation and Others (AZAPO) v. President of the Republic of South Africa*, 1996 (8) BCLR 1015 (CC); 1996 (4) SA 671 (CC) at paras 683–685.

32 See Report of the Inter-American Commission on Human Rights on the Situation of Human Rights in El Salvador, para. 77, quoted by D Cassel "Lessons from the Americas: guidelines for international responses to amnesties for atrocities" 59 *Law and Contemporary Problems* 4 (1996) at 214.

33 See *AZAPO*, n. 31.

34 Act 34 of 1995.

35 Chapter 4, Section 21 paragraph 7 (a) of the Act.

of a core crime under international law, namely, crimes against humanity? Is there a possibility to make grants of amnesty less controversial and more acceptable both in domestic, foreign and international forums?

This volume seeks therefore to provide a comprehensive answer to the foregoing questions, with the view of suggesting a model approach to amnesty that will strengthen its legal status under international law. It will be demonstrated that the customary nature of crimes against humanity does not facilitate a clear determination of the nature of States obligations in respect thereof; and that this legal vacuum has played in favour of States in granting amnesty to criminals against humanity. It will then be argued that amnesty for such crimes is, in general, in contradiction with the Nuremberg spirit behind the prohibition against the most serious crimes of international concern, and therefore, legally invalid under international law.

The significance of this book is at least threefold. First, it may provide national bodies with guidelines in granting legally valid and acceptable amnesties; and may provide international institutions with a better approach in suppressing grants of amnesties in respect of serious human rights offences. Second, the fact that potential perpetrators know that the amnesty they have received can still be invalidated or ignored by an international or a foreign court, or even by a newly elected national government, may have a diminishing effect on large-scale human rights violations. Finally, this book is addressed to academics, students, legal practitioners, political scientists, politicians, and all those who are concerned with accountability for gross human rights violations.

Scope and Limits of this Book

In order to achieve the objectives of this book, chapters two and three will provide a general background to the subject by defining the concept of amnesty and that of crimes against humanity as a core crime under international law. In this respect, chapter two will examine, among others, the origin, meaning, evolution, object and consequences of amnesty, whereas chapter three will define crimes against humanity in terms of their historical legal foundations, their content, their gravity and the legal obligations attached to them. It will be argued at this point that such crimes are of the kind that offends the conscience of mankind and constitutes a threat to international peace and security. As a consequence, international law imposes legal obligations on individuals as well as on States to refrain from committing such crimes.

Under chapter four, the nature of individual obligations in respect of crimes against humanity will be discussed. In this regard, the principle of individual criminal responsibility will be elaborated as the expression of the individual duty in respect of this offence. It will be demonstrated that the principles of criminal responsibility do no admit amnesty as a ground for excluding personal criminal liability for serious international crimes, including crimes against humanity.

In chapter five, an attempt will be made to identify the nature of States' duties as regards the prosecution of serious crimes and to determine the effect of amnesty on such duties. Here, it will be determined whether States' legal duties to prosecute and punish the perpetrators of these crimes are mandatory or only permissive under international law. The determination of such duties will be made with reference, on the one hand, to treaties which have a bearing on crimes against humanity such as the 1949 Geneva Conventions, the 1948 Genocide Convention, the 1984 Torture Convention and the 1998 Rome Statute; and to general human rights conventions and customary international law, on the other hand.

Chapter six will critically address the South African amnesty mechanisms as an example of the application of the concept of amnesty as enunciated in chapter two to offences that may otherwise be qualified as crimes against humanity. This case study will highlight the difficulties encountered by the South African courts in interpreting an amnesty law in conformity with international law duties attached to crimes against humanity.

The crux of this volume is embodied in Chapter seven, which will seek to establish the legal status of amnesty with regard to crimes against humanity. In this chapter, various principles and provisions of international law will be relied upon to demonstrate that amnesties granted to offenders of crimes against humanity are fundamentally illegal under international law. This argument will be developed by presenting crimes against humanity as part of *delicti jus gentium* and as a *jus cogens* offence. It will then be argued that the values underlying the prohibition of these crimes, as well as other serious crimes under international law, are of such a fundamental importance that no exceptional circumstance can justify their commission. Recent developments in the practice of amnesty before the ICTY and domestic forums, as well as in the practice of the United Nations as regards the establishment of the Special Court for Sierra Leone (SCSL), will be relied upon to ultimately invalidate amnesty for crimes against humanity under international law.

Finally, chapter eight will close this book with a summary of the major parts thereof, followed by a brief exposition of the main arguments developed therein. A few suggestions intended to make grants of amnesty less controversial under international law will be made in conclusion of this volume.

THE CONCEPT OF AMNESTY

Meaning, Forms and Purpose of Amnesty

Meaning and Forms

Meaning

The word amnesty is derived from the Greek word *amnestia* or *amnesis*, which means forgetfulness, oblivion,[1] or to lose memory. It is an act of sovereign power designed to apply the principle of *tabula rasa* to past offences, usually committed against the State, in order to end proceedings already initiated or that are to be initiated, or verdicts that have already been pronounced.[2] In this sense, the Black's Law Dictionary defines amnesty as:

> A sovereign act of forgiveness of past acts, granted by a government to all persons (or to certain classes of persons) who have been guilty of crime or delict, generally political offences,—treason, sedition, rebellion, draft evasion,—and often conditioned upon their return to obedience and duty within a prescribed time. [...] Included in the concept of pardon is 'amnesty', which is similar in all respects to a full pardon, insofar as when it is granted both the crime and punishment are abrogated.[3]

Thus, offences to which amnesty generally applies include political delicts such as treason, sedition or rebellion, draft evasion. In this regard, amnesty is to be distinguished from another term to which it is closely related, namely pardon.

---

1 See N. Weisman "A history and discussion of amnesty" 4 *Columbia Human Rights Law Revue* 1 (1972) at 529; see also N.J. Kritz, chap. I, n. 3 at 551.
2 N. Weisman, n. 1, at 529; see also El Salvador Supreme Court Judgment on Amnesty Law, Proceedings 10–93 of 20 March 1993, reprinted in N.J. Kritz, chap. I, n. 3 at 551.
3 H.C. Black *Black's Law Dictionary* 6th ed. (1992) at 82–83.

Faustin Z. Ntoubandi, Amnesty for Crimes against Humanity under International Law, pp. 9–37.
© 2007, *Koninklijke Brill NV. Printed in The Netherlands.*

Pardon is defined as:

> An executive action that mitigates or sets aside punishment for a crime. An act of
> grace from governing power which mitigates the punishment the law demands for the
> offence and restores the rights and privileges forfeited on account of the offence. [...]
> A pardon releases offender from entire punishment prescribed for offence and from
> disabilities consequent on his convictions; it reinstates his civil liberties.[4]

Although both amnesty and pardon grew out of the general pardoning power of
the governing authority of the State, they have different origins and purposes.[5]
The decision to grant amnesty is usually a legislative act while a pardon is an
executive act granted by the Head of State.[6] As stated earlier, amnesty deals with
offences of a military or political nature which are generally committed against
the State, while pardon is usually granted to individuals who have been convicted
of an infraction (generally common crimes) against the peace and security of the
State.[7] If this approach is correct, then it can be argued that the main difference
between amnesty and pardon is that the former may be granted before any conviction or punishment has been pronounced, whereas the latter only takes place
after the benefactor has already been convicted and punished. Nevertheless, as will
be demonstrated later in this chapter, amnesty overlooks the offence and prevents
the beneficiary from being punished. Pardon, on the contrary, does not overlook
the offence; it is usually granted after the punishment has been meted out, and
aims at either remitting such punishment, or putting an end to the execution of a
penalty, though in other respects the effects of the conviction remain in existence.[8]
Amnesty promotes peace or reconciliation while pardon provides a discretionary
mechanism for sidestepping the court. It usually involves obtaining something useful from the beneficiary of the pardon, or preventing or correcting a mistake in
the conviction of an innocent person.[9] Amnesty has its origin in early attempts to
re-establish peace between warring States or between the State and rebels, and to
ensure lasting victory over conquered territory. Pardon originates in the absolute
power of sovereigns.[10]

A more complete picture of the distinction between amnesty and pardon is
expressed in the thoughts of the Count of Peyronnet, Minister of Charles X, King
of France. He once stated that:

> Amnesty is abolition, forgiveness. Pardon is indulgency, piety. [...] When Thrasybulus
> overturned the thirty tyrants, he established a law that the Athenians christened with
> the title of amnesty, which means forgiveness. It was ordered in it that nobody should

---

4   *Id.* at 1113.
5   A. O'Shea *Amnesty for Crime in International Law and Practice* (2002) at 2.
6   See C. Pilloud (ICRC) *Commentary on the Additional Protocols of 8 June 1977 to
    the Geneva Conventions of 12 August 1949* (1987), Commentary of Article 6 (5) of
    Additional Protocol II at 1402.
7   N. Weisman, n. 1 at 530.
8   C. Pilloud, n. 6 at 1402.
9   See A. O'Shea, n. 5 at 2–3.
10 *Id.* at 3.

feel uneasy for his past actions and it is from there that we have inherited the act and even the name. Amnesty does not restore, it erases. Pardon does not erase, it abandons and restores. Amnesty turns to the past and destroys even the first trace of the sea. Pardon turns to the future, and preserves the past and everything it has produced. Amnesty, with the exception of accusation, does not suppose anything. Pardon supposes crime.... In political accusations the contrary is more often seen; for if the State does not forgive, neither will individuals; and if he remains an enemy, individuals will also remain enemies. Pardon is more judicial than political. Amnesty is more political than judicial. Pardon is an isolated favor more convenient to individual acts: amnesty is a general absolution more convenient to collective acts. Amnesty is sometimes an act of justice; and sometimes an act of prudence and ability. There is more to be found in amnesty than in pardon, a certain seal of generosity and of force imposed by the people, which gains fame to the prince, when applied. Amnesty surpasses pardon in that it does not leave behind any legitimate motive of resentment.[11]

Black's Law Dictionary further elaborates on this distinction as follows:

The distinction between amnesty and pardon is one rather of philological interest than of legal importance. [...] This is so as to their ultimate effect, but there are incidental differences of importance. They are of different character and have different purposes. The one overlooks offence; the other remits punishment. The first is usually addressed to crimes against the sovereignty of the State, to political offences, forgiveness being deemed more expedient for the public welfare than prosecution and punishment. The second condones infractions of the peace of the State. Amnesty is usually general, addressed to classes or even communities—a legislative act, or under legislation, constitutional or statutory—the act of the supreme magistrate. [...] 'pardon' applies only to the individual, releases him from the punishment fixed by law for his specific offence, but does not affect the criminality of the same or similar act when performed by other persons or repeated by the same person.[12]

Nevertheless, this distinction is not always made in that certain definitions of amnesty tend to include pardon in their scope. A Salvadorian court stated for example that:

[A]mnesty consists in the pardon or forgiveness of a crime granted by the Public Power—by virtue of the right of grace—in determined cases prescribed by law, which extinguishes completely the action and the penalty, and eliminates the quality of condemned in favor of whom or whose it is decreed.[13]

This definition rather emphasizes the legal consequences of both pardon and amnesty. In fact, the two concepts share the same consequences in law. They both result in a person obtaining immunity from criminal or civil legal consequences of his criminal deeds. Both may take their effect at any stage of legal proceedings. They both do not affect the legality of the act done, but merely release the accused from trial or a guilty person from the legal consequences of his admittedly illegal act.[14]

---

11 See Judgment of the Salvadorian Supreme Court on the Amnesty Law, excerpts in N.J. Kritz, chap. I, n. 3 at 552.
12 H.C. Black, n. 3 at 1113.
13 See El Salvador Supreme Court of Justice Decision on the Amnesty Law in N.J. Kritz, chap. I, n. 3 at 551.
14 A. O'Shea, n. 5 at 2.

However, for the present study, the distinction between pardon and amnesty is important, not only because of the nature of the crime involved, i.e. crimes against humanity, but also because of the general political context in which amnesty usually takes place. Therefore, amnesty will be used interchangeably with indemnity, which, according to Black's Law Dictionary, means "immunity from the punishment of past offences",[15] whereas reference to pardon will connote the discretionary power of grace of the executive branch of the State.

Forms

Amnesty has been used throughout centuries as a technique designed for ending insurrections, civil wars and international wars.[16] However, in recent years, it has been mainly used in emerging democracies as a political tool for enabling transitions from authoritarian to democratic governments.[17]

As a technique for ending wars, amnesty is usually granted either to all persons guilty of a particular offence committed during the war or in connection with the war, or only to certain categories of war offenders. Thus amnesty may be general or limited depending on its scope, internal or external and depending on the nature of the conflict to which it applies.

General amnesty, which is usually granted at the end of situations of armed conflict, provides immunity for all wrongful acts committed during the war by the belligerents themselves, the members of their forces and their subjects.[18] It usually covers all classes of offenders and may either be unconditional or contain conditions which the recipients must satisfy before it becomes effective. Limited or particular amnesty usually provides immunity only for specific offences or special groups of offenders; it can apply, for example, only to political offences committed by the enemy before or during the war,[19] or only to military personnel.

Internal amnesties are frequently granted after revolutions or civil wars by municipal authorities, and are political acts of primarily domestic significance, whereas external amnesties are those which are usually included in treaties of peace after international wars.[20]

---

15 H.C. Black, n. 3 at 769.
16 See e.g., the various amnesties granted by the American government, ranging from the "full, free and entire pardon" to the participants in the Whiskey Rebellion of 1794 to the amnesty granted to American citizens and soldiers in 1868 after the American civil war, and in 1950 after the Korean War, in N. Weisman, n. 1, at 530–533; see also the reciprocal amnesty clause of the Evian Declaration of 1962 in which France and Algeria undertook to grant amnesty to those who committed offences during the Algerian war of independence.
17 Examples of transitional societies, which made use of amnesty include, Argentina, Uruguay, Chile, El Salvador, Nicaragua, and South Africa.
18 A.M. de Zayas, Amnesty clause, in R. Bernhardt (ed.), *Encyclopaedia of Public International Law* vol. 1 (1992) at 148.
19 *Id.*
20 *Id.*

Purpose of Amnesty

One of the basic requirements of justice is that criminal offenders must not be allowed to go unpunished. However, in peace-making processes, justice is not always the most viable option and many statesmen have given priority to the political goal of healing, reuniting and reconciling a society destroyed by years of hatred and conflicts. Therefore, this central idea of national reconciliation and reunification is usually advanced as the main purpose of amnesty. These basic objectives of amnesty were already present in the amnesty proclamation of 7 September 1867, in which the then American President Andrew Johnson remarked:

> A retaliatory or vindictive policy attended by unnecessary disqualifications, pains, penalties, confiscation, and disenfranchisements, now as always could only tend to hinder reconciliation among the people and national restoration, while it must seriously embarrass, obstruct and repress energies and national industry and enterprise.[21]

While expanding on the goal of amnesty, many jurists unanimously recognize that one of the main objectives of amnesty is to maintain social peace. Thus, Eduardo Novoa Monreal states in this respect that amnesty deals with an institution born to solve difficulties that originate in cases of profound social or political changes, especially in cases of revolutionary or abnormal situations.[22] Carlos Fontán Balestra argues that amnesty is a politically prevailing measure of a general character, which signifies the forgiveness of a crime in order to re-establish peace and social harmony;[23] while José E. Sobremonte Martínez maintains that amnesty is an instrument of peace.[24]

Furthermore, international law links amnesty to the goal of restoring peace and reconciliation. From this perspective, Article 6 (5) of Additional Protocol II encourages national authorities to grant the 'broadest' possible amnesty at the end of hostilities in non-international armed conflicts. In its commentary of Additional Protocol II, the International Committee of the Red Cross (ICRC) specifies that the object of Paragraph 5 is to encourage "gestures of reconciliation, which can contribute to re-establishing normal relations in the life of a nation which has been divided."[25]

More significant in this regard is the memorandum of the drafters of the South African Amnesty Act of 1995,[26] which spells out the objectives of the amnesty provision in the following terms:

---

21 Proclamation No. 15, 15 Stat. 711 (Sept. 7, 1867) quoted by N. Weisman, n. 1 at 539.
22 El Salvador Supreme Court of Justice Decision on the Amnesty Law in N.J. Kritz, chap. I, n. 3 at 552.
23 Id.
24 Id.
25 C. Pilloud, n. 6 at 1402.
26 See chap. I, n. 34.

The divisions and strife of the past have generated the commission of gross violations of human rights, and the legal institution of amnesty is in terms of the said clause to be invoked as a method of reuniting the South African people who were deeply divided as a result of the commission of such violations. As will appear from the provisions of the laws of twenty or more countries, the countries concerned for differing reasons have in recent years invoked the legal institution of amnesty. The objective of this Bill is the promotion of national unity and reconciliation and the granting of amnesty to be provided for in terms of this Bill, is directed at the achievement of this objective.[27]

Meanwhile, the Salvadorian Supreme Court unanimously held in its judgment on amnesty that amnesty seeks to guarantee social and political peace. It made the following statement:

In modern times, the right of grace is a manifestation of society to recognize to all citizens the right of forgiveness, and what is pursued is the facilitation of social rehabilitation. Within this evolution, the broadest manifestation of the right of grace supposes forgiveness of a crime that has been committed, for it extinguishes the corresponding penalty and all its effects, all of which constitutes the institution of amnesty. This concept is considered a collective grace that seek to warrant social and political peace, inasmuch as it constitutes the juridical expression of a political act that allows for the opening of a democratic process that favors national consensus, the primordial objective of which is the neutralization of an internal crisis—a non international armed conflict—or the consolidation of the termination of an international armed conflict.[28]

It follows from the developments above that the main purpose of amnesties is to create conditions for peace, national reconciliation or reunification, rehabilitation and restoration within a divided State at the end of a non-international armed conflict. In the context of an international armed conflict, amnesty is used as a means of consolidating the termination of war and of establishing a lasting peace.

However, whether amnesty ever successfully reached its objective is quite difficult to assess. What is important to observe with Arsanjani[29] is that recent grants of amnesty tend to deviate from its main objectives. In his words:

[A]mnesties have sometimes been a critical component of a package for reaching a settlement in a divided State. Although the beneficiaries of amnesties have largely been governments and military officials, rebels and other regime opponents have also benefited from amnesties, and supported them. Amnesty has also served as the price for getting rid of tyrants and their associates in situations of quagmire and in the face of the unwillingness of the international community to pay the price necessary for stopping serious domestic violence. The controversial amnesty laws of Uruguay, Argentina, Chile, El Salvador, Peru and Honduras, to mention a few, attest to the present condition of Realpolitik and the impotence of the larger community to address serious domestic violations of internationally protected human rights.[30]

---

27   The full text of the memorandum is available at http://www.org.za/back/justice.htm as annex to the Promotion of National Unity and Reconciliation Act 34 of 1995.
28   See N.J. Kritz, chap. I, n. 3 at 551–552.
29   Senior Legal Officer, Office of Legal Affairs, United Nations Secretariat.
30   See "The international criminal court and national amnesty laws" 93 *The American Society of International Law* (2000) at 65; (Report of the Proceedings of the 93rd Annual Meeting held in Washington D.C. between 24 and 27 March 1999).

Such amnesties, which deviate from their main objectives, are usually suspected of aiming at shielding notorious criminals from prosecution, thus raising the issue of their lawfulness and their legitimacy that this study will attempt to resolve. Various amnesties granted in the past two decades are of this kind.

Historical Background of Amnesty

Historically, the right of grace was initially an act of individual clemency of theocratic origin. The divine nature of grace was linked to the sacred character of the King, as a divinity or as an intermediary between divinity and mankind.[31] However, with the birth of constitutional proceedings, a parallel idea developed which recognised the power of clemency as an attribute of the sovereign power of the people. It was then admitted that it is the people who has the faculty to grant clemency throughout its different manifestations. Thus, individual grace developed in a parallel form with collective grace, the real predecessor of modern amnesty.[32]

Thus, the history of modern amnesty may be divided in three significant time-periods: the pre-World War II period, the period covering World War II trials, and that covering immediate post-World War II conflicts. During this time-frame, recourse to amnesty clauses in international peace treaties decreased as a result of important developments in international law,[33] while increasing significantly in the context of civil war, insurrection or political uprising.

Amnesties in Pre-World War II Conflicts

At the end of the Peloponnesian War in 404 BC, which saw the victory of the Spartans over the Athenians, an oligarchic provisional government was established in Athens. It consisted of thirty officials who became known as the 'Thirty Tyrants' because of the ruthless nature of their rule. Within eight months they executed 1,500 persons and banished 5,000 others.[34] Thrasybulus, an Athenian general, led a revolt, which resulted in the fall and expulsion of the Tyrants. After the revolt, Thrasybulus proposed an amnesty law, which forbade any accusation or punishment of Athenian citizens for wrongs and offences committed on either side before the expulsion of the Tyrants. The Tyrants and their agents were excepted. The citizens of Athens were requested to take an oath to respect amnesty and the first man who violated

---

31 See El Salvador's Supreme Court Judgment on the Amnesty Law in N.J. Kritz, chap. I, n. 3 at 551.

32 *Id.*

33 Especially as a result of the Kellogg-Briand Pact of 1928, which forbids war as an instrument of international politics; and the regulations dealing with the *Jus in Bello* as contained in the Geneva Conventions of 1949.

34 N.G.L. Hammond *A History of Ancient Greece to 322 B.C.* quoted by A O'Shea, n. 40 at 6.

the provision on the amnesty was executed.[35] By this act, the general intended to "erase civil strife from memory by the imposition of legal oblivion."[36]

The practice of imposing 'legal oblivion' then developed in Europe in the context of armed conflicts in opposition to a principle developed by Vitoria and Suarez, according to which the theological origins of international law recognize the right of the victor to punish the vanquished in war.[37]

Writing on the responsibility of commanders and soldiers for acts committed during war, Grotius stated that:

> [G]enerals are responsible for the things which have been done while they were in command; and all the soldiers that have participated in some common acts, as the burning of a city, are responsible for the total damage.[38]

However, he further indicated that undisclosed crimes be remitted and that "in peace it is not fitting to follow up former wrongs".[39]

Grotius' proposition of remitting undisclosed crimes found its application in Europe at the end of 'The Thirty Years War' (1618–1648), which is believed to have been one of the bloodiest armed conflicts in the modern history of Europe.[40] It arose out of the revolt of Bohemia over religious questions and engulfed the Holy Roman Empire and its neighbours.[41] When this war came to an end in 1648, the belligerents met at Münster and Osnabrück for peace negotiations, which gave birth, on 24 October, to the Westphalia Peace Treaty. Article 2 of this treaty used the words 'oblivion', 'amnesty' and 'pardon' without any further distinction. It stated:

> That there shall be on the one side and the other a perpetual oblivion, amnesty, or pardon of all that has been committed since the beginning of these troubles [...] in words, writings, and outrageous actions, in violence, hostilities, damages and expenses.[42]

On the basis of Article 2 of the Westphalia Peace Treaty, amnesty became an important element of peace settlements and the practice of incorporating an amnesty clause in European peace agreements became common throughout the 17th and 19th Centuries. Therefore, the majority of subsequent peace treaties would make provision for an amnesty clause, either expressly or tacitly.

Three important peace treaties signed between France and other Powers during the 17th century made provision for an amnesty clause.

The Treaty of the Pyrenees of 7 November, 1659 signed by France and Spain provided in its Article IV that "whatsoever hath been done, or hath happen'd

---

35   *Id.*
36   Y. Walter *Encyclopaedia Britannica* vol. I (1960) at 828.
37   A.M. de Zayas, n. 18 at 149.
38   A.M. de Zayas, n. 18 at 149, quoting *De jure belli ac pacis* Book III, Chapter X, paras III and IV.
39   *Id.*
40   See A. O'Shea, n. 5 at 7, quoting G. Pagès *The Thirty Years War 1618–48.*
41   *Id.*
42   www.yale.edu/lawweb/avalon/westphal.htm.

upon occasion of the present Wars, or during the same, shall be put into perpetual oblivion."[43]

Likewise, the Treaty of Nijmegen of 10 August and 17 September, 1678 concluded between France and the Netherlands after Louis XIV failed to conquer the northern part of the Netherlands, provided in Article III as follows: "[t]here shall be perpetual friendship between the said king and state, and their subjects, and no resenting of damages, or offences during the war."[44]

Finally, the Treaty of Ryswick concluded on 20 September, 1697 between France and Great Britain contained an amnesty clause in its Article III to the effect that:

> [A]ll Offences, Injuries, Damages, which the said King of Great Britain and his Subjects, or the said most Christian King and his Subjects have suffered from each other during this War, shall be forgotten, so that neither on account of them, or for any other cause or pretence, neither Party, or the Subjects of either, shall hereafter do, cause or suffer to be done any Hostility, Enmity, Molestation or Hindrance to the other, by himself or others, secretly or openly, directly or indirectly, by color, by Right or way of fact.[45]

The most significant peace treaties of the 18th Century, which contained an amnesty clause, are the Treaty of Aix-La-Chapelle of 18 October, 1748, the Treaty of Hubertsburg of 15 February, 1763, and the Treaty of Paris of 1763.

The Treaty of Aix-La-Chapelle was concluded between Great Britain, France, Spain, Sardinia, Modena, the Republic of Genoa and the United Provinces in order to put an end to the War of Austrian Succession. Article II of this agreement stipulated that there shall be a general oblivion of "whatever may have been done or committed during the war, now ended...."[46]

Similarly, the Treaty of Hubertsburg, which ended the Seven Years War ignited in 1756 by Austria in its desire to recover Silesia contained a very extensive amnesty clause, similar to that of the Westphalia Treaty of 1648.[47] It is stated in Article II of this document that:

> Both sides shall grant a general amnesty and totally wipe from their memory all hostilities, losses, damages and injuries whatever their nature, committed or sustained on either side during the recent disturbances. Hostilities shall never more be alluded to nor shall any compensation be claimed under any pretext or in any name. No subject on either side shall ever be troubled but shall enjoy this amnesty and all its effects to the full, despite the decrees sent out and published; all orders for confiscation shall be withdrawn and goods confiscated or sequestrated shall be returned to their owners, from whom they were taken during the recent disturbances.[48]

---

43 A. Axelrod and C.L. Phillips *Encyclopaedia of Historical Treaties and Alliances* Vol. I (2001) at 50.
44 *Id.* at 54.
45 *Id.* at 60.
46 See Fred L. Israel (ed.), *Major Peace Treaties of Modern History 1648–1967*, vol. I (1967) at 272.
47 See the amnesty clause of the Westphalia Treaty in subsection 4.1 below.
48 See A. Axelrod n. 43 at 92.

Moreover, Article 1 of the Treaty of Paris of 10 February, 1763 that ended the Anglo-French conflict over North America contained an amnesty provision to the effect that:

> [T]here shall be a general oblivion of everything that may have been done or committed before, or since the commencement of the war, which is just ended.[49]

The first half of the 19th century was mainly dominated by the struggle against the French hegemony under Emperor Napoleon. However, peace treaties concluded during this period; namely, the Treaty of Luneville of 1801 between Austria and France and the Treaty of Amiens of 1802 between England and France, did not provide for amnesty.[50]

Conversely, amnesty was contemplated in the Treaty of Peace and Amity of 30 May, 1814 signed between France and Great Britain, which ended the Napoleonic wars. Article 16 of this treaty stipulated that:

> [T]he High Contracting Parties, desirous to bury in entire oblivion the dissensions which have agitated Europe, declare and promise that no individual, of whatever rank or condition he may be, in the Countries restored and ceded by the present Treaty, shall be prosecuted, disturbed, or molested, in his person or property, under any pretext whatsoever, either on account of his conduct or political opinions, his attachment either to any of the Contracting Parties or to any Government which has ceased to exist, or for any other reason, except for debts contracted towards individuals, or acts posterior to the date of the present Treaty.[51]

Similarly, the Treaty of Adrianople of 2/14 September, 1829 which ended the Russo-Turkish war over the question of the independence of Greece from the Ottoman Empire contained an amnesty clause in its Article 13 which stipulated that:

> By re-establishing relations of sincere friendship the Contracting Powers grant a general pardon and full and entire amnesty to all those of their subjects of whatever condition they might be who in the course of the war [might] have taken part in military operations....[52]

The second half of the 19th century was dominated by the successive victories of the Prussian army under Otto von Bismarck, over Denmark, Austria and France. Keeping in line with the amnesty tradition, the Treaty of Peace signed between Austria and Prussia in Prague on August 23, 1866 provided for amnesty in its Article 10 paragraph 3.[53] However, peace treaties signed between Germany and Denmark and between Germany and France following Bismarck victories over

---

49 *Id.* at 119; see also www.historicaldocuments.com/TreatyofParis1763.htm for the full text.
50 Full texts available at www.napoleon-series.org/research/government/diplomatic/c_luneville.html and www.napoleon-series.org/research/government/diplomatic/c_amiens.html respectively.
51 Full text of the Treaty available at www.napoleon-series.org.
52 See Fred L. Israel (ed.), *Major Peace Treaties of Modern History 1648–1967*, vol. II (1967) at 937–938.
53 See full text available at www.zum.de/psm/div/ostsee/mowat24.php3.

these nations contained no amnesty provisions.[54] Events that followed the fall of Bismarck in 1890, would lead up to the First World War.

The 20th century is characterized by a general change of attitude towards granting amnesty. In effect, after World War I, the Allied and Associated Powers opposed any idea of general amnesties for the German war criminals. The only amnesty clause provided for in Article 6 of the Conditions of Armistice signed on 11 November, 1918 was that which the German Government was to observe in respect of persons in all areas from which the German armies were to evacuate.[55] In contrast to the general practice observed in previous peace treaties, the Versailles Peace Treaty of 28 June, 1919 which put an end to World War I did not include any amnesty clause. On the contrary, the punishment of persons suspected of having committed acts in violation of the laws and customs of war was contemplated in Articles 227 to 230 of the Treaty. Article 227 provided for the punishment of the German Kaiser, while in Article 228 the German Government recognized the rights of the allied military courts to have jurisdiction over German war criminals. However, due to divergence of opinions among the Allied on the applicable law, no prosecution took place.

Nevertheless, there has been a limited grant of amnesty in relation to World War I. For example, the Treaty of Brest-Litovsk signed on 3 March, 1918 between Germany, Austria-Hungary, Bulgaria Turkey and the Soviet Union provided for a general amnesty clause in its Articles 23 to 27.[56] The Treaty of Lausanne of 24 July, 1923 was accompanied by an Amnesty Declaration whose paragraphs IV and VI granted amnesty to the Turkish perpetrators of the Armenian massacres.[57]

Although recourse to amnesty was a general practice throughout the 17th till the 19th centuries, it is significant to remark that not all peace treaties contained an amnesty clause. The reason being that amnesty was most likely to be adopted as a measure when there was no clear victor, and where the negotiating parties had a firm and genuine determination to establish a lasting peace.[58]

After international law prohibited the use of force as an instrument of foreign policy and since the Kellogg-Briand Pact of 1928 became an established rule of international law, amnesty in peace treaties lost their validity. As a consequence, amnesty did not form a major component of World War II agreements.[59]

---

54 See e.g., the Treaty of Versailles of 26 February 1871 and the Treaty of Frankfort of 10 May 1871 between France and Germany; also the Treaty of Vienna of 30 October 1864 between Denmark, Austria and Prussia; full texts available in Fred L. Israel (ed.), n. 46 at 645, 651 and 611 respectively.

55 See www.firstworldwar.com/source/armisticeterms.htm.

56 See A. Axelrod, n. 43 at 419.

57 See *Treaties of Peace 1919–1923* vol. II, Carnegie Endowment for International Peace (1924), reprinted in www.lib.byu.edu/~rdh/wwi/1918p/lausanne.html.

58 A. O'Shea, n. 5, especially in Chapter 2 at 15.

59 *Id.* at 15–16.

Amnesties in Connection With World War II

The trend towards excluding amnesty clauses from peace agreements culminated in 1945 with the Charter of the International Military Tribunal, which provided for the individual criminal responsibility of persons responsible for crimes against peace, war crimes and crimes against humanity committed during World War II.[60] It is worth noting that the IMT Charter was not a peace treaty agreed upon between the Allied Powers and Germany; it was rather an instrument negotiated by the victors among themselves and imposed on the vanquished. Nevertheless, on the basis of the IMT Charter, subsequent agreements also put great emphasis on the trial and punishment of the Axis war criminals rather than on oblivion, pardon and amnesty. Thus, the Charter of the IMT for the Far East as well as Control Council Law No. 10 contained no amnesty clauses.[61]

Moreover, the individual Peace Treaties of 1947 concluded between the Allied Powers and other Axis Powers imposed on the latter the obligation to prosecute war offenders. For example, Article 6 of a peace treaty signed on 10 February, 1947 between the Allied Powers and Hungary provided, among others, as follows:

> Hungary shall take all necessary steps to ensure the apprehension and surrender for trial of:
>
> Persons accused of having committed, ordered or abetted war crimes and crimes against peace or humanity;
>
> Nationals of any Allied or Associated Power accused of having violated their national law by treason or collaboration with the enemy during the war.[62]

Similar wording was used in three other peace documents agreed upon by the Allied Powers on February 10, 1947; namely, in Article 5 of the peace treaty with Bulgaria, Article 6 of the peace treaty with Romania, and Article 9 of the peace treaty with Finland.[63]

Nevertheless, in relation to World War II, the practice of punishing war criminals did not completely eliminate that of granting amnesty. Amnesty clauses contained in individual peace agreements with other Axis Powers were negotiated only on behalf of those who fought for, or sympathized with, the Allied Powers. Thus, amnesty became a means by which the victors could exonerate from criminal liability their nationals or sympathizers who had committed criminal offences when resisting the Nazi hegemony. This one-sided approach to amnesty, which characterized the immediate post-war period, could be seen in amnesty clauses contained in peace agreements signed between the Allied and certain Axis Powers, which exonerated

---

60 Article 6 (a) (b) and (c) of the Charter of the Nuremberg Tribunal.
61 See Articles 1, 5 and 6 of the Charter of the International Military Tribunal for the Far East (1946), full text available at www.yale.edu/lawweb/avalon/imtfech.htm; see also Article II of Control Council for Germany, reprinted in 3 Official Gazette Control Council for Germany 50–55 (1946).
62 See Fred L. Israel (ed.), *Major Peace Treaties of Modern History 1648–2000*, vol. IV (2002) at 2557.
63 *Id.* at 2527, 2787 and 2618 respectively.

only crimes committed on behalf of the 'United Nations'.[64] Article 3 of the peace treaty with Hungary provided, for example, that:

> Hungary, which in accordance with the Armistice Agreement has taken measures to set free, irrespective of citizenship and nationality, all persons held in confinement on account of their activities in favor of, or because of their sympathies with, the United Nations [...] shall in future not take any measures or enact any laws which would be incompatible with the purposes set forth in this article.[65]

The same phraseology appeared in Article 3 of the peace treaty with Bulgaria, Article 4 of the peace treaty with Romania and Article 7 of the peace treaty with Finland.[66]

Consistent with this development, various countries adopted laws in connection with World War II, which granted amnesty for criminal acts committed by their nationals in furtherance of their anti-Nazi campaign. On 21 December 1945, for example, Austria issued a broad amnesty law providing immunity from trial and release from imprisonment to anti-Nazis and anti-fascists.[67] Similarly, on 8 May 1946, Czechoslovakia issued an amnesty law, which exonerated from punishment war criminals as well as all persons who committed atrocities against Germans during their expulsion from the Sudetenland in the summer of 1945. The amnesty law provided, among others, that:

> Any act committed between September 30th, 1938 and October 28th, 1945, the object of which was to aid the struggle for liberty of the Czechs and Slovaks or which represented just reprisals for actions of the occupying forces and their accomplices, is not illegal, even when such actions may otherwise be punishable by law.[68]

Furthermore, Article 30 of the French Law No. 51–18 of January 5, 1951 amnestied all acts committed by the French Resistance during the occupation of France by the German troops: it provided as follows:

> *Amnistie pleine et entière est accordée à tous faits accomplis postérieurement au 10 Juin 1940 et antérieurement au 1er Janvier 1946 dans l'intention de servir la cause de la libération du territoire, ou de contribuer à la libération définitive de la France.*[69]

Amnesties in Immediate Post-World War II Conflicts

Despite the successful example set by the trial of war criminals at Nuremberg, Tokyo and in occupied territories under Control Council Law No. 10, most

---

64 The meaning of 'United Nations' as used here is that of the Atlantic Charter of 1941.
65 See Fred L. Israel, n. 62 at 2554.
66 *Id.* at 2526, 2586, and 2617 respectively.
67 See A.M. de Zayas, n. 18 at 150.
68 *Id.*
69 Meaning: "full and entire amnesty is granted for all acts committed after 10 June 1940 and prior to 1 January 1946, with the intention of serving the cause of the liberation of the territory, or of contributing towards the permanent liberation of France", unofficial translation.

post-World War II armed conflicts were not accompanied by the punishment of war criminals. Instead, grants of amnesty as a means to bury the past and to facilitate a new beginning did not lose their validity; they remained common practice. This situation is evidenced by the amnesty law passed by the United States of America's government in 1950, which exonerated American soldiers from all crimes committed during the Korean War. Likewise, the Governments of France and Algeria agreed in Chapter II A. II of the Accords of Evian of March 19, 1962, to mutually forgive all crimes committed by their respective citizens during the Algerian war of independence.

The foregoing exposition demonstrates that amnesty evolved in the context of armed conflicts, as an exception to the right of the victor to punish the vanquished. Amnesty has been consistently used throughout centuries as part of general clauses in peace treaties, aiming at forgiving in all or in part, criminal offences committed during the war. However, the issue of its lawfulness has never been raised until very recently. This situation generates an important question that is of utmost interest for this volume: namely, whether amnesty, as it operated before World War II, was consistent with the existing laws and customs of war and, due to the adoption of the IMT Charter, whether it was consistent with the prohibition against crimes against humanity.

Status of Amnesty Under the Laws and Customs of War Before and After 1945

The laws and customs regulating the conduct of war as codified before 1945 did not provide for the responsibility of individuals for the atrocities committed during the war. The two most significant international legal instruments relating to war, namely, Hague Convention II of 1899 and Hague Convention IV Respecting the Laws and Customs of War on Land of 1907, did not codify the issue of individual liability for the violation of the laws and customs of war. Only State liability was contemplated under Article 3 of Hague Convention IV, which provided for pecuniary responsibility in the form of compensation to be borne by the State but not by the individual.[70] In addition, customary international law existing at the time did not either require that peace treaties contain amnesty clauses[71] nor affirmed the obligations of belligerents to punish members of their armed forces for committing acts in violation of the laws and customs of war. This situation would remain unchanged in the aftermath of World War I. After the first world conflict, two treaties were signed which provided for the prosecution of the authors of the atrocities committed during the war: namely, the Treaty of Versailles of 1919 and the Treaty of Sèvres of 1920. However, the Treaty of Lausanne of 1923 later

---

70   De Zayas, n. 18 at 150.
71   *Id.* at 148.

granted amnesty for the very crimes, which the Versailles and the Sèvres Treaties sought to punish.[72]

It can therefore be argued that amnesty clauses in peace agreements were not totally inconsistent with the international law of armed conflicts, as it existed before 1945. They are even sometimes held to have been entirely consistent with the Hague Conventions of 1899 and 1907;[73] the reason being that such laws and customs did not expressly provide for the punishment of individual offenders for violations of the laws of war, nor did they expressly reject the principle of post-war *tabula rasa* in peace negotiations. Although the use of amnesty clauses was not prescribed by any existing international legal text, it was nevertheless an acceptable practice among former belligerents. However, the perception changed as a result of the adoption of the Charter of the IMT of 1945 and, more importantly, as a result of the four Geneva Conventions of 12 August 1949, and the two Additional Protocols thereto of 10 June 1977.[74]

As already explained earlier on, the Charter of the IMT of 1945 created an obligation to prosecute war crimes as well as two newly defined crimes; namely, crimes against peace and crimes against humanity. On the basis of the Charter, the Nuremberg Tribunal, the Tokyo Tribunal and various Control Council Law No. 10 Tribunals were established to try crimes against humanity only when committed in connection with crimes against peace or in connection with war crimes.[75] Therefore, any form of general amnesty for war crimes would have been incompatible with the mandate of these Tribunals, and would have been extended to the two newly created crimes.

Likewise, an obligation to prosecute war criminals is contained in Article 49 of Geneva Convention I, Article 50 of Convention II, Article 129 of Convention III and Article 146 of Convention IV, in the following terms:

> The High Contracting Parties undertake to enact any legislation necessary to provide effective penal sanctions for persons committing, or ordering to be committed, any of the grave breaches of the present Convention [...] Each High Contracting Party shall be under the obligation to search for persons alleged to have committed, or to have ordered to be committed such grave breaches, and shall bring such persons regardless of their nationality, before its own courts....

Moreover, in terms of Article 51 of Convention I, Article 52 of Convention II, Article 131 of Convention III and Article 148 of Convention IV, States are prohibited from exonerating themselves or other States from their responsibility. Thus, an amnesty clause would undoubtedly be incompatible with these responsibility clauses.

---

72 Namely, the violation of established laws and customs of war and of the laws and principles of humanity.

73 A.M. de Zayas, n. 18 at 150.

74 *Id.*

75 It is worth noting here that crimes against humanity developed as an extension to war crimes, in order to cover atrocious acts committed by the Nazis against the civilian populations of Germany and occupied territories. Therefore, the two offences were connected until crimes against humanity evolved as a separate offence.

Various other documents negotiated within the framework of the United Nations appear to indicate that amnesty clauses in the area of war crimes and crimes against humanity will not be permitted. Among such documents are General Assembly Resolution 95 (1) of 11 December, 1946 relating to the Affirmation of the Principles of International Law Recognized by the Charter of the Nuremberg Tribunal, and the Convention on the Non-Applicability of Statutory Limitations to War Crimes and Crimes against Humanity, which entered into force on 11 November, 1970. In addition, States Parties to the Genocide Convention of 9 December, 1948 committed themselves to enacting appropriate legislations to provide effective penalties for genocide offenders. They stated further that alleged genocide offenders shall be tried by a competent tribunal of the State in the territory of which the act was committed, or by such international penal tribunal as may have jurisdiction with respect to those contracting parties, which shall have accepted its jurisdiction.

In contrast to the international documents referred to above, which are all silent on the issue of amnesty, Protocol II of 1977 Additional to the Geneva Conventions of 1949 opened the possibility of using amnesty in the limited context of civil war. To this effect, Article 6 (5) of Additional Protocol II provides as follows:

> At the end of hostilities, the authorities in power shall endeavor to grant the broadest possible amnesty to persons who have participated in the armed conflict....

Additional Protocol I, on the other hand, does not contain any provision relating to amnesty in situation of international armed conflicts.

Most recent amnesties have been granted by States in the context of civil wars or internal disturbances and on the basis of Article 6 (5) of Additional Protocol II. However, the question remains as to whether grants of amnesty under Article 6 (5) are compatible with the rules prohibiting war crimes and crimes against humanity. This issue is crucial because Article 6 (5) does not specify the nature of the crimes to which it applies. In addition, it is not clear whether there exists a difference between war crimes committed in international armed conflicts and war crimes committed in civil wars.

Justification or Motives for Amnesty

Although amnesty clauses in peace treaties have decreased since the Second World War, the motives for granting amnesty have not lost their validity. For centuries amnesties have always been granted with the view of facilitating the transition from war to peace, and their motives have differed according to the nature of the conflict. Amnesties have been granted over the years in respect of atrocities committed in at least three different contexts; namely, in the context of international armed conflict, in that of civil war and in the context of transition from dictatorship to democratic rule.

In the context of an international armed conflict, rehabilitation is usually raised as a justification for granting amnesty to those who violated military laws during the conflict. For example, the necessity to rehabilitate American soldiers, who violated the laws of war during the Vietnam War, was advanced by Weisman as justification for his call for amnesty. He held the view that:

> To deny amnesty now would mean that potentially over 100,000 young, educated Americans would be effectively ostracized from society. Not only would these individuals face jail sentences but they would also face a future life marred by the political and civil disabilities which accompany a felony conviction. As a result of these disabilities they would be denied the right to vote, hold public office, to become a member of one of the professions, or to work for the Government. The effect of their alienation would be felt collectively by family, friends, and those surrounding them. Consequently, the painful legacy of the war would continue to haunt [them] far into the future.[76]

However, in the context of a civil war, national reconciliation usually justifies recourse to amnesty. As mentioned earlier in this chapter, this was the concern raised by American President Andrew Johnson in his amnesty proclamation of September 7, 1867 when he stated that punishing war offenders "could only tend to hinder reconciliation among the people and national restoration".

The motives for amnesty in the context of a transitional society are legion and vary according to the political interests at stake. In the *AZAPO Case*,[77] for example, Mahomed DP justified recourse to amnesty by the South African Truth and Reconciliation Commission (TRC) as follows:

> The families of those unlawfully tortured, maimed or traumatized become more empowered to discover the truth, the perpetrators become exposed to opportunities to obtain relief from the burden of a guilt or anxiety they might be living with for many long years, the country begins the long and necessary process of healing the wounds of the past, transforming anger into a mature understanding and creating the emotional and structural climate essential for reconciliation and reconstruction...[78]

In this excerpt, Mahomed DP emphasizes the healing aspect of truth telling which will not only help the families of the victims to know of the circumstances in which their loved ones died, but will also free the perpetrators from guilt and anxiety. It is only after such a mutual relief has occurred that a suitable climate for reconciliation would be created. Therefore, in the opinion of Mahomed DP, knowing the truth about the past may serve as a justification for granting amnesty in that it may create a suitable climate required for reconciliation.

However, Schlunck gives a much rational argument of the reasons that may induce national decision-makers to grant indemnity for massive crimes and gross violations of human rights. Such reasons are: firstly, the existence of an asymmetric power structure within a given State; secondly, a prior commitment to grant indemnity; and thirdly, the lack of interest in accountability among the parties or their constituencies.[79] Schlunck finds transition from authoritarian rule to democracy difficult as long as the former political elite is still very powerful. In the case of El Salvador

---

76 See n. 1 at 538–539.
77 See chap. I, n. 31.
78 At para. 17.
79 See chap. I, n. 3 at 246–248.

for example, members of the old regime still dominated the new democratically elected ARENA government, which came to power after the twelve-year war. New democratic institutions such as the judiciary, the executive and the legislature were still dominated by agents of the old regime some of which were actively involved in gross human rights violations perpetrated during the old rule. The strength of the fraternity between military officers, government executives and judges made it impossible for the ARENA government to publish the findings of the ad hoc Commission that was established to examine the death squad-like activities and the human rights records of the military. Finally, having no means to fight against those forces, which were sympathetic to the old establishment, the reformists had no other choice than to issue a broad amnesty for 'political crimes'.[80] Thus, in the Salvadorian case, the existence of a parallel power structure clearly justifies the grant of a broad amnesty.

Secondly, amnesty may be justified by the existence of a prior commitment by the parties to forgive all their mutual crimes. For instance in EL Salvador and in South Africa, the national legislature enacted amnesty laws as a concession and political signal to the other side that they were ready to negotiate the parameters for the cessation of hostilities.[81] In the South African case, the ANC[82] leaders began claiming amnesty for ANC exiles in 1990 long before the peace talks started. The ANC made amnesty a precondition for a peace negotiation. The government, led by the apartheid National Party (NP), complied with the ANC claim and enacted two amnesty laws in 1990 and 1992. By 1994, when the ANC came to power to lead the government of national unity, it was in a weak position to claim the prosecution and punishment of the crimes committed by the Apartheid security forces. Consequently, prior political negotiations between the ANC and the NP shaped the conflict environment in favour of an indemnity for human rights abuse committed by both parties.[83]

Thirdly, the motive for granting amnesty for serious human rights violations may be that the parties concerned have no interest in accountability. After the Bosnian war for example, the Dayton Peace Accords were signed in Paris on 14 December, 1995 between the Republic of Bosnia and Herzegovina, the Republic of Croatia and the Federal Republic of Yugoslavia.[84] The peace treaty provided, among others, for the arrest and surrender of the major war criminals. However, the implementation of the treaty in Bosnia proved difficult because of the reluctance of the local authorities and large parts of the population to comply with its provisions. Similarly, several years after the conclusion of the treaty, no war criminal was apprehended in Republika Srpska. Thus, the non-compliance with the Dayton Accords is a

---

80 *Id.* at 246–247.
81 *Id.* at 248.
82 African National Congress, the first democratically elected party that came to power in 1994 after the fall of the Apartheid regime in South Africa.
83 A. Schlunck, chap. I, n. 3 at 248.
84 See the text of the treaty at http://www.google.com.

significant sign of lack of interest in prosecuting members of the former political leadership.[85] This attitude may well justify recourse to amnesty.

Scope of Amnesty: Extent and Limits

Amnesty clauses may be broad so as to cover a wide range of offences or offenders, or limited to some specifically defined crimes. However, they almost always contain some form of exceptions. This section will address the following questions: which category of persons are the beneficiaries of amnesty? To which acts or offences does amnesty apply? Can amnesty cover both criminal as well as civil liabilities?

In order to address these issues, a distinction shall be made between amnesty clauses in the context of international peace treaties and amnesty clauses as provided for in domestic legislation.

Amnesty in International Peace Treaties

Amnesty clauses in international peace treaties are generally broad enough to cover a wide range of offences committed during the conflict. For example, Article 2 of the Westphalia Peace Treaty of 1648 contained a broad formulation, which was extensive enough in scope to cover every single act that was committed in the context of the war. It read:

> That there shall be on the one side and the other a perpetual Oblivion, Amnesty, or Pardon of all that has been committed since the beginning of these Troubles, in what place, or what manner soever the Hostilitys have been practis'd, in such manner, that no body, under any pretext whatsoever, shall practice any Acts of Hostility, entertain any Enmity, or cause any Trouble to each other, neither as to Persons, Effects and Securitys, neither of themselves or by others, neither privately nor openly, neither directly nor indirectly, neither under the colour of Right, nor by way of Deed, either within or without the extent of the Empire, notwithstanding all Covenants made before to the contrary: That they shall not act, or permit to be acted, any wrong or injury to any whatsoever; but that all that has pass'd on the one side, and the other, as well as before as during the War, in Words, Writings, and Outrageous Actions, in Violences, Hostilitys, Damages and Expences, without any respect to Persons or Things, shall be entirely abolish'd in such manner that all that might be demanded of, or pretended to, by each other on that behalf, shall be bury'd in eternal Oblivion.[86]

Thus, this amnesty clause was very broad because it totally covered all persons who had committed offences before and during the war. It extended to all kinds of criminal and civil liabilities as well as all acts (physical or verbal, written or unwritten, etc) committed before and in the course of the conflict. It further prohibited all acts of retribution by any public or private person. However, it may

---

85 A. Schlunck, chap. I, n. 3 at 246.
86 www.yale.edu/lawweb/avalon/westphal.htm.

happen that the offences to be indemnified are limited to specific crimes, or that the amnesty clause is written in general or unclear terms so as to leave a margin of freedom to each belligerent to determine the scope of its applicability. With respect to the latter, Pierre F. Simon indicates that except otherwise provided for in a peace treaty, an amnesty clause, which has been written in general and unclear terms always seem to cover the following three grounds:

1. Cessation of all prosecutions and all repressive actions in respect of damages that were caused before and during the war by the citizens of any of the belligerent States.[87] Such damages as well as any claim thereof must somehow have a certain connection with the war. However, any private obligation entered into before the war by the citizens of different warring States (for example, an obligation to pay a certain amount of money) subsists during the war and must be honoured notwithstanding the provision on amnesty. Similarly, debts contracted during the hostilities by a prisoner of war during his captivity are not affected by the amnesty clause.[88]

2. Cessation of prosecutions and of all repressive actions against the authors (be they members of the belligerent armed forces, members of a resistance movement or even civilians who have committed offences in the exaltation of patriotism) of wounds, homicides, other acts of violence, damages to property, etc.[89] Consequently, amnesty does not cover crimes and delicts, which have no connection with the laws and customs of war or those committed outside the context that induced the grant of amnesty. Thus, common crimes are usually excluded from the scope of amnesty. However, amnesty may extend to civilian offenders whose crimes are tolerated by the laws and customs of war, under the condition that their acts were motivated by their patriotic sentiments. But, if they have acted only with the intention to cause damage, their conduct, notwithstanding the situation of war, falls within the ambit of common crimes, to which amnesty does not extend. Moreover, acts of violence, damages to property, etc, committed by members of the armed forces or by civilians within the territory of a neutral State are excluded from the ambit of amnesty.[90]

3. Release of all political prisoners and renunciation of all subsequent prosecutions for political offences committed during the war; such clauses are generally referred to as political amnesty clauses.[91]

In sum, when a peace treaty is silent or unclear as to the content, extent and limits of an amnesty clause, it can be admitted that amnesty does not extend beyond:

1. Offences committed before or during the war, which have connections with the war;

---

[87] P.F. Simon "La clause d'amnistie dans les traités de paix" 26 *Revue Générale de Droit International Public* (1919) at 250.
[88] *Id.*
[89] *Id.*
[90] *Id.* at 252.
[91] *Id.* at 253.

2. Offences or delicts tolerated by the laws and customs of war and not committed within neutral territory, to the exclusion of common or ordinary crimes;

3. Political and military acts as well as political offences committed during the conflict by the nationals of each belligerent, to the exception of desertion, treason, or any other damageable act of the same order.

Amnesty in Domestic Instruments

Amnesty laws enacted at the end of civil war, insurrection or political turmoil are generally limited to the so-called political offences committed in the course of these conflicts. However, they may extend to certain ancillary offences usually referred to in amnesty clauses as related common or ordinary crimes. Each legal order applies different criteria in distinguishing between political crimes and ancillary common or ordinary crimes. For example, the following elements may be taken into consideration in classifying these two categories of offences: the nature of the offences, the circumstances of their commission, the objectives to be achieved and sometimes the relationship between the act and the objectives pursued.[92]

The South African legislature applied similar criteria to determine the scope and content of its Amnesty Law of 1995.[93] In fact, the South African Constitution of 1993[94] only provided that in order to advance reconciliation and reconstruction, amnesty shall be granted in respect of acts, omissions and offences associated with political objectives committed in the course of the conflict of the past.[95] It gave no definition of the expressions 'conflicts of the past' or "acts, omission and offences associated with political objectives"; instead, it left this task to the national parliament. The subsequent Amnesty Law of 1995 later defined acts associated with political objectives in a very broad manner so as to cover both apartheid and common criminals.[96]

Conversely to the South African approach to amnesty, other countries defined the scope of their amnesty legislation on the basis of a distinction between two categories of crimes, namely political and related common crimes on the one hand, and international crimes on the other hand. This approach led them to exclude the latter category from the ambit of amnesty. For example, the Guatemalan National Reconciliation Law of 18 November, 1996 that formed part of a peace agreement, which ended the forty-year brutal civil war in Guatemala, applied to both political and related common crimes. However, exception was made for the most serious

---

92 See M.R. Rwelamira in M.R. Rwelamira and G. Merle (ed.), *Confronting Past Injustices: Approaches to Amnesty, Punishment, Reparation and Restitution in South Africa and Germany* (1996) at 15.

93 See chap. I, n. 34.

94 Act 200 of 1993.

95 Epilogue to the 1993 Constitution.

96 See chapter 6 below for more details on the South African amnesty law.

crimes such as forced disappearances, torture and genocide.[97] Similarly, the Honduras Amnesty Law Decree No. 87–91 of July 1991, which accorded indemnity for criminal offences committed in the 1980's by members of the military forces, covered both political and related common crimes, while excluding forced disappearances.[98]

However, the Chilean Amnesty Decree of 1978[99] did not find it necessary to exclude serious crimes. This document granted a blanket amnesty to all persons responsible for torture, disappearances, abduction, extra-judicial executions, murder, kidnapping and assault, which were committed during the State of Siege between 11 September, 1973 and 10 March, 1978. The connection between such crimes and a political motive or objective was irrelevant, and the only offences to which amnesty did not apply were infanticide, armed robbery, rape, incest, fraud, embezzlement, dishonesty, and drunk driving.[100]

Moreover, the Argentina Law of National Pacification of 1983[101] granted amnesty to all persons responsible for the crimes committed with terrorist or subversive motivation or objective between 25 May, 1973 and 17 June, 1982. The Law covered different categories of perpetrators, namely the authors, participants, instigators, accomplices and accessories, as well as connected crimes such as related common crimes and related military crimes.[102] Nevertheless, crimes of economic subversion were excluded from the scope of the Amnesty Law.[103]

Finally, the Salvadorian Law on General Amnesty for the Consolidation of Peace[104] stated in its Article 1:

> A broad, absolute and unconditional amnesty is granted in favour of all those who in one way or another participated in political crimes, crimes with political ramifications, or common crimes committed by no less than twenty people, before January 1st 1992, regardless of whether proceedings against them for the perpetration of these crimes have commenced or not, or whether they have received a sentence as a consequence. This amnesty will cover all those who participated as direct or indirect perpetrators or as accomplices in the above-mentioned crimes. The pardon will extend to those referred to in Article 6 of the Law of National Reconciliation...

In sum, amnesty generally covers persons who have committed offences in the course or in relation to a specific conflict. While amnesty clauses in international peace treaties tend to exclude common crimes from their operation, some domestic amnesties do not differentiate between political crimes and common crimes; it is

---

97   N. Roht-Arriaza and L Gibson "The developing jurisprudence on amnesty" 20 *Human Rights Quarterly* 1 (1998) at 852.
98   *Id.* at 854.
99   Decree Law No. 2.191 of 18 April 1978.
100   See N. Roht-Arriaza and L. Gibson, n. 97 at 847.
101   Law No. 22.924 of 22 September 1983, see text in N.J. Kritz, chap. I, n. 3 at 477–479.
102   Article 1.
103   Article 4.
104   Decree No. 486 of 20 March 1993.

sufficient that the crime was committed in the course of the conflict. However, domestic as well as international amnesties converge in excluding private obligations, such as the obligation to pay a certain amount of money, or to pay a debt contracted during the conflict, from the scope of amnesty.

Legal Effects and Consequences of Amnesty

The granting of amnesty has significant consequences on the ability of the judiciary to perform its sovereign task within a given democratic society, namely that of applying the law. Among these, are its derogatory effect from the application of the law, the discharge of criminals from individual liability and the discontinuance of all proceedings in relation to the crimes allegedly committed.

Derogatory Effects

One of the legal consequences of amnesty is to derogate, with retroactive effect, from the normal operation of the law. Commentators, State practice as well as court decisions concurred in recognizing the derogatory effects of amnesty.

According to Puig Peña, amnesty supposes the derogation of the penal law or of the efficiency of the law with relation to particular cases to which it is applied.[105] In the 19th Century Luis Silvela stated that it was a real transitory derogation of the law.[106] Similarly, Gustavo Zagrebeisky declares that amnesty must be appreciated, more as a manifestation of the faculty of grace as an exception to legal ordainment, than as a corrective instrument of law; adding that in as much as amnesty constitutes a temporal derogation with retroactive effects of some rules of law, it can be likened to the retroactivity of penal laws when they favour a convict of a determined crime.[107]

Developing the same argument, the Salvadorian Supreme Court of Justice adds that amnesty is the legislative competence or repeal form of legislation with retroactive and temporal effects.[108]

Meanwhile, the French *Grand Dictionnaire Encyclopédique Larousse* defines amnesty so as to highlight its effects on prosecutions as well as on convictions. It reads as follows:

> *Amnistie: acte du législateur qui a pour effet d'éteindre l'action publique ou d'effacer une peine prévue pour une infraction et, en conséquence, soit d'empêcher ou d'arrêter les poursuites, soit d'effacer les condamnations.*[109]

---

[105] See the Salvadorian Supreme Court in its judgment on the Amnesty Law, excerpts in N.J. Kritz, chap. I, n. 3 at 553.

[106] *Id.*

[107] *Id.*

[108] *Id.*

[109] Volume I (1982) at 414.

Thus, amnesty is defined as an act of the legislative power, whose effect is either to end the public prosecution of certain offences or to cancel the penalties thereon, so that no more prosecutions will be instituted and those already instituted will be discontinued and any conviction for such offences will be quashed. Therefore, amnesty impacts not only on the liability of the perpetrator, but on the court proceedings as well; both on the prosecution phase and on the conviction phase.

Effects on the Personal Liability of the Perpetrator

The basic consequence of amnesty in respect of the responsibility of an offender is to discharge him from personal liability, be it civil or criminal. Thus, the Salvadorian Law on General Amnesty for the Consolidation of Peace indicated in its Article 4 (e) that "[t]he amnesty granted by this law extinguishes all civil responsibilities," whereas the Argentina Law of National Pacification[110] extinguished both civil and criminal responsibilities of the alleged perpetrators. Article 1 of the latter document granted the benefits of amnesty for 'all criminal activities' which took place between 25 May, 1973 and 17 June, 1982 in the following terms:

> No one can be interrogated, investigated, summoned to appear or enjoined in a manner because of imputations or suspicions of having committed the crimes or participated in the actions referred to in Article 1 of this Law, or on suspicion of knowledge of them, or of their circumstances, their authors, participants, instigators, accomplices, or accessories.[111]

On the other hand, under Article 6, alleged perpetrators were discharged of their civil liability in the following manner: "[u]nder the force of the present Law, civil actions arising from the crimes and acts comprised in Article 1 are also nullified."[112]

However, in certain cases, the scope of amnesty may be broad enough to also include vicarious liability that may be incurred by a third party as a result of the perpetrator's initial act, omission or offence. As will be demonstrated later on,[113] the South African Amnesty Law is of this kind.

Procedural Effects

Once amnesty has been granted in respect of a particular offence all court proceedings in relation thereto must be discontinued. In pre-conviction cases, the proceedings are stopped and cancelled, while in post-conviction cases the sentence lapses and becomes void, followed by the release of the condemned.

---

110 See n. 101 above.
111 Article 5, text reproduced in N.J. Kritz, chap. I, n. 3 at 477.
112 *Id.* at 478.
113 See particularly chapter 6 below.

Several national amnesty laws provide for formal and procedural effects of amnesty in different ways. For example, the formal and procedural effects of the Salvadorian Amnesty Law of 1993 appeared in its Article 4 as follows:

The amnesty and pardon granted by this law function in the following manner:

a) For those convicted of a crime, which deprives them of liberty, the judge or court carrying out the sentence will officially decree the release of those condemned, without having to pay bail. The same procedure will apply to the court taking up the case, even if the sentence has not been executed;

b) For those absentees convicted of a crime for which they are to be deprived of liberty, the competent judge or court shall immediately cancel the order of arrest against them, without restriction, the discontinuance of the case, in favour of those prosecuted, by annulling the punitive act, and ordering the immediate release of those involved;

c) In the case of those who as yet have not entered into legal proceedings, when the process begins against them for crimes committed (crimes mentioned in this amnesty), those accused can oppose the case by petitioning a dismissal in their favour, if captured they would be placed under the jurisdiction of the appointed judge who would decree their release.

By the same token, the Inter-American Commission on Human Rights' Report on Argentina's Full Stop and Due Obedience Laws highlighted the impact of amnesty on fundamental rights, when it held in respect of the right to fair trial that:

The effect of passage of the Laws and the Decree was to cancel all proceedings pending against those responsible for past human rights violations. These measures closed off any judicial possibility of continuing the criminal trials intended to establish the crimes denounced; identify their authors, accomplices and accessories after the fact, and impose the corresponding punishments. The petitioners, relatives of those injured by the human rights violations have been denied their right to a recourse, to a thorough and impartial judicial investigation to ascertain the facts.

What is denounced as incompatible with the Convention are the legal consequences of the Laws and the Decree with respect to the victims' right to a fair trial. One of the effects of the disputed measures was to weaken the victim's right to bring a criminal action in a court of law against those responsible for these human rights violations.[114]

The consequences of amnesty according to the description given above are therefore very clear. When amnesty has been granted in respect of an act, omission or offence, the perpetrator thereof is freed from criminal liability arising out of the commission of such a crime and can no longer be prosecuted in respect thereof. Such a perpetrator is equally freed from any civil liability for damages sustained by the victim and no civil suits can successfully be filed against her. In case of the perpetrator being a State's employee, or any other person acting in the name of the State, the State is equally exempted from any vicarious liability in respect of any offence committed by such an employee or a person. Other bodies, organizations or persons are discharged from any vicarious liability arising as a consequence of

---

114 Report No. 28/92 of 2 October 1992 on the violation by Argentina Amnesty Law of Article 8.1 of the American Convention on Human Rights, reprinted in N.J. Kritz, chap. I, n. 3 at 536.

the perpetrator's act or omission. Furthermore, any legal suit pending against a person who has been granted amnesty must be discontinued and any conviction thereof must be cancelled and annulled.

In its summary of the legal consequences of amnesty, Domb stated that, in order to be effective, an amnesty should be based on the following principles:

> Prohibition of the institution of any criminal proceedings against any person, on the ground of suspicion of having performed the acts to which the amnesty applies;
> Prohibition of any administrative, disciplinary or other proceeding for the commission of the acts to which the amnesty applies;
> Inadmissibility of any civil suits based on claims arising from the acts to which the amnesty applies;
> Quashing of all prosecutions and convictions for the acts to which the amnesty applies, and release of persons detained on the basis of such convictions.[115]

However, it is worth mentioning here that amnesty does not have any consequence on matters which are not connected to the conflict that induced the grant of indemnity. Thus, claims based upon a debt contracted, or an injury received, prior to the conflict, and which have no links to the conflict are not annulled by the amnesty clause, unless such a clause has been extended to embrace the relinquishment of all claims whatsoever. The same rule holds for debts contracted during the conflict, as well as for injuries or damages sustained during the conflict, but which are not related to it.

Finally, amnesty impacts negatively on the fundamental rights of the aggrieved party to seek reparation for damages or injuries sustained as a result of the perpetrator's act, omission or offence. This aspect of the consequences of amnesty has been at the heart of fierce criticisms levelled against the institution of amnesty in post-conflicts democracies.[116]

Critics of Amnesty

According to Scharf, amnesty may be a necessary bargaining chip to induce human rights violators to agree to peace and relinquish power.[117] This is what happened in Haiti where the military leaders agreed to relinquish power to allow the return of the democratically elected civilian president Jean-Bertrand Aristide, in return for full amnesty for the members of the regime and a lifting of economic sanctions imposed by the United Nations Security Council. An agreement to that effect was signed with the support of the United Nations Security Council, which later declared that it constituted the only valid framework for resolving the crisis

---

115 F. Domb, Treatment of war crimes in peace settlements—prosecution or amnesty? in Y. Dinstein and M. Tabory (ed.), *War Crimes in International Law* (1996) at 305.
116 See the South African amnesty case in AZAPO in chapter 6 for example.
117 "The amnesty exception to the jurisdiction of the international criminal court" 32 *Cornell International Law Journal* 3 (1999) at 509.

in Haiti.[118] The amnesty deal was a success: President Aristide (who was in exile in the United States) returned to Haiti and reinstated a civilian government; the military leaders, headed by General Cedras, left the country, while many members of the armed forces surrendered their arms. Consequently, most of the human rights violations stopped with practically no resistance or bloodshed.[119]

Notwithstanding this successful result, the institution of amnesty has increasingly become controversial in the past two decades; especially in the context of post-traumatic transitional societies.[120] Areas of criticisms are legion and range from violations of fundamental human rights[121] to breaches of international legal obligations.[122] In certain cases the amnesty law has been simply abrogated.[123] However, almost all criticisms levelled against the institution of indemnity converge on one point: the call for prosecution as an indispensable ingredient for establishing the rule of law in emerging democracies, and as a means for achieving the goals of the United Nations Charter, namely the maintenance of international peace and security.

---

[118] See the Pact of New York of 16 July 1993 (Doc. 26297) between the representatives of President Aristide and the rebels, which provided for amnesty for gross human rights violations; see also Security Council Resolution 948 of 15 October 1994, which approved the New York Pact; or else Scharf, n. 117 at 509.

[119] See Scharf, n. 117 at 509–510.

[120] Examples abound of amnesty grants, which have been criticized throughout the world on grounds such as breach of fundamental human rights, breach of international conventions and breach of national legal orders; Argentina, El Salvador, Chile, or South Africa have all passed amnesty laws whose legality has been challenged before the courts.

[121] See e.g., the *AZAPO* cases.

[122] See e.g., the Inter-American Commission on Human Rights' decision on the Uruguayan *Ley de Caducidad* Report no. 29/92 of 2 October 1992, reproduced in N.J. Kritz, chap. I, n. 3 at 605; see also its decision on the Argentina Full Stop and Due Obedience Laws, Report No. 28/92, Reproduced in N.J. Kritz, chap. I, n. 3 at 533.

[123] See e.g., the Argentina Amnesty Nullification Law No. 23.040 of 27 December 1983, which revoked the Amnesty Law of National Pacification of 22 September 1983 "as unconstitutional and declared irrevocably null", reproduced in N.J. Kritz, chap. I, n. 3 at 480. After the Amnesty Law was nullified, Argentina competent courts engaged criminal trials against members of the former military junta, which were the main target of the Amnesty Law. However, the prosecutions were halted by two newly-adopted legislative measures, namely: the Full Stop Law No. 23492 of 23 December 1986, which extinguished criminal prosecutions against any person who participated in the crimes committed during the military rule; and the Due Obedience Law No. 23521 of 4 June 1987, which exempted members of the military junta from punishment. The Supreme Court later upheld the validity of the latter law. Finally, Presidential Decree 1002/89 of 6 October 1989 and Decree 2741/90 of 29 December 1990 granted a full pardon to all persons who had been convicted, or were still being prosecuted as a result of the nullification of the Amnesty Law. On 17 August 2003, on a sudden move, the Senate adopted another Nullification Law with a majority of 43 votes against 7 and 1 abstention This law nullifies the Full Stop Law as well as the Due Obedience Law, thus allowing the court to resume prosecutions against the authors of the crimes committed during the "Dirty War" between 1976 and 1983. On 14 June 2005, the Supreme Court finally abrogated the amnesty laws (www.yahoo.fr/actualités consulted on 15 June 2005).

Justifications of the merits of prosecutions over amnesties are based on various grounds. Cassese states that amnesty violates due process. He believes that when justice is not rendered the victims are inclined to take the law into their own hands to exact retribution and to draw attention to the denied historical fact. For these reasons, he favours prosecution and justice over amnesty and revenge.[124] Examples exist that may illustrate recourse to self-help as a consequence of a lack of prosecution. On 25 May, 1926 in Paris, Shalom Schwartzbard gunned down Simon Petlyura, a former member of the Ukrainian armies responsible for the pogroms during the Russian civil war that claimed about a hundred thousand victims between 1917 and 1920. Similarly, Talaat Bey, the great killer of the Armenian pogroms of 1915 was shot to death by Tehlirian in the streets of Berlin in 1921. The two perpetrators immediately and voluntarily surrendered themselves to the police after their crime and insisted on being put on trial. Each used his trial as a forum to show the world what crimes had been committed against his people and gone unpunished.[125] Another example is that of Haitian citizens who committed acts of violence and assassination against the former members of the military regime who were granted amnesty.[126]

Likewise, Scharf comments that prosecuting persons responsible for violations of international humanitarian law may discourage future human rights abuses, deter vigilante justice[127] and reinforce respect for law and the new democratic government.[128] He further warns against the international community encouraging or endorsing amnesty for human rights abuses in the following term:

> [T]here is a risk that rogue regimes in other parts of the world will be encouraged to engage in gross abuses.
>
> For example, history recorded that the international amnesty given to the Turkish officials responsible for the massacre of over one million Armenians during World War I encouraged Adolf Hitler some twenty years later to conclude that Germany could pursue his genocidal policies with impunity. In his speech to his Chief Commanders and Commanding Generals of 22 August 1939, he is reported to have remarked: "Who after all is today speaking about the destruction of the Armenians?" Richard Goldstone, former prosecutor of the ICTY, has concluded that the failure of the international community to prosecute Pol Pot, Idi Amin, Saddam Hussein, and Mohammed Aidid, among others, encouraged the Serbs to launch their policy of ethnic cleansing in the former Yugoslavia with the expectation that they will not be held accountable for their international crimes.[129]

---

124 "Reflections on international criminal justice" 61 *The Modern Law Review* 1 (1998) at 1.
125 See A. Cassese, n. 124 at 1, quoting H. Arendt *Eichmann in Jerusalem: A Report on the Banality of Evil.*
126 See M.P. Scharf, n. 117 at 513.
127 That is a form of justice rendered by a self-appointed committee for the maintenance of justice and order in an imperfectly organized community.
128 M.P. Scharf, n. 117 at 512.
129 *Id.* at 514.

More importantly, the United Nations Commission on Human Rights' Report on the Consequences of Impunity held the view that failure to prosecute perpetrators of human rights abuses breeds contempt for the law and encourages future violations. And that impunity can induce victims to resort to self-help and take the law into their own hands, which in turn exacerbates the spiral of violence. The Commission concluded that impunity is a major reason for continuing human rights violations throughout the world.[130]

Summary

As demonstrated above, amnesty has been applied almost regularly throughout the past five centuries, and has served various political purposes. It has covered different kinds of offences, ranging from mere political delicts to the most serious offences of international concern. If early definitions of amnesty expressed the idea of lasting forgetfulness and perpetual oblivion for wrongs and offences previously committed, modern-time amnesties tend to deviate from this. In fact, according to O'Shea:

> Amnesty has become integrated into the general project of obtaining and preserving the truth for future generations, so that forgetfulness and oblivion have become antiquated factors in the perceptions of the role of amnesty.[131]

However, the political origin of the decision to grant amnesty, its mode of operation together with the criticisms and challenges surrounding its modern institution have led many commentators to question its legal status. Is amnesty a political or a legal institution? Can there be any limitation to the State's sovereign power to grant amnesty? Where can such limitations be found? Can jurisdictional immunity based on national amnesty be opposable before a foreign or an international court? All these issues become more crucial when amnesty impacts on the prosecution of the very crimes, which the international community has pledged to eradicate, and when it is supported, encouraged and even negotiated by the United Nations.

In order to provide a legal framework within which to address the issues raised by the institution of amnesty, the next chapters will attempt to define crimes against humanity as a serious offence under international law, which imposes certain obligations on both the individual and the State, and to determine the legal status of amnesty with respect to such crimes.

---

130 See UN Doc E/CN.4/1990/13, excerpts in N.J. Kritz, chap. I, n. 3 at 474; it is worth mentioning here that the Human Rights Commission has been replaced by the Human Rights Council, established by the United Nations General Assembly Resolution 60/251 of 15 March 2006. The Human Rights Council has hitherto held five sessions; the last one having been held from 11 to 18 June, 2007.

131 See n. 5 at 4.

CRIMES AGAINST HUMANITY IN INTERNATIONAL LAW

Introduction

The term 'crimes against humanity' first appeared in international law under Article 6 (c) of the Nuremberg Charter. Though the expression 'crimes against humanity' was new in international law in 1945, with its meaning and content still controversial, its source is believed to be traceable as far back as to older international documents such as the Hague Conventions No. II of 1899 and No. IV of 1907, Respecting the Laws and Customs of War on Land,[1] which spoke of the 'laws of humanity'. The words 'laws of humanity' would later undergo a slow and gradual development throughout World War I, until its first legal application by the IMT at Nuremberg under the appellation of 'crimes against humanity'. The legal content and meaning ascribed to this new offence in 1945 would later be expanded and explained by subsequent national and international jurisdictions, international instruments and the work of international lawyers, until the adoption in 1998 of the Rome Statute which established the first permanent international criminal court in history.

This Statute, which is viewed by many as the first genuine move by the international community to tackle the most serious crimes, has brought more clarification to the definition of the concept. It has also addressed some of the most important legal issues that have dominated the debate on this offence since its first legal consideration by the Nuremberg Tribunal in 1945. These legal issues are, *inter alia*: the question of the legality of crimes against humanity, its connection to a situation of war, the nature, content and limits of this offence, and the mental element required for its commission. Maybe the greatest merit of the Rome Statute is to have put an end to the use of ad hoc tribunals to respond to pressing human rights violations.

---

[1] Hereinafter, Hague Conventions.

Faustin Z. Ntoubandi, Amnesty for Crimes against Humanity under International Law, pp. 39–79.
© 2007, *Koninklijke Brill NV. Printed in The Netherlands.*

The present chapter examines the content, meaning and limits of crimes against humanity as they have evolved since their first legal elaboration by the Nuremberg Tribunal. International and national jurisprudence, international instruments, State practice and doctrinal works are used in this text to clarify definitional issues raised in the context of this offence. The interest here is twofold: first, to expose the gravity or seriousness of acts of crime against humanity in order to understand the reasons of its international criminalization and secondly, to determine the status of crimes against humanity as a core crime under international law. For this purpose, two phases in the evolution of the concept of crimes against humanity shall be addressed: firstly, the period before World War II characterised by the emergence of the concept in the form of the 'laws' or 'principles of humanity'; secondly, the period stretching from the end of World War II till the adoption of the Rome Statute, which witnessed the first legal qualification of crimes against humanity as a core crime under international law.

The Gestation Phase

During this phase, which is the period preceding World War II, two fundamental events occurred that are of utmost importance for the emergence of the offence of crimes against humanity: the adoption of the Hague Conventions of 1899 and 1907 and the beginning of World War I in 1914.

The 1899 and 1907 Hague Conventions

Before the earliest form of crimes against humanity was incorporated in the Hague Conventions under the appellation 'laws of humanity', the roots of this offence were already discernible in the ethics of Plato, Socrates and Aristotle, and in the ideas of natural law and natural justice propounded by St. Augustine and St. Thomas Aquinas.[2] Balthazar Ayala, one of the earliest international lawyers, wrote in 1582 that nothing could justify mass killing of innocents.[3] Alberico Genttili later referred to the 'common law of humanity' as the protector of humankind.[4] Hugo Grotius, known as the father of modern international law, called for the brotherhood of mankind, while Samuel Pufendorf argued in 1688 that human beings owed each other the duties of humanity. Moreover, Jeremy Bentham, who first used the concept 'international law', proposed in 1789 the codification of norms of international behaviour.[5]

---

2   See B.B. Ferencz, Crimes against humanity, in R. Bernhardt (ed.), *Encyclopaedia of Public International Law* vol. I (1992) at 869.

3   *Id.*

4   *Id.*

5   *Id.* at 870.

The emergence of humanitarianism[6] that directly preceded the advent of the Hague Conventions of 1899 and 1907 put more emphasis on the protection of human rights by codes and constitutions. In 1863, Francis Lieber, a law professor at Columbia College in New York, produced a draft code regulating the conduct of the United States' armies in the fields, which simultaneously became the United States first official pronouncement on the rules of land warfare and a model law for humanitarian warfare.[7]

The ideas of humanity developed by international lawyers referred to above as well as the works of Francis Lieber would find international expression in the Hague Conventions and Declarations of 1899 and 1907. These documents embody international humanitarian rules regulating the conduct of war, and place limitations on combatants in respect of their choice of weapons. The rules contained in the Hague Conventions and Declarations are generally referred to as *jus in bello*.

Hague Convention (II) of 1899 and Hague Convention (IV) of 1907 both contain in their preamble an identical provision generally referred to as the Martens Clause,[8] which reads:

> Until a more complete code of the laws of war has been issued, the high contracting Parties deem it expedient to declare that, in cases not included in the Regulations adopted by them, the inhabitants and the belligerents remain under the protection and the rule of the principles of the laws of nations, as they result from the usages established among civilised peoples, from the laws of humanity and the dictates of the public conscience.[9]

This provision, which has been subject to many conflicting interpretations,[10] is the first treaty provision to proclaim that there may exist principles or rules of customary international law resulting not only from State practice, but also from the laws of humanity and the dictates of public conscience.[11] However, rules and principles of customary international law resulting from the laws of humanity and the dictates of public conscience were originally envisaged, in the Martens Clause, to apply

---

6 Movement that emphasises the protection of human rights and lobbies for their embodiment in binding treaties; see also G. Scharzenberger and E.D. Brown *The Manual of International Law* 6th ed. (1976) at 90.

7 See B.B. Ferencz, n. 2 at 870; also R.S. Hartigan *Lieber's Code and the Law of War* (1983) at 31–73.

8 For the origin, legal significance and legal value of this clause, see A. Cassese "The Martens Clause: half a loaf or simply pie in the sky?" 11 *European Journal of International Law* 1 (2000) at 187–216; T. Meron "The Martens Clause, principles of humanity, and dictates of public conscience" 94 *American Journal of International Law* 1 (2000) at 78–89.

9 Preamble to Convention (IV), reprinted in J.B. Scott *The Hague Conventions and Declarations of 1899 and 1907* (1915) at 100–132.

10 For a comprehensive summing-up and criticism of the existing interpretative approaches to the Martens Clause see Cassese, n. 8 at 189–192.

11 *Id.* at 188–189.

essentially in war times and only to lawful combatants in occupied territories.[12] Today, their application has been extended to peaceful situations and, when invoked in the interpretation of human rights and humanitarian law norms, they serve as restraining factors on the freedoms of States to do what is not expressly prohibited by treaty or custom.[13]

The principle of humanity is further reiterated in article 4 common to Hague Convention (II) of 1899 and (IV) of 1907 in the following terms:

> Prisoners of war are in the power of the hostile government, but not in that of the individuals or corps who captured them. They must be treated *humanely*. All their personal belongings, except arms, horses, and military papers remain their property.[14]

References to 'laws of humanity', 'dictates of public conscience' or 'humane' treatment of prisoners of war, made in the Hague Conventions, also appeared in earlier official statements issued by different European Governments in 1800 condemning brutal killings of the Christian minority by the Ottoman government. Such statements contained expressions such as 'laws' or 'principles of humanity'.[15]

The meaning of the word 'humanity', referred to as '*humanité*' in French, or '*Menschlichkeit*' in German, is at least twofold. Firstly, it connotes the human race or mankind as a whole—by the crime mankind is affected in one of its groups. Secondly, it refers to a peculiar nature of man and prescribes a certain quality of behaviour, which is best expressed in the term humanness[16]—by the crime mankind is affected in its spiritual essence. Thus, the expression 'laws' or 'principles of humanity' embodies the idea that some transcendental humanitarian principles exist beyond conventional law that are not subject to any form of violation.[17] Such an idea is also reflected in the South African word '*Ubuntu*', which was introduced in the post-amble of the South African Interim Constitution of 1993. In the words of Justice Mokgoro, '*Ubuntu*' fundamentally expresses transcendental values, which are best expressed in the idea of humanness, humanity, morality, fairness, social justice and human dignity.[18] This idea of transcendental values and principles stands as the precursor of the modern notion of crimes against humanity, and will later be advanced by the Allied Powers as a legal basis for the prosecution of persons responsible for the commission of atrocious acts during World War I.

---

12 *Id.* 197; it is worth mentioning that the Martens Clause was inserted in the preamble of the Hague Conventions for the only purpose of resolving a diplomatic deadlock; on the history of this clause see Cassese n. 8 at 193–198.
13 T. Meron n. 8 at 88.
14 See Convention (II) in J.B. Scott, n. 9 at 108.
15 L.S. Sunga *Individual Responsibility in International Law for Serious Human Rights Violations* (1992) at 41.
16 E. Schwelb chap. I, n. 8 at 195.
17 B. Van-Schaack "The definition of crimes against humanity: resolving the incoherence" 37 *Columbia Journal of Transnational Law* 3 (1999) at 795.
18 See *S v. Makwanyane and Mchunu* 1995 (6) BCLR 665 (CC); 1995 3 SA 391 (CC) at 308.

World War I and the Coining of the Term 'Crimes against Humanity'

The events of World War I that were determinant in respect of the development of the offence of crimes against humanity took place in two distinct scenes, which can be referred to as the Turkish theatre and the German theatre.

The Turkish Theatre

Shortly after the beginning of World War I in 1914, accounts of the massacres of Armenians by the Turks, and the massacres, persecutions and expulsions of the Greek-speaking population of Turkey were being given. On 28 May, 1915 the Allied Governments[19] issued a declaration condemning the massacres of the Armenian population in Turkey, denouncing them as "crimes against humanity and civilisation" for which the members of the Turkish Government together with the perpetrators of the massacres were to be held responsible.[20] The term 'crimes against humanity' as it appeared in the Allied Governments' declaration, was the result of a compromise solution reached by the representatives of Russia, Great Britain and France as regards the formulation of their official declaration condemning Turkey for the crimes committed against the Armenians. In fact, the draft text of the declaration prepared by Sergei Sazorov, the Russian representative, read as follows:

> In face of these fresh crimes committed by Turkey against Christianity and civilisation, Allied Governments announce publicly to Sublime Porte that they will hold all the members of the Ottoman Government, as well as such of their agents as are implicated, personally responsible for Armenian massacres.[21]

The British and French governments did not feel comfortable with the use of the expression "crimes committed by Turkey against Christianity and civilisation". The British preferred to see the massacres not as an issue of Christians against Muslims, but rather as that of civilisation versus barbarism. So, they proposed the removal of the word 'Christianity' from the declaration. The French advanced the idea of striking from the declaration both the words 'Christianity' and 'civilisation' so as to punish the culprits only for their 'crimes'.[22] To reconcile the different views held by each of the Allied Governments, Mr. Sazorov inserted in the declaration the expression 'against humanity and civilisation', thus coining for the first time the expression crimes against humanity.

When World War I ended in 1918, several arrests of Turkish war crimes suspects were made in order to give substance to the declaration of 1915. The Treaty of Sèvres signed in 1920 by the Allied Governments and the defeated Turkish government, carved up the Ottoman Empire and made provisions for the surrender of

---

19   Composed of the Governments of France, Great Britain, Russia and later, the United States of America.
20   E. Schwelb, chap. I, n. 8 at 181.
21   G.J. Bass, chap. I, n. 26 at 115.
22   *Id.* at 116.

the authors of the Armenian massacres and for their trial before an international tribunal for crimes against humanity and civilisation.[23] Unfortunately, the treaty was not ratified and did not come into force. Consequently, no trial took place and most of those detained under the Treaty were later set free due to lack of legal evidence against them.[24] Finally, the Treaty of Lausanne, which was signed in July 1923 replacing the Treaty of Sèvres, destroyed all hope of punishing the authors of the Armenian massacres by making no provisions for war criminals.[25] Instead, it granted amnesty for all offences committed between 1914 and 1922.[26]

The German Theatre

From the beginning of World War I, German troops committed serious war crimes against citizens of the Allied Powers. The citizens of Belgium, France, Great Britain and America suffered most from German atrocities. It is believed that the German occupation of northern France and the war that ensued claimed between 1.4 million and two million French victims. The German submarine and air warfare against Britain claimed the life of at least 950,000 British nationals. Similarly, the sinking of neutral ships by German U-boats later brought the United States of America into the war, causing the death of at least 100,000 Americans.[27] Furious at the atrocities committed against their nationals, and at the scale of destruction caused by German troops in territories under German occupation, the Allied Powers envisioned to put German officials on trial for aggression and other war crimes as soon as the war ended, including the German Kaiser Wilhelm II of Hohenzollern.

An armistice put an end to World War I on November 11, 1918. Kaiser Wilhelm II abdicated and flew to the Netherlands, where asylum was granted to him at Doorn.[28]

In January 1919, the Commission on the Responsibilities of the Authors and on Enforcement of Penalties for Violations of the Laws and Customs of War (Commission) was created at the Preliminary Peace Conference in Paris. The mandate of the Commission was, among others, to inquire into and to report upon the breaches of the laws and customs of war committed by the German Empire and their allies Turkey and Bulgaria, during the war.[29] On 29 March, 1919 the Commission issued a report; chapter II of which condemned Germany and her allies for committing acts in violation of "established customs, and the clear dictates of humanity". The report continued by recommending the criminal prosecution of

---

23 *Id.* at 135.
24 *Id.* at 138.
25 *Id.* at 144.
26 E. Schwelb, chap. I, n. 8 at 182.
27 G.J. Bass, chap. I, n. 26 at 58.
28 B.B. Ferencz *An International Criminal Court, a Step Towards World Peace—A Documentary History and Analysis: Half a Century of Hope* vol. I (1980) at 32.
29 E. Schwelb, chap. I, n. 8 at 180.

"all persons belonging to enemy countries [...] who have been guilty of offences against the laws and customs of war or the laws of humanity".[30]

During the discussions leading to the creation of an international criminal tribunal that would try the authors of the atrocities committed during the war, a divergence arose between the Allied Governments with respect to the legal basis for prosecution. In fact, international law as it operated then, did not proscribe the very act of waging war, and there existed no precedent for holding leaders individually responsible for crimes perpetrated during a war of aggression. Mindful of this reality, Britain, France, Russia and associated powers such as Belgium, pushed for the trial of German criminals, including Wilhelm II for, among others, breaching the elementary laws and principles of humanity.[31]

But Mr. Robert Lansing and James Brown Scott, representing the United States of America, opposed the report presented by the majority of the Commissioners on the grounds that the word 'laws of humanity' had been improperly inserted in the report.[32] They argued that the 'laws of humanity' were uncertain and not well established enough to form the basis of prosecution. In addition, they maintained that holding the Kaiser personally responsible was unprecedented and would pierce the veil of sovereign immunity from suit and prosecution, which "a Monarch and Chief of State enjoy according to the municipal law of every civilised country and also according to the Common Law of Nations".[33] In their memorandum rejecting the creation of an international tribunal to prosecute the Kaiser, Lansing and Scott wrote:

> The laws and customs of war are a standard certain, to be found in books of authority and in the practice of nations, [...] The laws and principles of humanity vary with the individual, which, if for no other reason, should exclude them from consideration in a court of justice, especially one charged with the administration of criminal law.[34]

They also argued that aggression was not a crime against positive law and that a formal reprimand was sufficient rather than holding the aggressors personally responsible.

The American view prevailed at the Peace Conference of Paris in 1919. The resulting treaty signed at Versailles in June finally made provision for the trial of war criminals, but omitted to expressly mention the term 'laws' or 'principles of humanity' in its final document as basis for criminal prosecution. The Versailles Treaty nevertheless contained four clauses dealing with war crimes, namely Articles 227–230. While Article 228 focused on the prosecution of German soldiers of lesser rank who had committed acts in violation of the laws and customs of war, Article 227 provided for the trial of the Kaiser. It read as follows:

---

30 *Id.* at 181.
31 G.J. Bass, chap. I, n. 26 at 58–92.
32 E. Schwelb, chap. I, n. 8 at 181.
33 G.J. Bass, chap. I, n. 26 at 101.
34 *Id.* at 103.

The Allied and Associated Powers publicly arraign William II of Hohenzollern, formerly German Emperor, for a supreme offence against international morality and the sanctity of treaties.[35]

The Allied and Associated powers signed the Versailles Treaty on 28 June, 1919. Efforts were later made by the victorious Powers to try the German Emperor. But, despite repeated requests by the English and French respective Governments, the Dutch Government refused to hand over the Kaiser for trial. Kaiser Wilhelm II remained in exile in Holland where he finally died of old age.[36] Germany, which had reluctantly signed the Versailles Treaty on 26 June, 1919 denounced it a month later as a *Diktat* and, as a result it refused to be bound by Articles 227–229 and to surrender its nationals to be tried by the Allied Powers for war crimes.[37] Instead, it came out with a compromise solution of trying the accused before its own highest court in Leipzig. This proposition was agreed upon by the Allied Powers in February 1920. But by 1922, the unwillingness of Germany to punish its nationals became clear; only a few trials took place, in which the accused were either acquitted or received light sentences.[38] Finally, no trial for the violation of the 'laws and principles of humanity' took place and the German and Turkish officials went unpunished.

The gestation phase shows that the expression 'crimes against humanity' is derived from notions such as 'laws of humanity', 'basic principles of humanity', 'dictates of humanity' or 'dictates of public conscience'. While this phase did not make the violation of the laws and principles of humanity an offence under the law of nations, thus permitting some of the most notorious criminals in the history of mankind to go unpunished, it has at least set the tone of what would become known in 1945 as a revolution in international law, namely the criminalization of acts that contradict the laws of humanity.

World War II and the Legal Construction of Crimes against Humanity

The need to criminalize violations of the laws and principles of humanity became imperative in 1945, after the world discovered the nature and scale of the crimes committed during World War II by the Nazis against German Jews, Catholics, Gypsies and others. In order to punish these horrendous crimes, which were said to be unprecedented in modern world history, the Allies[39] agreed to establish an international military tribunal to try the major German war criminals. The Nuremberg Charter was adopted, which made provisions for crimes against

---

35 *Id.* at 76.
36 *Id.* at 87.
37 B.B. Ferencz n. 28 at 32.
38 G.J. Bass, chap. I, n. 26 at 79–82.
39 Composed of the Representatives of France, Great Britain, the United States and the Soviet Union.

humanity and for the prosecution of individuals responsible for their commission. As already mentioned above, the Nuremberg Charter was the very first document to make use of the term 'crimes against humanity' as devised by Mr. Sazorov, and to make it a crime under international law. The concept would then be explained and clarified by the Nuremberg Tribunal, the Tokyo Tribunal[40] and the tribunals established under Control Council Law No. 10.[41] The works of subsequent international tribunals such as the Yugoslavia Tribunal[42] or the Rwanda Tribunal[43] and that of national jurisdictions[44] contributed in shaping the meaning of crimes against humanity. Legal opinions of national and international lawyers together with the deliberations of international bodies such as the United Nations International Law Commission (ILC) have also contributed in giving meaning to the offence of crimes against humanity.

What follows is a cursory account of the legal history of the offence of crimes against humanity and of the most significant features of its development since 1945.

Crimes against Humanity in the Nuremberg Charter

Background to the Charter

Soon after the rise of the Nazi party to power on January 30, 1933 measures were taken by its leadership to secure for themselves total power. This goal was to be achieved in a ruthless manner through the persecution and purge of all political opponents inside Germany. Thus, on the night of 30 June, 1934 in what would later be known as 'the Night of the Long Knives', an estimated 200 Trade Unionists, Communists, Bolshevists, Social-Democrats, Church leaders and all those considered as potential threats to the Nazi rule, were brutally murdered by

---

40   The Tokyo Charter was adopted in 1946 by Special Proclamation of the Supreme Commander for the Allied Powers in the Pacific. This instrument established the International Military Tribunal for the Far East, for the prosecution of war criminals in the Pacific Theatre.

41   It was promulgated in 1945 by the Allied Control Council of Germany for the punishment of minor German criminals found guilty of the crimes within the jurisdiction of the Nuremberg Tribunal.

42   The International Criminal Tribunal for the former Yugoslavia was established on 25 May 1993 by Security Council Resolution 827, for the Prosecution of Persons Responsible for Serious Violations of International Humanitarian Law Committed in the Territory of the Former Yugoslavia since 1991; the Statute for the International Criminal Tribunal for the former Yugoslavia (hereinafter, Yugoslavia Statute) was subsequently adopted by resolution S/RES/808 (1993).

43   See chap. I, n. 12.

44   See e.g., the Israeli Supreme Court in *Eichmann*, chap. I, n. 23 at 239; the French *Cour de Cassation* in *Fédération Nationale des Déportés et Internés Résistants et Patriotes and Others v. Klaus Barbie*, in 78 *International Law Reports* (1988) at 125; the Canadian Supreme Court in *Regina v. Imre Finta* (1994) 1 Supreme Court of Canada (SCR) 701 1994.

the SS[45] in the execution of the 'cleansing action' ordered by German Chancellor Hitler.[46] Already in March and April 1933, Communists and Socialists were massively arrested and interned in Dachau, the first concentration camp set up on 22 March.[47] Other disliked minorities such as the Jews and the so-called 'useless eaters'[48] would later join them.

The execution of a policy referred to as 'the solution to the Jewish question' as developed and implemented by the Nazi rulers in Germany stirred the world community to anger. Under this anti-Semitic policy, Jews were regarded as internal enemies of Germany, and it was held that the salvation and rebirth of the country was to be achieved through the destruction of Germany's enemies.[49] Jews were then being persecuted, arrested, dispossessed, deported, interned or exterminated.[50] What is here relevant to the development of crimes against humanity is the fact that all the criminal acts described above were committed by Germans against Germans, and in a relatively peaceful situation. Therefore, they were not covered by the traditional notion of war crimes which, at that time, were unanimously recognised as an established offence under international law. Crimes against humanity would later be defined to cover the crimes perpetrated by German against Germans, since such crimes did not fall within the ambit of war crimes, as it was then understood.

Traditionally, the concept of war crimes refers to the breach of the *jus in bello* as embodied in the Hague Conventions of 1899 and 1907 or in the Geneva Conventions of 12 August, 1949. These documents regulate the conduct of war by restraining the choice of weapons used by the parties in conflict, and by limiting the behaviour of the soldiers taking part in the conflict. They provide basic humanitarian rules for the protection of civilians as well as all other persons not taking an active part in the conflict, and for the treatment of prisoners of war. Since the laws and customs of war are only applicable in a situation of armed conflict and directed to an external enemy, the crimes committed by the Nazi government against German nationals could not be qualified as war crimes. They were to be embodied in a newly crafted notion: that of crimes against humanity.

In the years preceding his accession to the chancellorship, Hitler had developed his 'world view' (*Weltanschauung*) that would later form the basis of the Nazi government international policy. His vision of the world was based on two main principles: firstly, the destruction of the Jewry that was to take place through waging war against Russia to annihilate the 'Jewish Bolshevism'; secondly, the acquisition of a new 'living space' (*Lebensraum*) in Eastern Europe in order to salvage

---

45 *Schutzstaffel* or Protection Squad; the Nazi security armed forces.
46 I. Kershaw *Hitler: 1889–1936 Hubris* (1999) at 505–517.
47 *Id.* at 463–464.
48 Name given by the Nazi to the crippled and those affected by genetic diseases, who were to be exterminated.
49 I. Kershaw n. 46 at 134.
50 For more details on the treatment of Jews see in general IMT 22 *Trial of the Major War Criminals before the International Military Tribunal* (1947), (Hereinafter IMT Reports).

Germany.[51] In Hitler's vision, the theory of *Lebensraum* would justify territorial conquest and would serve as a means of uniting in the German Reich the so-called ethnic Germans (*Volksdeutsche*) who were scattered throughout Eastern Europe.[52] The implementation of Hitler's worldview by the Nazi regime would precipitate the world into a second atrocious conflict only twenty years after World War I.

Condemnations Immediately Preceding the Adoption of the Charter

When World War II started in 1939, the German army occupied countries such as Poland, France, the Union of Soviet Socialist Republics, Yugoslavia, Belgium, Austria, Czechoslovakia, Greece, etc, in the territory of which the persecutions of the Jewish population were extended. Barbarous acts committed against the Jews of occupied territories were fiercely criticised and condemned by writers, politicians, statesmen and organisations, who promised to investigate, try and punish the authors thereof.[53]

Thus, between 1942 and 1945, several condemnations of German atrocities were expressed in discussions, in semi-official and official statements and proclamations. For example, on 17 December, 1942 a declaration denouncing inhuman treatments of Jews in German-occupied countries was made on behalf of the Governments of Belgium, Czechoslovakia, Greece, Luxembourg, the Netherlands, Norway, Poland, the United States, the United Kingdom, the Union of Soviet Socialist Republics, Yugoslavia, and the French National Committee. It reads:

> From all the occupied countries Jews are being transported, in conditions of appalling horror and brutality, to Eastern Europe. [...] The above mentioned Governments and the French National Committee condemn in the strongest possible terms this bestial policy of cold-blooded extermination. They declare that such events can only strengthen the resolve of all freedom-loving peoples to overthrow the barbarous Hitlerite tyranny. They reaffirm their solemn resolution that those responsible for these crimes shall not escape retribution and to press on with the necessary practical measures to this end.[54]

In 1943, an inter-governmental agency which was established under the appellation of the United Nations War Crimes Commission, recommended to the Allies[55] that the retributive action against the Nazi regime and other Axis Powers should not only be restricted to the traditional violations of the laws and customs of war; but that it should also be extended to other crimes committed against civilians of the occupied countries and of Axis countries themselves.[56] Reference to crimes committed against civilian populations of the Axis countries would later appear in the

---

51   I. Kershaw, n. 46 at 250.
52   *Id.* at 248.
53   E. Schwelb, chap. I, n. 8 at 183.
54   *Id.* at 184.
55   Composed of France, Great Britain, the Union of Soviet Socialist Republic, the United State of America and other countries opposing the Nazi camp.
56   The crimes committed against civilians would later be referred to in Article 6 (c) of the Nuremberg Charter as 'crimes against humanity'.

Instrument of Surrender of Italy signed at Malta on 29 September, 1943 under the appellation of 'analogous offences'. Article 29 of this Instrument obliged Italy to arrest and surrender to the United Nations, all persons suspected of having committed war crimes and 'analogous offences'. The expression 'war crimes or analogous offences' also appeared in Article 2 of the Berlin Declaration signed on 5 June, 1945 which confirmed the defeat of Germany and that officially ended World War II.[57] The term 'analogous offences' foreshadowed what would later become 'crimes against humanity' in the Nuremberg Charter.

On 1 February, 1945 the United States under Secretary of State expressed the U.S. State Department's call for the punishment of all German criminal acts, "including offences wherever committed against [...] minority elements, Jewish and other groups, and individuals".[58]

On 2 May, 1945 the President of the United States issued an Executive Order providing for the participation of the United States to the prosecution of the authors of the war and of the atrocities committed during the war. The Order used the words 'atrocities' and 'war crimes'.[59] It is sometimes assumed that the word 'atrocities' would later become 'crimes against humanity'.

The examples of declarations and condemnations referred to above gradually grounded and reinforced the need of inserting in the Nuremberg Charter a provision criminalizing acts not falling within the ambit of war crimes. Therefore, in preparation of the trial of the Nazi leadership, Justice Robert H. Jackson, Chief Counsel of the United States in the Prosecution of the Axis War Criminals classified the legal charges against Nazi criminals in three groups, corresponding to three different categories of acts. Group one contained "atrocities and offences against persons or property, constituting violations of International Law, including the laws, rules, and customs of land warfare". Group two included: "invasions of other countries and initiation of war of aggression in violation of International Law or treaties". Group three comprised "Atrocities and offences, including atrocities and persecutions on racial or religious grounds, committed since 1933." He justified the choice of the third group in the following manner:

> This is only to recognise the principles of criminal law as they are generally observed in civilised states. These principles have been assimilated as a part of International Law at least since 1907. The Fourth Hague Convention provided that inhabitants and belligerents shall remain under the protection of the rules of the principles of the law of nations, as they result from the usage established among civilised peoples, from the laws of humanity and the dictates of public conscience.[60]

What is of valuable interest in this assertion is that the prohibited acts falling within the generic term 'crimes against humanity' were deemed to be universally recognised as crimes under the penal law of all civilised nations. Therefore, it was

---

57 E. Schwelb, chap. I, n. 8 at 185.
58 *Id.* at 186.
59 *Id.* at 187.
60 *Id.*

contended that the Nuremberg Charter did not create a new offence, but rather, it made a universal legal recognition of already existing crimes. This view would later be expanded in Nuremberg to reject allegations that the Nuremberg Charter violated the principles of legality when it criminalized crimes against humanity.[61] In fact in addressing the defence claim of *ex post facto* law, the Nuremberg Tribunal concluded:

> The Charter is not an arbitrary exercise of power on the part of the victorious nations, but in the view of the Tribunal, as will be shown, it is the expression of international law existing at the time of its creation; and to that extent is itself a contribution to international law.[62]

The three categories of charges retained by Justice Jackson would respectively be included in the Nuremberg Charter under the headings of 'War crimes', 'Crimes against peace' and 'Crimes against humanity'.

In November 1943, the Allies signed the Moscow Declaration that provided for the prosecution of Nazi war criminals. The Declaration stipulated that minor war criminals be judged and punished in countries where their alleged crimes were committed, and that major war criminals would be tried and punished by a joint decision of the Governments of the Allies.[63] On August 8, 1945 the Allies gave effect to the Moscow Declaration by adopting the London Agreement,[64] which established the Nuremberg Tribunal. The Agreement also stressed that the existence

---

61 Critics to the Nuremberg Charter argued, however, that the setting aside of the German positive national law through the ad hoc promulgation by the victors of newly enacted norms, as well as the double standard of applying such norms exclusively to the vanquished violated the principle of legality. On these grounds, they concluded that criminal responsibility should not have been extended from war crimes which existed under positive international law, to crimes against peace and crimes against humanity which did not exist. Such an extension, according to critics, constituted a violation of the prohibition against ex post facto law which is embodied in the maxims *nullum crimen sine lege* and *nulla poena sine lege*; for further details on the principle of legality in the Nuremberg Charter, see e.g., Bassiouni *International Criminal Law: Crimes* 2nd ed. (1999) at 559–561; S. Glaser "Le principe de la légalité des délits et des peines et les procès de criminels de guerre" 28 *Revue de Droit Pénal et de Criminologie* (1947–8) at 230–238; A Cassese *International Criminal Law* (2003) at 139–158; *The Hostages Cases* in 11 *Trial of War Criminals under Control Council Law No. 10* (1950) at 1238–42; *Flick and Others* in 11 *Trial of War Criminals under Control Council Law No. 10* (1950 at 1189; Motion adopted by all Defence Council on 19 November 1945 stressing that the Nuremberg Tribunal applied ex post facto law in *IMT Reports*, n. 50 at 168–9.
62 *IMT Reports*, n. 50 at 461.
63 Preamble of the Agreement for the Establishment of an International Military Tribunal as reproduced in *IMT Reports*, n. 50 at 13.
64 Agreement for the Prosecution and Punishment of the Major War Criminals of the European Axis Powers and Charter of the International Military Tribunal; on the legality of the Charter see e.g., *Reports of the Trial of the Major War Criminals before the International Military Tribunal* vol. I (1947); S. Glaser "Le principe de la légalité en matière pénale notamment en droit codifié et en droit coutumier" 46 *Revue de Droit Pénal et de Criminologie* 899 (1966).

of the Tribunal was not to prejudice the jurisdiction of any national or occupation courts. The Nuremberg Charter was later annexed to the London Agreement and provided a legal structure and basis for prosecutions before the IMT.[65]

Article 6 of the Nuremberg Charter made provision for three categories of crimes, namely: crimes against peace, war crimes and crimes against humanity. These crimes were defined as followed:

Article 6 (a):

> Crimes Against Peace: namely, planning, preparation, initiation or waging of a war of aggression, or a war in violation of international treaties, agreements or assurances, or participation in a common plan or conspiracy for the accomplishment of any of the foregoing.

Article 6 (b):

> War Crimes: namely, violations of the laws or customs of war. Such violations shall include, but not be limited to, murder, ill-treatment or deportation to slave labour or for any other purpose of civilian population of or in occupied territory, murder or ill-treatment of prisoners of war or persons on the seas, killing of hostages, plunder of public or private property, wanton destruction of cities, towns or villages, or devastation not justified by military necessity.

Article 6 (c):

> Crimes Against Humanity: namely, murder, extermination, enslavement, deportation and other inhumane acts committed against any civilian population before or during the war, or persecutions on political, racial, or religious grounds in execution of or in connection with any crime within the jurisdiction of the Tribunal, whether or not in violation of the domestic law of the countries where perpetrated.[66]

These clauses thus established the principle of individual criminal responsibility in international law. The crimes defined therein were related to each other in that they were made punishable only when committed in preparation or in furtherance of a war of aggression. Nevertheless, they covered different grounds; Article 6 (a) penalised the act of starting an illegal war while Article 6 (b) was directed to criminal acts committed in furtherance of that war. Article 6 (c) was a novelty because, for the first time, it criminalized certain acts of war committed by a State against its own citizens.[67]

Soon after the recognition of crimes against humanity as an offence under international law, it became essential to define its content, limits and ambit. The definitional work focused mainly on the following aspects: the qualification of crimes against humanity as an offence, the elements of the offence required for its existence, its

---

65 M.C. Bassiouni "Crimes against humanity: the need for a specialised convention" 31 *Columbia Journal of Transnational Law* 3 (1994) at 459.

66 R.H. Jackson (United States Representative at the International Conference on Military Trials) *Report to the President of The United States*, in *Trial of War Criminals* (1945) at 8–9.

67 The 1899 and 1907 Hague Conventions only covered situations in which the warring parties were of different nationality.

connection to war, and the nature of the acts to include in the repertoire of acts of crime against humanity. In this process, customary law, conventional law as well as jurisprudential and doctrinal works all concurred to shape the contours of crimes against humanity as it exists today.

Inhumanity of Acts of Crime against Humanity

One of the most basic requirements for the existence of a crime against humanity is the inhumanity of the act involved. Inhumanity is often defined as synonymous to brutality or barbarousness,[68] or simply as the opposite of the word 'humanity' as defined earlier on in this chapter. However, in the context of criminal law the notion of inhumanity is a subjective notion,[69] which is often associated with other subjective concepts such as the gravity of an act or the scale of its commission. Since all acts of crime are inhumane in nature, the inhumanity of an act of crime against humanity would be measured with reference to the degree of outrage or indignation associated with its commission, rather than with reference to existing legal standards.

Article 6 (c) of the Nuremberg Charter spoke of "inhumane acts committed against any civilian population". In his opening speech in Nuremberg, Justice Jackson qualified inhumane acts as those which have 'repercussions reaching across international frontiers', or those that pass "in magnitude or savagery any limits of what is tolerable by modern civilisations".[70] Therefore, two aspects of inhumanity clearly emerge, which constitute the foundation of crimes against humanity: they are gravity and scale.

The Gravity or Seriousness Requirement

In common language, gravity refers to the character of what is important or serious. Applied to the case in question here, the issue would be to evaluate, in a more precise way, the degree of gravity or seriousness that is necessary for a criminal act to reach the status of crimes against humanity. An ILC's Report has tried to address this issue by holding the following views:

> [F]or an internationally wrongful act to become a crime [...], not only must it be extremely serious but the international community must decide that it is to be included. Extreme seriousness is too subjective a criterion and leaves room for considerable uncertainty.[71]

---

68 See *The Concise Oxford Dictionary* 9th ed. (1995) at 700.
69 A notion that varies according to individual judgement; or a notion without any objective criteria of determination.
70 Full text available at www.courttv.com/archive/casefiles/nuremberg/jackson.html.
71 ILC 47th Session, 13th Report on the Draft Code of Crimes against the Peace and Security of Mankind, by Special *Rapporteur* Mr. Doudou Thiam, UN Doc A/CN. 4/466, 1995 at 4 para. 4.

Legal scholars, as well as national and international tribunals also addressed the question of the gravity of crimes against humanity.

In 1965 for example, Jankelevitch, then Professor of moral philosophy at La Sorbonne University, France, qualified as 'imprescriptible' the crimes committed at Auschwitz by the Nazis. He described those crimes as "*une chose innommable et terrifiante, une chose dont on détourne la pensée et que nulle parole humaine n'ose décrire*".[72] Similarly, Mansfield, while referring to the Nazi crimes, pointed out that "certain acts committed against our fellow human beings are so terrible, so intrinsically evil that they represent a crime to the human race, to humanity as a whole".[73]

In *Regina v. Imre Finta*,[74] the Canadian Supreme Court held the view that inhumane acts must display a 'dimension of cruelty and barbarism'.

Of all these descriptions, maybe the most correct and complete qualification of the grave character of crimes against humanity is the one given by the Yugoslavia Tribunal in *Prosecutor v. Drazen Erdemovic*.[75] In this case, the first Trial Chamber of the Tribunal made the following statement:

> Generally speaking, crimes against humanity are recognised as very grave crimes, which shock the collective conscience. The indictment supporting the charges against the accused at the Nuremberg Trial specified that the crimes against humanity consti-tuted breaches of international conventions, domestic law, and the general principles of criminal law as derived from the criminal law of all civilised nations. The Secre-tary-General of the United Nations, in his report which proposed the Statute of the International Tribunal, considered that 'crimes against humanity refer to inhumane acts of *extreme gravity*, such as wilful killing, torture or rape, committed as part of a widespread or systematic attack against any civilian population on national, political, ethnic, racial or religious grounds' [...] In 1994, the International Law Commission asserted that 'the definition of crimes against humanity encompasses inhumane acts of a *very serious character* involving widespread or systematic violations aimed at the civilian population in whole or in part' [...] Crimes against humanity are serious acts of violence which harm human beings by striking what is most essential to them: their life, liberty, physical welfare, health, and or dignity. They are inhumane acts that by their extent and gravity go beyond the limits tolerable to the international com-munity, which must perforce demand their punishment. But crimes against humanity also transcend the individual because when the individual is assaulted, humanity comes under attack and is negated. It is therefore the concept of humanity as victim, which essentially characterises crimes against humanity.[76]

Indeed, the gravity of the crimes against humanity seem not only to constitute an element of their qualification, but also, provide a basis for their internationalisation in that the whole of mankind is targeted through the persons who are the victims of such acts. Thus, the gravity of the acts constitutes a qualitative factor that shall

---

72 Meaning "something nameless and terrifying, [...] something no human word can describe" n. 9 at 37.
73 L. Mansfield, chap. I, n. 10 at 293–341.
74 See n. 44.
75 ICTY, Case No. IT-96-22-T.
76 Judgment of 29 November, 1996 at para. 28.

be combined with a quantitative component in order to give a complete picture of what amounts to an inhumane act.

Scale of the Commission

In 1965 Professor Jankelevitch wrote the following notes on crimes against humanity: *"ce crime-lá est incommensurable á quoi que ce soit d'autre"*.[77] The *Concise Oxford Dictionary* defines incommensurable as something having no common standard of measurement, something utterly disproportionate or not comparable in respect of magnitude. If this definition were to apply to crimes against humanity, it would connote the vastness of the number of victims of this offence. The idea of the vastness of the victims of crimes against humanity is commonly embodied in the words 'widespreadness', 'immensity of the criminal enterprise', 'methodical plan or policy' and "importance of the means required to commit the offence" which is generally referred to as 'systematicity'.

What is important to note with regard to this quantitative component of crimes against humanity is the fact that the requirement of widespreadness and systematicity was applied for the first time in the definition provided for by the Statute of the Rwanda Tribunal. It was not contained in the Nuremberg Charter, although the Nuremberg Tribunal stressed that "[t]he policy of terror was certainly carried out on a vast scale; and in many cases was organised and systematic."[78]

Article 3 of the ICTR Statute defines crimes against humanity as:

> [...] the following crimes when committed as part of a widespread or systematic attack against any civilian population on national, political, ethnic, racial or religious grounds: murder; extermination; enslavement; deportation; imprisonment; torture; rape; persecution on political, racial or religious grounds; other inhumane acts.

The mention of a "widespread or systematic attack against any population" as the broader context within which crimes against humanity must occur logically involves the commission of multiple acts by several peoples against a multitude of victims. The Rwanda Tribunal defined the word 'widespread' as "a massive, frequent, large scale action, carried out collectively with considerable seriousness and directed against multiple victims", while the term 'systematic' was defined as "organised action, following a regular pattern, on the basis of a common policy" and requiring 'substantial public or private resources'.[79] Should this approach therefore be understood as implying that the legal existence of crimes against humanity is solely subject to the existence of a multiplicity of victims? In other words, could a single violating act committed by a perpetrator be sufficient to constitute an act of crime against humanity?

---

77 Meaning "this crime is incommensurable with anything else" see *Le Monde* (3 January 1965) under the rubric "Opinion libre" at 3.
78 See E. Schwelb, chap. I, n. 8 at 203.
79 See *Prosecutor v. Jean Paul Akayesu* Rwanda Tribunal Case No ICTR-96-4-T, TC I Judgment of 2 September, 1998 at para. 204.

With respect to the first question raised above, Article 18 of the 1996 Draft Code of Crimes against the Peace and Security of Mankind[80] provided the following definition:

> A crime against humanity means any of the following acts, when committed in a systematic manner or on a large-scale and instigated or directed by a Government or by any organisation or group: murder; extermination; torture; enslavement; persecution on political, racial, religious or ethnic grounds; institutionalised discrimination on racial, ethnic or religious grounds involving the violation of fundamental human rights and freedoms and resulting in seriously disadvantaging a part of the population; arbitrary deportation or forcible transfer of population; arbitrary imprisonment; forced disappearance of persons; rape, enforced prostitution and other forms of sexual abuse; other inhumane acts which severely damage physical or mental integrity, health or human dignity, such as mutilation and severe bodily harm.

The Draft Code's approach to the quantitative component of crimes against humanity differs from that of the ICTR Statute in that the word 'widespread' has been replaced with 'large-scale'. The ILC explained its rejection of the word 'widespread' by asserting as follows:

> [T]he use of the term large-scale [...] is sufficiently broad to cover various situations involving the multiplicity of victims, for e.g., as a result of the cumulative effect of a series of inhumane acts or the singular effect of an inhumane act of extraordinary magnitude.

It further explained that large-scale implies "that the acts are directed against a multiplicity of victims"; and that this "requirement excludes an isolated inhumane act committed by a perpetrator acting on his own initiative and directed against a single victim."[81]

With regard to the second question, namely whether a single act can constitute a crime against humanity, it shall be noted that the jurisprudence that developed immediately after World War II has not been consistent on this issue. The American Military courts established under Control Council Law No. 10 for the Punishment of Persons Guilty of War Crimes, Crimes against Peace and against Humanity (Control Council Law No. 10), generally required the massive nature of the act.[82] These courts made the existence of crimes against humanity subject to the commission of several criminal acts on a substantial number of victims. In contrast, the British courts did not find the mass element essential to the definition, with respect to either the number of acts or the number of victims. They usually held that "what counted was not the mass aspect but the link between the act and the

---

80 Adopted by the International Law Commission in its 48th Session, Report A/48/10 of 1996.
81 International Law Commission Commentary of the Draft Code of Crimes against the Peace and Security of Mankind, 48th Session 1996, GA Official Records; 51st Session: Supp. No. 10 A/51/10, at 4.
82 See *The Prosecutor v. Dusko Tadic*, Yugoslavia Tribunal Case No IT-94-1-T, TC II Judgment of 7 May, 1997 at para. 649.

cruel and barbarous political system, specifically, the Nazi regime".[83] Moreover, the *Tadic* ICTY stated that:

> Clearly, a single act by a perpetrator taken within the context of a widespread or systematic attack against a civilian population entails individual criminal responsibility and an individual perpetrator need not commit numerous offences to be held liable. Although it is correct that isolated, random acts should not be included in the definition of crimes against humanity, that is the purpose of requiring that the acts be directed against a civilian *population* and thus, even an isolated act can constitute a crime against humanity if it is the product of a political system based on terror or persecution.[84]

Trial Chamber II of *Tadic* thus confirmed an earlier view adopted by Trial Chamber I in the *Vukovar Hospital Case*[85] reinforcing the position that a single act can constitute a crime against humanity under certain conditions. The *Vukovar Hospital* judgement had previously held that:

> Crimes against humanity are to be distinguished from war crimes against individuals. In particular, they must be widespread or demonstrate a systematic character. However, as long as there is a link with the widespread or systematic attack against a civilian population, a single act could qualify as a crime against humanity. As such, an individual committing a crime against a single victim or a limited number of victims might be recognized as guilty of a crime against humanity if his acts were part of the specific context identified above.[86]

Therefore, while the number of victims may play an important role in the determination of crimes against humanity, the number of criminal acts committed is irrelevant so long as they form part of the required specific context.

Motives for the Perpetration of Crimes against Humanity

In criminal law, the motive of a crime broadly refers to the impulse that led the perpetrator to act, or to the feeling that animated him. The motives generally characterising a crime against humanity appear in various texts that define this offence, and are contained in the phrase "on political, racial or religious grounds".[87] Motive, which is required for the commission of genocide, a particular form of crime against humanity, combines specific acts of genocide with a specific "intent

---

83   *Id.*
84   *Id.*
85   *Mile Mrksic, Miroslav Radic, Veselin Sljivancanin ("Vukovar Hospital")* Yugoslavia Tribunal Case No IT-95-13-R 6 of 3 April 1996.
86   *Id.* at para. 30.
87   E. Schwelb, chap. I, n. 8 at 224, quoting Article 6 (c) of the Nuremberg Charter; Article 5 (c) of the Tokyo Charter that does not contain religious grounds; Article II (c) of Control Council Law No. 10; Article 18 of the 1996 Draft Code that added ethnic grounds; Article 5 of the Yugoslavia Statue; Article 3 of the Rwanda Statute that added national and ethnic grounds; Chapter (I) and (II) of the Danish Act of 12 July, 1946 concerning the punishment of war crimes.

to destroy, in whole or in part, a national, ethnical, racial, or religious group".[88]
Is this element of intentionality therefore a determinant factor for the qualification
of all other crimes against humanity?

On this point, two schools of thought coexist. For the first, a discriminatory
motive is required for all crimes against humanity, whereas for the second, certain
acts may exist independently of any discriminatory motive.

Requirement of a Discriminatory Motive

The position holding that all crimes against humanity require an underlying
discriminatory motive was adopted for the first time in the definition provided
by the Rwanda Statute. In fact, all the crimes cited in this text are preceded by
the condition of intentionality "on national, political, ethnic, racial or religious
grounds".[89] Neither the Nuremberg Charter nor any other subsequent document
requires discriminatory motive for all acts of crime against humanity. Only the
Rwanda text holds that acts of murder, extermination, enslavement, deportation,
imprisonment, torture, rape; as well as that of persecution, occur as a result of
the identification of the victims with a particular racial, religious, ethnic, political
or national attribute. The Canadian Supreme Court in *Regina v. Imre Finta*[90] corroborated this approach when it held that a crime against humanity differed from an
ordinary crime because it is "undertaken in pursuance of a policy of discrimination
or persecution of an identifiable group or race". This argument leads to arguably
admitting that discriminatory motives stem from a pre-existing segregationist plan,
policy or ideology that targets a specific category of peoples in such a way that
all criminal acts committed against such peoples in a systematic or large-scale
manner are in furtherance of that plan, policy or ideology. Therefore, the existence
of a criminal policy establishes the specificity of acts of crimes against humanity
in relation to those of other crimes of similar importance, such as war crimes or
crimes against peace. For a better understanding of the discriminatory motive of
crimes against humanity, the subsequent paragraphs will identify the nature of the
criminal policy or ideology and the identity of its authors and targets.

In his report[91] to the President of the United States Justice Robert Jackson, the
US representative at Nuremberg, expressed his intention to prosecute top Nazi
"officials and organisations responsible for originating the criminal policies" of
the Nazi regime. Such criminal policies consisted of, amongst others, planning,
organising and executing acts of oppressions, large-scale murders, wholesale
confiscation of property, persecution of the greatest enormity on racial, political
and religious grounds, the liquidation of all religious and moral influences, the
violation of international agreements; all these as "preparatory to the launching

---

88 Article II of the Genocide Convention.
89 See Article 3 of the Rwanda Statute.
90 See n. 44.
91 Text reproduced in 39 *American Journal of International Law* (1945) at 180.

of an international course of aggression [...] with the evil intention of capturing the form of the German State as an instrumentality for spreading" criminal rule to other countries.[92] Such discriminatory policies were embodied in slogans such as killing of 'useless eaters' under which all aged, insane, and incurable people were transferred to special institutions where they were coldly murdered;[93] the 'final solution of the Jewish question', which meant the extermination of the Jews; and the search of a 'living space' for the surplus of the German population which could only be achieved through a war of aggression and occupation of neighbouring States. Also, the policy of 'ethnic cleansing'[94] carried out in former Yugoslavia as part of achieving the ideology of a 'Greater Serbia'[95] bore the seal of a careful organisation and planning. Thus, premeditation and planning are the core elements of the crime against humanity.

As to the proof of the existence of a particular discriminatory policy, Trial Chamber II of *Tadic* stated that:

> [S]uch a policy need not be formalised and can be deduced from the way in which the acts occur. Notably, if the acts occur on a widespread or systematic basis that demonstrates a policy to commit those acts, whether formalised or not.[96]

Here, the ICTR attempted to demonstrate that the way in which criminal acts are committed, namely their large-scale and systematic occurrence constitute the yardstick by which to measure the existence of a policy to commit crimes against humanity. Nevertheless, some authors argued that the existence of a policy presupposes the use of public power and resources of a state's public personnel acting under public or legal authority, or under colour of public authority, to engage in conduct designed to carry out policies, or perform acts in furtherance of which, if committed by another person, would be criminal.[97] Shall this contention therefore, be understood to imply that only a State entity or a public authority can commit a crime against humanity?

The argument that a discriminatory policy must be that of a State is a legacy of the particular historical context of World War II. In fact, Nazi Germany made use of State institutions, means, personnel and State powers to achieve their goals. This is, without any doubt, the reason why Article 6 of the Nuremberg Charter had jurisdiction only over persons "acting in the interests of the European Axis countries", but not over those acting in the interests of any other group separated from the countries concerned. State sources of discriminatory policy were also

---

92 *Id.* at 184–185.
93 E. Schwelb, chap. I, n. 8 at 201.
94 *Tadic*, n. 82 at paras. 147–153.
95 *Id.* at paras. 85–101.
96 *Id.* at para. 653.
97 See M.C. Bassiouni *Crimes against Humanity in International Criminal Law* (1999) at 249.

emphasised by the French *Cour de Cassation* in *Klaus Barbie*[98] when it defined crimes against humanity as:

> [I]nhumane acts and persecution committed in a systematic manner in the name of a state practising a policy of ideological supremacy, not only against persons by reason of their membership of a racial or religious community, but also against the opponents of that policy, whatever the form of their opposition.[99]

It is worth mentioning that a shift has been made in recent decisions so as to extend the source of discriminatory policy to organisations or groups other than the State. In *Tadic* for example, Trial Chamber II held that the law of crimes against humanity has evolved to take into account forces which have de facto control[100] over a particular territory but without international recognition or formal status of a *de jure* State, or by a terrorist group or organisation.[101] This position was later confirmed in *prosecutor v. Kupreskic et al.*[102] The reasons for requiring a discriminatory policy from a State, an organisation or a group was explicitly given by the ILC in the following terms:

> This alternative is intended to exclude the situation in which an individual commits an inhumane act while acting on his own initiative pursuant to his own criminal plan in the absence of any encouragement or direction from either a Government or a group or organisation. This type of isolated criminal conduct on the part of a single individual would not constitute a crime against humanity. [...] The instigation or direction of a Government or *any* organisation or group, which may or may not be affiliated with a Government, gives the act its great dimension and makes it a crime against humanity imputable to private persons or agents of a State.[103]

Consequently, one could agree with Paust that acts perpetrated by the following groups cannot amount to crimes against humanity: governmental actors whose crimes are not pursuant to or in furtherance of a State or organisational policy, private unorganised actors and private actors who do not act pursuant to or in furtherance of a State or organisational policy.[104]

---

98   See n. 44 at 125.

99   *Id.* at 127–128.

100 Groups which have a de facto control over a particular territory without, *ipso facto*, claiming formal status of a *de jure* State are usually referred to as *de facto* regimes; for more details on this notion see notably J.A. Frowein *Das de facto-Regime im Völkerrecht* (1968); M. Schoiswohl "De facto regimes and human rights obligations—the twilight zone of public international law?" 6 *Austrian Review of International and European Law* (2001) at 45–90.

101 *Tadic*, n. 82 at para. 654.

102 Yugoslavia Tribunal Case No IT-95-16-T, TC II Judgment of 14 January, 2000 at paras. 551–552 and 553–555; also *Prosecutor v. Tihomir Blaskic*, Case No IT-95-14, TC Judgment of 3 March, 2000 at para. 205.

103 Report of the International Law Commission on the Work of its 43rd Session (1991) at 94.

104 J.J. Paust, Content and contours of genocide, crimes against humanity, and war crimes, in Sienho Yee and Tieya Wang (eds.), *International Law in the Post-Cold World War, Essays in Memory of Li Haopei* (2001) at 291.

Whereas a discriminatory policy may come from different sources, it must nevertheless aim at the same target; namely, a civilian population.

The requirement that a crime against humanity be committed against a civilian population has been laid down by Article 6 (c) of the Nuremberg Charter. This text referred to 'any civilian population' as the possible victims of inhumane acts. The expression 'any civilian population' has been subsequently employed in several other documents dealing with the crime in consideration here. These are, *inter alia*, Article II (c) of Control Council Law No. 10, Article 5 (c) of the Tokyo Charter, Article 5 of the ICTY Charter, Article 3 of the ICTR Charter and Article 7 (1) of the ICC Statute. Mention of 'any civilian population' as the target of crimes against humanity automatically excludes acts directed against military personnel. Therefore, the prime interest here is to determine what the expression 'civilian population' entails.

First, it is essential to note that the inclusion of the word 'any' before 'civilian population' calls for a broad interpretation of civilian population. This means that, "crimes against humanity can be committed against civilians of the same nationality as the perpetrator, against stateless civilians, as well as against civilians of a different nationality."[105] As to the word 'civilian', Article 3 Common to the 1949 Geneva Conventions gives a broad view of the category of people that can be classified as civilians. This clause makes a distinction between combatants and non-combatants. While the word 'combatants' generally refers to persons actively engaged in fighting, the category of non-combatants is defined as "[p]ersons taking no active part in the hostilities, including members of armed forces who have laid down their arms and those placed hors de combat by sickness, wounds, detention, or any other cause".[106] This approach was corroborated in *Tadic* when the Prosecution defined the term 'civilian' as covering "all non-combatants within the meaning of common Article 3" of the Geneva Conventions.[107] However, Trial Chamber II of *Tadic* rejected an immediate application of Common Article 3 of the Geneva Conventions in the context of crimes against humanity, arguing that the rules contained in the Conventions were part of the laws and customs of war and could only be applied to crimes against humanity by analogy.[108] The use of the analogical approach thus provided guidance to the Tribunal to answer the question of whether a person who is not a military affiliate in the traditional sense of the term, but who is actively involved in the conduct of hostilities due to his membership of some resistance movement or group, can be qualified as a civilian for the purpose of crimes against humanity. In resolving this tricky issue, the Tribunal simultaneously relied on the reasoning of the French *Cour de Cassation* in *Barbie* and that of Trial Chamber I in its Review of the Indictment Pursuant to

---

105   *Tadic*, n. 82 at para. 635.
106   See the International Committee of the Red Cross *Basic Rules of the Geneva Conventions and their Additional Protocols* (1983) at 52; also *Tadic*, n. 82 at para. 639.
107   *Tadic*, n. 82 at para. 637.
108   *Id.* at para. 639.

Rule 61 of the Rules of Procedure and Evidence in *Mile Msksic, Miroslav Radic, and Veselin Sljivancanin*[109] to reach the conclusion that:

> [T]he presence of those actively involved in the conflict should not prevent the characterisation of a population as civilian and those actively involved in a resistance movement can qualify as victims of crimes against humanity [...] although crimes against humanity must target a civilian population, individuals who at one time performed acts of resistance may in certain circumstances be victims of crimes against humanity [...] patients in a hospital, either civilians or resistance fighters who [have] laid down their arms, [can be] considered victims of crimes against humanity.[110]

This conclusion seems to differentiate between members of the armed forces who constitute a stable and permanent body and whose normal and professional activities include making war, and other individuals who, due to certain circumstances, organise themselves into a group such as a resistance movement, to conduct some activities not necessarily part of their usual day to day occupation.

In contrast to the views expressed in *Tadic*, which exclude members of the armed forces from the ambit of crimes against humanity it is worth noting that with reference to Article 6 (c) of the Nuremberg Charter, the British courts of occupation applied crimes against humanity in all cases where the perpetrator and the victim were of the same nationality, regardless of whether the victim was civilian or military.[111] Therefore, the inclusion of all non-combatants within the meaning of Common Article 3, as well as members of a resistance movement or group as part of a 'civilian' population susceptible of being victims of crimes against humanity, constitutes an evolution in the definition of crimes against humanity. What therefore does the word 'population' entail for the purpose of crimes against humanity?

It is argued that the significance of the term 'population' contained in the definition of crimes against humanity is twofold. Firstly, it indicates that a larger body of victims is visualised, meaning that this offence is of a collective nature. Secondly, it excludes single or isolated acts committed against individuals from the scope of this offence, no matter how cruel or repulsive they may be.[112] Consequently, the term 'population' gives full meaning to the adjectives 'widespread' and 'systematic' and, by the same token, helps to differentiate between crimes of an international concern which are likely to affect the stability of mankind as a whole, and crimes of a domestic concern which only affect national security and order. The United Nations War Crimes Commission advanced this idea when it stated that:

> As a rule systematic mass action, particularly if it was authoritative, [is] necessary to transform a common crime, punishable only under municipal law, into a crime against humanity, which thus became also the concern of international law. Only crimes which either by their magnitude and savagery or by their large number or by the fact that a similar pattern was applied at different times and places, endangered the international community or shocked the conscience of mankind, warranted intervention by States

---

109 *Vukovar Hospital*, n. 85.
110 *Tadic*, n. 82, at para. 643.
111 *Id.* at para. 640.
112 See E. Schwelb, chap. I, n. 8 at 191; or *Tadic*, n. 82 at para. 644.

other than that on whose territory the crimes had been committed, or whose subjects had become their victims.[113]

Therefore, for the purpose of crimes against humanity, the term 'population' covers all individual members belonging to a larger group, targeted collectivity, be it political, religious, racial, or cultural, to the exclusion of any other person.

The foregoing sections have explained the position that holds that discriminatory motive is required for all crimes against humanity. However, as it will appear in the following paragraphs, this view is not shared unanimously.

Partial Rejection of a Discriminatory Motive

Article 6 (c) of the Nuremberg Charter created two distinct categories of crimes against humanity; it spoke of murder, extermination, enslavement, deportation, and other inhumane acts committed against any civilian population (first category) or persecutions on political, racial, or religious grounds (second category); with the conjunction 'or' indicating a difference between the two categories. These two groups are generally referred to as crimes of a murder type for the first category, and crimes of a persecution type for the second category.[114] The same distinction is operated by Control Council Law No. 10;[115] the ILC's Report on the Principles of International Law Recognised by the Charter of the Nuremberg Tribunal and the Judgement of the Tribunal adopted in 1950;[116] and the Yugoslavia Statute.[117]

Unlike the ICTR Statute that incorporated a special element of motive for the two categories of crimes, the texts referred to above require a particular motive only for the persecution type crimes, which target individuals only by reason of their race, religion, ethnicity or political affiliation. The justification behind this distinction is given by the doctrine. For Ratner and Abrams, crimes of a murder type are so heinous and so grave that, if committed in a mass or systematic way, the reason for commission is irrelevant.[118] While for de Hemptinne, applying the discriminatory requirement to the two groups of crimes is to confuse crimes against humanity with genocide, in that only genocide aims at a group for its specificity.[119]

Ratner and Abrams seem to imply that although persecution type crimes are grave, an additional motive is required before one can speak of crime against humanity. In contrast, the degree of gravity and hate inherent in acts of crime of a murder type is such that these acts, when perpetrated in a systematic and widespread manner

---

113 *Tadic*, n. 82 at para. 644.
114 E. Schwelb, chap. I, n. 8 at 191–195.
115 (1945), Article II(c).
116 UN GAOR, 5th Session Supp. No. 12, UN Doc A/1316 (1950) (Hereinafter, Nuremberg Principles), see in particular Principle VI (c).
117 See n. 42, Article 5.
118 See *Accountability for Human Rights Atrocities in International Law: Beyond the Nuremberg Legacy* (1997) at 63.
119 "La définition du crime contre l'humanité par le TPIY" 9 *Revue Trimestrielle des Droits de l'Homme* 36 (1998) at 766–770.

exclude per se any motive requirement as an element of liability. De Hemptinne, on the other hand, seems to highlight the persecutory nature of the crime of genocide, whose commission is subject to the existence of a special motive, namely that of 'intent to destroy in whole or in part' an identified group.

Despite the fact that Article 5 of the ICTY Statute provides for an underlying discriminatory motive only for crimes against humanity of a persecution type, the interpretation of this clause by Trial Chamber II in *Tadic* once produced the effects of the ICTR Statute which requires a motive for crimes against humanity of a murder type as well. The Tribunal argued in this respect that:

> Significantly, discriminatory intent as an additional requirement for all crimes against humanity was not included in the Statute of this International Tribunal as it was in the Statute for the International Tribunal for Rwanda, the latter of which has, on this very point, recently been criticised. Nevertheless, because the requirement of discriminatory intent on national, political, ethnic, racial or religious grounds for all crimes against humanity was included in the *Report of the Secretary-General*, and since several Security Council members stated that they interpreted Article 5 as referring to acts taken on a discriminatory basis, the Trial Chamber adopts the requirement of discriminatory intent for all crimes against humanity under Article 5.[120]

The decision of Trial Chamber II would later be overturned by the Appeals Chamber, which, in its subsequent consideration of the question, finally rejected the requirement of a discriminatory criterion for all crimes against humanity, making such a requirement only available for crimes of a persecution type. The Appeals Chamber held that "[d]iscriminatory intent need only be shown in relation to persecution crimes" and that the requirement of proof of the accused's motives is not necessary as a substantive element of crimes against humanity.[121]

In sum, at least as it stands to date, the majority view rejects the requirement of discriminatory motive for crimes of a murder type but retains it only for crimes of a persecution type. The provisions of the Rome Statute on this issue lends credence to the contention that discriminatory motive is only required for crimes against humanity of a persecution type.[122]

Connection to War

Crimes against humanity were not initially perceived as autonomous offences capable of being committed in all times. The Nuremberg Charter spoke of this offence as acts committed "in execution of or in connection with any crime within the jurisdiction of the Tribunal";[123] with "any crime within the jurisdiction of the Tribunal" meaning war crimes and crimes against peace, which were the princi-

---

120 See n. 82 at para. 652.
121 See *Tadic*, Appeals Chamber of the Yugoslavia Tribunal, Case No. IT-94-1-A, Judgment of 15 July 1999 (hereinafter *Tadic* (1999)) at paras. 272, 283, 292, and 305.
122 See Article 7 (1) (h).
123 Article 6 (c).

pal offences aimed at by the IMT Charter.[124] The consequence of associating the three categories of crimes within the meaning of the Charter was to make crime against humanity a subsidiary crime. Article 5 (c) of the Tokyo Charter as well as the more recent Article 5 of the ICTY Statute retained the war nexus requirement. The existence of a nexus between crimes against humanity and war raises one fundamental question: can a crime against humanity exist outside a situation of armed conflict?

Before answering this question, and for a better understanding of this element, it is important to address the rationale behind the war connection.

Justification of the War Connection

It is agreed that international law, as it stood in 1945, did not provide a legal basis for the competence of an international court to adjudicate crimes committed by the German State against its own citizens.[125] Respect for human rights formed part and parcel of the domestic competence of sovereign States and arguing for the contrary was seen as an illegal interference into domestic affairs. It was therefore necessary to link these crimes to an element that would render them justiciable from an international law point of view. The linkage to war crimes and to crimes against peace was therefore unavoidable. The choice of the latter two categories of offences was justified by the fact that the atrocities committed by the German Reich against German citizens "were based on identical factual manifestations of conduct falling within the traditional meaning of war crimes, but they were extended to the civilian population of the country that had committed these violations."[126] It was also intended to strengthen the validity of crimes against humanity with regard to the requirements of the principle of legality.[127] Justice Robert H. Jackson further elaborated on the rationale behind the connection between crimes against humanity and a situation of war as follows:

> The reason that this program of extermination of Jews and destruction of the rights of minorities becomes an international concern is this: it was a part of a plan for making an illegal war. Unless we have a war connection as a basis for reaching them, I would think we have no basis for dealing with atrocities. They were a part of the preparation

---

124 This appeared in the expressions used throughout the Charter; such as "Agreement for the Prosecution and Punishment of the *Major War Criminals* of the European Axis", with Article 1 stipulating that there shall be established an International Military Tribunal for their trial; in the Preamble and in Articles 3, 4 and 6 mention was made of '*war criminals*', etc. In all these places the term '*war criminals*' was used in the wider sense to include not only violations of the laws and customs of war, but also crimes against peace and crimes against humanity, see E. Schwelb, chap. I, n. 8 at 200.

125 M. Bettati, Le crime contre l'humanité, in H. Ascensio, E. Decaux et A. Pellet (ed.), *Droit International Pénal* (2000) at 308.

126 M.C. Bassiouni, n. 97 at 24–25.

127 *Id.* at 30.

for war or for the conduct of the war in so far as they occurred inside of Germany and that makes them our concern.[128]

The result of the war connection was to limit the prosecution of crimes against humanity to those acts perpetrated after the war had officially been declared; that is, atrocities that occurred in the course of World War II. In interpreting the Charter, the Nuremberg Tribunal virtually omitted the phrase 'before or during the war' contained in the Charter, thus limiting the ambit of Article 6 (c). It generally came to the conclusion that inhumane acts perpetrated prior to the formal declaration of war could not constitute crimes against humanity, unless it has been proven that they had some sort of connection with the war. This restrictive approach appeared in the Tribunal's opinion on crimes against humanity when it stated that:

> With regard to crimes against humanity, there is no doubt whatever that political opponents were murdered in Germany before the war and that many of them were kept in concentration camps in circumstances of great horror and cruelty. The policy of terror was certainly carried out on a vast scale; and in many cases was organised and systematic. The policy of persecution, repression and murder of civilians in Germany before the war of 1939, who were likely to be hostile to the Government, was most ruthlessly carried out. The persecution of Jews during the same period is established beyond all doubt. To constitute crimes against humanity, the acts relied on before the outbreak of war must have been in execution of, or in connection with, any crime within the jurisdiction of the Tribunal. The Tribunal is of the opinion that revolting and horrible as many of these crimes were, it has not been satisfactorily proved that they were done in execution of, or in connection with, any such crimes. The Tribunal cannot, therefore, make a general declaration that the acts before 1939 were crimes against humanity within the meaning of the Charter, but from the beginning of the war in 1939 war crimes were committed on a vast scale, which were also crimes against humanity; and in so far as the inhumane acts charged in the Indictment, and committed after the beginning of the war did not constitute war crimes, they were all committed in execution of, or in connection with, the aggressive war, and therefore constituted crimes against humanity.[129]

The Nuremberg Tribunal thus considered the war connection both as an element of the definition of the offence and as an element of its competence. However, it did not clarify whether acts of crimes against humanity must occur only in the course of an international conflict. In other words, the Tribunal did not rule on whether this offence applies identically to both international and internal conflicts. With regard to this aspect of the war nexus, there are various arguments today that call for the extension of crimes against humanity to both international and internal conflicts. The most authoritative statement on this issue is provided by the jurisprudence of the ICTY Tribunal, which held that what is inhumane and forbidden in international conflicts cannot be regarded as humane and admissible in internal conflicts.[130] This

---

128 Quoted by B. Van-Schaack, n. 17 at 799.
129 E. Schwelb, chap. I, n. 8 at 203–204.
130 *Drazen Erdemovic*, n. 75 at para. 121 or else M. Bettati, n. 125 at 309.

opinion gives weight to the ICTY Statute, which spoke of the crimes "committed in armed conflicts, whether international or internal in character".[131]

Decline of the War Connection

The war connection criterion was first abandoned in Control Council Law No. 10 Article II (c), which defined crimes against humanity as:

> Atrocities and offences, including but not limited to murder, extermination, enslavement, deportation, imprisonment, torture, rape, or other inhuman acts committed against any civilian population, or persecutions on political, racial or religious grounds, whether or not in violation of the domestic laws of the country where perpetrated.

The removal of the link between crimes against humanity on the one hand, and war crimes and crimes against peace on the other hand, set in motion the beginning of the development of crimes against humanity as an autonomous offence. Various domestic and international documents would follow suit. For example, Articles 211 (1) and 212 (1) of the 1992 French *Nouveau Code Pénal* as well as the Israeli statute used to prosecute Adolf Eichmann did not connect crimes against humanity to a situation of war.[132] By the same token, the ICTR Statute Article 3 and the 1996 Draft Code of Crimes against the Peace and Security of Mankind Article 18, did not require the war connection. The jurisprudence of the ICTY has also played an important role with regard to this development. Despite an exigency of the war connection in Article 5 of the ICTY Statute, the ICTY did not strictly apply such a requirement in its judgement, arguing that:

> [C]ustomary international law no longer requires any nexus between crimes against humanity and armed conflict [...] Article 5 was intended to reintroduce this nexus for the purposes of this Tribunal. Accordingly, its existence must be proved, as well as the link between the act or omission charged and the armed conflict.[133]

Recent arguments have justified the severance of the war nexus by the recognition of the fact that crimes against humanity are capable of being committed not only in situations of armed conflicts of an international or national character, but also in situations of peace.[134] Apartheid stands as an example of crimes against humanity that can be committed in relatively peaceful times.[135] The final blow to the war nexus came from Article 7 of the Rome Statute, which made it definitively redundant for the purpose of crime against humanity.

However, this does not necessarily lead to the disappearance of a context within which crimes against humanity must be committed. A substitute for the war

---

131 Article 5.
132 S.R. Ratner and J.S. Abrams, n. 118 at 51.
133 *Tadic*, n. 82 at para. 627.
134 Amicus brief of the US Government before the Yugoslavia Tribunal, mentioned in S.R. Ratner and J.S. Abrams, n. 118 at 54.
135 Article 1 of the Apartheid Convention.

connection has appeared in the ICTR Statute in that the ICTR has the power to prosecute persons for crimes "when committed as part of a *widespread or systematic attack* against any civilian population".[136] A variant of this formulation can also be found in Article 7 of the Rome Statute, which defined crimes against humanity as "any of the following acts when committed as part of a *widespread or systematic attack* directed against any civilian population with *knowledge of the attack*". The Rome Statute defined the expression "attack directed against any civilian population" as a course of conduct involving the multiple commission of any act of crime against humanity against any civilian population, pursuant to or in furtherance of a State or organisational policy to commit such an attack.[137] Such an attack must be either widespread or systematic. The expression 'knowledge of the attack', which relates to the criminal intent or *mens rea* of a perpetrator, has been explained by the ICTY; what follows is the clarification of this element.

Criminal Intent or **Mens Rea**

Contrary to the criminal motive which refers to the impulse or feeling that led a perpetrator to commit a crime, *mens rea* characterises the degree of consciousness, or the mental or psychological state, exhibited by a person at the very moment he is engaging in a criminal conduct.[138] This mental or psychological element of a criminal offence is embodied in the common law principle *actus non facit reum, nisi mens sit rea*, meaning that a person cannot be convicted and punished in a proceeding of a criminal nature unless it can be shown that he had a guilty or evil mind.[139] A common law or statutory definition of a criminal offence generally requires that the offender displays a particular state of mind at the moment of the commission of a crime. He may act maliciously, fraudulently, with some particular intent, or knowingly.[140] Intent and knowledge constitute the *mens rea* required for crimes against humanity; that is the intent to commit an act and the knowledge of the circumstances that make the act a criminal offence.

'Knowledge' as the required *mens rea* for crimes against humanity, appeared in the definition contained in the ICC Statute. Article 7 of the Statute speaks of acts "committed as part of a widespread or systematic attack against any civilian population with knowledge of the attack." The Statute further defines knowledge as "awareness that a circumstance exists or a consequence will occur in the ordinary course of events."[141] While the doctrine interprets this definition as to imply either criminal

---

136 Article 3.
137 Article 7 (2) (a).
138 See S.R. Ratner and J.S. Abrams, n. 118 at 61.
139 H.A. Palmer and H. Palmer *Harris Criminal Law* 19th ed. (1954) at 19.
140 *Id.*
141 Article 30 (3).

intent or criminal negligence,[142] a much more complete and extensive analysis of knowledge as the required *mens rea* for crimes against humanity is provided for by the jurisprudence of international tribunals, namely the ICTY and the ICTR. Knowledge as *mens rea* displays three aspects, namely knowledge of the criminal context, knowing participation in that context and proof of the awareness.[143]

The first aspect implies that the perpetrator knows of both the general context in which his criminal acts were committed and of the link between his acts and that context.[144] As explained above, the general context for crimes against humanity is that of a widespread or systematic attack against a civilian population. Therefore, to have the necessary *mens rea*, an accused must know of the existence of this general context of attack, and must be aware that his individual criminal conduct fits within that context. The ICTR stressed this aspect of knowledge when it held that:

> Part of what transforms an individual's act into a crime against humanity is the inclusion of the act within a greater dimension of criminal conduct; therefore an accused should be aware of this greater dimension in order to be culpable thereof. Accordingly, actual or constructive knowledge of the broader context of the attack, meaning that the accused must know that his act is part of a widespread or systematic attack on a civilian population and pursuant to some kind of policy or plan, is necessary to satisfy the requisite *mens rea* element of the accused.[145]

With regard to the second aspect of knowledge, namely the question of knowing participation in the criminal context, the ICTY held that it is not necessary for the accused to be "identified with the ideology, policy or plan in whose name mass crimes were perpetrated, nor even that he supported it. It suffices that he knowingly took the risk of participating in the implementation of the ideology, policy or plan."[146] Knowing participation in this context may take the following forms: the accused consciously agreed to accept and perform functions which resulted in his collaboration with the authors of a criminal ideology, policy or plan; he received orders relating to such an ideology, policy or plan and lastly, through his intentional acts or omissions he contributed in the commission of crimes in furtherance of the criminal ideology, policy or plan.[147] According to the Trial Chamber of *Tadic*, the decision to participate shall be made consciously and must be coupled with a requirement of intent, which involves awareness of the act of participation.[148]

---

142 See e.g., S. Stirling-Zanda "The individual criminal responsibility of judicial organs in international law in the light of international practice" 48 *Netherlands International Law Revue* 1 (2001) at 80.
143 See *Blaskic*, n. 102 at paras. 246–259.
144 *Id.* at para. 247.
145 *The Prosecutor v. Clément Kayishema and Obed Ruzindana*, ICTR, Case No. 95-1-T, Judgment of 21 May 1999 at para. 134.
146 *Blaskic*, n. 102 at para. 257.
147 *Id.*
148 See n. 82 at para. 674.

Lastly, it is submitted that evidence of *mens rea* is required before guilt can be ascribed. In its jurisprudence, the ICTR stressed the difficulty of ascertaining the mental or psychological factor of a crime against humanity in the absence of a confession from the accused.[149] Nevertheless, Trial Chamber I of this Tribunal held that intent can be inferred from a certain number of presumptions of fact,[150] while Trial Chamber I of the ICTY held in *Blaskic* that "knowledge [...] may be inferred from the concurrence of a number of concrete facts."[151] Therefore, these two opinions concur to reject all attempts to presume the *mens rea* necessary for crimes against humanity. The implications are that the guilty mind may be inferred from factual circumstances. These can be, for example, the historical and political circumstances in which the acts of violence occurred; the functions of the accused when the crimes were committed or his responsibilities within the political or military hierarchy; the scope and gravity of the acts perpetrated; the nature of the crimes committed; the degree to which they are common knowledge; or the existence of a pattern of conduct.[152]

Another important aspect of *mens rea* for a crime against humanity is intent. To 'intend' literally means to 'aim at', with the terms 'intention' and 'intentional' referring to the consequences which are aimed at by acts or omissions.[153] However, an act or omission is 'intentional' when it is voluntarily done or omitted in order to produce the consequences, which it does in fact produce.[154] To meet the element of *mens rea* for crimes against humanity, the jurisprudence of international tribunals as well as international criminal law requires a combination of knowledge with criminal intent. For example, Trial Chamber I held in *Blaskic* that "[f]or the underlying crimes to be constituted, a mental factor specific to crimes against humanity must be adjoined to the required criminal intent";[155] whereas Article 30 (1) of the Rome Statute stipulates that "unless otherwise provided, a person shall be criminally responsible and liable for punishment for a crime within the jurisdiction of the Court only if the material elements are committed with intent and knowledge."

However, proof of the criminal intent differs according to the type of crime involved. The following discussion on various acts constituting crimes against humanity shall highlight their specific underlying criminal intent where necessary.

---

149 See *Akayesu*, n. 79 at para. 523.
150 *Id.*
151 At para. 259.
152 See *Akayesu*, n. 79 at paras 523–524; *Tadic*, n. 82 at para. 657; and *Prosecutor v. Radovan Karadzic and Ratko Mladic* Cases No IT-95-5-R 61 & IT-95-18-R 61, Consideration of Indictment in terms of Rule 61 of the Rules of Procedure and Evidence at para. 94.
153 H.A. Palmer and H. Palmer, n. 139 at 21.
154 *Id.*
155 See n. 102 at para. 244.

Repertoire of Acts of Crime against Humanity

As already explained earlier in this study, various international legal texts, ranging from the Nuremberg Charter to the more recent Rome Statute, have established two broad categories of acts constituting crimes against humanity, namely crimes against humanity of a murder type and crimes against humanity of a persecution type. However, due to the occurrence of new forms of acts that shock the conscience of mankind and to the jurisprudence of ad hoc tribunals, the list of acts of crimes against humanity has amplified to cover a huge variety of conduct. The Statute of the IMT of Nuremberg enumerated six acts: murder, extermination, enslavement, deportation, other inhumane acts or persecution. Article 3 of the ICTR Statute added three other acts to the Nuremberg list: namely, torture, rape, and imprisonment. Article 7 of the Rome Statute recently produced a much more complete list of acts constituting crimes against humanity, by adding to the two precedent lists the following: forcible transfer of population, other severe deprivation of physical liberty, sexual slavery, enforced prostitution, forced pregnancy, enforced sterilisation, sexual violence, enforced disappearance of persons and apartheid. To this list shall be added the crime of genocide.[156] Genocide is also a crime against humanity but of a particular kind, which requires for its commission specific acts combined with a specific *mens rea*.[157]

A summary account of the most significant features of some acts constituting crimes against humanity is given below.

Murder Type of Crimes against Humanity

Among the crimes against humanity that are listed as the murder type, are the following:

Murder and Extermination

These crimes involve a deliberate taking of a person's life, and represent the core crimes against humanity. The prohibition against murder and extermination is contained in all international instruments dealing with crimes against humanity. According to the Israeli definition of crimes against humanity, death through

---

156 See Article 19 of the 1991 Draft Code of Crimes against the Peace and Security of Mankind adopted at the ILC 43rd Session, which made genocide a crime against humanity, UN Doc A/CN.4/L.459 (1991).

157 Article II of the 1948 Genocide Convention lists five acts of genocide which are: killing members of a group, causing serious bodily or mental harm to members of the group, deliberately inflicting on the group conditions of life calculated to bring about its physical destruction in whole or in part, imposing measures intended to prevent births within the group and forcibly transferring children of the group to another group. Any of these acts must be committed with the special intent to destroy, in whole or in part, a national, ethnical, racial or religious group as such.

means such as starvation is also tantamount to deliberate killing.[158] A Report of the Preparatory Commission for the ICC fixes the conditions under which murder and extermination constitute a crime against humanity.[159] According to this document, for the crime of murder to exist, the perpetrator must kill one or more persons. His conduct must be committed as part of a widespread or systematic attack directed against a civilian population, and he must know that his conduct was part of or was intended to be part of a widespread or systematic attack against a civilian population.[160] The requirements of murder are also applicable to extermination, the only difference being that the latter includes infliction of conditions of life calculated to bring about the destruction of a part of the population.[161]

Enslavement

The Supplementary Convention on the Abolition of Slavery, the Slave Trade, and Institutions and Practices Similar to Slavery[162] defines slavery as "the status or condition of a person over whom any or all of the powers attaching to the right of ownership are exercised".[163] Article 1 of this instrument calls for the elimination of "institutions and practices similar to slavery", including debt bondage, serfdom, and various types of exploitation of women and children. Article 7 (1) (d) of the Elements of Crimes of the ICTY Statute which endorsed the Slavery Convention's definition of enslavement, further defined the expression "powers attaching to the right of ownership" to include purchasing, selling, lending or bartering one or more persons or imposing on them a similar deprivation of liberty.

Deportation or Forcible Transfer of Population

This conduct refers to the unlawful and forced removal of a population from its State of residence to another State, through expulsion or any other coercive means and without grounds permitted by international law.[164] The latter disposition would mean that justified displacements such as those aimed at in Article 49 of the fourth Geneva Convention of 12 August, 1949 are permitted. These are for example, evacuation in case of emergency or natural disaster threatening the life and well-being of the population, or displacement when the security of the population or imperative military reasons so demand. Deportation is an act, which formed part of the core crimes prosecuted at Nuremberg. It has also been

---

158 See *Eichmann*, chap. I; n. 23 at 239.
159 See International Law Commission Finalised Draft Text on the Elements of Crime (hereinafter, Elements of Crimes), Doc PCNICC/2000/1/Add.2, of 2 November 2000.
160 *Id.* Article 7 (1) (a).
161 *Id.* Article 7 (1) (b).
162 As adopted by the Economic and Social Council Resolution 608 (XXI) of 30 April, 1956, entered into force on 30 April, 1957 (hereinafter Slavery Convention).
163 Article 7 (a).
164 See M. Bettati, n. 125 at 313.

included in the ICTY and ICTR Statutes, the 1954 and 1996 Draft Codes, as well as in the ICC Statute.

Imprisonment or Other Severe Deprivation of Physical Liberty

In order to be a crime against humanity, imprisonment must presumably occur without any due process.[165] Control Council Law No. 10, the 1954 and the 1996 Draft Codes, the ICTY and ICTR Statutes, all include imprisonment in their list of specific acts of crimes against humanity. Article 7 (1) (e) of the Rome Statute added to imprisonment 'other severe deprivation of physical liberty' contrary to fundamental rules of international law. The implication of this prohibition seems to be that preventive detentions in order to control the spread of infectious diseases or for any other sanitary or security reasons would be permitted.

Torture

This offence is defined separately in international conventions[166] and constitutes one of the core crimes against humanity. The drafters of the Rome Statute define torture to mean inflicting severe physical or mental pain or suffering upon a person under the custody or control of the perpetrator. This excludes pain or suffering arising out of lawful sanctions.[167] Acts of torture are also prohibited by the Universal Declaration of Human Rights (UDHR)[168] which states that "no one shall be subjected to torture or to cruel, inhuman or degrading treatment or punishment".[169] Similarly, the ACHR[170] makes torture or cruel, inhuman or degrading punishment or treatment a crime under the Convention, and requires that all persons deprived of their liberty be treated with respect for the inherent dignity of the human person.[171] Moreover, the Torture Convention goes further and imposes legal obligations not only on individuals, but also on States. In terms of this instrument, States Parties are under the duty to take appropriate measures to prevent the commission of torture, and to punish alleged torturers, including public officials or any other persons acting in an official capacity.[172] It is sometimes submitted that torture as

---

165 S.R. Ratner and J.S. Abrams, n. 118 at 70.
166 See, e.g., the Convention against Torture and Other Cruel, Inhuman, or Degrading Treatment or Punishment (hereinafter, the Torture Convention), G.A. Res. 39/46, U.N. Doc. A/39/51 (1984), see also J.H. Burgers and H. Danelius *The United Nations Convention against Torture: A Handbook on the Convention against Torture and Other Cruel, Inhuman or Degrading Treatment or Punishment* (1988).
167 Elements of Crime, n. 159 Article 7 (1) (f).
168 GA Res. 217 A (III) of 10 December 1948, UN Doc A/810 at 71 (1948).
169 Article 5.
170 Adopted in San José on 22 November 1969, OASTS 1, OEA/ser.L./V/II.23, doc.21 of 1979.
171 Article 5 (2).
172 See Articles 2, 5, 7 and 8.

an international crime has reached the status of *jus cogens*, thus justifying States in assuming universal jurisdiction over it wherever committed.[173] However, to be qualified as a crime against humanity, torture has to be committed on a large scale and with the required *mens rea*.

Sexual Crimes

Conduct amounting to this category of crime includes *Rape, sexual slavery, enforced prostitution, forced pregnancy, enforced sterilisation, and sexual violence.*

Rape leads to the violation of the physical integrity of the victim and therefore constitutes a crime against humanity. This offence is defined in the *Akayesu Case* as a physical invasion of a sexual nature, committed on a person under circumstances, which are coercive.[174] Rape is part of sexual violence, which involves physical invasion of the human body through penetration or insertion of an object into a person's natural orifices and it includes forced participation in prostitution. Rape has been massively and systematically used as an instrument of "ethnic cleansing intended to humiliate, shame, degrade and terrify entire ethnic groups" in the conflict in Yugoslavian.[175] Its prohibition under international humanitarian law can be found in instruments such as Control Council Law No. 10, the 1996 Draft Code and the ICC Statute.

The definition of *sexual slavery* provided by the Rome Statute is similar to that of enslavement, the only difference being that the person owned is caused by the perpetrator to engage in acts of a sexual nature.

Enforced prostitution means forcibly or coercively causing a person to engage in acts of a sexual nature, with the intention of obtaining a pecuniary or any other advantage from the sexual act.[176]

Forced pregnancy is defined by the Rome Statute as confining a woman who is forcibly made pregnant, with the intent of affecting the ethnic composition of any population or carrying out any grave violations of international law.[177]

Enforced sterilisation means depriving a person of biological reproductive capacity without any medical or hospital treatment or justification and carried out without the genuine consent of the person concerned.[178]

The Rome Statute defines *sexual violence* as committing or causing a person to engage in an act of a sexual nature by force, or by threat of force or coercion

---

173 See Lord Browne-Wilkinson in *UK House of Lords: Regina v. Bartle and the Commissioner of Police for the Metropolis and Others Ex Parte Pinochet*, 38 *International Legal Materials* 581 (1999) at 589.
174 At para. 598.
175 See T. Meron "Rape as a crime under international humanitarian law" 87 *American Journal of International Law* (1993) at 424.
176 See Elements of Crime, n. 159 Article 7 (1) (g)-3.
177 *Id.* Article 7 (1) (g)-4.
178 *Id.* Article 7 (1) (g)-5.

against such person; or by taking advantage of a coercive environment or such person's incapacity to give genuine consent.[179]

Other Inhumane or Inhuman Acts

The expression 'inhumane act' or 'inhuman act' appears in several international documents.[180] However, there is no unanimous definition of what constitutes inhumane or inhuman acts. These crimes are sometimes described as those for which motive is not relevant.[181] In the *Medical Case*,[182] a Control Council Law No. 10 court adopted a test based on 'the dictate of public conscience' as a standard for determining what amounts to inhumane or inhuman acts. This led the court to find that medical experimentation constituted an inhuman act. Inhumane acts are sometimes defined to cover the destruction and plundering of private property. At Nuremberg, the International Military Tribunal found Alfred Rosenberg, Minister of the Occupied Eastern Territories, and Walter Funk, Minister of Economics, Plenipotentiary-General for War Economy and President of the *Reichbank*, guilty of acts of plunder of Jewish property, including the transfer of property of concentration camp victims.[183] Nevertheless, the doctrine holds that the words 'other inhumane acts' would cover only serious crimes of a character similar to murder, extermination, enslavement and deportation, to the exclusion of offences to property.[184] A more recent document defines inhumane acts as those of a character similar to all other listed acts of crimes against humanity.[185] In this sense, the word 'other inhumane acts', used in connection with crimes against humanity would include both murder type and persecution type crimes. However, it is essential to note that there seems to be a similarity between 'inhumane acts' constituting crimes against humanity and 'inhuman treatment', which amounts to an act of torture.[186] The latter concepts have been clarified by both the European Human Rights Commission and the European Court of Human Rights as treatment that "deliberately causes severe suffering, mental or physical."[187] The European Court also stressed that the ill treatment must attain a minimum level of severity to qualify as inhuman or ill

---

179 *Id.* Article 7 (1) (g)-6.
180 See Article 6 (c) of the Nuremberg Charter; Article II (1) (c) of Control Council Law No 10; Article 5 of the Yugoslavia Statute; Article 3 of the Rwanda Statute and Article 7 (1) (k) of the Rome Statute.
181 S.R. Ratner and J.S. Abrams, n. 118 at 71.
182 In G.K. McDonald and O. Swaak-Goldman (ed.), *Substantive and Procedural Aspects of International Criminal Law: The Experience of International and National Courts Documents and Cases* (2000) at 1781.
183 See IMT Reports, n. 50 at 295–296.
184 E. Schwelb, chap. I, n. 8 at 191.
185 Rome Statute Article 7 (1) (k).
186 See in particular the 1984 Torture Convention.
187 See *Soering v. United Kingdom*, Series A No. 161, Application No. 14038/88 (7 July 1989), Judgment reprinted in 11 *European Human Rights Reports* 439 (1989) at 489 para. 104.

treatment, with the assessment of this minimum depending on all the circumstances of the case, such as the duration of the treatment, its physical or mental effects and, in some cases, the sex, age and state of health of the victim, etc.[188]

Enforced Disappearance of Persons

Enforced disappearance generally refers to the situation in which a person is clandestinely arrested, detained or abducted, with the authorisation, support or acquiescence of a State or a political organisation. Such arrest, detention or abduction is accompanied by a refusal to acknowledge the deprivation of freedom or to give information on the fate or whereabouts of the detainee. The intention behind such acts is to remove the victim from the protection of the law for a prolonged period of time.[189] The Inter-American Convention on the Forced Disappearance of Persons[190] and Article 212–1 of the French New Penal Code[191] also outlaw enforced disappearance of persons.

Persecution Type of Crimes against Humanity

Persecution

This term originally appeared in the Nuremberg Charter and in Control Council Law No. 10, and later, in the ICTY, the ICTR and the ICC Statutes. It is worth noting with the ICTY that, though often used, the term persecution has never been clearly defined in international criminal law nor known as a crime in the world's major criminal justice systems.[192] This is probably the reason why the authors of the ICC Statute endeavoured to gather jurisprudential and doctrinal elements to define this crime. For Bassiouni, persecution means the following:

> State action or policy leading to the infliction upon an individual of harassment, torment, oppression, or discriminatory measures, designed to or likely to produce physical or mental suffering or economic harm, because of the victim's beliefs, views, or membership in a given identifiable group [religious, social, ethnic, linguistic etc.], or simply because the perpetrator sought to single out a given category of victims for reasons peculiar to the perpetrator.[193]

---

188 See *The Republic of Ireland v. United Kingdom* Series A No 25 (18 January 1978), Judgment reprinted in 2 *European Human Rights Reports* 25 (1978) at 79 para. 162.
189 Elements of Crime, n. 159 Article 7 (1) (i).
190 See paragraph 6 of the Preamble reprinted in 33 *International Legal Materials* (1994) at 1429–1430.
191 See chap. I, n. 22.
192 *Tadic*, n. 82 at para. 694; also M.C. Bassiouni *Crimes against Humanity in International Criminal Law* (2000) at 327.
193 M.C. Bassiouni, n. 192 at 327.

Meanwhile, the ICTY held that:

> Because the persecution type is separate from the murder type of crimes against humanity it is not necessary to have a separate act of an inhumane nature to constitute persecution; the discrimination itself makes the act inhumane.[194]

Therefore, it is grave violations of fundamental rights that constitute persecution, even though, as already demonstrated, discriminatory motives are required for the existence of this crime. This is to say that the crime of persecution covers a variety of acts. It encompasses a variety of both enumerated acts such as murder, rape, sexual assault, torture, inhuman treatment, deportation and transfer of population; and non-enumerated acts such as those of a physical, economic or judicial nature that violate an individual's right to the equal enjoyment of his basic rights.[195]

Using all the elements developed above, the Rome Statute defined persecution as intentional and severe deprivation of fundamental rights contrary to international law by reason of the identity of the group or collectivity, or targeting such group or collectivity on the basis of their race, political affiliation, nationality, ethnicity, culture, religion, gender, or on other grounds that are universally recognised as permissible under international law.[196] Given this definition, it would seem appropriate to classify apartheid in the rubric of crimes against humanity of a persecution type because it was a State-wide system of racial discrimination that targeted specific groups, merely by reason of their identity or race.[197]

The Case of Apartheid

As stated above, apartheid may be qualified as persecution based on race and thus as a conduct amounting to crime against humanity. This is because apartheid is generally seen as a widespread and systematic policy of racial discrimination implemented with the commission of widespread and systematic inhumane acts.[198] As to the legal status of apartheid, many authoritative instruments concur to make systematic racial discrimination a crime under international law.[199] Above all, Article I of the Apartheid Convention makes apartheid a crime against humanity for which organisations, institutions and individuals may be held criminally liable. Article II lists inhuman acts that form part of 'the crime of apartheid'. These are, among

---

194 *Tadic*, n. 82 at para. 695.
195 *Id.* at paras 699–713.
196 Elements of Crime, n. 159 Article 7 (1) (h).
197 R.C. Slye "Apartheid as a crime against humanity: a submission to the South African Truth and Reconciliation Commission" 20 *Michigan Journal of International Law* 1 (1998) at 280.
198 *Id.* at 300.
199 E.g. Article 2 (2) of the 1996 International Covenant on Economic, Social and Cultural Rights; the 1966 International Convention on the Elimination of All Forms of Racial Discrimination; the 1973 Apartheid Convention; Article 20 of the 1991 Draft Code of Crimes against the Peace and Security of Mankind and Article 7 of the 1998 Rome Statute.

others, the denial to members of a racial group the right to life and liberty of person by murdering them, inflicting upon them serious bodily and mental harm, subjecting them to torture or to cruel, inhuman or degrading treatment or punishment, or by arbitrarily and illegally imprisoning them; the deliberate imposition on a racial group of condition of living calculated to cause its physical destruction in whole or in part; adopting legislative or any other measures designed to divide the population along racial lines and to prevent racial groups from participating in the political, social, economic and cultural life of the country.

The prohibition against apartheid as systematic racial discrimination is believed to be a *jus cogens* norm[200] to which no derogation is allowed, since apartheid stands in contradiction with the basic principles upon which the United Nations rests. *Jus cogens* are peremptory norms of international law, which binds all states irrespective of their consent. Other human rights norms, which are believed to have reached the status of *jus cogens*, are the prohibition against genocide, slavery, and torture.[201] Other international criminal instruments criminalizing apartheid include, the Convention on the Non-Applicability of Statutory Limitations to War Crimes and Crimes against Humanity,[202] which extends the definition of crimes against humanity to cover acts of eviction by armed attack or occupation, and inhuman acts resulting from the policy of apartheid. In addition, the Rome Statute defines apartheid as inhuman acts analogous to those aimed at in its Article 7 (1)[203] committed in the context of an institutionalised regime of systematic oppression and domination by one racial group over any other racial group or groups with the intention to maintain such regime.[204]

As regards the required *mens rea* for the crime of apartheid, the Apartheid Convention is not as specific as the Genocide Convention. It only states that inhumane acts in furtherance of this crime shall be committed "[…] for the purpose of establishing and maintaining domination by one racial group of persons over any other racial group of persons".[205] Since the Convention has never been interpreted by any court of law there is no clear indication as to the exact *mens rea* required for the crime of apartheid. Nevertheless, one can infer from the definition provided by the Rome Statute that in addition to the elements of *mens rea* required for other persecution type crimes, namely knowledge and discriminatory intent, the crime of apartheid would require a further specific requirement: that of maintaining or supporting an institutionalised regime of oppression by one racial group over another.

---

200 See the meaning of this term in chapter 7.
201 See Draft Convention against Torture and Other Cruel, Inhuman, or Degrading Treatment or Punishment reprinted in 23 *ILM* 5, 1027 (1984).
202 See chap. I, n. 17.
203 Meaning all acts of crimes against humanity as listed above.
204 Article 7 (2) (h).
205 Article 2.

Summary

In light of the foregoing exposition, crimes against humanity exists whenever at least one of the acts referred to above is committed as part of a widespread or systematic attack directed against a civilian population. Such an attack must result from a group, state or organisational policy or plan, and the accused must act with the required *mens rea*, i.e. knowledge of the attack and intent to commit the incriminated act for the murder type crimes, or knowledge and discriminatory motive for the persecution type crimes. However, this definition fails to address all criminal action targeting civilian populations and perpetrated by a group of persons in a widespread and systematic manner. Of particular interest to the world community today is terrorism; especially, the case of a terrorist act of the magnitude of that of September 11, 2001 which targeted innocent civilians. Since such an act is committed as part of the policy of terror formulated by a particular group, and directed against a civilian population with the intention to inflict more harm as possible, would it not be suitable to refer to it as a form of crime against humanity? This can easily fall within the rubric of either murder type crimes or "inhuman acts intentionally causing great suffering or serious injury to body or to mental or physical health".

Our conclusion is that crimes against humanity form part of the *delicti jus gentium*[206] in that their commission does not only affect individual victims, but also the international community at large. They are therefore concerned with both States and individual conduct, hence the imposition of certain duties on both the individual and the State to refrain from the commission of such crimes. The Nuremberg Tribunal recognised individual duties as well as States duties by virtue of international law in the following way: "[t]hat international law imposes duties and liabilities upon individuals as well as upon States has long been recognised."[207] The nature, content, scope and limits of such duties in respect of crimes against humanity are defined in the next two chapters.

---

206 Serious crimes of international concern, or crimes against the law of nations; this concept is examined in chapter 7.
207 See G.K. McDonald and O. Swaak-Goldman, n. 182 at 337–338.

INDIVIDUAL CRIMINAL LIABILITY FOR CRIMES
AGAINST HUMANITY

Introduction

Criminal liability arises out of the violation of an existing duty towards the community as a whole. In international law, customary and conventional norms impose certain obligations on both the State and the individual. Such norms, which are contained in various treaties, agreements, protocols, conventions, covenants and statutes, obligate States and persons to abstain from committing certain acts, which are likely to disturb the peace and security of mankind. International law documents containing penal provisions apply directly to individuals and require each State to establish mechanisms for individual criminal liability for the crimes they prohibit. International treaties dealing with torture, genocide, slavery, war crimes and crimes against humanity are of this kind. Therefore, the principle of individual criminal responsibility for crimes against humanity is entrenched in international law and, *mutatis mutandis*, in domestic law.

This chapter will attempt to identify the sources of individual criminal responsibility for crimes against humanity in international law, and to assess the mechanisms for attributing or rejecting liability whenever an act constitutive of such an offence is committed. The aim here is to demonstrate that because of the fact that crimes against humanity are a serious international offence par excellence, the principle of individual criminal liability for its commission is entrenched in international law, and that such a principle calls for the prosecution and punishment of all offenders irrespective of their status or office. Consequently, no form of domestic limitation—be it based on office, sovereignty, immunity, amnesty or pardon—shall prevent the competent courts from hearing cases dealing with the alleged commission of this crime. It will be shown that the chain of liability for crimes against humanity includes the decision-maker who initiates the criminal policy, the intermediary who facilitates the implementation of such a policy and

Faustin Z. Ntoubandi, Amnesty for Crimes against Humanity under International Law, pp. 81–111.
© 2007, *Koninklijke Brill NV. Printed in The Netherlands.*

the subordinate who actually executes that policy. Great emphasis will be placed on the responsibility of higher State officials and powerful leaders in that they constitute the main target of statutory limitations such as immunity and amnesty. Finally, it will be concluded that the principle of individual criminal liability for crimes against humanity the implementation of which is part and parcel of State's duties under international law, calls for some sort of sanction.

Legal Sources of Individual Criminal Liability

The source of the criminal liability of individuals in international law can be traced as far back as 1649, when the British Parliament set up a special High Court to try King Charles I for the breach of certain fundamental norms of national and international law. At the conclusion of the summary proceedings the Court discovered that the King could be condemned to death for breaching "[...] the fundamental law of this Kingdom, [...] the general law of all nations, and the unanimous consent of all rational men in the world."[1]

Echoing the idea of holding individuals criminally liable for violating the law of nations, Alberico Gentili (1552–1608) proposed that war could be waged as punishment for "cases in which a sovereign or a nation does wrong" and in instances where a private individual has done wrong and his sovereign or nation has failed to repair his fault.[2] In commenting on the legality of war, Hugo Grotius (1563–1645) suggested that:

> [A] community and/or its rulers may be held responsible for the crime of the subject if they knew of it and took no such preventive measures as stood in their power to employ. And the same responsibility is incurred by a community and/or its ruler if they do not abide by the principle *aut dedere aut punire*.[3]

Later on, Christian Wolff (1679–1754) proposed that if a sovereign oppresses his subjects, foreign rulers possess the right of interceding on behalf of the unfortunates. He recommended that such measures of humanitarian intervention be limited to peaceful actions.[4]

Despite all the doctrinal works advocating individual liability for the violation of international law, no proper legal text existed which fixed the mechanisms of individual responsibility. Consequently, sovereigns who were indicted for violating international law were either impeached or were not properly tried and punished.[5]

However, the views expressed above by Gentili, Grotius and Wolff will have their first legal consecration in the 1919 Versailles Peace Treaty, which put an end

---

1 A.G.D. Levy "Criminal responsibility of individuals and international law" 12 *The University of Chicago Law Revue* 4 (1945) at 320.
2 *De Jure Belli Libri Tres, I, XXI* of 1598, as quoted by A.G.D. Levy, n. 1 at 322.
3 *Id.* at 323.
4 *De Jure Naturae et Gentium Libri Octo, 8, III, 4* of 1750, as quoted by A.G.D. Levy, n. 1 at 324.
5 *Id.* at 319.

to World War I. In effect, Articles 227–30 of this Treaty provided for the personal criminal responsibility of the authors of the war. Of utmost importance was Article 227, which arraigned the German emperor "for a supreme offence against international morality and the sanctity of treaties".[6] But in 1919, the most dominant view on the principle of responsibility for the violation of international norms was that sovereign States incurred vicarious responsibility for internationally wrongful acts committed by their agents, while personal criminal liability was a matter of domestic jurisdictions.[7] This view was advanced at the Preliminary Peace Conference in Paris in 1919 by the United States' members of the Commission on the Responsibility of the Authors of the War and on Enforcement of Penalties (Commission) to support their reservations to the Commission's Report recommending the criminal prosecution of all persons responsible for the violation of the laws and customs of war, and the laws of humanity committed during World War I. Regarding the personal criminal responsibility of the German Kaiser, the U.S. Commissioners argued, among others, that as agents of the people who are the only depository of the sovereignty of any State, heads of State were responsible only to the people for the illegal acts which they might have committed. Consequently, they should not be responsible to any other sovereign.[8] It was therefore rather an exception in earlier times when pirates and slave traders were recognised as the enemies of all mankind who could be punished by any captor.[9] Consequently, the division among the members of the Commission on the legal basis for the responsibility of the Kaiser hindered his trial.

Nevertheless, the American position on the criminal responsibility of individuals for the violation of international law would change in 1945 with the adoption of the Charter of the International Military Tribunal. In fact, Article 6 of the Charter set the basis of individual criminal liability for war crimes, crimes against peace and crimes against humanity. Subsequent international human rights and humanitarian law instruments as well as the work of international tribunals will later establish the mechanisms and modalities of individual criminal liability for the most serious crimes in international law i.e., war crimes, crimes against humanity, genocide or the crime of aggression.

In general, the principle of individual criminal liability for crimes against humanity finds its sources in human rights and humanitarian law treaties, and is expressed in various international criminal law instruments establishing the parameters of the acquisition of criminal responsibility. The first substantive rules setting the basis of individual criminal liability for crimes against humanity were established by the Nuremberg Charter; they were subsequently developed in the judgments of the IMT, and finally introduced in the corpus of international law by the Nuremberg Principles.

---

6 E. Schwelb chap. I, n. 8 at 183.
7 R. Jennings and A. Watts *Oppenheim's International Law* 9th ed. vol. I (1992) at 159–166.
8 G.K. McDonald and O. Swaak-Goldman, chap. III, n. 182 at 52.
9 See B.B. Ferencz, chap. III, n. 2 at 870.

The Nuremberg Charter, Judgements and Principles

Since the provisions of the Versailles Treaty on the personal liability of the German Kaiser for violating the laws and customs of war and the laws of humanity were never enforced, the Nuremberg Charter remains the first international instrument to hold State officials directly and individually liable for violating their international duties. This view is shared by the many commentators who believe that the Charter is the true legal source of individual responsibility for war crimes, crimes against peace and crimes against humanity.[10] In order to better grasp the quasi-universal role played by the Nuremberg Charter—its Judgements and Principles—in establishing individual criminal responsibility for these crimes, it is perhaps important to clarify the status of this document under international law. Defining the legal status of the Charter is fundamental for today's understanding of the rationale underlying the strict legal proscription of certain international crimes, such as crimes against humanity.

The Nuremberg Charter as Source of International Obligations

In terms of Article 38 (1) of the Statute of the ICJ, the following are sources of international law: international conventions or treaties, international customs, general principles of law recognised by civilised nations, judicial decisions and the teachings of the most highly qualified publicists of various nations.

In international law a treaty or convention exists "when two or more independent sovereign states treat a subject matter with one another and reach an agreement with the intention of giving it legal validity".[11] There exists two types of treaties: contractual treaties which are generally bilateral treaties between two parties, governing a special object affecting the particular interests of the State-parties, and law-making treaties, which are multilateral conventions designed to lay down general rules of conduct binding on a large number of States in the same manner as domestic legislation.[12] Such treaties create law when they are declaratory of existing rules or when non-parties accept them as binding because they regard such treaties as the embodiment of principles of international custom.[13]

Custom as the oldest source of international law requires a consistent, uniform and general State practice coupled with the belief that such practice is rendered

---

10 See e.g. L.S. Sunga, chap. III, n. 15 at 36.
11 P.K. Menon "Primary, subsidiary and other possible sources of international law" 1 *Sri Lanka Journal of International Law* (1989) at 114; see also Article 2 (1) (a) of the 1969 Vienna Convention on the Law of Treaties, which defines the word 'treaty' as "an international agreement concluded between States in written form and governed by international law, whether embodied in a single instrument or in two or more related instruments and whatever its particular designation".
12 P.K. Menon, n. 11 at 117.
13 D.W. Greig *International Law* 2nd ed. (1976) at 17.

obligatory by the existence of a rule of law requiring it.[14] This mental element is usually referred to as *opinio juris sive necessitatis*.

General principles of law recognised by civilised nations are seen by jurists, such as Verdross as a means of incorporating principles of natural law into the international area, while others, such as Guggenheim, believe that such principles reiterate those principles previously covered in treaties and customs.[15] In elaborating on this notion, Lord Phillimore of the United Kingdom who co-authored Article 38 (1) of the Statute of the ICJ stated that general principles refer to "those which were accepted by all nations *in foro domestico*, such as principles of procedure, the principle of good faith, and the principle of *res judicata*, etc".[16]

With reference to the definitions given above, it is generally accepted that treaties proscribing crimes against humanity, war crimes and genocide are of the category of law-making treaties in that they impose legal obligations on the international community as a whole.[17] In this sense, the Charter of the IMT was a law-creating treaty. The drafters, prosecutors and judges regarded the Nuremberg Charter both as a custom-creating act and as an instrument codifying the state of custom at that time.[18] In fact, in 1945 the existence of customary international law required some affirmation in subsequent State practice that a given act supported by *opinio juris* represented the expression of a binding obligation. On the basis of this argument it was commonly contended and accepted that the fact that four victorious nations signed the Nuremberg Charter and nineteen others subsequently acceded to it evidenced those States' *opinio juris* in respect of the crimes defined in the Charter.[19] Therefore, it can be argued that, even in the absence of any precedent in international law, the obligations contained in the Nuremberg Charter were generally accepted as binding not only upon sovereign States but also upon private individuals.

However, if one strictly applies the above definitions of 'international custom' and 'general principles of law' to certain provisions of the Charter—especially to those dealing with individual criminal liability for the Charter's crimes—it would become clear that holding responsible State officials directly accountable for crimes against humanity was not a common State practice in international law. This practice was therefore an innovation in 1945, when crimes against humanity became an offence under international law. Nevertheless, the Nuremberg Charter can be said to have been a custom-creating instrument, as it would later be evidenced by numerous subsequent international and national documents modelled on it, which made private

---

14 M. Dixon and R. McCorquodale *Cases and Materials on International Law* 3rd ed. (2000) at 27.

15 See J. Black-Branch, Sovereign immunity under international law: the case of Pinochet, in D. Woodhouse *The Pinochet Case: A Legal and Constitutional Analysis* (2000) at 96–97.

16 *Id.* at 97.

17 See e.g., D.W. Greig, n. 13 at 9.

18 M.C. Bassiouni, chap. III, n. 97 at 83.

19 *Id.*

persons, including constitutionally responsible State leaders, personally answerable for war crimes, crimes against peace or crimes against humanity.

Individual Criminal Liability Under the Nuremberg Charter

Articles 6, 7 and 8 of the Nuremberg Charter first established the legal basis for individual liability for crimes against humanity.

Article 6 of the Charter listed acts that might give rise to personal liability and named the categories of offenders that they were aimed at. It provided that:

> Leaders, organisers, instigators, and accomplices participating in the formulation or execution of a common plan or conspiracy to commit any of the foregoing crimes [crimes against peace, war crimes or crimes against humanity] are responsible for all acts performed by any person in execution of such plan.

Article 7 further made official position irrelevant for all the crimes listed in the Charter. It read:

> The official position of defendants, whether as Heads of State or responsible officials in Government Departments, shall not be considered as freeing them from responsibility or mitigating punishment.

Moreover, Article 8 rejected the defence of superior order for the crimes contained in the Charter. It stated:

> The fact that the defendant acted pursuant to order of his Government or of a superior shall not free him from responsibility, but may be considered in mitigation of punishment if the Tribunal determines that justice so requires.[20]

The principle of individual criminal liability for the crimes defined in the Charter would later be reiterated in more or less the same language in Control Council Law No. 10,[21] and in the Tokyo Charter.[22]

In its judgements, the Nuremberg Tribunal offered one of the most convincing arguments on the rationale of holding individuals criminally liable for the Charter crimes, when it opined that:

> It was submitted that international law is concerned with the actions of sovereign States, and provides no punishment for individuals; and further, that where the act in question is an act of State, those who carry it out are not personally responsible but are protected by the doctrine of the sovereignty of the State. In the opinion of the Tribunal, both these submissions must be rejected. That international law imposes duties and liabilities upon individuals as upon States has long been recognised [...] the very essence of the Charter is that individuals have international duties which transcend the national obligation of obedience imposed by the individual States. He who violates the laws of war cannot obtain immunity while acting in pursuance of the

---

20 G.K. McDonald and O. Swaak-Goldman, chap. III, n. 182, vol. II Part I at 63.
21 Articles II (2) and II (4) (a) and (b).
22 Article 5 (c) and Article 6.

authority of the State, if the State in authorising action moves outside its competence under international law.[23]

It further elaborated on individual liability by making the following statement:

Crimes against international law are committed by men, not by abstract entities, and only by punishing individuals who commit such crimes can the provisions on international law be enforced.[24]

In his Hague lectures, Sir Arthur Watts echoed the view expressed above in the following way:

For international conduct, which is so serious as to be tainted with criminality to be regarded as attributable only to the impersonal State and not to the individuals who ordered or perpetrated it is both unrealistic and offensive to common notions of justice.[25]

An additional ruling by a Control Council Law Court definitively solidified the basis of individual criminal liability for war crimes, crimes against peace and crimes against humanity in international law. This Court held that:

The question of the responsibility of individuals for such breaches of international law as constitute crimes, has been widely discussed and is settled in part by the judgement of the International Military Tribunal. It can no longer be successfully maintained that international law is concerned only with the actions of sovereign States and provides no punishment for individuals.[26]

The principles of individual criminal liability as provided for by the Nuremberg Charter and interpreted in the judgements of the Nuremberg Tribunal were adopted by the ILC of the United Nations in 1950, which established them as "Principles of International Law Recognised in the Charter of the Nuremberg Tribunal and the Judgement of the Tribunal". As to the legal status of this instrument, it is worth observing that it was adopted on the basis of United Nations General Assembly Resolution 177 (II), paragraph (a) of 21 November, 1947 which directed the ILC to formulate the Nuremberg Principles. Since such Principles had already been previously 'affirmed' by General Assembly Resolution 95 (I) of 11 December, 1946 the Commission was merely required to 'formulate' them, rather than to 'ascertain' them.[27] One may therefore ague that, being the product of a General Assembly resolution, the Nuremberg Principles do not have a legally binding force per se.[28]

---

23 I. Brownlie *Principles of Public International Law* 4th ed. (1990) at 562.

24 *United States v. Flick et al.*, chap. III, n. 61, reprinted in *Law Reports of the Trial of the Major War Criminals Before the International Military Tribunal* (1947) at 171, 223.

25 *1994–III Recueil Des Cours: Collected Courses of The Hague Academy of International Law*, vol. 247 of the Collection (1995) at 82.

26 *Law Reports of the Trial of the Major War Criminals Before the International Military Tribunal* vol. 9–1 (1947) at 3–5.

27 See introductory note to the text of the Nuremberg Principles, available at www.deoxy.org/wc/wc-nurem.htm.

28 See discussion in chapter 5 on the legal force of United Nations resolutions.

However, their insertion in subsequent treaties, such as the Rome Statute of 1998, has elevated them to the status of legally binding principles as far as State Parties to such treaties are concerned.

Nuremberg Principle VI made crimes against peace, war crimes and crimes against humanity punishable under international law while Principle I made any "person who commits an act which constitutes a crime under international law [...] responsible therefore and liable to punishment." Principle III made official capacity irrelevant for the relevant crimes, whereas Principle IV excluded the defence of superior order in the following terms:

> The fact that a person acted pursuant to orders of his Government or of a superior does not relieve him from responsibility under international law provided a moral choice was in fact possible to him.

Principle VII made complicity in the commission of the Charter's crimes a crime under international law, while Principle II prescribed the irrelevance of domestic law with regard to the Charter's crimes; the latter provided as follows:

> The fact that internal law does not impose a penalty for an act that constitutes a crime under international law does not relieve the person who committed the act from responsibility under international law.

On the basis of the IMT Charter and of the Nuremberg Principles, several other international legal documents developed, which made private individuals as well as State authorities directly and personally answerable for the breach of certain international obligations. Some of these documents are discussed below.

The Progeny of Nuremberg

Among the international instruments that provide for individual criminal liability on the basis of the Nuremberg Charter are: the Genocide Convention, the four Geneva Conventions of 12 August, 1949 and their Additional Protocols of 1977, the Apartheid Convention, the Draft Code of Crimes against the Peace and Security of Mankind, the ICTY Statute, the ICTR and the ICC Statutes.

The Genocide Convention unanimously adopted on 9 December 1948 by the General Assembly of the United Nations made genocide a crime under international law, which the contracting parties undertake to prevent and punish.[29] Article II of the Convention defines genocide as:

> (A)ny of the following acts committed with intent to destroy, in whole or in part, a national, ethnical, racial or religious group, as such: a) Killing members of the group; b) Causing serious bodily or mental harm to members of the group; c) Deliberately inflicting on the group conditions of life calculated to bring about its physical destruction in whole or in part; d) Imposing measures intended to prevent births within the group; e) Forcibly transferring children of the group to another group.

---

29 See Article I of this Convention.

Article III lists acts of genocide, which are punishable under international law. These are genocide, conspiracy to commit genocide, direct and public incitement to commit genocide, attempt to commit genocide and complicity in genocide. Article IV, which is very relevant here, provides for individual liability by making all persons, whether they are constitutionally responsible leaders, public officials or private individuals, punishable for any act enumerated in Article III. Article V enjoins the contracting parties to provide, among others, effective penalties for persons guilty of any act of genocide.

The definition above requires two conditions to be fulfilled before an individual can be held personally and criminally liable for committing acts of genocide. Firstly, there must be an act as prescribed by Article III of the Convention. Secondly, any such act must be committed with a special *mens rea*; that is the intent to destroy, in whole or in part, a national, ethnical, racial or religious group as such. In this sense, genocide differs from the crime against humanity by persecution[30] for which a discriminatory intent is also required, and to which genocide is the closest crime. In the crime against humanity by persecution, the perpetrator targets its victims merely because they belong to a distinct group and without seeking to destroy such a group, while genocide denies the existence of a group as such and seeks its partial or total destruction.[31] Despite the existence of strong arguments that consider genocide as a crime against humanity,[32] the distinction above highlights the difference between the two offences. In general, the prohibition against genocide protects groups from destruction or extermination, while the prohibition against crimes against humanity protects any civilian populations from persecutions irrespective of their belonging to a particular racial, ethnical, religious or national group.[33] The difference between the two crimes is further strengthened by the 1998 Rome Statute as well as the 1996 Draft Code of Crimes, which include crimes against humanity and genocide in two separate headings. This separate inclusion upholds the view held by the Trial Chamber of *Akayesu*, according to which the two "crimes have different purposes and are, therefore, never co-extensive".[34] However, despite the existence of a clear difference between the two crimes, many commentators hold the view that genocide is a crime against humanity in its more aggravated form.

The Geneva Conventions of 12 August 1949 establishes the system of grave breaches that constitutes the basis of individual criminal liability not only for the

---

30 See Chapter III above for the content and contour of this crime.
31 See *Prosecutor v. Akayesu*, chap. III, n. 79 at para. 522.
32 See e.g., Article 7 of the 1968 Convention on the Non-Applicability of Statutory Limitations to War Crimes and Crimes against Humanity; Article 1 (1) of the European Convention on the Non-Applicability of Statutory Limitation to Crimes Against Humanity and War Crimes of 1974, in *European Treaty Series* No. 82; see also T. Meron "International criminalization of internal atrocities" 89 *American Journal of International Law* (1993) at 557, and *Prosecutor v. Tadic*, chap. III, n. 82 at paras. 622–655.
33 W.A. Shabas, The crime of genocide in the jurisprudence of the international criminal tribunal, in Fisher-Ipsen and Wolf *Bochumer Schriften zur Friedenssicherung und zum Humanitären Völkerrecht* Band 38 (2000) at 461.
34 See chap. III, n. 79 at para. 469.

direct perpetrators of grave breaches of the laws of war, but also for their superiors. Acts constituting grave breaches of the Conventions are defined in detail in Article 50 of Convention I,[35] Article 51 of Convention II,[36] Article 130 of Convention III[37] and Article 147 of Convention IV.[38] They are, among others, wilful killing, torture or inhuman treatment such as biological experiments, wilfully causing great suffering or serious injury to body or health, extensive destruction or appropriation of property not justified by military necessity and carried out unlawfully and wantonly, unlawful deportation, the transfer or confinement of a protected person, the taking of hostages.

As far as the responsibility *ratione personae* is concerned, the Geneva Conventions provide for the responsibility of any person who violates the 'grave breaches' system of protection set in the Conventions. In order to monitor the implementation of the Geneva Conventions, States-Parties undertake to enact legislation to provide effective penal sanctions for persons committing or ordering to be committed, any of the acts constitutive of grave breaches of the Conventions.[39] The Hague Convention of 1954 for the Protection of Cultural Property in the Event of Armed Conflict uses similar wordings when it provides for individual liability for breaches of that Convention.[40] Moreover, Article 86 (2) of Protocol I Additional to the 1949 Geneva Conventions and relating to the Protection of Victims of International Armed Conflicts provides that superiors are not absolved from penal or disciplinary responsibility for any breach of the Conventions or of the Protocol committed by their subordinates, 'if they knew or had information' enabling them to conclude that the subordinate was about to commit or was committing such a breach and if no measures were taken to prevent or punish the breach.

The Geneva Conventions are generally believed to be the codification of the customary law of war. Various acts defined in the system of 'grave breaches' such as killings, inhuman treatments, unlawful deportations, the transfer or confinement of protected persons are also acts of crime against humanity, especially when committed on a widespread or systematic manner with the required *mens rea*. Therefore, the violation of the system of 'grave breaches' as established by the Geneva

---

35 Convention (I) for the Amelioration of the Condition of the Wounded and Sick in Armed Forces in the Field, 6 UST 311, TIAS No. 3362, 75 UNTS 31.

36 Convention (II) for the Amelioration of the Condition of Wounded, Sick and Shipwrecked Members of Armed Forces at Sea, 6 UST 3217 TIAS No. 3363, 75 UNTS 85.

37 Convention (III) Relative to the Treatment of Prisoners of War, 6 UST 3316, TIAS No. 3364, 75 UNTS 135.

38 Convention (IV) Relative to the Protection of Civilian Persons in Time of War, 6 UST 3516, TIAS No. 3365, 75 UNTS 287.

39 Article 49 of Convention I; Article 50 of Convention II; Article 129 of Convention III and Article 146 of Convention IV.

40 Article 28 states: "The High Contracting Parties undertake to take, within the framework of their ordinary criminal jurisdiction, all necessary steps to prosecute and impose penal or disciplinary sanctions upon those persons, of whatever nationality, who commit or order to be committed a breach of the present Convention".

Conventions committed with the required knowledge and intent may constitute a basis for individual criminal liability for crimes against humanity.

Similarly, the Apartheid Convention created criminal liability for individuals, representatives of the State, members of organisations and institutions (regardless of their motive or place of residence) when they either commit, participate in, directly incite, and conspire in the commission of acts of apartheid; or when they directly abet, encourage or co-operate in the commission of the crime of apartheid.[41] This would mean according to Slye that "an individual or organisation that had no intention of supporting apartheid might be criminally liable for acts that had the unintended effect of encouraging apartheid."[42] Finally, Article 4 granted jurisdiction to prosecute persons found guilty of the crime of apartheid, regardless of their nationality or the location where the crime was committed.

As demonstrated above, the principle of individual criminal liability for crimes against humanity is entrenched in international law. It is embodied in international customs and treaties and has been extensively developed by jurisprudential and doctrinal works. These sources of law have also established mechanisms governing the attribution or rejection of individual criminal liability. Such mechanisms will be dealt with below.

Parameters of Individual Criminal Attribution

Crimes against humanity are a type of offence whose commission requires a careful organisation and the involvement of different categories of people belonging to various strata of society. Therefore, each criminal act committed in furtherance of a criminal enterprise will differ according to the degree of involvement of the perpetrator in the commission of that crime. In general, a crime may be committed either directly or indirectly. In the first case, the author of the criminal act is believed to be a direct perpetrator; in the second case, one deals with an indirect perpetrator. In the case of direct perpetration of a crime, which is usually characteristic of the situation of low-level executants in situations of mass criminal actions, the perpetrator is directly and physically involved in the actual commission of the crime. In contrast, in the case of an indirect perpetration of a crime, the action of the perpetrator is remote from the actual scene of the crime and, in certain cases he is not even connected to the crime perpetrated. Decision-makers fit well into the category of indirect perpetrators. In between, stands a third group generally referred to as facilitators whose task is to help or assist in various ways in the commission of crimes.

Since crimes against humanity can only be committed pursuant to a State, organisational or group policy,[43] it therefore requires a combined and concerted effort of the direct perpetrator, the facilitator and the indirect perpetrator. Thus,

---

41 Article 3.
42 See chap. III, n. 197 at 293.
43 See Chapter III above.

international criminal law creates criminal liability for acts committed in a collective context and in a systematic manner. Accordingly, participation constitutes the basis of responsibility for crimes against humanity in international law. The form and extent of participation will determine the degree of individual criminal liability of each perpetrator.

Participation as Basis of Liability: Extent of Participation

Participation as basis of individual criminal liability for the most serious international crimes was first established by the Nuremberg Charter; it was later restated in various other international instruments.[44] The principles governing participation as basis of liability in international law were set forth by a Canadian court in *Ramirez*,[45] a case involving torture. In interpreting the word 'committed' contained in Article F (a) of the 1951 Convention Relating to the Status of Refugees, the Canadian Federal Court established, *inter alia*, that for a crime of persecution to be committed, personal and knowing participation in persecutorial acts are required; that membership in an organisation which is directed to a limited, brutal purpose, such as secret police activity, may by necessity point to personal and knowing participation; that mere presence at the scene of persecutorial acts does not qualify as personal and knowing participation; and finally that the existence of a shared common purpose and the knowledge that all the parties have of it is sufficient evidence of complicity.[46] Some of these principles were further developed by Trial Chamber II of the ICTY in *Tadic*. In this case, the Tribunal adopted the following views while interpreting Article 7 (1) of its Statute relating to individual criminal responsibility:

> [A] person may only be criminally responsible for conduct where it is determined that he knowingly participated in the commission of an offence [and] his participation directly and substantially affected the commission of that offence through supporting the actual commission before, during, or after the incident.[47]

Knowing participation is defined as 'awareness' of the act of participation coupled with a conscious decision to participate.[48] This implies that a person cannot be held

---

44 See e.g., Articles 2 (3) (e) and 16 of the 1996 Draft Code of Crimes against the Peace and Security of Mankind; Article 3 (a) of the Apartheid Convention; Article 6 (1) of the ICTR Statute and Article 25 (3) (a), (b), (c), (d) of the Rome Statute.
45 *Ramirez v. Canada: Minister of Employment and Immigration*, 1992 2 Federal Court 306, 89 DLR (4th) 173, 135 NR 390 (CA).
46 J. Rikhof "Crimes against humanity, customary international law and the international tribunals for Bosnia and Rwanda" 6 *National Journal of Constitutional Law* (1996) at 254.
47 *Tadic*, chap. III, n. 82 at para. 692.
48 *Id.* at para. 674 as confirmed in *Prosecutor v. Zlatko Aleksovski* Case No IT-95-14-1, '*Lasva Valley*', TC I Judgment of 25 June 1999 at para. 61.

criminally liable when he provided assistance to the perpetrator without knowing that his actions would facilitate the commission of the crime.

In addition, participation must be direct and substantial. Direct and substantial participation involves a contribution that facilitates the commission of a crime in some significant way, or a contribution that has an effect in the commission of a crime.[49] Such contribution includes for example, providing the perpetrator with the means, which enable him to commit the crime.[50] Participation gives rise to criminal responsibility only when the crime is actually committed or at least attempted.[51] However, it may take different forms depending on whether it occurred at the decision-making level or at the level of the actual carrying out of the decision.

Forms of Participation

The Nuremberg Charter,[52] the Genocide Convention,[53] the Apartheid Convention,[54] the 1996 Draft Code of Crimes against the Peace and Security of Mankind,[55] the 1993 ICTY Statute,[56] the 1994 ICTR Statute,[57] and the 1998 ICC Statute[58] are among the international legal documents that criminalize both participating in the formulation or the execution of a criminal policy, and conspiring to commit a crime. They also address various ways in which an individual may incur liability for participating in a crime or otherwise for contributing significantly to the commission of a crime. These are participation by commission, by complicity or by attempt to commit a crime.[59] In all these circumstances, the participation of an accomplice must be of the nature that facilitates the commission of a crime in some significant way, irrespective of the form of participation involved.

Participation by the Commission of a Crime

According to the Trial Chamber of the ICTY in *Kunarac*,[60] a person 'commits' a crime "when he or she physically perpetrates the relevant criminal act or engenders

---

49 *Tadic*, chap. III, n. 82 at para. 688.
50 ILC 1996 Report on the Draft Code of Crimes against the Peace and Security of Mankind, Commentary of Articles 2 (3) (d) and (e).
51 G.K. McDonald and O. Swaak-Goldman, chap. III, n. 182, vol. II Part I at 340.
52 Article 6.
53 Articles II, III and IV.
54 Article 3 (a) and (b).
55 Article 2.
56 Article 7 (1).
57 Article 6 (1).
58 Article 25.
59 G.K. McDonald and O. Swaak-Goldman, chap. III, n. 182, vol. II Part I at 340.
60 *Prosecutor v. Dragoljub Kunarac, Radomir Kovac and Zoran Vukovic*, Cases Nos. IT-96-23 and IT-96-23/1 '*Foca*', Judgment of 22 February 2001.

a culpable omission in violation of a rule of criminal law."[61] This implies that, a crime against humanity may be committed by means of an act or an omission. In the first case, an individual incurs criminal liability for "the affirmative conduct of performing an act in violation of the duty to refrain from performing such an act".[62] This form of participation amounts to a direct or immediate perpetration, which is referred to in the Rome Statute as commission '... as an individual'.[63] In the second case individual criminal liability results from the failure "to perform an act in violation of the duty to perform such an act";[64] with the word 'commit' generally referring to intentional rather than merely negligent or accidental conduct.

Regarding individual criminal liability by commission, it is unlikely that a head of State or senior government or military senior official will be in a position where he will be directly and personally committing a crime against humanity. Mainly low-level executioners are likely to be directly involved in the commission of this offence. However, this does not mean that senior State officials cannot be found guilty for the commission of a crime against humanity. During the Nuremberg trials the basis of the guilt of senior political leaders such as Goering, Ribbentrop and Rosenberg for war crimes and crimes against humanity, was not direct participation in the commission of the crimes they were accused of. It was rather their participation in conferences at which policies of slave labour, persecution, or extermination were agreed upon.[65] Many other Nazi officials were condemned on the basis of their belonging to criminal organisations such as the SS or the Gestapo. Consequently, direct participation of the most senior civilian Nazi officials was never proved[66] and need not be proved in order to hold them personally liable for the Nazi crimes.

Therefore, in almost all cases, only low-level perpetrators are likely to be convicted for participation by the commission of a crime, while the guilt of the most senior officials will likely be more difficult to prove because of their remoteness from the scene of the crime. However, they may be found guilty for the commission of a crime against humanity on the basis of their belonging to a criminal group, or of their participation in the meetings of such groups.

Participation by Complicity in a Crime

Co-perpetration (jointly with another person) and perpetration by means (through the instrumentality of another person) are part of participation by complicity in a crime. This form of participation includes acts such as: ordering the commission of a crime; failure to prevent or repress the commission of a crime; aiding or abetting;

---

61 At para. 390.
62 G.K. McDonald and O. Swaak-Goldman, chap. III, n. 182, vol. II Part I at 340.
63 Article 25 (3) (a).
64 G.K. McDonald and O. Swaak-Goldman, chap. III, n. 182 vol. II Part I at 340.
65 L.C. Green "Command responsibility in international humanitarian law" 5 *Transnational Law and Contemporary Problems* 2 (1995) at 329–335.
66 *Id.* at 331.

planning or conspiring to commit a crime; direct and public incitement to commit a crime. The most relevant of these acts of participation are explained below.

Planning

Planning is defined as "implying that one or several persons contemplate designing the commission of a crime at both the preparatory and execution phases."[67] In this sense the word 'planner' shall be understood to include not only the persons who took part in the formulation of an original criminal plan, but also persons who, through their personal action, were able to modify the original criminal plan to render it more effective. It seems that complicity for planning to commit a crime against humanity arises only when the execution of the criminal plan has commenced, since it would be legally difficult to punish an accused for his mere criminal thoughts or for a crime that has not at least been attempted.

Ordering

A person may also be held individually liable for giving the unlawful *order* to commit a crime against humanity.[68] Ordering implies a superior-subordinate relationship between the person giving the order and the one receiving and executing it, with the person in a position of authority using his power to convince another to commit an offence.[69] In *Eichmann*, the Israeli District Court of Jerusalem highlighted what the position of authority in the Nazi government entailed when it stated:

> It is well known that in the Nazi regime, based as it was in the principle of leadership, every rank, apart from Hitler himself, both received and gave orders. And, as is common to any hierarchical regime an order becomes increasingly detailed and elaborated as it passes down from one level to the next.[70]

This finding led the Court to argue that those who issued orders were more responsible than those who actually carried them out, and that:

> [T]he degree of responsibility generally increases as we draw further away from the man who uses the fatal instrument with his own hands and reach the higher levels of commands.[71]

The ILC later corroborated the Israeli Court's approach when it remarked that:

---

67 G.K. McDonald and O. Swaak-Goldman, chap. III, n. 182, vol. II Part II at 1626.
68 Report of the Secretary General of the United Nations on the Yugoslavia Statute quoted in M.C. Bassiouni, chap. III, n. 97 at 436.
69 G.K. McDonald and O. Swaak-Goldman, chap. III, n. 182, vol. II Part II at 1627.
70 *Id.* at 2359–2360.
71 *Id.* at 2338.

[T]he superior who orders the commission of the crime is in some respects more culpable than the subordinate who merely carries out the order and thereby commits a crime that he would not have committed on his own initiative.[72]

Failure to Prevent or Repress the Commission of a Crime

Individual criminal responsibility for failure to prevent or repress the commission of a crime is specifically directed to all superiors holding a position of command over subordinates. The Report of the Secretary General of the United Nations on the ICTY Statute stressed that superiors should be held "responsible for failure to prevent a crime or to deter the unlawful behaviour of [their] subordinates."[73] The word 'superiors' includes the immediate superior of a subordinate as well as his other superiors in the military chain of command or governmental hierarchy. It also covers both military and civilian authorities who are in a position to exercise a degree of control over subordinates.[74]

In terms of Article 6 of the 1996 Draft Code of Crimes, the mechanism of the superior's personal responsibility for failure to prevent or repress the commission of a crime is activated when two criteria are fulfilled.

Firstly, a superior must have known or had reason to know in the circumstances at the time that a subordinate was committing or was going to commit a crime. Under this criterion, the required *mens rea* is either that the superior had actual knowledge that his subordinate was committing or was about to commit a crime, or that he had sufficient information to enable him to conclude under the circumstances at the time that his subordinate was committing or was about to commit a crime. A superior who ignores information which clearly indicates the likelihood of criminal conduct on the part of his subordinates is seriously negligent in failing to perform his duty to prevent or suppress such conduct, and in failing to make a reasonable effort to obtain the necessary information that will enable him to take appropriate action.

Secondly, the superior failed to take all necessary measures within his power to prevent or repress the criminal conduct of his subordinate. In this case, criminal responsibility is incurred only if a superior had a clear legal obligation to act coupled with the capacity to take the necessary measures to prevent or repress the unlawful conduct of his subordinates, and he failed to do so. He cannot incur criminal responsibility for failing to perform an act that was impossible for him to perform, even when knowledge of the unlawful conduct of his subordinate can be clearly established.

When these two criteria are met, a superior may be considered to be an accomplice to the crime and may incur personal liability for the crime committed by his subordinate. However, the liability of a superior does not relieve the subordinate

---

72   See n. 50, Comm. of Article 2 (3) (b).
73   See M.C. Bassiouni, chap. III, n. 97 at 436.
74   ILC Report, n. 50 Comm. of Article 6 at para. 4.

of his own criminal responsibility. In general, the duty of a superior to repress the unlawful conduct of his subordinate includes the initiation of disciplinary or penal sanctions against the alleged offender.[75]

Aiding and/or Abetting

This conduct covers any act, which contributes to the commission or attempted commission of a crime.[76] Aiding in the commission of a crime means giving assistance to someone who actually commits the crime, while abetting involves facilitating the commission of a crime by being sympathetic thereto.[77] The assistance shall be of a nature, which contributes directly and substantially to the commission of the crime; that is, an assistance that 'facilitates the commission of a crime in some significant way.[78] Such degree of assistance includes for example providing the means, which enable the perpetrator to commit the crime.[79] Assistance may occur either in physical form or in the form of moral support and encouragement,[80] and must have a substantial effect on the perpetration of the crime.[81] This would mean that the presence of the aider or abettor at the scene of the crime is qualified as moral support and encouragement only if it has a significant encouraging effect on the principal perpetrator. Moreover, the requirement of aiding or abetting can be fulfilled without the presence of the accomplice during the commission of the crime. This interpretation was given by the ICTR which considered that participation in the form of aiding and/or abetting may also consist in an omission.[82] In this case, the non-presence of the accomplice at the scene of the crime will amount to criminal participation only when it has a substantial effect in the realisation of the crime. This approach gives weight to the ICTY's ruling which held that the proof of a causal link between the conduct of the aider and abettor and the act of the principal perpetrator is not required;[83] nor is the proof of the existence of a common concerted plan required, since the principal perpetrator may not even know about the accomplice's contribution.[84]

---

75   *Id.* Comm. of Article 6 at para. 4.
76   K. Ambos, in O. Triffterer (ed.), *Commentary on the Rome Statute* (1999), Comm. of Article 25 at 481 para. 15.
77   See *Akayesu*, at para. 484; or G.K. McDonald and O. Swaak-Goldman, chap. III, n. 182 vol. II Part II at 1627.
78   ILC Report, n. 50 Comm. of Article 2 (3) (d).
79   *Id.* Comm. of Article 2 (3) (d); also Article 25 (3) (c) of the Rome Statute.
80   ICTY, *Prosecutor v. Anto Furundzija* Case No IT-95-17/1-T '*Lasva Valley*', TC Judgment of 10 December, 1998 at para. 231.
81   *Id.* at paras 235 and 249.
82   K. Ambos in O. Triffterer, n. 76 Comm. of Article 25 at 482 para. 17; see also *Akayesu*, chap. III, n. 79 at para. 548; or G.K. McDonald and O. Swaak-Goldman, chap. III, n. 182, vol. II Part II at 1627.
83   *Blaskic*, chap. III, n. 102 at para. 285.
84   *Tadic* (1999), chap. III, n. 121 at para. 229.

As regards the *mens rea* of this form of participation, a person aiding and/or abetting in the planning, preparation and commission or attempted commission of a crime against humanity must show the required intent to commit the crime; that is the intent to destroy in whole or in part a protected group[85] in the case of genocide. For other crimes against humanity, knowledge of the act of assisting coupled with the intent to provide assistance to the actual direct perpetrator is required.[86] The ILC's Report of 1996 on the Draft Code of Crimes elaborated on the requirement of knowing assistance when it stated that:

> [A]n individual who provides some type of assistance to another individual without knowing that this assistance will facilitate the commission of a crime would not be held accountable under the present paragraph.[87]

Therefore, to be found guilty as an aider and/or abettor, knowledge of the precise crime to be committed by the principal perpetrator is not a requirement; it is sufficient that the accused had intended to facilitate any crime that was in fact committed,[88] or attempted.

Incitement

An individual may incite another to commit a crime. Incitement can be public or private. Public incitement "requires communicating the call for criminal action to a number of individuals in a public place or [...by] means of mass communication such as radio or television"[89] or newspaper. This form of incitement has the potential to expand the reach of the call for criminal conduct in order to increase the number of individuals who will engage in mass criminal actions. In Rwanda for example, a daily programme broadcast by *La Radio Des Mille Collines* and calling for the extermination of Tutsis and moderate Hutus played an important role in broadening the execution of the genocidal plan formulated by the perpetrators. Similarly, the Nuremberg Tribunal convicted Julius Streicher, a Reich official, for the count on crimes against humanity for speaking and preaching hatred of the Jews, and for writing and publishing anti-Semitic articles in his weekly newspaper *'Der Stürmer'*. In this case the Tribunal argued as follows:

> Streicher's incitement to murder and extermination, at the time when Jews in the East were being killed under the most horrible conditions, clearly constitutes persecution on

---

85 Article II of the Genocide Convention.
86 *Blaskic*, at para. 286; *Tadic*, chap. III, n. 82 at para. 674; *Celebici Camp (Prosecutor v. Zdravko Mucic et al.* Case No. IT-96-21 Judgment of 9 October 2001) at para. 326; and *Aleksovski*, n. 48 at para. 61.
87 See Comm. of Article 2 (3) (d).
88 *Furundzija*, n. 80 at para. 246.
89 G.K. McDonald and O. Swaak-Goldman, chap. III, n. 182, vol. II Part I at 344.

political and racial grounds in connection with war crimes, as defined by the Charter, and constitutes a crime against humanity.[90]

Contrary to public incitement, private incitement to commit a crime occurs when an individual joins in planning or conspiracy to commit a crime.[91] Private incitement is closely related to instigation, which is a form of complicity that specifically targets a certain person or group of persons in private.[92]

In addition to public and private incitement, Article III (c) of the Genocide Convention speaks of 'direct and public' incitement to commit genocide, with the qualifier 'direct' requiring "specifically urging another individual to take immediate criminal action rather than merely making a vague or indirect suggestion."[93] Moreover, the Trial Chamber of *Akayesu* defined direct and public incitement to commit genocide as:

> [D]irectly provoking the perpetrator to commit genocide, whether through speeches, shouting or threats uttered in public places or at public gatherings, or through the sale or dissemination, offer for sale or display of written material or printed matter in public places or at public gatherings, or through the public display of placards or posters, or through any other means of audio-visual communication.[94]

As to the question of whether individual criminal liability based on public, private or direct incitement to commit crimes against humanity necessitates the actual or attempted realisation of any criminal act, two positions exist. The 1996 Draft Code of Crimes subjects individual criminal liability based on incitement to the actual or attempted commission of any of the listed crimes,[95] while the Rome Statute makes an exception in respect of genocide. In effect, Article 25 (3) (e) of this Statute does not require the actual commission or the attempted commission of genocide with regard to incitement. In terms of this provision, it is sufficient for a person to directly and publicly incite another to commit any act of genocide to incur individual liability for incitement, even if no crime is actually committed or attempted.[96] The ICTR upheld the position advanced by the Rome Statute when it ruled that:

> [G]enocide clearly falls within the category of crimes so serious that direct and public incitement to commit such a crime must be punished as such, even where such incitement failed to produce the result expected by the perpetrator.[97]

---

90 *International Military Trials: Nazi Conspiracy and Aggression* vol. II (1946) at 690–709; see also *Akayesu*, chap. III, n. 79 at para. 550.
91 G.K. McDonald and O. Swaak-Goldman, chap. III, n. 182, vol. II Part I at 344.
92 K. Ambos, in O. Triffterer, n. 76, Comm. of Article 25 at 486 para. 26.
93 ILC Report, n. 50 Comm. of Article 2 (3) (f) at para. 16.
94 See chap. III, n. 79 at para. 559.
95 This requirement is indicated by the words 'which in fact occurs' in Article 2 (3) (f) of the 1996 Draft Code of Crimes, or by the phrase 'which in fact [...] is attempted' contained in Article 25 (3) (b) of the Rome Statute.
96 K. Ambos, in O. Triffterer, n. 76, Comm. of Article 25 at 487 para. 29.
97 *Akayesu*, chap. III, n. 79 at para. 562.

However in a more recent case,[98] the ICTR was called to address the role of the media (print and radio media) in the Rwandan genocide as well as the related legal question of what constitutes individual criminal responsibility for direct and public incitement to commit genocide. In this respect, the Tribunal declared that three factors have to be considered in defining the elements of 'direct and public incitement to genocide' as applied to mass media, namely the purpose and context of the incitement, as well as the causal link between the incitement and the ensuing widespread killings of the victims.[99] It went on to stress the importance of the purpose and context of incitement in determining the intent to commit genocide, while recalling its findings in *Akayesu* with respect to the factor of causation that incitement is a crime regardless of whether it has the effect it intends to have.[100]

Therefore, in interpreting the requirement of a causal link between the media broadcast and publications and the commission of the crime of genocide, the Trial Chamber of the *Media Case* discovered an element of gravity which it highlighted in the following manner:

> In determining whether communications represent an intent to cause genocide and thereby constitute incitement, the Chamber considers it significant that in fact genocide occurred. That the media intended to have this effect is evidenced in part by the fact that it did have this effect.[101]

The Chamber finally ruled that the strong and racist language broadcast on the radio as well as the publication of communiqués and other writings calling on listeners and readers to exterminate the Tutsis indicate the accused's intent to commit the crime of genocide, and has caused the crimes to be committed.[102]

The following remarks may thus be made: mere incitement to commit genocide coupled with the specific intention to destroy a group in whole or in part, is required to incur criminal liability. The actual commission or attempted commission of any acts of genocide is not a requirement. For other crimes against humanity, it results from the 1996 Draft Code of Crimes that criminal liability for incitement is incurred only when the execution of a crime is at least commenced.

Participation by Attempting to Commit a Crime

Attempt to commit a crime criminalizes all conduct still at the commencement phase of the execution of a crime, and punishes them as completed offences.[103] There

---

98 See *The Prosecutor v. Ferdinand Nahimana, Jean-Bosco Barayagwisa and Hassan Ngeze* Case No ICTR-99-52-T, Judgment of 3 December, 2003 (hereinafter *the Media Case*).

99 *Id.* at paras 1000–1010.

100 *Id.* at paras 1011–1015.

101 *Id.* at para. 1029.

102 *Id.* at paras 1016–1039

103 See the Rome Statute Article 25 (3) (f), the 1996 Draft Code of Crimes Article 2 (3) (g). However, attempt was not recognised as a crime in the Nuremberg Charter, the Tokyo Charter, the Yugoslavia and Rwanda Statutes.

is attempt when the perpetrator who intends to commit a crime has commenced the execution of that crime but, for reasons independent of his own will, is unable to complete it.[104] But if he voluntarily and completely gives up the criminal purpose or abandons all efforts to commit the crime, or takes positive steps to oppose the wrongful decision or prevent the harm from occurring, he shall not be liable for punishment on the basis of attempt.[105] International criminal law as it operates today does not state under which circumstances abandonment is voluntary or at what stage of the commission abandonment is still admissible; it seems that this issue is left to be dealt with by the courts.[106]

Nevertheless, abandoning or opposing a criminal plan or policy may take various forms, ranging from express disagreement with the criminal plan or policy, to resignation from office. For example, acts of opposition against the criminal enterprise of the Nazi Government could clearly be inferred from the attitude of Schacht who was indicted at Nuremberg for a common plan or conspiracy to wage an aggressive war and for crimes against peace. The accused, who served successively as Commissioner of Currency, President of the *Reichbank*, Minister of Economics, Plenipotentiary General for War Economy, and Minister without Portfolio, was seen by many as a central figure in Germany's rearmament program. However, when he discovered the criminal plan behind this program, he attempted to slow down its speed. He vehemently opposed the Four-Year Plan aiming at making the German entire economy ready for war within four years and the appointment of the officials in charge of implementing this plan. He reduced the credit allocated to the Nazi Government to finance rearmament. As a result of his actions he was accused by the Nazi leadership, including Hitler, of upsetting the governmental plan with his financial methods. To express his total disagreement with the policy of rearmament, Schacht finally resigned from his positions as Minister of Economics and as Plenipotentiary General for War Economy. He later took part in the conspiracy to assassinate Hitler. The Nuremberg Tribunal found that through his actions, Schacht had attempted to prevent the Nazi from completing their crimes; consequently, he was acquitted of all counts of indictment.[107]

Attempt begins when the perpetrator has commenced the execution of a crime; that is, performing an act, which constitutes a significant step towards the completion of the crimes.[108] Therefore, preparatory acts such as planning or framing the criminal policy are not included in the rubric of 'attempt'.

Three conditions must therefore be fulfilled before a person can incur criminal liability for attempt: firstly, he must intend to commit a particular crime; secondly, he must act towards the commission of that crime and thirdly, the crime must not be completed for reasons independent of his personal will.[109] Since individual

---

104 G.K. McDonald and O. Swaak-Goldman, chap. III, n. 182, vol. II Part I at 347.
105 See Article 25 (3) (f) of the Rome Statute.
106 See K. Ambos, in O. Triffterer, n. 76, Comm. of Article 25 at 490 para. 36.
107 IMT Reports, chap. III, n. 50 at 552–556.
108 ILC Report, n. 50, Comm. of Article 2 (3) (g) at para. 17.
109 *Id.*

responsibility for attempt only arises when a person who intends to commit a crime takes a substantial step in commencing its execution it would be very difficult for a high ranking State official to be found guilty for attempt, since his action is sometimes only limited to planning and formulating criminal policies. Consequently, in most cases, only low-level direct executioners are likely to be found guilty for attempting to commit a crime against humanity.

Negation of Individual Criminal Liability

The principles of international criminal law are not only concerned with the extent to which criminal attribution may operate, they also deal with the circumstances under which an individual may be exempted from criminal liability despite his/her involvement in the commission of the crimes. International law provides various defences that an alleged perpetrator can rely upon to free himself/herself from liability. These are, for example, self-defence, incapacity, intoxication, duress or coercion and abandonment.

The Nuremberg Charter did not admit any form of defence for war crimes, crimes against peace and crimes against humanity. The possibility of admitting defences for the most serious crimes was first articulated in the 1996 Draft Code of Crimes, which entrusted the competent courts with the determination of the admissibility of defences in accordance with the general principles of law and in light of the character of each crime.[110] Nevertheless, the relevant provision did not expressly list specific admissible defences for the crimes contained in the Code. In justifying this omission, the ILC held the view that the title 'defence' given to Article 14 of the Draft Code was intended to cover both grounds justifying the wrongful act (so as to eliminate in all respects the criminal character of the act in question) as well as grounds excusing the perpetrator (leading to his exculpation).[111]

Contrary to the Draft Code, the Rome Statute does not speak of 'defences', but rather of 'grounds for excluding criminal responsibility'.[112] The reason given for the use of this expression is that article 31 of the Rome Statute is merely addressing substantive grounds for excluding criminal responsibility.[113] In addition to the substantive grounds,[114] this Statute provided for two other categories of exclusionary grounds, namely: additional grounds appearing elsewhere in the Statute[115] and other exclusionary grounds found in applicable international and national law that may be developed by the competent court.[116] Such a move, which in fact recognises all forms of defence existing in both national and international penal law, constitutes

---

110 Article 14.
111 ILC Report, n. 50, Comm. of Article 14 at para. 2.
112 See Article 31.
113 A. Eser, in O. Triffterer, n. 76, Comm. of Article 31 at 544 para. 15.
114 Listed in Article 31 (1) (a), (b), (c) and (d) of the Rome Statute.
115 Article 31 (2).
116 Article 31 (3).

a novelty in international law.[117] The form, nature, content and effects of some of the most established exclusionary grounds are discussed below. This is done with the intent of assessing their admissibility in respect of crimes against humanity.

Substantive Grounds for Excluding Criminal Liability

Article 31 (1) of the Rome Statute provides for four of the most firmly established grounds for excluding criminal liability; they are incapacity, intoxication, self-defence or defence of property and duress.

Incapacity

Incapacity is also sometimes referred to as insanity. Incapacity exists in two forms: *dementia naturalis*, meaning idiocy or absence of understanding from birth, without any lucid intervals; and *dementia accidentalis* or *adventicia*, which is insanity in the strict sense that may be partial or total, permanent or temporary.[118] Incapacity as a ground for excluding criminal liability contains two requirements: first, the existence of a mental disease or defect; second, such a mental disease or defect must be of the nature that destroys the capacity to either appreciate the unlawfulness of a conduct or to control it.[119] The requirement of a defective mental state seems to exclude momentary psychic disturbances such as sneezing, apoplexy or hysteria fit, which neither affects the cognitive or intellectual capacity of a person, nor make a person suffer. The mental defect must not be of the nature that impairs the person's capacity to appreciate the unlawfulness or nature of his conduct or to bring his conduct in conformity with the law; but rather, it must be of the nature that destroys it. Consequently, if a mental deficiency is in such a way that it annihilates the person's awareness of his acts, criminal liability is excluded for lack of intent, lack of human conduct or lack of culpability.[120] Incapacity as an admissible defence against charges of crimes against humanity is more likely to apply to direct perpetrators than to decision-makers whose acts of planning and designing a criminal policy require sane cognitive and intellectual capacities.

---

117 In fact, none of the main international criminal law documents, such as the Nuremberg Charter, the Apartheid Convention, the Genocide Convention, the Geneva Conventions and the 1977 Additional Protocol I, nor the 1996 Draft Code of Crimes Against the Peace and Security of Mankind, has expressly listed any particular defences nor justifying grounds for the crimes they have covered.

118 H.A. Palmer and H. Palmer, chap. III, n. 139 at 32.

119 A. Eser, in O. Triffterer, n. 76, Comm. of Article 31 at 545 para. 20.

120 *Id.* at 546 para. 23.

Intoxication

Intoxication implies a sort of excitement or acceleration beyond self-control, caused by consumption of an exogenic substance with toxic effects.[121] As in the case of mental disease or defect, intoxication must destroy the person's ability to appreciate the lawfulness of his acts or the ability to control his conduct in conformity with the requirements of the law.[122] Involuntary intoxication may lead to the exculpation of the accused. But if a person voluntary put himself in a state of non-responsibility by means of intoxication with the objective of committing a crime, intoxication cannot be successfully invoked as a defence.[123] If this form of defence is raised by a Head of State or a State minister with respect to a crime against humanity, his chances of success will be very slim; it can for example be rejected on the basis of grave dereliction of duty with serious criminal consequences.

Self-Defence, Defence of Another Person, Defence of Property

The ILC distinguishes between two contexts in which self-defence may be applied. Firstly, self-defence in the context of Article 51 of the Charter of the United Nations, which refers to the lawful use of force by a State in the exercise of the inherent right of individual or collective self-defence, and which would therefore not constitute aggression by that State. Secondly, self-defence in the criminal law context, which relieves an individual of responsibility for a violent act committed against another person that would otherwise constitute a crime.[124] Self-defence in the context of criminal law may be successfully raised by an accused who is charged with a crime of violence resulting in the victim's death or serious bodily harm, provided that the use of force was necessary to avoid an immediate threat of the accused own death or serious bodily harm[125] and that it was not disproportionate to the attack.[126]

Article 31 (1) (c) of the Rome Statute expressly provides for two other forms of self-defence, namely defence of another person who is endangered by an unlawful attack, and defence of property in war crimes. In these cases, the requirement is that the defence be reasonable in terms of being necessary as well as able to prevent the danger,[127] and proportionate to the degree of the attack. Therefore, the right to self-defence is not an unlimited right.

Self-defence as a ground for excluding criminal liability is unlikely to be successfully raised by persons holding higher State office in the context of crimes against

---

121 *Id.* at 547 para. 25.
122 *Id.* at 547 para. 26.
123 Article 31 (1) (b) of the Rome Statute.
124 ILC Report, n. 50 Comm. of Article 14 at para. 7.
125 *Id.* at para. 8.
126 G.K. McDonald and O. Swaak-Goldman, chap. III, n. 182, vol. II Part I at 379.
127 A. Eser, in O. Triffterer, n. 76, Comm. of Article 31 at 549 para. 32.

humanity. At least two reasons can justify this allegation. First, self-defence implies immediate or imminent personal danger or threat, which is usually not present at the stage of formulating, planning, or ordering the commission of a crime against humanity; therefore, only low-level direct perpetrators may raise this defence since the likelihood to face immediate or imminent threat is much greater in their situation. Second, crimes against humanity are a category of offences that generally requires a careful planning and a multitude of victims. Accordingly, the defence of oneself cannot reasonably justify the killing of many persons. In sum, self-defence as a ground for excluding liability is unlikely to be successfully raised by either a direct or an indirect perpetrator of a crime against humanity.

Duress or Coercion

Duress or coercion exists whenever a person is compelled to commit a criminal act. Referring to a United Nations War Crimes Commission's conclusion, the ILC stated that duress requires three essential elements, namely:

(a) [T]he act charged was done to avoid an immediate danger both serious and irreparable;
(b) [T]here was no other adequate means to escape;
(c) [T]he remedy was not disproportionate to the evil.[128]

This approach is echoed by Article 31 (1) (d) of the Rome Statute which requires that the accused raising duress as a defence be exposed to threat of imminent death or continuing or imminent serious bodily harm resulting in duress; that the act aiming at avoiding the threat be necessary (in terms that no other means are available),[129] reasonable (in terms of being able to reach the desired effect), and adequate (in terms of not being unreasonably disproportionate);[130] and that no intention to cause a greater harm than the one sought to be avoided is present.

As to the effect of duress or coercion on the person's criminal liability, it is important to distinguish between physical coercion and moral coercion. Physical coercion exists when physical force is used to compel someone to commit a crime; for example, when A seizes the hands of B and compels him to stab C. Moral coercion results from threats of personal violence; for example, being under the threat of being killed or having one's family member killed if one refuses to perform a criminal act. When an act is committed under physical coercion the *mens rea* element of the crime is negated and the accused may successfully rely on the defence of duress or coercion. In contrast, moral coercion does not generally afford complete defence to the commission of a criminal offence.[131] This general principle of domestic criminal law is likely to apply in international law as well.

---

128 ILC Report, n. 407 Comm. of Article 14 at para. 10.
129 A. Eser, in O. Triffterer, n. 76, Comm. of Article 31 at 551 para. 39.
130 *Id.* at 551–552 para. 39.
131 H.A. Palmer and H. Palmer, chap. III, n. 139 at 24.

In considering this exclusionary ground at Nuremberg, the IMT applied the test of "whether a moral choice was in fact possible" in order to determine the admission of duress as a ground of defence. This led the Tribunal in *re Krupp and Ten Others*,[132] to hold that the defence of duress is not supportable where the accused had no intention or will contrary to those who supposedly exerted the compulsion. This would mean, with reference to the example of physical coercion taken above, that it is sufficient that B shares the intention of A in respect of C to be criminally liable. The Tribunal further decided in *Einsatzgruppen*[133] that the defence of duress could only be supported if the seriousness of the injury that would have been suffered from refusing to carry out an order to act was close to the seriousness of the act committed in obedience to the order. This would mean according to Sunga that the plea of duress on the grounds that it was necessary to kill innocent victims to avoid a short period of imprisonment is unlikely to succeed.[134]

In the light of the foregoing, it would be unlikely that the defence of duress or coercion be admitted for offences as serious as crimes against humanity. However, in case such a defence is successfully raised in a specific case of a crime against humanity, it is doubtful whether it will relieve the perpetrator of all responsibility for his criminal conduct. It may nonetheless constitute an extenuating circumstance resulting in the imposition of a lesser punishment.[135] The defence of duress or coercion would not generally apply to high level State officials simply because their higher status gives them the authority to coerce rather than to be victims of coercion.

Additional Grounds for Excluding Criminal Liability

Article 31 (1) of the ICC Statute provides for additional grounds for excluding criminal liability, other than those expressly listed in subsections (a), (b), (c) and (d). The additional grounds, which appear elsewhere in the Statute, are abandonment,[136] exclusion of jurisdiction over persons under 18,[137] mistake of fact or mistake of law,[138] superior orders and prescription of law.[139] A cursory summary of these grounds is given below.

---

132 Judgment of the US Military Tribunal at Nuremberg reprinted in 15 *ILR* (1948) at 620.
133 See *re Ohlendorf and Others* reprinted in 15 *ILR* (1948) at 656.
134 L.S. Sunga, chap. III, n. 15 at 58–59.
135 ILC Report, n. 50, Comm. of Article 14 at para. 10.
136 Article 25 (3) (f).
137 Article 26.
138 Article 32.
139 Article 33.

Abandonment

As stated above, a person shall not be held liable for attempt to commit a crime if he/she abandons the effort to commit the crime or otherwise acts to prevent the completion of the crime, provided that he/she gives up the criminal purpose completely and voluntarily.[140]

Exclusion of Jurisdiction Over Persons Under Eighteen

This excluding ground relieves persons under eighteen of criminal liability, even when the *actus reus* and the elements of *mens rea* can be established. Persons under the age of eighteen are believed to fall under the category of 'minors'[141] or 'children'.[142] Such category of human beings is usually exempted from criminal liability because of their immaturity. Article 26 of the ICC Statute prohibits both the initiation of investigations and the exercise of the jurisdiction of the Court over persons under eighteen.[143] The *travaux préparatoires* of Article 26 shows that this provision was not intended to shield minors from criminal liability in general. It was rather intended to exclude the jurisdiction of the ICC over them with respect to the crimes provided for in the Statute, while giving national courts the possibility of exercising national jurisdiction over minors.[144] The drafters of the ICC Statute agreed that when national laws so provide, national courts may exercise jurisdiction over minors over fifteen and those not victimised in the sense of Article 8 (2) (b) (xxvi) or (e) (vii) of this Statute.[145] As regards youngsters under the age of fifteen years who are victimised under Article 8 (2) (b) (xxvi) or (e) (vii) it was concluded that such juveniles were already the victims of crimes violating international provisions established to protect them and that they should not be victimised a second time by being brought before a national criminal jurisdiction.[146]

The question of how to deal with children involved in the commission of war crimes and crimes against humanity received a particular attention during the drafting of the Statute of the SCSL. A provision entitled "jurisdiction over persons of fifteen years of age" was inserted in the Statute and provided that:

---

140 See section above on 'attempt to commit a crime'.
141 See the relevant provisions in the International Covenant on Civil and Political Rights (1966) GA Res. 2200A (XXI), UN Doc A/6316 (1966); the European Convention for the Protection of Human Rights and Fundamental Freedoms (1950) 213 UNTS 222; and in the American Convention on Human Rights, chap. III, n. 170.
142 See Article 1 of the Convention on the Rights of the Child adopted by GA Res. 44/25 of 20 November 1989.
143 R.S. Clark, in O. Triffterer, n. 76, Comm. of Article 26 at 498 para. 16.
144 *Id.* at 499 para. 20.
145 These provisions make it a war crime the act of conscripting or enlisting children under the age of fifteen years into the national armed forces or groups, or using them to participate actively in hostilities.
146 R.S. Clark, in O. Triffterer, n. 76, Comm. of Article 26 at 499 para. 21.

1) The Special Court shall have no jurisdiction over any person who was under the age of 15 at the time of the alleged commission of the crime. Should any person who was at the time of the alleged commission of the crime between 15 and 18 years of age come before the Court, he or she shall be treated with dignity and a sense of worth, taking into account his or her young age and the desirability of promoting his or her rehabilitation, reintegration into and assumption of a constructive role in society, and in accordance with international human rights standards, in particular the rights of the child.

2) In the disposition of a case against a juvenile offender, the Special Court shall order any of the following: care guidance and supervision orders, community service orders, counselling, foster care, correctional, educational and vocational training programmes, approved schools and, as appropriate, any programmes of disarmament, demobilization and reintegration or programmes of child protection agencies.[147]

Mistake of Fact or Mistake of Law

There is mistake of fact when a person reasonably believes in the existence of a situation, which in fact does not exist. Mistake of law is a false perception that a particular conduct is not prohibited and punished by the law.

Mistake of fact excludes criminal liability if the accused can prove that he acted under an honest and reasonable belief in the existence of a state of things which would have justified or excused his act, thus negating his *mens rea*.[148] Despite its absence in the Nuremberg Charter and in Control Council Law No. 10 this excluding ground was nevertheless successfully raised during the Nuremberg Trials. In the '*Ärtze-Urteil*' for example, German physicians were acquitted because they believed that the persons brought to them were sentenced to death and would be pardoned if they survived the medical experiments, during which they were at the disposal of the physicians.[149] Mistake of fact may also be relied upon as a ground for the mitigation of punishment in cases where the competent court decides that criminal liability is not excluded. The court will therefore determine the sentence while taking into account factors such as the gravity of the crime and the individual circumstances of the convicted person.[150]

In contrast, mistake of law is generally rejected as a valid ground for excluding criminal liability when it deals with the wrongful legal evaluation of a conduct.[151] Such rejection is partly due to the obligation put on the individual by the maxim *nemo ius ignorare censetur*[152] or *ignorantia iuris neminem scusat*[153] to seek to know the law, and partly because mistakes about the legal aspects of a crime

---

147 Article 7 of the Statute of the Special Court for Sierra Leone adopted pursuant to SC Res. 1315 of 14 August 2000 (as amended on 16 January 2002).
148 Rome Statute Article 32 (1).
149 O. Triffterer, in O. Triffterer, n. 76, Comm. of Article 32 at 557 para. 4.
150 Rome Statute Article 78 (1); or O. Triffterer, in O. Triffterer, n. 76, Comm. of Article 32 at 567 para. 27.
151 See Article 32 (2) of the Rome Statute.
152 Meaning "ignorance of the law is no excuse".
153 Meaning "ignorance of the law is no defence to anyone".

leave untouched the material elements or material prerequisites for justification or excuse.[154] Nevertheless, mistake of law may exclude criminal liability in two situations: firstly, when it negates the mental element required by the relevant crime—[155] in order to negate the mental element of a crime, the mistake must be unavoidable;—[156] secondly, when the accused is mistaken on the legal evaluation of an unlawful order in terms of Article 33 of the ICC Statute.

Superior Orders

The general rule established since Nuremberg is that the defence of superior orders does not relieve of criminal liability the defendant who committed a crime pursuant to orders of his government or of a superior. However, the court may consider such defence in mitigation of punishment if it determines that justice so requires. As in the case of duress, the test applied at Nuremberg was whether a moral choice was in fact possible.[157] Contrary to the position adopted in the Nuremberg Charter, the Rome Statute contemplates the possibility of excusing the subordinate who committed the Statute's crimes pursuant to superior orders when three cumulative conditions are satisfied. First, the defendant was under the legal obligation to obey orders of the relevant government or superior; secondly, he did not know that the order was unlawful; and thirdly, the order was not manifestly unlawful.[158] Orders to commit crimes against humanity or genocide are usually considered as examples of manifestly unlawful orders.[159] Accordingly, the defence of superior order cannot be successfully raised in respect of these two crimes.

In final analysis, one would argue that with the exception of prescription of law and abandonment, additional grounds for excluding personal liability are unlikely to be successfully opposed by a senior State official as a defence against allegations of war crimes, genocide and crimes against humanity, unless the defendant is a minor.

Other Grounds for Excluding Criminal Liability

This heading covers other defences which are generally admissible as excluding grounds by national laws, but which are neither explicitly recognised nor rejected by Article 31 (3) of the Rome Statute as grounds for excluding criminal liability. Among these defences are necessity and reprisals.

---

154 O. Triffterer, in O. Triffterer, n. 76, Comm. of Article 32 at 563 para. 15.
155 Article 32 (2) of the Rome Statute.
156 O. Triffterer, in O. Triffterer, n. 76, Comm. of Article 32 at 570 para. 38.
157 Article 8 of the Nuremberg Charter.
158 Article 33 (1).
159 Article 33 (2) of the Rome Statute.

Necessity

A state of necessity arises in circumstances not created by the defendant but in which he has to choose between a legal duty not to commit a crime and an overwhelming interest.[160] Such interest may either be personal, in which case one deals with personal necessity, or military, in which case one speaks of military necessity. The defence of personal necessity is generally accepted in domestic criminal laws, provided that the value the defendant sought to protect was greater than, or proportional to, the one he ignored and provided that he had no other choice. In these circumstances, the offence may either be justified or excused.[161] The plea of military necessity is usually raised in war crime trials. This plea was occasionally recognised during the Nuremberg Trials either as a possible ground for excluding criminal liability, or as a ground in mitigation of punishment.[162] However, in international criminal law it is unlikely that military necessity reasonably justifies the commission of crimes against humanity or of any other serious international crimes.

Reprisal

This refers to an act of self-help by the injured State, in retaliation for loss or injury suffered as a result of an original act committed by the offending State in breach of international law. It has the effect of suspending momentarily, in relation to the States involved, the observance of international law rules dealing with the issue involved.[163] The right of a State to have recourse to reprisal is limited by the principle of proportionality. A successful recourse to reprisal by a State would have the effect of protecting those who carry it out from incurring personal liability for any crime committed in relation to such a reprisal. However, this defence is prohibited by international humanitarian law[164] and is unlikely to be successfully opposed as justification for the commission of crimes which rise to the level of crimes against humanity. Therefore, any act of reprisal that resulted in the commission of crimes against humanity may create criminal liability not only for those who committed such crimes, but also for those who ordered its commission.

---

160 S.R. Ratner and J.S. Abrams, chap. III, n. 118 at 124.
161 H.A. Palmer and H. Palmer, chap. III, n. 139 at 25.
162 ILC Report, n. 50, Comm. of Article 14 at para. 11.
163 L.S. Sunga, chap. III, n. 15 at 60–61.
164 Article 46 of 1949 Geneva Convention I and Article 47 of Convention II prohibit the use of reprisals against the wounded, sick, shipwrecked persons, personnel, buildings or equipment protected by the Convention.

Summary

To conclude this chapter, it shall be noted that the bases of individual criminal liability as well as the parameters of individual criminal attribution in respect of crimes against humanity are clearly established in international law. They are valid for all categories of offenders irrespective of their legal status within a given State. In general, when the *actus reus* and the *mens rea* elements of crimes against humanity exist, and when the degree of participation in the commission of this offence as explained above has been clearly defined and established, the accused shall be liable for prosecution and punishment under international criminal law. This requirement of prosecution seems to exclude all forms of indemnity for crimes against humanity. However, the duty to establish the mechanisms of individual criminal responsibility and of prosecution rests on each individual State. Such a duty, which is based on the very serious character of the offence of crimes against humanity, calls for each State to prosecute and punish the perpetrators thereof. Unfortunately, many issues remain either unclear or unresolved as far as the nature, extent and limits of State obligations under international law in respect of crimes against humanity are concerned. The following chapter proposes to shed light on these fundamental questions.

STATES OBLIGATIONS IN RESPECT OF CRIMES AGAINST HUMANITY

Introduction

States' duties under international law may be derived from diverse international law instruments, which contain words and expressions such as 'obligation' to 'ensure rights', to 'provide a remedy' or the obligation to 'prosecute, punish or extradite'. These words and expressions usually invite individual States to take positive actions in response to certain conduct, which threaten the peace and security of the international community as a whole. Crimes against humanity are the kind of offence the commission of which threatens international peace and security. The scope, nature and implications of States' obligations in respect of this offence cannot be fully grasped if they are studied in isolation. They need to be integrated in the overall scheme of human rights protection in order to acquire their full meaning. The overall scheme of human rights protection includes international conventions or treaties; international custom; United Nations Security Council resolutions; reports, declarations and recommendation of various other international bodies; international and national courts' decisions; as well as the writings of international and national scholars.

The nature and scope of States obligations under international law are mainly defined in international conventions, or inferred from international custom. However, many other documents may provide reliable sources that suggest the existence of particular States obligations.

Conventional Sources of States Duties Under International Law

International conventions that clearly put certain duties on States to act may be classified in two broad categories: these are international criminal law conventions and general human rights conventions.

Faustin Z. Ntoubandi, Amnesty for Crimes against Humanity under International Law, pp. 113–149.
© 2007, *Koninklijke Brill NV. Printed in The Netherlands.*

International Criminal Law Conventions

International criminal law conventions are those that generally obligate States Parties to prosecute or extradite those who commit the offences defined therein.[1] At least twenty-four international offences are defined in several international instruments, which impose on States a duty to prosecute or extradite.[2] Among the international criminal law conventions that have a particular bearing on crimes against humanity are the following: the Geneva Conventions of 1949, the Genocide Convention, the Convention on the Non-Applicability of Statutory Limitations to War Crimes and Crimes against Humanity, the Apartheid Convention, the Torture Convention, and the Rome Statute.

The Four Geneva Conventions and their Additional Protocols

Four conventions were negotiated under the auspices of the ICRC in Geneva on 12 August, 1949 in order to codify the customary law of war.[3] They are Geneva Convention I;[4] Geneva Convention II;[5] Geneva Convention III;[6] and Geneva Convention IV.[7] As already pointed out above, each of these Conventions has developed a system of grave breaches, which amount to war crimes under international law and for which individuals incur criminal liability for their commission. Acts amounting to grave breaches of the Geneva Conventions may be committed both against persons and property. These are:

> [W]ilful killing, torture or inhuman treatment, including biological experiments, wilfully causing great suffering or serious injury to body or health, extensive destruction and appropriation of property, not justified by military necessity and carried out unlawfully and wantonly.[8]

---

1 M.C. Bassiouni and E.M. Wise *Aut Dedere Aut Judicare: The Duty to Extradite or Prosecute in International Law* (1995) at 73.

2 These offences are: aggression, war crimes, unlawful use of weapons, crimes against humanity, genocide, racial discrimination and apartheid, slavery and related crimes, torture, unlawful human experimentation, piracy, aircraft hijacking and related offences, crimes against the safety of international maritime navigation, use of force against internationally protected persons, taking of civilian hostages, drug offences, international traffic in obscene publications, protection of national and archeological treasures, environmental protection, theft of nuclear materials, unlawful use of the mails, interference with submarine cables, counterfeiting, corrupt practices in international commercial transactions, and mercenarism, in M.C. Bassiouni and E.M. Wise, n. 1 at 73–283.

3 See excerpts of the four Geneva Conventions in C. van den Wyngaert *International Criminal Law: A Collection of International and European Documents* (1996) at 5–15.

4 See chap. IV, n. 35.

5 See chap. IV, n. 36.

6 See chap. IV, n. 37.

7 See chap. IV, n. 38.

8 See Article 50 of Geneva Convention I and Article 51 of Geneva Convention II.

To this list, Geneva Convention III adds conduct such as compelling a prisoner of war to serve in the forces of the hostile Power, and wilfully depriving a prisoner of war of the rights of fair and regular trial prescribed in the Convention.[9] Geneva Convention IV completes the list by criminalizing acts of wilfully depriving protected civilians of the rights of a fair and regular trial, unlawful deportation or transfer and unlawful confinement of civilians, or the taking of civilians as hostages.[10]

The Geneva Conventions impose on States Parties an obligation to search for all perpetrators of grave breaches regardless of their nationality, and to either prosecute and punish them, or hand them over to another High Contracting Party for trial.[11] This clause, which is contained in the four Geneva Conventions, embodies two important principles of international criminal law, namely the principle of universal jurisdiction and the principle of *aut dedere aut judicare*.

The irrelevance of the nationality of the perpetrator as regards his prosecution by any State introduces the principle of universal jurisdiction in the system of grave breaches of the Geneva Conventions. Universal jurisdiction is based on the assumption that certain crimes are so heinous and depredatory that any State, in the territory of which the offenders thereof are found, is authorised to try and punish them.[12] In early times, universal jurisdiction applied to piracy and slave trading, which were considered to be morally reprehensible and involved violence to civilians and interference with commerce and navigation in the high sea.[13] Consequently, pirates and slave traders were considered *hostis humani generis*—enemy of all humanity—over which all States could exercise their jurisdiction. However, States could opt whether to punish such offenders or not, since universal jurisdiction is permissive rather than mandatory.[14]

Aut dedere aut judicare—extradite or prosecute—obligates States Parties to either prosecute offenders of grave breaches of the Conventions, or hand them over to a requesting State Party. This principle ensures that perpetrators of international crimes do not find safe haven anywhere in the world.[15] Unlike universal jurisdiction, the requirement embodied in *aut dedere aut judicare* is mandatory,[16] because it only gives two options to a State: either to extradite the offender to another State which is prepared to try him, or to have him prosecuted before its own courts.

As far as the nature of the obligations contained in the Geneva Conventions is concerned, many commentators agree that the duty to prosecute or extradite is

---

9 Article 130.
10 Article 147.
11 See Article 49 of Geneva Convention I; Article 50 of Geneva Convention II; Article 129 of Geneva Convention III and Article 146 of Geneva Convention IV.
12 N. Roht-Arriaza, chap. I, n. 24 at 25.
13 *Id.*
14 *Id.*
15 *Id.*
16 *Id.*

absolute and is not subject to any form of limitation.[17] Therefore, States Parties can under no circumstances grant perpetrators of grave breaches immunity or amnesty from prosecution. However, the State's duty arising out of the Geneva Conventions is subject to the characterization of a particular conflict (non-international armed conflict, conflict of an international character, international armed conflict); a characterization which makes the applicability of international humanitarian law very controversial to certain categories of victims. The Geneva Conventions distinguish between two categories of conflicts, international conflicts and conflicts not of an international character. The first category includes cases of declared war or any other armed conflict which may arise between two or more of the High Contracting Parties, even if the state of war is not recognised by one of them, and cases of partial or total occupation of the territory of a High Contracting Party, even if the said occupation meets with no armed resistance.[18] Although the second category of conflicts is not defined in the four Geneva Conventions, provision is made for the application by State Parties of minimum standards of humanity whenever they occur.[19]

On the other hand, two Protocols were adopted on 8 June 1977 which supplemented the four Geneva Conventions and reinforced the protection of victims in armed conflicts contained in the system of grave breaches. They are Protocol (I) Additional to the Geneva Conventions of 12 August 1949, and Relating to the Protection of Victims of International Armed Conflicts, and Protocol (II) Additional to the Geneva Conventions of 12 August 1949, and Relating to the Protection of Victims of Non-International Armed Conflicts.[20]

Additional Protocol I extends the system of grave breaches to all victims of international armed conflicts.[21] It also imposes on States a general obligation to repress or suppress breaches resulting from a failure to act, when it provides that Parties to the Conventions and parties to the conflict shall repress grave breaches and take measures necessary to suppress other breaches of the Convention or of the Protocol, which result from the failure to act when under the duty to do so.[22] This provision reinforces similar provisions already contained in Geneva Convention I,[23] Geneva Convention II,[24] Geneva Convention III,[25] and Geneva Convention IV,[26] which distinguish between grave breaches of the Conventions and (simple) breaches of the Conventions.

---

17 See M.P. Scharf "The letter of the law: the scope of the international legal obligation to prosecute human rights crimes" 59 *Law and Contemporary Problems* 4 (1996) at 43.
18 Article 2 common to the four Geneva Conventions.
19 Article 3 common to the four Geneva Conventions.
20 Texts reprinted in C. Pilloud, chap. II, n. 6 at 3 and 1307 respectively.
21 Article 85 (2) provides that grave breaches of the Geneva Conventions are also grave breaches of the Protocol.
22 Article 86 (1).
23 Article 49.
24 Article 50.
25 Article 129.
26 Article 146.

In terms of the Geneva Conventions and Additional Protocol I, grave breaches must be repressed. This implies the obligation to enact legislation laying down effective penal sanctions for perpetrators of such breaches.[27] In this respect, the provisions of the Geneva Conventions also apply to Additional Protocol I.[28] As regards breaches other than grave breaches the parties to the Convention undertake to suppress them. Suppression of such breaches may take the form of penal or disciplinary sanctions and is the responsibility of the authority on which those committing such breaches depend, or the power to which they belong.[29] However, this obligation does not detract from the right of States under customary law, as reaffirmed in the writings of a number of publicists, to punish serious violations of the laws of war under the principle of universal jurisdiction.[30] Moreover, Additional Protocol I, Article 88 (1) requires co-operation between all Parties to the Geneva Conventions in order to respect and ensure respect for international humanitarian law. It provides that:

> The High Contracting Parties shall afford one another the greatest measure of assistance in connection with criminal proceedings brought in respect of grave breaches of the Conventions or of this Protocol.

In all, the obligations arising from the Geneva Conventions and Additional Protocol I are so compelling that many authors share the view that they are absolute and cannot be derogated from.[31]

Additional Protocol II protects all victims of non-international armed conflicts. Non-international armed conflict is defined as "a situation in which hostilities break out between armed forces or organised armed groups within the territory of a single State."[32] In such circumstances Additional Protocol II applies as rules of humanitarian law, aiming at securing fundamental guarantees for individuals in all circumstances.[33] In this sense, Additional Protocol II has the same humanitarian purpose as Article 3 common to the four Geneva Conventions,[34] which was envisaged to remove the distinction between international and non-international armed conflicts.[35] However, as already mentioned above, States duties in respect of grave breaches of the Geneva Conventions and of Additional Protocol I do not extend to the situation of non-international armed conflicts envisaged in Additional Protocol II. This is probably because Additional Protocol II is silent on the punishment of grave breaches.

---

27 C. Pilloud, chap. II, n. 6 at 1010.
28 See Article 85 (1) of Additional Protocol I.
29 C. Pilloud, chap. II, n. 6 at 1011.
30 *Id.*
31 A. Schlunck, chap. I, n. 3 at 39.
32 C. Pilloud, chap. II, n. 6 at 1320.
33 *Id.* at 1328.
34 Common Article 3 safeguards basic humanitarian principles in situations of armed conflicts of a non-international character.
35 See *Travaux Preparatoires* in C. Pilloud, chap. II, n. 6 at 1328.

Nevertheless, recent developments in the laws of armed conflict have seen an increased indiscriminate application of the rules and principles of international humanitarian law both to the Geneva Conventions' international conflicts and conflicts not of an international character on the one hand, and to Additional Protocol II non-international armed conflicts, on the other. This has resulted in the blurring of the distinction between all these categories of conflicts.[36] The rationale behind this new trend was clearly explained by the Appeals Chamber of the ICTY in *Tadic* when, called to address the issue of whether the accused could be held criminally liable for breaches of international humanitarian law allegedly committed in an internal armed conflict, it answered in the affirmative,[37] stating that:

> [C]ivil wars have become more frequent, not only because technological progress has made it easier for groups of individuals to have access to weaponry but also on account of increasing tension, whether ideological, inter-ethnic or economic; as a consequence the international community can no longer turn a blind eye to the legal regime of such wars. [I]nternal armed conflicts have become more and more cruel and protracted, involving the whole population of the State where they occur: the all-out resort to armed violence has taken on such a magnitude that the difference with international wars has increasingly dwindled. [...] Gradually the maxim of Roman law *hominum causa omne jus constitutum est* (all law is created for the benefit of human beings) has gained a firm foothold in the international community as well. It follows that in the area of armed conflict the distinction between interstate wars and civil wars is losing its values as far as human beings are concerned. Why protect civilians from belligerent violence, or ban rape, torture or the wanton destruction of hospitals, churches, museums or private property, as well as proscribe weapons causing unnecessary suffering when two sovereign States are engaged in war, and yet refrain from enacting the same bans or providing the same protection when armed violence has erupted 'only' within the territory of a sovereign State? If international law, while of course duly safeguarding the legitimate interests of States, must gradually turn to the protection of human beings, it is only natural that the... dichotomy should gradually loose its weight.[38]

The view of the Tribunal has been generally upheld and seems to have been consecrated in Article 8 (2) (c)–(f) of the Rome Statute.

Contrary to war crimes, the applicability of the rules prohibiting crimes against humanity is not made subject to the existence of any particular conflict. As already demonstrated in Chapter 3, Subsection 4.2 above, the severance of the war nexus has made these crimes capable of being committed in all situations (in international wars, non-international wars and in peace time), whereas Article 7 (2) (a) of the Rome Statute makes it clear that they can be committed by States as well as by non-State entities.

---

36 The most salient aspects of these developments are analysed by T. Meron, The Humanization of the law of war, in 301 *Recueil Des Cours* (2003) at 49–60.

37 *Prosecutor v. Tadic* a/k/a 'Dule', Case No IT-94-1-AR72, Decision on the Defence Motion for Interlocutory Appeal on Jurisdiction, Appeal Chamber judgment of 2 October, 1995, at paras 128–137.

38 At para 97.

The Genocide Convention

Adopted on 9 December, 1948, the Genocide Convention entered into force on January 12, 1951 and has been widely ratified.[39] This instrument provides an unambiguous definition of genocide and lists acts that are punishable under the Convention.[40] Before one can speak of the crime of genocide, the perpetrator must commit one of the punishable acts listed in the Convention with the specific intent to destroy in whole or in part a national, ethnical, racial, or religious group as such.[41] Like the Geneva Conventions, the Genocide Convention imposes an absolute obligation on States to prosecute the Convention's offenders.[42] Such an obligation is contained in Article 4, which states that "[p]ersons committing genocide or any of the other acts enumerated in article 3 shall be punished..." Moreover, Article V requires States to 'provide effective penalties' for persons found guilty of genocide. Nevertheless, the State duty under the Genocide Convention to prosecute and punish exists only if the intention to destroy, in whole or in part, a racial, ethnical, national or religious group can be inferred.

The Genocide Convention is believed to belong to the category of *ius cogens*, in that it contains norms of international law that existed in the form of international customary law prior to their introduction in the text of the Convention.[43] Consequently, the offence of genocide is punishable both under the Genocide Convention and under international customary law. Would this therefore imply that international customary law imposes on States the obligation to prosecute and punish genocide in the same way as the Genocide Convention does?

An answer to this question depends on whether the widespread condemnation of genocide is followed by the State practice of prosecuting and punishing genocide offenders, as evidence of the existence of the prohibition against acts of genocide. There exist today several precedents of prosecution and punishment of genocide. The Nuremberg Tribunal, the ICTY, the ICTR as well as several Rwandan domestic courts and bodies involved in the trial of genocide offenders, are evidence of the States practice in respect of prosecuting and punishing genocide.[44] In addition, during the deliberations leading to the adoption of the Rome Statute, genocide was the only offence that all delegations accepted to submit to the jurisdiction of the

---

39 As of 9 October, 2001, 133 States are Parties to the Genocide Convention; status of ratification available on www.unhchr.ch/html/menu3/b/treaty1genhtm.
40 See previous chapter for more details.
41 *Id.*
42 M.P. Scharf, n. 17 at 44; or A. Schlunck, chap. I, n. 3 at 31; or Genocide Convention Article 1 which states that the parties *confirm* that genocide is a crime under international law.
43 A. Schlunck, chap. I, n. 3 at 31.
44 To this shall be added the deal struck in March 2003 between the United Nations and the Government of Cambodia for the prosecution of the Khmer Rouge who allegedly participated in the Cambodian genocide.

international criminal court. This unanimous agreement reflects the general attitude of the majority of the United Nations Member States in respect of genocide.

In light of the foregoing, one can arguably declare that the duty to prosecute and punish the crime of genocide exists both in conventional international law and in customary international law. Consequently, all States are bound by such duty and no derogation is permitted.

The Torture Convention

The Torture Convention,[45] which entered into force on 26 June, 1987 defines torture as:

> [A]ny act by which severe pain or suffering, whether physical or mental, is intentionally inflicted on a person for such purposes as obtaining from him or a third person information or a confession, punishing him for an act he or a third person has committed or is suspected of having committed, or intimidating or coercing him or a third person, or for any reason based on discrimination of any kind, when such pain or suffering is inflicted by or at the instigation of or with the consent or acquiescence of a public official or other person acting in an official capacity. It does not include pain or suffering arising only from, inherent in or incidental to lawful sanctions.[46]

The Torture Convention requires States Parties to ensure that acts of torture, attempt to commit torture, complicity or participation in torture are offences under their domestic criminal law.[47] Each State Party is also required to take measures necessary to establish its jurisdiction over torture in cases where, among others, the alleged offender is its national or when the offence is committed in the territory under its jurisdiction or on board of a ship or aircraft registered in that State.[48] Article 7 requires each State Party to extradite alleged offenders, or, if they choose not to do so, prosecute them as if they had committed an ordinary offence of a serious nature under the domestic law of that State.

As regards the nature of the obligations contained in the Torture Convention, a few observations shall be made. In contrast to the strong language of the Geneva Conventions and the Genocide Convention, which requires States to 'suppress' violation of the conventions, provide 'effective penal sanctions' or 'effective penalties' for their violations or 'search' offenders, 'bring them before the courts' and 'punish' them, the language of the Torture Convention seems to be less compelling. In fact, it only requires each State Party to make torture 'punishable by appropriate penalties', to 'establish its jurisdiction' over the offence or to "submit the case to its competent authorities for the purpose of prosecution." The use of such wordings seems to privilege the interpretation that the Torture Convention does not explicitly

---

45 See chap. III, n. 166.
46 Article 1.
47 Article 4.
48 Article 5.

require prosecution and punishment.[49] However, in the opinion of its drafters, the Torture Convention was intended to make torture a grave offence punishable by severe penalties as they apply to the most serious offences under the domestic legal system.[50] In addition, it is suggested that the prohibition against torture did not start with the Convention. On the contrary, "the Convention is based upon the recognition that [acts of torture] are already outlawed under international law."[51] Therefore, it is assumed that the aim of the Convention is to strengthen the already existing prohibition by a number of supportive measures.[52] On the basis of this assumption, it would seem that the prohibition against torture is binding as a rule of international law both for States Parties to the Convention and for non-States Parties. However, the obligation to prosecute and punish, or extradite contained in the Convention does not seem to have an absolute character as in the case of genocide. This is because the practice of States in this respect is quasi non-existent, and because the use of torture as a means of intimidation, punishment, or as a means of obtaining information is still common practice all over the world.

The Apartheid Convention

As already explained above,[53] Article II of this Convention lists inhuman acts amounting to the crime of apartheid, while Article IV requires States Parties to declare apartheid and those engaging in it as criminal and to take steps to prevent, 'prosecute' and 'punish' violators thereof in accordance with their jurisdiction. Article V contemplates the enforcement of the Convention by means of an 'international penal Tribunal' and Article IX requires States Parties not to regard apartheid as a political offence in the matter of extradition.

As far as the nature of the prohibition against apartheid is concerned, it is important to note that the conduct prohibited under the Apartheid Convention is also proscribed under other international human rights instruments;[54] with the difference that the violations enunciated in human rights instruments are not generally qualified as criminal.[55] In addition, the qualification of apartheid as a crime against humanity,

---

49 See M.P. Scharf, n. 17 at 46 quoting D. Orentlicher.
50 See J.H. Burgers and H. Danelius, chap. III, n. 166, annotation of Article 4 at 129.
51 *Id.* at 1.
52 *Id.*
53 See previous chapters for more details on the content of this Convention.
54 See e.g., Articles 2, 4, 7, 13 and 16 of the Universal Declaration of Human Rights, which provides, *inter alia*, that everyone is entitled to all the rights and freedoms set forth in the Declaration without distinction of any kind, such as race, colour; among the rights set forth are: freedom from servitude, freedom from discrimination and a guarantee of equal protection of the laws, freedom of movement and residence, freedom of inter-racial marriage; or the International Covenant on Civil and Political Rights, Articles 1, 2, 12, 14, etc.
55 See M.C. Bassiouni and D.H. Derby "Final report on the establishment of an international criminal court for the implementation of the Apartheid Convention and other relevant international instruments" 9 *Hofstra Law Review* (1981) at 532.

and as an offence entailing international criminal responsibility suggests that the international community as a whole has an interest in prosecuting and punishing apartheid. Therefore, the obligation of States to criminalize, prosecute and punish acts of apartheid is binding both on States Parties and non-parties as a general rule of international law. However, the lack of State practice as regards the prosecution and punishment of apartheid offenders,[56] the relatively low level ratification of the Apartheid Convention and the fact that the Convention requires States to exercise their duties only according to their own rule of jurisdiction, concur to remove any mandatory character from the exigencies of the Apartheid Convention.

The Rome Statute

The Rome Statute is the last of the several international conventions that impose obligations upon States Parties with respect to war crimes, aggression, genocide and crimes against humanity. This instrument was signed at a United Nations Diplomatic Conference of Plenipotentiaries on the Establishment of an International Criminal Court on 16 July, 1998 by 120 votes for, 21 abstentions, and 7 votes against.[57] It entered into force on 1st July, 2002 with 139 State signatories and 89 ratifications.[58] States' duties in respect of the crimes defined in the Rome Statute are contained in the express text of the Statute. In fact, the Statute makes provision for two important principles that govern the relationships between the ICC and domestic courts on the one hand, and between the ICC and States Parties to its Statute on the other hand. These are the principle of complementarity and the principle of co-operation.

The principle of complementarity, which defines the nature of the relationship between the ICC and national jurisdictions is stated in the Preamble of the Statute in these terms:

> Affirming that the most serious crimes of concern to the international community as a whole must not go unpunished and that their effective prosecution must be ensured by taking measures at the national level and by enhancing international co-operation,

---

56 Even the democratically elected new South African government, composed mainly of the racial group which suffered more from apartheid policy decided not to prosecute perpetrators of apartheid; instead, they held the view that: "sharing [...] the international community's basic moral and legal position on apartheid [the recognition of apartheid as a crime against humanity] should not be understood as a call for international criminal prosecution of those who formulated and implemented apartheid policies. Indeed, such a course would militate against the very principles on which this commission was established", see S. de Villiers, chap. I, n. 2 at 94.

57 The United States of America, China, India, Vietnam, Bahrain, Libya and Israel voted against, see T. Puurunen "The committee on amnesty of the South African truth and reconciliation commission—a new model of conflict resolution" 9 *The Finnish Yearbook of International Law* (1998) at 338.

58 See www.unorg/icc consulted on 29 March 2003.

> Determined to put an end to impunity for the perpetrators of these crimes and thus to contribute to the prevention of such crimes,
>
> Recalling that it is the duty of every State to exercise its criminal jurisdiction over those responsible for international crimes.[59]

Article 1 of the Statute reiterates this principle in the following terms:

> An International Criminal Court [...] shall be a permanent institution and shall have the power to exercise its jurisdiction over persons for the most serious crimes of international concern [...] and shall be complementary to national criminal jurisdictions.

Therefore, one may infer from the provisions above that the primary duty of achieving the goals set forth in the Preamble of the Rome Statute lies with each individual State Party, with the ICC itself only playing a secondary role.

The second principle is contained in Article 86 which carries the title 'general *obligation* to cooperate'. This principle obligates States Parties to "cooperate fully with the Court in its investigation and prosecution of crimes within the jurisdiction of the Court."

The Preamble's use of wordings such as "the most serious crimes [...] must not go unpunished", 'effective prosecution must be ensured', "it is the duty of every State to exercise its [...] jurisdiction over [...] crimes" is reminiscent of the language of the Geneva Conventions and that of the Genocide Convention that impose an absolute obligation on States Parties to either prosecute or extradite offenders of the crimes defined therein. Reference to such wordings leads many authors to argue that once a State has become party to the Rome Statute, it cannot justify refraining from investigating, prosecuting and punishing the Statute's offenders. Speaking about the prohibition against the application of statutory limitations to the crimes defined in the Statute, Lattanzi argues that States duties under the Rome Statute are 'inderogable' and 'non-negotiable'.[60]

Concerning the obligation to co-operate with the ICC in the investigation and prosecution of the crimes defined in the Statute, it is important to note that such an obligation may well extend to non-State Parties. This possibility is contemplated in Article 12 (3)[61] and Article 87 (5)[62] of the Statute. However, in the absence of a co-operation agreement with the Court, the binding character on third-States of

---

59   See chap. I, n. 6 at 4.

60   See F. Lattanzi, The International Criminal Court and national jurisdictions, in M. Politi and G. Nesi *The Rome Statute of the International Criminal Court: A Challenge to Impunity* (2001) at 185.

61   In terms of this provision, a State non-party to the Statute may accept the jurisdiction of the Court in respect of a crime; in this case, the State concerned is under the obligation to co-operate with the Court.

62   This provision makes it possible for third-States to be bound by the provisions of the Statute through ad hoc agreements.

the obligation to co-operate may still be inferred from the modality of referral to the Court, and from the nature of the offences defined in the Statute.[63]

With respect to the modality of referral to the ICC, Article 13 of the Rome Statute designates three bodies that are competent to refer a matter to the Court. These are: a State Party, the Security Council acting under Chapter VII of the United Nations Charter, and the Prosecutor of the Court. When a situation, which threatens international peace and security is referred to the Court by the Security Council, all members of the United Nations—including States Parties and non-parties to the Rome Statute—are under the obligation to co-operate. In this case, the Security Council resolution referring the matter to the Court is the source of the obligation to co-operate for all members of the United Nations.[64]

As far as the nature of the crimes defined in the Statute is concerned, genocide, war crimes or crimes against humanity are the most serious crimes for which certain clear obligations already exist in international law. As pointed out above, the Geneva Conventions as well as the Genocide or the Apartheid Convention obligate States Parties to investigate, prosecute and punish offenders of the crimes they define. Consequently, States non-parties to the Rome Statute, but parties to these Conventions will be bound by the duties arising out of the Statute because of the incorporation of war crimes, genocide or crimes against humanity in its provisions.[65] This is because of the assumption that the obligations of third-States that originate from the Geneva Conventions, the Genocide or the Apartheid Convention have automatically been transferred to the Rome Statute.

General Human Rights Conventions

General human rights conventions do not expressly oblige States Parties to punish violations of the rights they protect, however, they require them to respect and ensure the rights enumerated therein, and to provide remedies when such rights are violated. The major human rights conventions containing a general obligation to respect and ensure rights are: the International Covenant on Civil and Political Rights (ICCPR)[66] the European Convention for the Protection of Human Rights and Fundamental Freedoms (ECHR),[67] and the ACHR.[68] Other human rights instru-

---

63 See G. Nesi, The obligation to cooperate with the International Criminal Court and States not Party to the Statute, in M. Politi and G. Nesi, n. 60 at 222.

64 *Id.*; see also for example Security Council Resolution 1593, adopted on 31 March 2005 referring the Darfour situation to the Prosecutor International Criminal Court for investigation: in this case any decision taken by the Prosecutor will bind all UN members, including Sudan which is not Party to the ICC Statute.

65 See G. Nesi, in M. Politi and G. Nesi, n. 60 at 222.

66 See chap. IV, n. 141.

67 *Id.*

68 See chap. III, n. 190.

ments such as the African Charter on Human and Peoples' Rights (ACHPR)[69] and the UDHR[70] guarantee the obligation to provide a remedy in case of human rights violations.

The International Covenant on Civil and Political Rights

This instrument protects, among others, the right of all peoples to self-determination,[71] the inherent right to life,[72] the right to liberty and security of the person;[73] it also protects everyone from torture[74] and slavery.[75] States are required to respect and to ensure to all persons the rights recognised in the ICCPR, to provide legislative or other measures in order to give effect to the Covenant and to provide effective remedy to victims of the violations.[76] Article 28 establishes a Human Rights Committee to monitor compliance with the Covenant, while Article 40 entrusts the Committee with the power, among others, to receive reports of compliance from States Parties to the Covenant, and to issue general comments on any alleged violation of the rights contained therein.

The Human Rights Committee issued three comments that have been repeatedly put forward as a justification to the claim that there exists a positive duty on States to punish violators of the Covenant. Firstly, in reaction to a claim of alleged acts of torture perpetrated in Zaire, the Committee commented that Zaire was:

> [U]nder the duty to [...] conduct an inquiry into the circumstances of torture, to punish those found guilty of torture and to take steps to ensure that similar violations do not occur in the future.[77]

Secondly, in response to a communication of alleged extra-legal executions in Surinam, the Committee insisted that the government of Surinam takes "effective steps [...] to investigate the killings [...] and to bring to justice any persons found to be responsible."[78] Finally, in its comment on the situation of human rights in Uruguay in March 1993, the Committee stated that the obligation of States Parties under Article 2 (3) of the Covenant is "to ensure that victims of past human rights

---

69 Adopted on 27 June 1981, OAU Doc. CAB/LEG/67/3 rev.5, 21 *ILM* 58 (1982), entered into force on 21 October 1986. Text available at www1.umnedu/humanrts/instree/z1afchar. htm.

70 See chap. III, n. 190.

71 Article 1.

72 Article 6.

73 Article 9.

74 Article 7.

75 Article 8.

76 Articles 2 and 3.

77 See *Muteba v. Zaire* Comm. No. 124/1982, 39 UN GAOR Supp. No. 40 Annex XIII, UN Doc A/39/40 (1984); see also M.P. Scharf, n. 17 at 48–49.

78 See *Boaboeram v. Surinam* Comm. Nos 146/1983 and 148–154/1983, 40 UN GAOR Supp No. 40, Annex X, UN Doc A/40/40 (1985).

violations have an effective remedy."[79] In addition, in a case involving forced disappearance in Uruguay, the Committee urged the government of Uruguay to take effective steps to bring to justice any person found responsible.[80]

Moreover, in elaborating on the nature of the obligation flowing from Article 7 (2) and (3) of the ICCPR, which prohibits torture or any cruel, inhuman or degrading treatment or punishment, the Human Rights Committee commented that amnesties covering acts of torture:

[A]re generally incompatible with the duty of States to investigate such acts; to guarantee freedom from such acts within their jurisdiction; and to ensure that they do not occur in the future.[81]

Whether the Committee's pronouncements imply a duty to prosecute violators is not quite clear. However, each State's understanding of the nature of the Covenant's obligation at the moment of its ratification may be decisive in determining the existence of a duty to prosecute.

It is suggested that during the negotiations of the ICCPR, the delegates specifically considered and rejected a proposal that would have required States to prosecute violators of the Covenant.[82] Therefore, for the States that originally signed the Covenant, the Human Rights Committee's comments do not create any binding obligation to prosecute and punish violators of the Covenant. For example, such States would interpret the Committee's comment on Zaire in respect of the duty to punish persons guilty of torture, as a call for the use of any alternative measures short of criminal prosecution, including:

[D]ismissal from the military or loss of military rank, cancelling government pensions, banning the perpetrator from public office, and/or requiring the payment of damages through administrative fines or civil proceedings.[83]

Similarly, the Committee's general comment that amnesties 'are generally incompatible' with the duty of States to investigate may be interpreted to mean for example that amnesties that are accompanied by investigations, identification of perpetrators, purging of the perpetrators from the positions of authority and compensation of victims, would be acceptable.[84]

In contrast, States that newly adhered to the ICCPR, as well as a number of commentators, tend to consider the Human Rights Committee's comments as Covenant

---

[79] UN Human Rights Committee, UN Doc CCPR/C/79/Add.19 (1993) at 11.

[80] See *Quinteros v. Uruguay* Comm. No. 107/1981, 38 UN GAOR Supp. No. 40, Annex XXII, UN Doc A/38/40 (1983).

[81] General Comment No. 20 (44), UN Doc CCPR/C21/Rev.1/Add.3 at 15 (April 1992); see also M.P. Scharf, n. 17 at 49.

[82] M.P. Scharf, n. 17 at 49.

[83] *Id.* at 50.

[84] *Id.*

jurisprudence, arguing that the Cold War context of the legislative history of the Covenant has become obsolete.[85]

In sum, no provision in the ICCPR clearly suggests that the right to a remedy against human rights violations implies the duty to prosecute perpetrators by means of criminal law.[86] Moreover, the Committee's decisions are only interpretative guidelines for the rights contained in the Covenant and in this respect they lack any legally binding character. On the basis of the Committee's comments referred to above, one may conclude that the duties to respect and ensure rights and to provide a remedy recognised in the Covenant, require States Parties to adopt at least any of the following measures: investigation into the alleged violations of the Covenant rights, punishment of the offenders and compensation of the victims, and adoption of preventive measures to halt violations of the Covenant's rights.

The European Convention on Human Rights

This document states in its Article 1 that States Parties have the obligation "to secure within their jurisdiction the rights and freedoms defined" in the Convention. Among these rights and freedoms are: the right to be protected by law, the right to liberty and security of the person, freedom from torture, inhuman or degrading treatment or punishment, and freedom from slavery or servitude.[87]

In *Ireland v. The United Kingdom*,[88] which concerned cases of human rights violations by the British security forces, the European Court of Human Rights held that States Parties have the duty to prevent and remedy breaches of the Convention in order to secure the rights defined therein. However, it did not put an injunction on the UK to prosecute the authors of the violations.[89]

Article 13 of the ECHR provides for the right to a remedy every time any conventional right or freedom is violated. It states in these respect that:

> Everyone whose rights and freedoms as set forth in [the] Convention are violated shall have an effective remedy before a national authority notwithstanding that the violation has been committed by persons acting in an official capacity.

The European Court of Human Rights established the following general principles for the interpretation of Article 13:

---

85 See e.g., D. Orentlicher "Settling accounts: the duty to prosecute human rights violations of a prior regime" 100 *Yale Law Journal* 8 (1991) at 2568.

86 A. Sclunck, chap. I, n. 3 at 41.

87 Articles 2, 5, 3 and 4 respectively.

88 Appl. No. 00005310 of 18 January 1978, text of the judgment available in 25 *European Convention on Human Rights* (ser. A 1978).

89 See 25 *European Convention on Human Rights*, n. 88 at 159.

(a) [W]here an individual has an arguable claim to be the victim of a violation of the rights set forth in the Convention, he should have a remedy before a national authority in order both to have his claim decide and, if appropriate, to obtain redress;

(b) [T]he authority referred to in Article 13 need not be a judicial authority but, if it is not, the powers and the guarantees which it affords are relevant in determining whether the remedy before it is effective;

(c) [A]lthough no single remedy may itself entirely satisfy the requirements of Article 13, the aggregate of remedies provided for under domestic law may do so;

(d) Article 13 does not guarantee a remedy allowing a Contracting State's law as such to be challenged before a national authority on the ground of being contrary to the Convention or equivalent domestic norms.[90]

The European Court also pointed out that the word 'remedy' within the meaning of Article 13 does not mean a remedy bound to succeed, but simply an accessible remedy before an authority competent to examine the merits of a complaint,[91] and that 'effective remedy' must mean a remedy that is as effective as can be.[92]

It appears that neither the text of the ECHR nor the jurisprudence of the European Court of Human Rights insist on any specific form of effective remedy to be awarded under Article 13. The definition of the content of the words 'effective remedy' would therefore vary according to the circumstances of the case, and according to the Contracting States' available provisions on remedies.

The American Convention on Human Rights

The obligation to respect and ensure rights appears to be more compelling in the ACHR. In its landmark ruling in the *Velasquez Rodriguez Case*,[93] the Inter-American Court of Human Rights assumed a duty to prosecute human rights violations under the Convention. The case concerned allegations of torture and disappearance in which Manfredo Velasquez, a student activist had been arrested, tortured, executed and disappeared by the Honduran security forces. The Inter-American Court found the Honduran government responsible for violating the rights to life, to humane treatment and to personal liberty, which are all protected under the ACHR. In so doing, the Court interpreted the duty to ensure rights set forth in Article 1 (1) of the Convention in the following way:

> This obligation implies the duty of the States Parties to organise the governmental apparatus and, in general, all the structures through which public power is exercised, so that they are capable of juridically ensuring the free and full enjoyment of human rights. As a consequence of this obligation, the States must prevent, investigate and punish any violation of the rights recognised by the Convention and, moreover, if

---

90 See *Leander v. Sweden*, Appl. No. 9248/81 (1987) 9 *European Human Rights Reports* (1987) at 433 para 77.

91 See *Lorsé v. Netherlands*, Appl. No. 52750/99 (2003) 37 *European Human Rights Reports* 3 (2003) at 105 para. 96.

92 *Id.* at para. 78.

93 See 4 *Inter-American Court of Human Rights* (ser C) No. 4 at 174 (1998).

possible attempt to restore the right violated and provide compensation as warranted for damages resulting from the violation.

On the basis of this reasoning, the Court found the Honduran government to be in breach of its duties under the Convention and ordered it to pay compensation to the victim's relatives. This interpretation renewed the debate on the right to a remedy contained in several human rights instruments, and its implication on the scope of the States duty to prosecute and punish human rights abusers. Since the Inter-American Court of Human Rights' interpretation of the Convention is binding on the Parties, one can assume that the obligation flowing from the ACHR requires some sort of investigation into the facts, prosecution and reparation. However, certain commentators argue that the fact that the Inter-American Court of Human Rights did not insist that the Honduran government criminally prosecute the persons responsible for the disappearance of Manfredo Velasquez, implies that in addition to criminal prosecutions, other forms of disciplinary action or punishment may be inflicted.[94]

The African Charter on Human and Peoples' Rights

The ACHPR[95] obligates States Parties to recognise the rights, duties and freedoms contained in the Charter and to adopt measures to give effect to them in their domestic law.[96] The right to a remedy is contained in Article 7, which provides that every individual shall have the right to have his cause heard, including:

> The right to an appeal to competent national organs against acts violating his fundamental rights as recognised and guaranteed by conventions, laws, regulations and customs in force.

On the other hand, Article 14 (6) requires compensation of the victim in case of miscarriage of justice.

Article 30 establishes the African Commission on Human and Peoples' Rights as the implementing organ designed to promote human and peoples' rights in Africa and to ensure their protection. However, the Commission is not given a clear mandate to order remedies for human rights violations. It is only entrusted, among other things, with the power to "ensure the protection of human and peoples' rights under conditions laid down by the [...] Charter."[97] Nevertheless, the Commission has interpreted its mandate to promote and ensure rights so as to include the competence to order provisional measures in its Rules of Procedures[98] and to

---

94 M.P. Scharf, n. 17 at 51.
95 See n. 69.
96 Article 1.
97 Article 45 (2).
98 See *Dagli v. Togo* Communication 83/92, see excerpts in Institute for Human Rights and Development *Compilation of Decisions on Communications of the African Commission*

order compensation.[99] It is suggested that in recommending that decrees be nullified, the African Commission has gone a step further than the European Court of Human Rights in its interpretation of ensuring the protection of rights.[100]

In 1998, a Protocol to the ACHPR on Human and Peoples' Rights was adopted, which established an African Court on Human and Peoples' Rights to complement the protective mandate of the African Commission.[101] This instrument defines the competence of the new Court to order a remedy in its Article 27:

> (1) If the Court finds that there has been violation of a human or peoples' rights, it shall make appropriate orders to remedy the violation, including the payment of fair compensation or reparation;
>
> (2) In cases of extreme gravity and urgency, and when necessary to avoid irreparable harm to persons, the Court shall adopt such provisional measures as it deems necessary.

It is important to note here that the competence of the African Court on Human Rights in terms of Article 27 reflects the position held by the Commission in the *Dagli* and *Mekongo* cases.

The Universal Declaration of Human Rights

The right to a remedy is also guaranteed in the UDHR,[102] Article 8 of which provides that:

> [E]veryone has the right to an effective remedy by the competent national tribunals for acts violating the fundamental rights granted to him by the constitution or by law.

The right to a remedy in domestic law systems usually implies both remedies of a civil law nature and remedies of a penal law nature. The UDHR does not seem to favour any form of remedy. Moreover, it obligates States to facilitate access to national court systems in cases of alleged human rights violations. Whether the UDHR creates a duty to criminally prosecute human rights offenders depends mainly on the legal opinion maintained by each State which voted in favour of its adoption. In general, two views coexist as to the legal character of the Declaration. The first holds that this instrument, which is based on a General Assembly resolution, only represents recommendations on principles of human rights and freedoms and

---

on Human and Peoples' Rights: Extracts from the Commission's Activity Reports 1994–2001.

99 See *Mekongo v. Cameroon* Communication 59/91; see excerpts in *Compilation of Decisions of the African Commission* n. 98 at 61–62.

100 See F. Viljoen, Overview of the African regional human rights system, in C. Heyns (ed.), *Human Rights Law in Africa* (1998) at 155.

101 See OAU Doc OAU/LEG/EXP/AFCHPR/PROT (III) of 9 June 1998, Articles 1 and 2.

102 See chap. III, n. 168, text available at www.unorg/Overview/rights.html.

thus, cannot have any binding legal effect.[103] The second view, which developed after the adoption of the two Covenants of 1966, holds that the UDHR has become a legally binding document. Proponents of this thesis claim that the Declaration may be regarded as an authoritative United Nations Charter interpretation; as laying down general principles of law in the sense of Article 38 (1) (c) of the ICJ Statute; or as embracing *in toto* rules of customary international law without, however, having that status in relation to the implementation and kinds of enforcement of its provision.[104] To adduce evidence of their claim, they highlight the adoption of various regional human rights instruments as well as domestic constitutions containing a charter of fundamental rights which are all premised on the UDHR. They also insist on the fact that international and domestic courts have given effects to such rights.[105]

Summary

To sum up this section, it shall be argued that international criminal law conventions such as the 1949 Geneva Conventions and Additional Protocol I of 1977, the Genocide Convention, the Torture and Apartheid Conventions and the Rome Statute, express a clear and unambiguous obligation to prosecute the crimes contained therein. In certain cases, such as in the Rome Statute, the obligation to prosecute assumes a mandatory character. In contrast, general human rights conventions such as the ICCPR, the ECHR, the ACHR and the ACHPR, are not explicit on the States' duty to prosecute. Instead, they all require States Parties to remedy human rights violations. A remedy pertains to the means by which a right is enforced or a violation of a right is prevented, redressed or compensated; remedies can vary from the right to lodge a complaint to a criminal court to monetary compensation.[106] In this sense, the rights to a remedy contained in the foregoing human rights instruments may be interpreted to imply the States duty to investigate, prosecute, compensate or punish human rights violations. Depending on the circumstances of the case, the right to a remedy may involve the States' duty to criminally prosecute human rights offenders.[107]

---

[103] See B. Simma *The Charter of the United Nations: A Commentary* 2nd ed., vol. II (2002) at 926.
[104] *Id.*
[105] *Id.*
[106] A. Schlunck, chap. I, n. 3 at 44–45.
[107] This precedent is set by the Inter-American Court of Human Rights in the *Velasquez Case*.

Customary Law Sources of States Duties

As demonstrated in chapter one, crimes against humanity emerged from the customary law of armed conflicts. In 1945, the drafters of the Nuremberg Charter, as well as the prosecutors and judges of the Nuremberg Tribunal held the view that the Charter was a custom-creating act, which codified the state of custom as it existed at that time. Therefore, in the absence of a specialised convention on crimes against humanity, customary international law remains the only reliable source of States obligations to prosecute this offence.

It has also been shown earlier in chapter three that for a particular conduct to create custom there must be a combination of an objective element with a subjective or psychological element. An objective element refers to a settled practice of States, while a subjective or psychological element is the feeling that in acting as they do, States are fulfilling a legal obligation.[108] This element is embodied in the maxim *opinio iuris sive necessitatis.*

Given that customary law is as binding as treaty law,[109] it would be important to first clarify the elements of international custom before determining whether such elements exist in respect of crimes against humanity. The aim here is to find out whether crimes against humanity has reached the status of international customary law necessary to create a binding obligation to prosecute its violation.

State Practice in Respect of Crimes against Humanity

The ICJ held in the *North Sea Continental Shelf Cases*[110] that, for an act to be accorded the weight of international custom, the act concerned must amount to a settled practice and must be carried out in such a way as to be evidence of a belief that such practice is rendered obligatory by the existence of a rule of law requiring it. The first element, namely a settled practice, implies that a State has carried out a particular act in a consistent, uniform and general manner, and over a certain period of time.

Definition and Content of Practice

State practice can be defined as any act or statement by a State from which views about customary law can be inferred.[111] The practice of States includes:

108　See ICJ, *North Sea Continental Shelf Cases* (*Federal Republic of Germany v. Denmark/ Federal Republic of Germany v. The Netherlands*), in *Reports of Judgments, Advisory Opinions and Orders*, 3 (1969) (hereinafter ICJ Reports) at 44 para. 77.

109　M.P. Scharf, n. 17 at 56.

110　ICJ *Reports*, n. 108.

111　M. Dixon and R. McCorquodale, chap. IV, n. 14 at 27.

[N]ot only their external conduct with each other, but is also evidenced by such internal matters as their domestic legislation, judicial decisions, diplomatic dispatches, internal government memoranda, and ministerial statements in parliament and elsewhere.[112]

External conduct of States means practice in the international arena through diplomatic protests, economic or military coercion, recourse to arbitration or international forums.[113] Such practice is as diverse as to include the following: diplomatic correspondence, including declarations of government policies; press communiqués; official manuals dealing with legal questions (for example manuals of military law); orders to the armed forces, such as rules of engagement; votes in international organisations; the observations of Governments on projects produced by the ILC or similar bodies; pleadings before international tribunals, etc.[114]

Moreover, States practice may take the form of either a positive act or an omission. Positive acts consist of verbal acts or statements. While a formal statement of position by a head of State or Government, or a formal diplomatic communication at the highest level, plainly must be taken seriously, a statement by junior diplomats or technicians carries less weight.[115] There is omission whenever a State abstains from acting positively; for example, it is believed that States' abstention from prosecuting foreign diplomats suspected or accused of crimes contributed substantially to the creation of rules of diplomatic immunity.[116]

Whose Practice is Required?

Mendelson defines a rule of customary international law as:

[O]ne which emerges from and is sustained by, the constant and uniform practice of States and other subjects of international law, in their international relations, in circumstances which gives rise to a legitimate expectation of similar conduct in the future.[117]

This definition suggests that not only State's practice is required for the development of customary rules; the practice of other entities may contribute to the formation of customary international law also. Such other entities include, for example, non-governmental international organisations such as Amnesty International, the Institute of International Law or the International Law Association; multinational and national corporations; or even individuals.[118]

---

112 R. Jennings and A. Watts, chap. IV, n. 7 at 26.
113 N. Roht-Arriaza, chap. I, n. 24 at 39.
114 I. Brownlie, chap. IV, n. 23 at 5.
115 M.H. Mendelson, The formation of customary international law, in 272 *Recueil des Cours* (1998) at 205.
116 *Id.* at 207.
117 *Id.* at 188.
118 *Id.* at 203.

Uniformity of Practice

In its judgement in the *North Sea Continental Shelf Cases*, the ICJ required a practice to be 'extensive and virtually uniform'[119] before one can speak of international custom. There is uniformity when the various instances of practice are essentially similar and consistent, both internally and collectively.[120] A practice is consistent internally when each State whose conduct is under consideration had behaved in the same way on virtually all of the occasions on which it was engaged in the conduct in question; whereas collectively consistent means that "different States must not have engaged in substantially different practice."[121] In addition, it is submitted that for a customary law rule to emerge, only substantial uniformity is required, not complete uniformity.[122] The ICJ adopted this line of reasoning in the *Fisheries Case*.[123] In this instance, the Court questioned the existence of a uniform State practice in limiting closing lines in bays to a length of ten miles, and remarked that although certain States have adopted a ten-mile closing line for bays:

> [B]oth in their national law and in their treaties and conventions, and although certain arbitral decisions have applied it as between these States, other States have adopted a different limit. Consequently, the ten-mile rule has not acquired the authority of a general rule of international law.[124]

Generality of Practice

As an element of custom, general practice implies the quantity of a particular practice and the continuity or duration of such a practice.[125]

Quantity of Practice

The ICJ requires a particular practice not only to be 'virtually uniform', but also 'extensive'. 'Extent' of practice raises two important issues: the issue of the amount of practice necessary to create a customary rule and that of the number of States required to participate in a particular practice. In respect to the latter, it is generally admitted that two States are sufficient to create particular customary law, such as regional and local customs, while more than two States are required for the creation of other forms of custom, such as universal and general customary laws.[126] As regards the amount of practice necessary to create a customary law rule, one distinguishes between universal practice and general practice. Universal

---

119 See ICJ *Reports*, n. 108 at 43 para. 74.
120 M.H. Mendelson, n. 115 at 212.
121 *Id.*
122 I. Brownlie *Principles of Public International Law* 5th ed., (1998) at 5.
123 (*Norway v. United Kingdom*) ICJ *Reports* (1951).
124 *Id.* at 116 para. 131.
125 P.K. Menon, chap. IV, n. 11 at 119.
126 M.H. Mendelson, n. 115 at 215.

practice requires all States to agree to a rule before it can reach the status of customary law, whereas general practice requires only the consent of the majority of States.[127] While the former creates universal customary law, the latter creates general customary law.

Universal customary law are "rules of customary law which are binding on all members of the international community, without exception". Examples of such rules include the prohibition of the use of force, except in self-defence, and the rule of *Pacta Sunt Servanda*.[128]

General customary law refers to:

> [A] set of rules, which, being supported by a sufficiently uniform and extensive prac-
> tice, bind all States [...] without its being necessary to show that the particular State
> allegedly bound by the rules has participated in its formation or application, or has
> otherwise accepted it.[129]

Universal practice is not usually required for a custom to be established; general practice is sufficient.[130] However, in its effects, general custom is similar to universal custom, the difference being that, in the case of general custom there is a possibility for a State to opt out by means of a persistent objector. A persistent objector is a safeguard for the State which does not participate in or acquiesce to a particular usage, but which is indeed positively opposed to it.[131] The basic effect of this principle is that:

> [A] State which manifests its opposition to a practice before it has developed into a
> rule of general international law can, by virtue of that objection, exclude itself from
> the operation of the new rule.[132]

For a persistent objection to be valid, a State must fulfil two conditions: first, the objection must be expressed from the early stages of the rule and maintained up to its formation and beyond. Second, the objection must be maintained consistently, in order to protect the position of other States, which may have come to rely on the position of the objector.[133] In addition, the objector should not benefit from its own inconsistencies; thus, if a State at times objects, and at other times invokes the rule, its conduct is no longer consistent and other States may be justified to believe that the objector no longer opposes the rule.[134] On occasions, the ICJ has made use of this principle. In the *Fisheries Case* for example, the Court was called to examine the United Kingdom's invocation of an alleged general rule of international law limiting closing lines in bays to a length of 10 miles. After the Court held that

---

127   P.K. Menon, chap. IV, n. 11 at 121.
128   M.H. Mendelson, n. 115 at 217.
129   *Id.* at 218.
130   I. Brownlie, n. 122 at 6.
131   M.H. Mendelson, n. 115 at 227.
132   *Id.*
133   M.E. Villiger *Customary International Law and Treaties: Manual on Theory and Practice of the Interrelation of Sources* Revised 2nd ed., (1997) at 35.
134   *Id.*

the ten-mile rule has not acquired the authority of a general rule of international law, it added that the ten-mile rule was inapplicable to Norway, because she had always opposed any attempt to apply it to the Norwegian coast.[135]

In addition to general practice, a certain amount or frequency of repetition of State practice is necessary to create a customary law rule. In respect of this element, it is submitted that where the evidence of *opinio iuris* is particularly strong, or in areas of customary international law where some States are particularly influent, a single act may be sufficient to establish a settled state practice.[136]

Continuity or Duration of Practice

The Roman law conceived customary law as the product of a long usage, while the English common law requires customary law to be immemorial, dating back "to the time whereof man's memory runneth not to the contrary".[137] A dissenting judge of the Permanent Court of International Justice adopted this approach in the European Commission of the *Danube Case*, when he required an immemorial usage before a customary rule could arise.[138] Likewise, the ICJ concluded in *The Right of Passage Case* that:

> [P]ractice having continued over a period extending beyond a century and a quarter unaffected by the change in regime [...] satisfied that that practice was accepted as law by the parties and has given rise to a right and a correlative obligation...[139]

Nevertheless, if there is a general consensus that the passage of a certain amount of time is necessary before an international law rule becomes a custom, various commentators as well as court decisions no more require immemorial practice. Brownlie points out for example, that a long practice is not necessary for a customary law rule to be created;[140] whereas Menon argues that "the traditional requirement of the time element is irrelevant in the formation of a rule of customary international law today."[141] Moreover, the principle of sovereign rights over the continental shelf took more or less 18 years to reach the status of international custom. The United States President Harry Truman first proclaimed it in 1951. In the same year, an Umpire in the *Abu Dhabi* arbitration case held that the doctrine had not yet assumed "the hard lineaments or the definitive status of an established rule of international law". In 1958, the Geneva Convention on the Continental Shelf recognised this entitlement on the part of coastal States and in 1969 it was acknowledged to be part of customary law by the ICJ in the *North Sea Continental Shelf*.[142] In this

---

135 ICJ *Reports*, n. 123 at 116 para. 131.
136 J. Rikhof, chap. IV, n. 46 at 251, quoting Akehurst.
137 See Statute of the Westminster of 1275, quoted by M.H. Mendelson, n. 115 at 209.
138 See dissenting opinion of Judge Negulesco in PCIJ Series B, No. 14 (1927) at 44.
139 ICJ *Reports* (1960) at 6 para. 40.
140 See e.g., I. Brownlie, n. 122 at 5.
141 P.K. Menon, chap. IV, n. 11 at 120–121.
142 M.H. Mendelson, n. 115 at 219.

case, Denmark and the Netherlands claimed that Germany was bound to apply the rule set out in Article 6 (2) of the Geneva Convention on the Continental Shelf of 1958. This clause provides that in the absence of an agreement or countervailing special circumstances, the continental shelf between two adjacent States is to be determined in accordance with the principle of equidistance. However, the difficulty was that Germany had signed the Convention, but had not ratified it. The claimants sought to circumvent this difficulty by arguing, among others, that the adoption of the provision in question in 1958 had 'crystallised' an 'emerging rule of customary law' or, alternatively, that a new rule had emerged since 1958, based partly on the Convention itself and partly on subsequent State practice. The ICJ rejected this argument and held, among others, that:

> [E]ven without the passage of any considerable period of time, a very widespread and representative participation in the convention might suffice of itself, provided it included that of States whose interests were specially affected.[143]

It went on to argue that:

> Although the passage of only a short period of time is not necessarily, or of itself, a bar to the formation of a new rule of customary international law [...] an indispensable requirement would be that within the period in question, short though it might be, State practice, including that of States whose interests are specially affected, should have been both extensive and virtually uniform...[144]

This led the Court to conclude that the use of the equidistance principle for the delimitation of continental shelf between adjacent States had not reached the Status of established customary law.[145] Consequently, Germany was not bound by such a rule.

Thus, State practice amounts to custom whenever State entities or any other recognised entities have observed a particular conduct for a certain amount of time, and have performed such conduct in a uniform and extensive manner. However, a settled practice alone is indeterminate in the formation of custom. It is necessary to make sure that States are acting because they have a legal conviction that they are obliged to act; hence, the requirement of a subjective or psychological element.

Opinio Iuris Sive Necessitatis

Various terms are used to designate this element. Article 38 (1) (b) of the Statute of the ICJ refers to it as general practice *accepted law*. Brownlie calls it a *sense of legal obligation*.[146] It is also sometimes referred to as a practice that is obligatory or as a *conception that the practice is required by, or consistent with, prevailing*

---

143 ICJ *Reports*, n. 108 at 42 para. 73.
144 At para. 74.
145 At para. 81.
146 See chap. IV, n. 23 at 8.

international law.[147] The *opinio iuris* requirement suggests that the necessity of a particular conduct is shared by various international actors and is supported by official statements that such conduct is permitted or forbidden by international law.[148] The ICJ shared this view in its judgements when it held that:

> Not only must the acts concerned amount to a settled practice, they must also be such, or be carried out in such a way, as to be evidence of a belief that this practice is rendered obligatory by the existence of a rule of law requiring it.[149]

The ICJ usually assumes the existence of an *opinio juris* on the basis of evidence of a general practice, or a consensus in the literature, or the previous determination of the Court or other international tribunals.[150]

Human rights instruments in the form of conventions, declarations and resolutions of the United Nations General Assembly may also provide evidence of an evolution of the *opinio iuris* among the United Nations Members States to investigate and punish human rights abuse.[151] In this respect, one can argue that the creation of ad hoc international tribunals or the establishment of a permanent international criminal court is the expression of States' repulsion of atrocities committed in international and internal conflicts. For example, during the debates of the Preparatory Committee on the Establishment of the ICC, a voluntary association of Like-minded States[152] was formed, which advocated the creation of a strong, independent and effective court. The fact that such a heterogeneous group of States, with different social, religious, cultural and political backgrounds and traditions, united behind the common goal of criminal prosecution for serious crimes suggests the intention to break with the past, where indemnity was the norm. However, the reluctance of some key players, such as the United States of America, to commit themselves to prosecuting international crimes, should not be interpreted to mean that they are in favour of letting international offenders go unpunished. In other circumstances, The United States have shown strong support for criminal prosecutions for the core crimes in international law. For example, they played a leading role in establishing the Nuremberg Tribunals and in prosecuting the Nazi war criminals. They pushed for the establishment of the Yugoslavia and the Rwanda ad hoc Tribunals and during the negotiations of the Dayton Accords they opposed the inclusion of an

---

147 See e.g. Brierly and Hudson respectively as quoted by I. Brownlie, chap. IV n. 23 at 8.
148 M. Dixon and R. McCorquodale, chap. IV, n. 14 at 28.
149 See *North Sea Continental Shelf Cases*, n. 108 at 77.
150 See I. Brownlie, chap. IV, n. 23 at 8.
151 A. Schlunck, chap. I, n. 3 at 46–47.
152 This group was chaired by Canada and was composed of Australia, Austria, Argentina, Belgium, Brazil, Brunei, Costa Rica, Chile, Croatia, Czech Republic, Denmark, Egypt, Finland, Germany, Ghana, Greece, Hungary, Italy, Ireland, Latvia, Lesotho, Liechtenstein, Lithuania, Malawi, Malta, Netherlands, New Zealand, Norway, Philippines, Portugal, Samoa, Senegal, Singapore, Slovakia, Slovenia, Solomon Islands, South Africa, South Korea, Spain, Sweden, Switzerland, Trinidad and Tobago, U.K., Uruguay and Venezuela.

amnesty clause that could have the effect of shielding Serb leaders from criminal prosecution for war crimes and crimes against humanity. More recently, they insisted on the prosecution of the alleged authors of the Lockerbie bombings. All these examples are sufficient to establish the American general *opinio iuris* in respect of punishing international crimes.

Moreover, one commentator points out that evidence of *opinio iuris* may be deduced from the conclusion of treaties or voting records in international fora, up to the point where practice and *opinio iuris* cannot be clearly distinguished from each other.[153] In this regard, the widespread ratification of the Genocide Convention as well as the Security Council unanimous agreement on the subject-matter jurisdiction of the ICTY and the ICTR Statutes indicate the UN Member States' *opinio iuris* in respect of the crimes contained in these documents. Likewise, the high level of co-operation among States in prosecuting offenders or extraditing them to the ICTY and ICTR translates into practice their conviction that at least genocide and war crimes must be punished at an international level. Does this also hold true for crimes against humanity? In other words, is the dual requirement of practice and *opinio iuris* sufficient enough in respect of crimes against humanity to give rise to the resulting State's duty to prosecute such crimes?

Evaluation

Many contemporary commentators argue that the two elements of custom, namely States practice and *opinio iuris*, need not be strictly applied as they once were.[154] Thus, the objective component of customary international law does not require that a practice be followed universally. Only general practice is required. According to the general practice requirement, a custom may be established by the practice of a majority of States or that of a limited number of States, or it can relate to certain areas of importance to States directly concerned in that area.[155] The latter is very true for the so-called special custom the development of which requires a special practice and fewer actors in the international scene.[156] The establishment of the IMT in Nuremberg in 1945 by a limited number of Allied Nations is an example of a special practice. General practice in respect of acts of crime against humanity may be inferred from several examples of domestic and international prosecutions that suggest an evolving custom in this direction.

---

153 See B. Simma and A.L. Paulus "The responsibility of individuals for human rights abuses in internal conflicts: A positive view" 93 *American Journal of International Law* 2 (1999) at 306–307.
154 See e.g., J. Rikhof, chap. IV, n. 46 at 247.
155 See A.A. D'Amato "The concept of special custom in international law" 63 *American Journal of International Law* (1969) at 212–213.
156 J. Rikhof, chap. IV, n. 46 at 250.

In 1983 for example, Argentina initiated trials against its former State officials for widespread torture, forced disappearances and arbitrary imprisonment committed as part of the military's 'dirty-war' against left wing opponents.[157] The *Pinochet Case*[158] followed suit with the British House of Lord's ruling that the doctrine of immunity of foreign State officials that has always been an obstacle to criminal prosecution of exiled statesmen does not cover acts of torture committed by a former head of States. Moreover, soon after its reunification in 1990 Germany embarked on the investigation and prosecutions of former East German officials for violation of fundamental principles of human rights in connection with the killing of East German citizens attempting to flee to the West.[159] Likewise, in 1991, Ethiopia initiated prosecutions for genocide and crimes against humanity against former president Mengitsu Haile-Mariam and his most senior officials.[160] Serbs officials have been prosecuted in Croatia for Crimes against humanity and war crimes committed as part of the policy of 'ethnic cleansing'. Israel,[161] France[162] and Canada[163] have also initiated trials for crimes against humanity perpetrated during World War II. As already mentioned above, the international evidence of investigation and prosecution of crimes against humanity is provided by the widespread acceptance of the subject-matter jurisdiction of the ICTY and the ICTR, as well as the quasi-universal co-operation of individual States in bringing perpetrators to trial. This commitment manifests a form of political awareness of the majority of the United Nations Members States that massive crimes shall not go unpunished. To this shall be added the trials conducted in 1945 under the Nuremberg Charter, the Tokyo Charter and under Control Council Law No. 10. The latest move towards the recognition of a duty to prosecute crimes against humanity, genocide and war crimes is the establishment of a permanent international criminal court.

On the basis of the foregoing developments, it can be argued that there exists a general State practice of prosecuting and punishing offenders of crimes against humanity. Such a practice has been established by a limited number of States in the territory of which crimes against humanity have been perpetrated.

Likewise, the element of duration does not require a practice to be observed from time immemorial in all circumstances. Thus, a practice which has been followed over a very short period of time may establish custom. For example, the prohibition against genocide, which is sometimes referred to as a particular form of crimes against humanity[164] became part of customary international law at the moment

---

157 See S.R. Ratner and J.S. Abrams, chap. III, n. 118 at 147–149.
158 See chap. III, n. 173.
159 See S.R. Ratner and J.S. Abrams, chap. III, n. 118 at 150.
160 *Id.* at 153; Mengistu Haile-Mariam has since been tried *in absentia* and found guilty of crimes against humanity and genocide by an Ethiopian court on 12 December, 2006; he was subsequently sentenced to life imprisonment.
161 See *Eichmann*, chap. I, n. 23 at 239.
162 *Barbie*, chap. III, n. 44 at 125.
163 See *Finta*, chap. III, n. 44.
164 See e.g., J. Rikhof, chap. IV, n. 46 at 256.

of the adoption of the Genocide Convention in 1948. Article I of the Genocide Convention corroborates the customary nature of the criminalization of genocide when it specifies that States parties 'confirm' the criminal character of genocide. In its Advisory Opinion of May 28, 1951 on *Reservations to the Convention on the Prevention and Punishment of the Crime of Genocide*, the ICJ further held that "the principles underlying the Convention are recognised by civilised nations as binding on States, even without any conventional obligation" and that the "Convention was adopted for purely humanitarian and civilizing purpose."[165] What is significant in the Court's approach is that in 1948, State practice with respect to punishing individuals for the commission of genocide was very limited in terms of the number of the States involved, in terms of the amount of practice and in terms of the passage of time.[166] Consequently, genocide developed as a special custom with little State practice and a strong sense of legal obligation.

The development of crimes against humanity followed the same patterns as that of genocide. Before crimes against humanity became an offence in 1945 no State practice in respect of punishing its offenders existed. Instead, the majority of States accepted that crimes against humanity was punishable as violating the customary rules of war as contained in the 1899 and 1907 Hague Conventions.[167] Therefore, the lack of a special convention confirming the customary nature of crimes against humanity shall not be taken as a justifying ground to forego to punish the offenders thereof.

As regards the subjective or psychological component of customary international law, it has been argued in the foregoing sections that official statements, the signing of treaties as well as voting records in international gatherings are strong evidence of States *opinio iuris*. Therefore, the worldwide condemnation of crimes against humanity that spread before and after its first legal appearance in 1945, as well as the adoption of various legal instruments condemning this offence are evidence of a settled *opinio iuris* with regard to this crime.[168]

Consequently, in applying the elements of customary international law to crimes against humanity the following conclusions can be reached: the offence of crimes against humanity was developed by a small number of States. Being a special custom, crimes against humanity does not require a great amount of State practice for its further development. The time factor in determining State practice in this area might be short. Being by themselves a strong evidence of *opinio iuris* crimes against humanity do not require an important State practice.[169] They are therefore customary international law crimes par excellence.

---

165 *Reservations to the Convention on the Prevention and Punishment of the Crime of Genocide* Advisory Opinion of 28 May 1951, *ICJ Reports* (1951) at 23 paras. 2 and 3.
166 J. Rikhof, chap. IV, n. 46 at 263.
167 See chapter 3 above on the discussion of the evolution of the concept of crimes against humanity.
168 I. Brownlie, n. 122 at 513; see also chapter 3 above.
169 See J. Rikhof, chap. IV, n. 46 at 251–252.

Summary

To conclude this section, one can argue that the question is no more whether State practice and *opinio iuris* regarding the prosecution of crimes against humanity can be established, but rather whether they are sufficient enough to create a binding customary international law obligation to prosecute. Thus, in the views of Simma and Paulus, there are sufficient practice and *opinio iuris* for the emergence of an international customary law duty to prosecute crimes against humanity.[170] Moreover, Bassiouni and Wise contend that the duty under customary international law to prosecute or extradite offenders of war crimes and crimes against humanity exists as an exception to the rule that, "in the absence of a treaty, the surrender of a fugitive cannot be demanded as of right."[171] Therefore, a customary law duty to prosecute crimes against humanity is part and parcel of international law. As to the nature of States' obligations to prosecute this offence, one may agree with Roht-Arriaza that although the Nuremberg Charter and its subsequent codification by the ILC and approval by the United Nations General Assembly make perpetrators of crimes against humanity liable for punishment, they do not by their terms require States to punish such crimes; they merely permit such prosecutions, and provide their legal basis.[172] Consequently, at this stage of its development, the customary law duty to prosecute crimes against humanity is permissive, rather than mandatory.

Other Sources of States Obligations Under International Law

Other sources that may provide evidence of the State obligation to prosecute crimes against humanity include United Nations resolutions, Reports and declarations of international organisations, and court decisions.

United Nations Resolutions

As a source of State obligations in international law, the United Nations resolutions include binding resolutions of the Security Council and non-binding resolutions of the General Assembly. Such resolutions may provide reliable evidence of the emergence of a customary law norm.

---

170   See n. 153 at 310.
171   See n. 1 at 21.
172   See chap. I, n. 24 at 51.

General Assembly Resolutions

Two forms of General Assembly resolutions are of valuable importance for crimes against humanity. These are the resolutions adopted by a majority vote and those that prescribe principles of international law.

The resolutions of the General Assembly when adopted by a majority vote may constitute evidence of customary rules. The Resolution affirming the Nuremberg Principles[173] is an example of such resolutions. Likewise, in the area of State obligations in respect of serious human rights violations, the General Assembly unanimously passed a resolution in 1985, which adopted the Declaration of Basic Principles of Justice for Victims of Crimes and Abuse of Power.[174] This resolution recommends that States Members "enact and enforce legislation proscribing acts that violate internationally recognised norms relating to human rights" and "establish and strengthen the means of detecting, prosecuting and sentencing those guilty of crimes."[175] With regard to the scope of this Declaration, the General Assembly requested a group of experts to develop principles of implementation designed to establish and strengthen the means of detecting, prosecuting and sentencing those guilty of crimes. The Implementation Principles call upon States to:

> [C]conduct impartial investigations as soon as possible into all deaths and serious physi-
> cal and mental injuries apparently caused by law enforcement, military, administrative,
> medical and other professional personnel and into all deaths and serious physical and
> mental injuries apparently in custody or in public institutions [... and to] prosecute
> persons who victimise others by committing serious crimes or extradite such persons
> to another State having jurisdiction.[176]

In addition, the Implementation Principles request States to provide compensation to victims of crimes violating international human rights instruments and of crimes against humanity.[177] Being a unanimous General Assembly resolution drafted under the auspices of the United Nations Economic and Social Council, these Implementation Principles provide reliable evidence that States accept the norms in question. Moreover, in 1989 the United Nations Economic and Social Council adopted the Principles on the Effective Prevention and Investigation of Extra-Legal, Arbitrary, and Summary Executions, which was endorsed by the General Assembly.[178] These principles provided that governments shall make extralegal, summary or arbitrary executions punishable by appropriate penalties, investigate all suspected cases and extradite or prosecute those involved. They set out international standards for

---

173   See chap. III, n. 116.
174   GA Res. 40/34, 40 UN GAOR Supp. No. 53 at 213, UN Doc A/40/53 (1985) reprinted in M.C. Bassiouni (ed.), *International Protection of Victims* (1988) at 201.
175   Articles 4 (c) and (d) respectively.
176   Principles R4(d).5 and R4(d).6.
177   Principle 18.2.
178   ECOSOC Res. 1989/65 of 24 May 1989, Annex ECOSOC Off. Rec. 1989, Supp. No. 1 p. 5 (1990) endorsed by GA Res. 44/162 of Dec. 15, 1989, GAOR 44th Sess, Supp. No. 49 p. 235 (1990).

investigating and prosecuting grave violations of human rights. The standards for investigation prohibit, among others, the invocation of superior power to justify participation in extralegal, arbitrary or summary executions, as well as the granting of immunity from prosecution to any person allegedly involved in such acts. Moreover, such principles required that fair and adequate compensation be paid to the families and dependent of victims. This is yet more evidence that in their statements and behaviour in international bodies States are committed in making investigation and prosecution of grave human rights violations legally obligatory.

As to the second form of General Assembly resolutions, namely those prescribing principles of international law, they may be regarded as an authoritative interpretation of the United Nation Charter when they deal with a particular issue contained in the Charter.[179] The theoretical base for the interpretative power of the General Assembly is laid down by Article 10 of the United Nations Charter which provides that the Assembly may discuss and make recommendations on any matters or questions within the scope of the Charter. This provision, together with Article 11 authorizing the Assembly to make recommendations on general principles of cooperation in the maintenance of international peace and security, has sometimes been interpreted as giving the General Assembly the authority to issue binding resolutions.[180]

As example of General Assembly resolutions prescribing principles of international law, one can mention Resolution 96 (I) on the Crime of Genocide of 11 December 1946, which affirmed that:

> Genocide is a crime under international law which the civilised world condemns, and for the commission of which principals and accomplices—whether private individuals, public officials or statesmen, and whether the crime is committed on religious, racial, political or any other grounds—are punishable.[181]

To this example, one can add a General Assembly resolution of 1970 on War Criminals and Crimes against Humanity, which called on States to take appropriate measures to arrest and extradite war criminals and persons who have committed crimes against humanity and to agree that such crimes should not be subject to statutes of limitations.[182] This was followed in 1973, by the adoption by the General Assembly of a further resolution on the Principles of International Co-operation in the Detection, Arrest, Extradition, and Punishment of Persons Guilty of War Crimes and Crimes against Humanity.[183] These principles establish a duty to prosecute

---

179 I. Brownlie, n. 122 at 14.
180 See B. Simma *The Charter of the United Nations: A Commentary* vol. I, 2nd ed., (2002) at 257–287; also B. Sloan *United Nations General Assembly Resolutions in our Changing World* (1991) at 59–60; or else the Uniting for Peace Resolution (GA Res. 377 (V) of Nov. 3, 1950, GAOR (V) Supp. No. 20, at 10.
181 G.K. McDonald and O. Swaak-Goldman, chap. III, n. 182, vol. II Part I at 81.
182 GA Res. 2712, 15 Dec 1970, UNGA Res. 2538 (XXIV) reprinted in M.C. Bassiouni, chap. I, n. 29 at 698.
183 GA Res. 3074 (XXVIII), 28 UN GAOR Supp. No. 30 at 79, UN Doc A/9030 (1973).

and stipulate that crimes against humanity, wherever they are committed, shall be subject to investigation and the persons against whom there is evidence shall be subject to tracing, arrest, trial, and punishment.[184]

In short, General Assembly resolutions and recommendations do not have any binding force per se. Therefore, States are not under a strict duty to co-operate, even though it is sometimes admitted that once a State has approved a resolution or a recommendation, it is under a certain obligation to co-operate, assist and to act in good faith in the implementation of adopted resolutions and recommendations.[185] Nevertheless, these resolutions are of utmost importance in that they express the *opinio iuris* of the majority of the United Nations members in respect of crucial legal matters. However, in its Advisory Opinion on the *Legality of the Threat or Use of Nuclear Weapons Case*,[186] the ICJ opened a possibility for General Assembly resolutions (not only expressing the official position of States, but also) having a binding character on States under certain circumstances. In this case, the World Health Organisation requested the ICJ to give an advisory opinion on whether the use of nuclear weapons by a State in war or any other armed conflict would be a breach of its obligations under international law, including the Constitution of the World Health Organisation. In examining customary international law to determine whether the prohibition of the threat or use of nuclear weapons flows from that source of law, the Court noted that:

> General Assembly resolutions, even if they are not binding, may sometimes have normative value. They can, in certain circumstances, provide evidence important for establishing the existence of a rule or the emergence of an *opinio juris*. To establish whether this is true of a given General Assembly resolution, it is necessary to look at its content and the conditions of its adoption; it is also necessary to see whether an *opinio juris* exists as to its normative character. Or a series of resolutions may show the gradual evolution of the *opinio juris* required for the establishment of a new rule.[187] [e.g., the Genocide Convention and the Convention on the Rights of the Child, in terms of the importance of their ratifications]

The Court further stressed that:

> Examined in their totality, the General Assembly resolutions put before [it] declare that the use of nuclear weapons would be "a direct violation of the Charter of the United Nations"; and in certain formulations that such use 'should be prohibited'.[188]

To this pronouncement, one can add the ICJ's holding in the *Nicaragua Case*[189] that certain General Assembly resolutions, especially those prohibiting the threat or use

---

184 Principle I.
185 M. Dixon and R. McCorquodale, chap. IV, n. 14 at 52.
186 Advisory Opinion of 8 July 1996 reprinted in 17 *Human Rights Law Journal* 7–10 (1996) at 253–396.
187 At para. 70.
188 At para. 71.
189 *Case Concerning Military and Paramilitary Activities in and against Nicaragua (Nicaragua v. United States of America)* ICJ Judgment of 27 June 1986, available at www.icj-cij.org/icjwww/icases/inus/inus_ijudgment/inus_ijudgment_19860627.pdf.

of force against the territorial integrity or political independence of any State (e.g. Resolution 2625 (XXV) entitled "Declaration on Principles of International Law concerning Friendly Relation and Cooperation among States in Accordance with the Charter of the United Nations"), may contain rules and principles of customary international law having a universal application.[190] According to the Court, the attitude of States towards such resolutions can be interpreted as the expression of their *opinio juris* to accept and respect the rules contained therein.[191]

Security Council Resolutions

Contrary to the resolutions adopted by the General Assembly, those of the Security Council are usually binding on States because they create international rights and obligations.[192] Binding obligations upon States to prosecute international crimes are created by the Security Council resolutions on the basis of Chapter VII of the United Nations Charter which allows recourse to such resolutions when a situation threatens international peace and security. In 1992 for example, the Security Council adopted a resolution requiring Libya to surrender to the United States or the United Kingdom for trial two Libyan nationals suspected of bombing an American aeroplane.[193] In 1993, a similar resolution was issued, calling for the arrest and prosecution of Somali Warlord Mohamed Farrah Aidid who was suspected of the murder of 24 United Nations peacekeepers.[194] Moreover, the Security Council resolutions establishing the Rwanda and Yugoslavia Tribunals[195] imposed an obligation on all States Members of the United Nations to fully co-operate with these Tribunals in the arrest and surrender of indicted criminals. Richard Goldstone, former Chief Prosecutor of the ICTY stressed the binding character of Security Council resolutions when he declared, during the negotiations of the Dayton Accord, that the Tribunal would not be bound by any clause offering immunity to indicted war criminals. He added that the Tribunal would not discontinue its proceedings against such criminals, unless the Tribunal's Statute was amended by the Security Council.[196] Moreover, it is argued that notwithstanding any amnesty that might have been included in the Dayton Accord, the parties to the Accord would still be bound by their obligations to arrest and surrender indicted war criminals to the Tribunal.[197]

---

190   Paras. 187–195 and 203–205.
191   See especially para. 188.
192   I. Brownlie, n. 122 at 15.
193   SC Res. 748, SCOR 1992.
194   SC Res. 837, SCOR 1993.
195   See chap. I, n. 12 and chap. III, n. 42 respectively.
196   See M.P. Scharf, n. 17 at 59, quoting Roger Cohen's article "UN in Bosnia: Black Robes Clash with Blue Hats" NY Times 25 April 1995.
197   M.P. Scharf, n. 17 at 60.

Reports of International Organisations

The international organisations whose reports and declarations may be relied upon as sources of State obligations under international law to prosecute include the ILC, the United Nations Human Rights Committee and the Secretary-General of the United Nations.

In 1950 for example, the ILC affirmed that the principles developed in the Nuremberg Charter and in the judgements of the Nuremberg Tribunals were principles of international law. In this respect, Nuremberg Principle II provides that:

> The fact that internal law does not impose a penalty for an act which constitutes a crime under international law, does not relieve the person who committed the act from responsibility under international law.

Likewise, at the 1993 World Conference on Human Rights, a Final Declaration and Programme of Action was adopted, which reaffirmed the duty of States to investigate allegations of forced disappearance and to prosecute the perpetrators thereof. This duty includes the necessity to abrogate legislation leading to impunity for those responsible for grave violations of human rights such as torture, and prosecute such violations, thereby providing a firm basis for the rule of law.[198] Moreover, a report of the Secretary-General of the United Nations stated that the law applicable in armed conflict is that part of conventional international humanitarian law, which has become part of international customary law.[199] It further declared that the law applicable in armed conflict can be found, among others, in the Geneva Conventions, the Genocide Convention and in the Nuremberg Charter.[200]

Decisions of International and National Tribunals

The jurisprudence of international, regional and national courts may also provide evidence of the state of the law in that a coherent body of jurisprudence will have important consequences for the law[201] and may improve the quality of a legal provision. Therefore, the judgements of courts are reliable sources of States' rights and obligations.

Permanent as well as ad hoc international tribunals or courts provide valuable opinions and judgements that may be relied upon as authoritative bases of States obligations in respect of certain serious crimes. The ICJ's Advisory Opinion on *Reservations to the Convention on the Prevention and Punishment of the Crime of*

---

198 Final Declaration and Programme of Action, 1993 World Conference on Human Rights, Part II 60, UN Doc A/Conf/57/24 reprinted in 32 *ILM* 166 (1993).

199 See Report of the Secretary-General Pursuant to Paragraph 2 of Security Council Resolution 808 of 3 May 1993, recommending the establishment of the Yugoslavia Tribunal, reprinted in G.K. McDonald and O. Swaak-Goldman, chap. III, n. 182 vol. II Part I at 289.

200 *Id.* at 289–290.

201 I. Brownlie, n. 122 at 19.

Genocide is of this kind. In addition, the rulings of the ad hoc ICTY and ICTR have been strongly relied upon by the drafters of the ICC Statute to include sexual crimes among the acts constitutive of crimes against humanity. In the *Furundzija Case*[202] for example, the ICTY held that the prohibition against torture has acquired the status of *Jus Cogens* and, as a consequence, "every State is entitled to investigate, prosecute and punish or extradite individuals accused of torture, who are present in a territory under its jurisdiction."[203]

Decisions of national courts are also reliable sources of law, which have strong evidential values. Municipal decisions in the *Papon, Touvier, Barbie* or *Eichmann Cases* have helped to shape the contours of the offence of crimes against humanity. Similarly, the drafters of the ICC Statute extensively relied on the interpretation of the *mens rea* element of crimes against humanity by a Canadian Court in the *Finta Case*, for their statutory definition of this element in the Statute.

Moreover, the decision of the Inter-American Commission on Human rights in the *Velasquez Case*, as well as its 1992 ruling that the laws restricting or prohibiting prosecutions of the military in El Salvador, Uruguay, and Argentina violate the ACHR, may be relied upon as sources of a State's duty under international law to prosecute and punish.

However, the decisions of national and regional jurisdictions in respect of the most serious crimes are usually very limited and lack any binding character. It is hoped that the creation of a permanent international criminal court will help to establish a consistent and coherent body of jurisprudence that will shed light on the nature of States' obligations with respect to the most serious crimes of international concern.

Conclusion

The concluding arguments with respect to this chapter are that international law imposes certain duties on individual States to punish grave violations of human rights. The nature of such duties is either clearly stated in criminal and human rights law conventions, or is inferred from custom, the practice of international organisations and the judgements of national and international tribunals.

Parties to an international criminal law convention are generally required to proscribe, repress or suppress a particular conduct. They are required to enact legislation necessary to provide effective or adequate penalties; to take the necessary steps to ensure that the offence is punished in accordance with its gravity; to make it a criminal offence punishable by severe penalties; to take all measures to search, discover, prosecute and punish offenders or else to extradite them, etc. Criminal law conventions use language binding the parties to co-operate to the

---

202 See chap. IV, n. 80.
203 At para. 156.

fullest possible extent in repressing prohibited conduct.[204] The Geneva Conventions, the Genocide Convention and the Torture Convention are among the treaties which contain an explicit obligation to prosecute.

However, international criminal law conventions are very limited in their application, due partly to States' reluctance to subject their officials to criminal prosecutions or extradite them. Hence a growing recognition of States' obligations based on general human rights conventions, which are less compelling. Human rights treaties such as the ICCPR, the ACHR or the ECHR all require States Parties to respect and ensure rights, and to provide a remedy when a right is violated. This duty to ensure rights provides States with alternative measures of punishment such as the establishment of investigative commissions to identify offenders and victims, the non-criminal sanction of the offenders and the payment of compensation to the victims.

Customary international law establishes permissive jurisdiction to prosecute offenders of crimes against humanity both internally and internationally. This argument is supported by a strong *opinio iuris* that can be inferred from an extensive collection of United Nations resolutions as well as the reports or commentaries of international organisations calling for the prosecution of crimes against humanity. To this shall be added the judgements of national and international tribunals as well as the writings of several scholars that insist on the punishment of the perpetrators of crimes against humanity. However, a consistent and uniform State practice has not yet developed to support the existence under customary international law of a mandatory duty to prosecute and punish offenders of crimes against humanity. The gap between the widespread *opinio iuris* calling for States to prosecute the most serious crimes and the relatively limited State practice in this respect has led to the development of a culture of protecting notorious criminals through the granting of amnesty. The extension of this practice to the most egregious crimes in international law raises a crucial issue, which is the main concern of this volume, namely whether amnesty can be legally compatible with the overall responsibility of individuals and States in international law as defined in the preceding sections. In other words, is it legally acceptable to argue that, in the absence of a mandatory obligation to prosecute crimes against humanity, the perpetrators thereof shall be rewarded with an amnesty?

In order to find an objective answer to this concern, it is fundamental to inquire firstly into the legal approach to amnesty as developed by countries which have made use of this mechanism, and secondly into the place of amnesty within the international law corpus of rules. As far as the first aspect of the inquiry is concerned, the intention here is not to study all available cases of amnesty, but rather to focus on a specific case, namely the South African experience, which has a particular legal significance and ramification for crimes against humanity (viz. apartheid).

---

[204] M.C. Bassiouni and E.M. Wise, n. 1 at 8–9.

AMNESTY LAW IN SOUTH AFRICA: THE ASSERTION OF AN AMNESTY EXCEPTION TO THE GENERAL PROHIBITION OF CRIMES AGAINST HUMANITY

Introduction

Like many post-political conflict amnesties, the South African amnesty was the product of a political compromise, which later received legal validation from the competent national authorities. However, like any other political enterprise of this kind, the South African indemnity system cannot be said to have been a perfect institution, hence the various criticisms that surrounded its operation. Among these is the Constitutional Court's argument in the *AZAPO Case*, which held that amnesty constitutes an exception to peremptory norms of *jus cogens* and that an Act of Parliament takes precedence over such norms.

In light of the South African experience, this chapter will attempt to examine the legal status of amnesty nationally in respect of the core crimes under international law. This will be done by arguing that in most cases national objectives of reconciliation as well as national laws are heavily relied upon as a yardstick in the process of assessing the lawfulness of amnesty legislation, whereas recourse to international law is made in a selective manner so as to advance immediate national interests. It will be contended that any evaluation of the lawfulness of amnesty with respect to core crimes such as war crimes, genocide, terrorism, torture and crimes against humanity should not disregard the importance of international law, which is an integrated system of law that does not only prohibit the commission of such crimes, but also reject all forms of exception to the prohibition thereof.

Faustin Z. Ntoubandi, Amnesty for Crimes against Humanity under International Law, pp. 151–183.
© 2007, *Koninklijke Brill NV. Printed in The Netherlands.*

Political Background to the South African Amnesty

Brief History of Apartheid

The policy of apartheid was introduced in South Africa in 1948 after the Afri-
kaner-dominated National Party (NP), led by Dr. Daniel Malan took over the reign
of power. Apartheid had two significant features: complete racial segregation and
ethnic 'self-determination' within the homelands.[1] This involved the separation of
every facet of life: residence, amenities, transport, education and politics. Soon
after its successful election, the NP government adopted a series of measures
aimed at institutionalising the Afrikaner's ideology of apartheid. Among these
were the Prohibition of Mixed Marriages Act passed by Parliament in 1949, which
outlawed marriages between South Africans of European origin and other South
Africans. Next, came the Population Registration Act, designed to allocate every
person to one of three racial groups: White, Coloured or African. This Act was
considered a cornerstone of apartheid.[2] The Suppression of Communism Act, the
Group Area Act, the Native Labour Act, the Black Affairs Administration Act,
the Labour Restriction Act, the Bantu Education Act, the Separate Amenities Act,
the Terrorism Act, the Riotous Assembly Act, the Gathering and Demonstrations
Act, the Protection of Information Act, the Publication and Control Act and the
various Pass Laws followed.[3] The NP further consolidated its power as well as its
ideology by removing all non-whites from the electorate.[4]

The first wave of public protests against the apartheid system started in the
1950's. Thus, in June 1952, two political organisations, the ANC and the South
African Indian Congress, responded to the Government's segregationist measures by
organising a passive resistance campaign against the apartheid system. A Freedom
Charter was adopted on 26 June, 1955 which called for the recognition of equality among all South African national groups as well as of equal rights.[5] In 1959,
the Pan-African Congress was founded as a forum for all African opponents to
apartheid. On 21 March, 1960 a peaceful protest march, organised in Sharpeville
in reaction to the pass laws, was brutally repressed by the security forces, which
left 67 demonstrators killed, 186 wounded and thousands arrested.[6]

The condemnation of apartheid grew world-wide in the 1960's. The Organisation of African Unity (today's African Union) implicitly banned apartheid in its

---

1   A. Schlunck, chap. I, n. 3 at 189.
2   See M. Meredith *Nelson Mandela: A Biography* (1997) at 81; also A. Krog *Country of
    my Skull* (1998) at 106.
3   M. Meredith, n. 1 at 93; see also A. Krog, n. 1 at 106.
4   See e.g., The Separate Registration of Voters Bill introduced in March 1951 removed the
    Coloureds of the Cape Province from the common roll by which they had been entitled
    to vote since 1853.
5   A. Schlunck, chap. I, n. 3 at 189, quoting T.G. Karis.
6   M. Meredith, n. 1 at 173.

Charter,[7] while African States undertook to eliminate apartheid.[8] The United Nations Secretary General, Dag Hammarskjoel criticized the apartheid policy following his visit to South Africa in 1961. In 1962, the United Nations General Assembly called for economic sanctions against South Africa. Furthermore, the International Olympic Committee suspended South African athletes from the Olympic Games in 1964,[9] whereas apartheid was branded a crime against all humanity by 1968.[10]

The NP government's response to this world-wide criticism was to ban all anti-apartheid movements and to engage in ruthless repression of any civic uprising. As a consequence, many political leaders and opponents of the apartheid regime were arrested and jailed, while those still at large chose the route to exile. On 16 June, 1976 the shooting by police officers of black schoolchildren who were protesting against new laws making the use of Afrikaans mandatory at school sparked another wave of violence, which left at least 600 people dead and 4,000 wounded.[11] This was followed a year later by the death of the black consciousness leader Steve Biko in the hands of the security police. These two events outraged the international opinion. Demands of economic boycotts and sanctions against South Africa grew and were discussed in Washington and Westminster. The United Nations Security Council banned all arms deals with South Africa. Foreign investors began to withdraw foreign capital. Several prominent companies terminated their business in South Africa and those which remained faced intense criticism from anti-apartheid groups.[12]

The 1980's were dominated by civil unrest following the limited constitutional reform of September 1983, which created a tri-cameral system of representation for the White, Indian and Coloured minorities, while excluding the black majority group. The United Democratic Front was established and stood at the forefront of protest against the new constitutional reform. This political movement was very active in organising and co-ordinating protest marches and civil disobedience actions.[13] In the meantime, sporadic guerrilla attacks organised by the military branch of the ANC and widespread unrest in black townships threatened internal peace and security, as well as the already shaky economy.[14] This led President P.W. Botha, as from 1986, to rule the country through emergency laws, which gave the security police wide discretionary powers to curtail civil liberty rights. The conflict between the black opposition and the white government escalated when police forces started making

---

7 Article 2 (1) (d) of the 1963 Charter of the Organisation of African Unity banned all forms of colonisation.
8 See Preamble of the 1981 ACHPR, para. 9.
9 A. Schlunck, chap. I, n. 3 at 189.
10 See Preamble and Article 1 (b) of the 1968 Convention on the Non-Applicability of Statutory Limitations to War Crimes and Crimes against Humanity, also Article 1 of the Apartheid Convention of 1973.
11 M. Meredith, n. 1 at 329.
12 *Id.* at 339–340.
13 A. Schlunck, chap. I, n. 3 at 190.
14 M. Meredith, n. 1 at 348, 354, 359 and 360.

use of arbitrary detention, torture, killings and disappearance as a deterrent tactic. The ANC and other opposition groups responded with systematic terror attacks and sabotage against governmental institutions or infrastructure and the assassination of proponents of the white political establishment.[15]

In the mid-eighties, the apartheid leadership realised that apartheid was doomed to failure. In fact, the ANC and the Communist Party had decided to create military units, which were learning guerrilla warfare tactics and were being trained in neighbouring countries. Such paramilitary units, generally referred to by the acronym MK were threatening to make South Africa ungovernable and to wage an armed struggle within the country.[16] Above all, the once most prosperous economy in the world was choking under international sanctions. Under these threats, the government felt the need to open a channel of dialogue with the black opposition leadership. Beginning 1984, first contacts were made between the Minister of Justice Hendrik Coetsee and Nelson Mandela, one of the most prominent ANC leaders, who was serving a life imprisonment term.[17]

In 1989, President Botha was forced to resign and was replaced by Mr. F.W. de Klerk, the reformer. In his first political moves, President de Klerk dismantled the national security management system, lifted the ban on all major political parties and opposition groups and decided to release Mr. Mandela from prison.[18] These courageous moves put an end to more than forty years of apartheid and, at the same time, opened the doors for political negotiations for a multiracial and democratic future of South Africa.

Political Negotiations and Commitment to Amnesty

Upon his release, Mr. Mandela toured South Africa and many foreign countries to explain his views and position upon the transition process, whereas the ANC engaged in preliminary peace talks with the de Klerk government. These talks resulted in two preliminary agreements: the Groote Schuur Minute of 4 May, 1990 and the Pretoria Minute of 6 August, 1990.[19] In these agreements, the parties committed themselves to discussing the concept of such offences in the South African context, including the possibility of granting immunity in respect of such offences to alleged perpetrators present both inside and outside of South Africa.[20]

On 14 September, 1991 the National Peace Accords were signed between the government, the ANC and the Inkhata Freedom Party,[21] as a follow up to the

---

15 A. Schlunck, chap. I, n. 3 at 190–191.
16 See generally M. Meredith, n. 1, particularly at chapters 9 and 16.
17 A. Schlunck, chap. I, n. 3 at 190.
18 *Id.*
19 The texts of these documents are reproduced in 6 *South African Journal on Human Rights* (1990) at 318–324.
20 Para. 1 of the Groote Schuur Minute.
21 This party was the most important political contender to the ANC during the transitional negotiation process, hereinafter IFP.

Groote Schuur and the Pretoria Minutes. These accords laid out, among others, the fundamental democratic principles previously agreed upon by the parties, the code of conduct for political parties and organisations, and the measures to facilitate socio-economic development. The Convention for a Democratic South Africa[22] was later established as a forum for political discussion whose work would later include the drafting of the Interim Constitution in 1993. The negotiations within this Convention stalled in December 1991 and eventually resumed in March 1993. It is worth mentioning here that the political negotiation process was conducted in the midst of brutal political murders and threats of destabilisation that drove the country to the brink of collapse. The negotiations between the NP and the government came to a standstill after members of the IFP killed 45 ANC supporters in the township of Boipatong on 17 June, 1992. Soon after these events, the ANC accused the security forces of fuelling the violence and withdrew from the negotiations. Unsuccessful attempts were made to restart the process. Finally, Mr. Mandela approached the United Nations to ask for assistance.

In September 1992, the United Nations Security Council established a United Nations Observer Mission to South Africa, and sent former U.S. Secretary of State, Cyrus Vance, as special representative to South Africa in an ultimate attempt to salvage the peace process.[23] Meanwhile, the United Nations Secretary-General was involved in monitoring the work of the Goldstone Commission[24] in an effort to prevent the occurrence of future political violence between members of the ANC and of the IFP. On conclusion of the Goldstone Commission's investigations, the Secretary-General of the United Nations recommended in his report to the Security Council a general amnesty for all offenders, among other things.

On 5 March, 1993 CODESA convened a new conference with broad representation for what was referred to as the Multiparty Negotiating Process. On 18 November, this organ adopted a series of constitutional principles, which would guide the country during the transitional period.[25] The work of the Multiparty Negotiating Process would produce an Interim Constitution[26] in November 1993 at Kempton Park.[27]

The first democratic parliamentarian elections in the history of the country were held between 26th and 29th April, 1994. As a result, a government of National Unity was elected. It was composed of the ANC, the IFP and the NP and was presided over by Nelson Mandela who had been nominated President of South Africa by the newly elected legislature. The latter appointed Mr. de Klerk, the head of

---

22 Generally referred to as CODESA.

23 A. Schlunck, chap. I, n. 3 at 196–197.

24 This Commission was established by the National Peace Accords, with the mandate to investigate past political violence and to recommend steps for prevention of such acts in the future.

25 A. Schlunck, chap. I, n. 3 at 198.

26 Constitution of the Republic of South Africa, Act 200 of 1993, text reproduced in B. de Villiers (ed.), *Birth of a Constitution* (1994) at 329.

27 See D. Basson *South Africa's Interim Constitution* (1994), introductory notes at xxi.

the NP, and Chief Buthelezi, chairman of the IFP, as members of the Cabinet of National Unity that was dominated by the ANC.[28] On 27 April of the same year the negotiated Interim Constitution designed to cover a transitional period of five years entered into effect.

Legal Bases of Amnesty

The origin of the South African Amnesty Law of 1995 can be traced as far back as to the first preliminary agreements between the ANC, the NP Government and various other important political groups. Such agreements produced two amnesty acts, which would later inform the drafters of the final Amnesty Law of 1995.

The Indemnity Act of 1990 and the Further Indemnity Act of 1992

Final agreement on the issues of amnesty and the definition of political offences[29] as agreed upon in the Groote Schuur Minute was reached by the end of 1990. As a follow-up to this agreement, the NP government passed an Indemnity Act[30] and set up a series of committees to deal with amnesty applications.[31] Section 1 of the Indemnity Act of 1990 empowered the State President to grant temporary immunity to anyone if he was "of the opinion that it is necessary for the promotion of peaceful constitutional solutions in South Africa or the unimpeded and efficient administration of justice." Section 2 (1) vested the State President with the power to "grant indemnity to any person or category of persons, either unconditionally or on the conditions he may deem fit, in respect of any event or category of events"; while Section 2 (2) dealt with the effect of amnesty, which is the prohibition of the institution of criminal as well as civil proceedings against any beneficiary thereof.

It is believed that the Indemnity Act of 1990 aimed mainly at granting immunity to members of the opposition movements who committed offences in the course of the struggle against apartheid, but that its extensive wording made it applicable to State officials as well.[32] Nevertheless, in 1992 the government realised that the Indemnity Act of 1990 did not sufficiently provide for the indemnification of all those who advised, directed, commanded, ordered or performed criminal acts in pursuit of a political objective. It therefore enacted, unilaterally and without

---

28 A. Schlunck, chap. I, n. 3 at 199.
29 The definition of 'political offences' is contained in *Government Gazette* 12834 of 7 November, 1990.
30 Indemnity Act 35 of 1990 reprinted in *Government Gazette* No. 12470 of 17 May, 1990.
31 See *Government Gazette* No. 12838 of 9 November, 1990.
32 See L. du Plessis, Amnesty and transition in South Africa, in A. Boraine, J. Levy and R. Scheffer (eds.), *Dealing with the Past: Truth and Reconciliation in South Africa* (1994) at 110.

consulting any major negotiating partners, the Further Indemnity Act[33] to cover the remaining categories of offenders.[34]

Like the 1990 Act, this additional Indemnity Act gave the State President extensive powers to decide on amnesty for criminal acts with political objectives, advised, directed, commanded, ordered, or performed before 8 October, 1990. In addition, the President could decide on the release of prisoners convicted and sentenced for committing offences with political objectives if he was of the opinion that such release might promote peace and reconciliation. As to its consequences, the Further Indemnity Act has the effect of nullifying both civil and criminal proceedings.

Unlike the Indemnity Act of 1990, that laid down clear guidelines in determining an offender's entitlement to amnesty or release, the Further Indemnity Act of 1992 established political motivation as the sole criterion for granting amnesty. Unlike the original definition of a political offence agreed upon with the ANC, the one contained in the new Act removed from consideration the criteria for evaluating what amounted to a political offence. It also eliminated the requirement to investigate the offence for which amnesty was being sought and to disclose to the public the crime involved.[35] According to some commentators, the application of the Further Indemnity Act resulted in the indemnification and the release of offenders who could not qualify under the 1990 Act.[36] More important, the Further Indemnity Act was widely seen as a kind of self-amnesty, which was kept in secret. In fact, under this Act, the amnesty power of the State President was to be exercised in consultation with an advisory body called the National Council on Indemnity, the composition of which was totally at his discretion. Applications were heard in camera and the applicants were sworn to secrecy in order to encourage prospective applicants to submit their case with confidence. The disclosure of any evidence presented to the Council was made an offence punishable by 12 months imprisonment.[37] In addition, the president was in no way bound by the advice of the National Council on Indemnity.[38]

Because of the secrecy that surrounded the granting of amnesty, the Further Indemnity Act was widely criticised. The Democratic Party, a parliamentary opposition, described it as "a charter for crooks, criminals and assassins."[39] While Professor du Plessis expressed the views that "[i]t is highly unlikely that the existing indemnity acts will survive constitutional review."[40]

However, with the coming into being of the Interim Constitution, the Indemnity Acts of 1990 and the Further Amnesty Act of 1992 became temporarily void in

---

33   Act 151 of 1992, *Government Gazette* No. 14401 of 9 November, 1992.
34   See L. du Plessis, n. 32 at 110.
35   See P. Parker "The politics of indemnities in South Africa" 17 *Human Rights Law Journal* 1–2 (1996) at 2.
36   See L. du Plessis, n. 32 at 111.
37   See P. Parker, n. 35 at 2.
38   See L. du Plessis, n. 32 at 111.
39   P. Parker, n. 35 at 1, quoting Reuter of 11 November, 1992.
40   See n. 32 at 108.

that the postscript to the Constitution designated the National Parliament as the sole authority competent to decide on the question of amnesty.

Amnesty Under the Interim Constitution

The Interim Constitution of 1993 contained a clause on National Unity and Reconciliation, which made provision for the granting of amnesty. This clause, which was inserted just before the Schedules, is generally referred to as post-amble, postscript or epilogue to the Interim Constitution. The origin of the amnesty clause in the Interim Constitution is not quite clear. However, according to Professor du Plessis,[41] the question of amnesty for acts associated with political objectives only came up at the final stage of the negotiation process as an issue in bilateral talks between NP government and the ANC alliance.[42] This view is corroborated in the following way by Desmond Tutu, Chairperson of the Truth and Reconciliation Commission (TRC) who saw the insertion of an amnesty clause in the Interim Constitution as an incentive to bring right wing political groups to the negotiating table in order to secure the country's first democratic elections:

> Amnesty made our election possible. The amnesty clause was inserted in the early hours of the morning after an exhausted night of negotiating. The last thing, the last sentence, the last clause was added: amnesty shall be granted through a process of reconciliation. And it was only when that was put in, that the *boere* signed the negotiations, opening the door to our elections.[43]

More compatible with the justification of amnesty given in chapter five is Professor Dugard's linkage of amnesty with the lack of a clear victor among the different parties to the political struggle in South Africa. In this respect, he wrote:

> The option of prosecution of the leaders of the Apartheid State before domestic courts was impossible as there were no victors in the process that brought to an end apartheid and the leaders of the apartheid State were themselves a party to the negotiated settlement. In essence the choice was between unconditional amnesty, favoured by the National Party, or conditional amnesty. The latter option was chosen.[44]

Nevertheless, the clause on National Unity and Reconciliation started with the presentation of the Constitution as a historical bridge between the past characterised by division, conflict, untold suffering and injustice, and a future founded on the recognition of human rights, democracy, peaceful co-existence and development opportunities for all South African, irrespective of colour, race, class, belief or sex. It went on to stress that the pursuit of national unity and peace required

---

41 L. du Plessis was the Convenor of the Technical Committee on Fundamental Rights at the Multiparty Negotiating Process.
42 See n. 32 at 109.
43 Quoted by A. Krog, n. 1 at 23.
44 J. Dugard "Is the truth and reconciliation process compatible with international law? An unanswered question" 13 *South African Journal on Human Rights* No. 2 (1997) at 258.

reconciliation between all South Africans and the reconstruction of society, and further that there is a need for understanding but not for vengeance, a need for reparation but not for retaliation, a need for *ubuntu* but not for victimisation. Reference to the necessity to grant indemnity as an integral part of the process of reconciliation and reconstruction is made in paragraph five of the post-amble of the 1993 Constitution as follows:

> In order to advance such reconciliation and reconstruction, amnesty shall be granted in respect of acts, omissions and offences associated with political objectives and committed in the course of the conflicts of the past. To this end, Parliament under this Constitution shall adopt a law determining a firm cut-off date, which shall be a date after 8 October 1990 and before 6 December 1993, and providing for the mechanisms, criteria and procedures, including tribunals, if any, through which such amnesty shall be dealt with at any time after the law has been passed.

Thus, those who framed this provision did not deal comprehensively and conclusively with the question of amnesty. The postscript can therefore be qualified as a declaration of their intention to resolve the issue of amnesty by legislation within a specific time. However, this declaration of intention had a constitutional value in terms of Section 232 (4) of the Constitution, which stated that:

> In interpreting this Constitution a provision in any Schedule, including the provision under the heading 'National Unity and Reconciliation', to this Constitution shall not by reason only of the fact that it is contained in a Schedule, have a lesser status than any other provision of this Constitution which is not contained in a schedule, and such provision shall for all purposes be deemed to form part of the substance of this Constitution.

It is therefore significant to observe here that the post-amble enjoyed the same status as other provisions included in the main text of the Interim Constitution and was meant to guide the courts in the interpretation of the provisions of the Constitution. It enjoyed higher status than the Preamble in that the latter could only be used as an aid in interpretation where the provisions of the Constitution appear to be unclear.[45]

The Promotion of National Unity and Reconciliation Act 34 of 1995

In order to give effect to the postscript of the Interim Constitution, Parliament passed a bill in November 1994, which established a TRC. On 19 July 1995, President Mandela signed the bill into law, which became known as the Promotion of National Unity and Reconciliation Act.[46] This Act covered persons who had not been granted indemnities under the Indemnity Act of 1990 and the Further

---

45 See D. Basson, n. 27 at 318.
46 See chap. I, n. 34, text available at www.polity.org/govdocs/legislationza (hereinafter the Amnesty Act).

Indemnity Act of 1992.[47] In addition, provision was made for the amnesties already granted under these two acts to be recognised.[48]

Section 2 (1) of the Amnesty Act established a TRC with the mandate to investigate gross violations of human rights,[49] which consisted of the killing, abduction, torture or severe ill treatment of any person, or any attempt, conspiracy, incitement, instigation, command or procurement to commit any of these acts.[50] The objectives of the Commission were to be achieved by three newly created subsidiary organs; namely, the Committee on Human Rights Violations,[51] the Committee on Amnesty[52] and the Committee on Reparation and Rehabilitation.[53]

The Committee on Human Rights Violations was entrusted with the task of investigating human rights violations, gathering information and receiving evidence of the violations thereof. It was required to keep record of such violations, to determine what articles have been concealed to hide human rights violations and to consider gross human rights violations for which indemnity had already been given or for which prisoners were released or had their sentences reduced for the purposes of reconciliation or to achieve peaceful solutions. In addition, this Committee could make recommendations as regards rehabilitation and reparation, witness protection program, institutions conducive to a stable and fair society and other measures to prevent future violations of human rights.[54]

The Committee on Reparation and Rehabilitation was established to consider matters referred to it by the two other Committees, and to gather evidence concerning the identity of victims, their fate, present whereabouts and the type of harms suffered by them. It could also recommend measures pertaining to reparations and rehabilitation of victims and was required to produce a comprehensive report of its activities, findings and recommendations.[55]

Section 19 of the Amnesty Act entrusted the Amnesty Committee with the power to decide on amnesty applications either on paper or after a public hearing. The most important requirements for the granting of amnesty were that the act, omission or offence must be connected with a political objective and be committed in the course of the conflicts of the past;[56] and that the applicant makes full disclosure of all relevant facts.[57]

In contrast to the basic tenets of amnesty as explained in the previous chapter, the South African amnesty has a distinctive feature in that it was not based on

---

47 See P. Parker, n. 35 at 2.
48 See Act 34 of 1995 as amended by the Promotion of National Unity and Reconciliation Amendment Act 87 of 1995, *Government Gazette* No. 16774 of 16 October 1995.
49 Section 1 (ix).
50 Section 1 (ix) (a) and (b).
51 Sections 12–15.
52 Sections 16–22.
53 Sections 23–27.
54 Section 14 of the Amnesty Act.
55 Section 25.
56 Subsection 20 (1) (b).
57 Subsection 20 (1) (c).

oblivion or forgetfulness. Instead, it was based on the concept of 'full disclosure'[58] of past wrongs so as to allow all South Africans to remember, and not to forget, the crimes committed in the past. This mechanism was believed to have the potential of helping the nation to reconcile with its past in order to secure a bright and co-existing future for all South Africans. In addition to giving a full account of his crimes, the applicant had to convince the Amnesty Committee that he was acting in support of a publicly known political organisation, the State or in furtherance of a coup d'état, and that his acts, omissions or offences had a political objective and was committed in the course of the conflict of the past.[59]

Scope of Amnesty

The Amnesty Act limited the grant of amnesty to "acts, omissions or offences associated with political objectives". Acts, omission or offences associated with political objectives consisted of:

> [A]ny act or omission which constitutes an offence or delict which was advised, planned, directed, commanded, ordered or committed within or outside the Republic during the period of 1 March 1960 to 5 December 1993 by:
>
> a.) [A]ny member or supporter of a publicly known political organisation or liberation movement on behalf of or in support of such organisation or movement, bona fide in furtherance of a struggle waged by such an organisation or movement against the State or any former State or another publicly known political organisation or liberation movement by civil war, insurrection or political turmoil;
> b.) [A]ny member of the security forces of the State or any former State in the course and scope of his or her express or implied authority directed against any publicly known political organisation or liberation movement engaged in a political struggle against the State or former State by civil war, insurrection or political turmoil, or against any members or supporters of such organisation or movement and which was committed bona fide with the objective of countering or otherwise resisting the said struggle; or
> c.) [A]ny persons who associated himself or herself with any act or omission committed for the purposes referred to in paragraph (a) and (b).[60]

However, the Act excluded privately motivated offences, by not including within its ambit any act, omission or offence committed:

> i.) For personal gain: provided that an act, omission or offence by any person who acted and received money or anything of value as an informer of the State or a former state, political organisation or liberation movement, shall not be excluded only on the grounds of that person having received money or anything of value for his or her information; or

---

58 *Id.*
59 Subsections 20 (1) (b) and 20 (2).
60 See Article 20 (2) of the Amnesty Act.

ii.) Out of personal malice, ill-will or spite, directed against the victim of the acts committed.[61]

In determining whether a particular act, omission or offence is associated with a political objective, the Committee on Amnesty applied the Norgaard principles,[62] which include the following criteria:

a.) The motive of the person who committed the act, omission or offence;
b.) The context in which the act, omission or offence took place, and in particular whether the act, omission or offence was committed in the course of or as part of a political uprising, disturbance or event, or in reaction thereto;
c.) The legal and factual nature of the act, omission or offence, including the gravity of the act, omission or offence;
d.) The object or objective of the act, omission or offence, and in particular whether the act, omission or offence was primarily directed at a political opponent or State property or personnel or against private property or individuals;
e.) Whether the act, omission or offence was committed in the execution of an order of, or on behalf of, or with the approval of, the organisation, institution, liberation movement or body of which the person who committed the act was a member, an agent or a supporter; and
f.) The relationship between the act, omission or offence and the political objective pursued, and in particular the directness and proximity of the relationship and the proportionality of the act, omission or offence to the objective pursued.[63]

In sum, two important aspects of the South African amnesty law are worth highlighting. Firstly, amnesty applied equally to both State officials and members of opposition movements. In fact, the definition of "acts or omissions associated with political objectives" as provided for by the Amnesty Law was wide enough to cover both persons who had committed serious criminal offences in furtherance of apartheid and persons who had violated the then existing South African criminal law code while opposing apartheid. Secondly, the Amnesty Act did not differentiate between common or ordinary crimes (i.e. offences such as acts of sabotage, invasion of privacy and offences against property committed by the liberation movements in violation of the South African national criminal law code) and serious international crimes (i.e., torture, disappearances, etc, committed in furtherance of the crime against humanity of apartheid). These two categories of crimes received an equal treatment under the heading "acts, omissions or offences associated with political objectives" and were both subject to amnesty. The only exception to amnesty provided for in the Amnesty Act concerned acts or omission committed for personal gain or personal gratification. As will be demonstrated later

---

61 See *AZAPO*, chap. I, n. 31 (hereinafter *AZAPO* 2) 1996 (8) BCLR at 1022 para. 5 G–H; see also Subsection 20 (3) (f) (i) and (ii) of the Amnesty Act.
62 These principles were drafted by Professor Carl Aage Norgaard who once served as President of the European Court of Human Rights. The Norgaard principles were used in the context of transition in Namibia to define political crimes. These principles require proportionality between the crime and the political motivation for committing it, in order for such crime to be qualified as political.
63 Article 20 (3) of the Amnesty Act.

in this book, the non-exclusion of serious international crimes from the purview of amnesty resulted in granting indemnity for such categories of crimes.

Effects of Amnesty

Sections 20 (7), 20 (8), 20 (9) and 20 (10) of the South African Amnesty Act made provision for the legal consequences of amnesty, which are individual on the one hand, and formal and procedural on the other.

Effects on the Personal Liability of the Perpetrator

The Amnesty Act exempted not only the direct perpetrator from personal criminal and civil liability, but it also exempted any third party from vicarious liability that he might have incurred as a result of the direct perpetrator's act, omission or offence. In this regard, Section 20 (7) provided that:

a.) No person who has been granted amnesty in respect of an act, omission or offence shall be criminally or civilly liable in respect of such act, omission or offence and no body or organisation or the State shall be liable, and no person shall be vicariously liable for any such act, omission or offence;

b.) Where amnesty is granted to any person in respect of any act, omission or offence, such amnesty shall have no influence on any criminal liability of any other person contingent on the liability of the first-mentioned person.

c.) No person, organisation or State shall be civilly or vicariously liable for an act, omission or offence committed between 1 March 1960 and the cut-off date by a person who is deceased, unless amnesty could not have been granted in terms of this Act in respect of such an act, omission or offence.

In general, the following consequences flow from Section 20 (7) of the Act: cancellation of all criminal and civil liabilities of the perpetrator in respect of any damages or injuries sustained by the victims of the acts for which amnesty has been granted. Cancellation of any criminal or civil liability that might be incurred by a civilian or a military commander who might have given order to commit the crimes, and exemption of the State or organisation of any pecuniary or moral responsibility, which it might have incurred as a result of the acts or omissions of its employees or members.

Formal and Procedural Effects

Section 20 of the Act provided for the formal and procedural effects of amnesty as follows:

(8) If any person:

a.) [H]as been charged with and is standing trial in respect of an offence constituted by the act or omission in respect of which amnesty is granted in terms of this section; or b.) [H]as been convicted of, and is awaiting the passing of sentence in respect of, or is in custody for the purpose of serving a sentence imposed in respect of, an offence constituted by the act or omission in respect of which amnesty is so granted, the criminal proceedings shall forthwith upon publication of the proclamation referred to in ss (6) become void or the sentence so imposed shall upon such publication lapse and the person so in custody shall forthwith be released.

(9) If any person has been granted amnesty in respect of any act or omission which formed the ground of a civil judgement which was delivered at any time before the granting of the amnesty, the publication of the proclamation in terms of ss (6) shall not affect the operation of the judgement insofar as it applies to that person.

(10) Where any person has been convicted of any offence constituted by an act or omission associated with a political objective in respect of which amnesty has been granted in terms of this Act, any entry or record of the conviction shall be deemed to be expunged from all official documents or records and the conviction shall for all purposes, including the application of any Act of Parliament or any other law, be deemed not to have taken place: provided that the Committee [on Amnesty] may recommend to the authority concerned the taking of such measures as it may deem necessary for the protection of the safety of the public.

In fact, Article 20 (8) nullified all pending criminal proceedings, convictions or sentences, which are related to the crimes for which amnesty has been granted. It also guaranteed the release of persons held in custody in connection with such crimes.

What is remarkable in respect of Section 20 is that the cancellation of all criminal and civil actions against an amnestied offender has the effect of negatively affecting any rights of claim that victims or third parties may legitimately have against alleged offenders. Mahomed D.P. clearly highlighted this extended effect of the amnesty law when he admitted that:

The effect of an amnesty undoubtedly impacts upon very fundamental rights. All persons are entitled to the protection of the law against unlawful invasions of their right to life, their right to respect for and protection of dignity and their right not to be subject to torture of any kind. When those rights are invaded those aggrieved by such invasions have the right to obtain redress in the ordinary courts of law and those guilty of perpetrating such violations are answerable before such courts, both civilly and criminally. An amnesty to the wrongdoer effectively obliterates such rights.[64]

However, the learned judge raised three sets of argument as a justification for the obliteration of fundamental rights by amnesty. Firstly, he contended that amnesty is necessary to know the truth about the past and that the public disclosure of the truth is reconciliatory through its positive psychological consequences for victims, their families and the perpetrators. Secondly, he contended that without amnesty the bridge to a liberal democratic society might not have been built. Thirdly, he held that amnesty for the State is justified by its service to remedial distributive justice.[65]

---

64 See *AZAPO 2*, at 1024 para. 9 H–I.
65 *Id.* at 1028 para. 17 B–E, para. 19 I and at 1039 para. C–F respectively; for a critical analysis of these justifications, see D. Moellendorf "Amnesty, truth and justice: AZAPO" 13 *South African Journal on Human Rights* (1997) at 285–290.

Challenging the Validity of Amnesty

Fearing that the amnesty legislation might conflict with their fundamental rights, the AZAPO, a political movement that took part in the struggle against the apartheid regime, together with relatives of political activists murdered during the apartheid era, approached the Constitutional Court in 1996 to challenge the constitutionality of various sections of the Amnesty Act.[66] Simultaneously, they applied to the Cape Provincial Division of the Supreme Court for an interdict against the TRC (in particular the Amnesty Committee) to refrain from granting amnesty pending the decision of the Constitutional Court on the validity of the Amnesty Act.[67] But the two jurisdictions reached similar conclusions and ruled in favour of the conformity of the Amnesty Act with the Interim Constitution. What follows is a discussion of the constitutional and legal analysis adopted by Cape Provincial Division and the Constitutional Court in deciding on the legal validity of amnesty.

The Amnesty Law Before the Supreme Court

As mentioned earlier, the applicants approached the Cape Provincial Division of the Supreme Court to seek a temporary interdict against the Amnesty Committee. In their claim they alleged that Sections 20 (7), 20 (8) and 20 (10) of the Amnesty Act were in conflict with various provisions of the Interim Constitution.[68] They contended further that the word 'amnesty' in the postscript of the Constitution was intended to cover criminal liability only and not civil liability also.

In terms of the applicable South African law, an interdict may be granted only after an applicant has fulfilled the following requirements:

> [N]amely a clear right or a right *prima facie* established, though open to some doubt: injury actually committed or reasonably apprehended and the absence of any other ordinary remedy. If the applicant fail to establish a clear right, but establish a *prima facie* right which is open to some doubt, it is then necessary for them to establish that the balance of convenience is in their favour.[69]

Therefore, in seeking to establish a clear right or a *prima facie* right entitling them to a temporary interdict, the applicants relied on various provisions of the Interim Constitution. Of utmost importance was the alleged violation of Section 22, which stipulated that: "[E]very person shall have the right to have justiciable disputes settled by a court of law or, where appropriate, another independent and impartial

---

66   *AZAPO 2*.
67   See *Azanian Peoples Organisation (AZAPO) and Others v. Truth and Reconciliation Commission* 1996 (4) SA 562 (hereinafter *AZAPO 1*).
68   Among the contested provisions are Subsections 7 (4) (a), 96 (1) and (3), 98 (2) and (3), 101 (3) (b), Section 22 and Constitutional Principle VI contained in Schedule 4 to the Constitution; these clauses deal in general with the function of the judiciary, the power and jurisdiction of the courts as well as the right of access to courts.
69   *AZAPO 1*, n. 67 at 568, para. J–569, and para. A.

forum." The applicants contended that as long as the effect of Section 20 (7) of the Amnesty Act was to bar them from seeking reparation before the competent courts, their right of access to court as entrenched in Section 22 was violated.

The court ruled on this point by conceding that the Amnesty Act in fact infringed upon the right of access to court, but argued further that such an infringement was justified by the need of reconciliation and reconstruction, which is spelt out in the epilogue of the Constitution.[70]

The applicants further claimed that the word 'amnesty' in the post-amble was intended to extinguish criminal liability only and not civil liability also. This argument turned out to be based on two passages of an article written by Professor Ziyad Motala, a prominent South African academic who suggested that amnesty for war crimes amounts to a violation of international law. In the words of this author:

> ... [I]n suspending and cancelling any civil action the victims of war crimes may bring against alleged offenders, the [Amnesty] Act violates a peremptory norm of international law which provides rights to individual victims of war crimes regardless of the attitude of the State.[71]

On the basis of the *jus cogens*[72] nature of the Geneva Conventions of 12 August 1949, which is believed to have entered into the corpus of customary international law, the learned author further claimed that:

> [T]he Act, to the extent that it grants amnesty to war crimes, violates a cardinal rule of international humanitarian law, namely that there can be no amnesty for war crimes.[73]

The court also rejected this contention by referring to two provisions of the Interim Constitution, namely Article 231 (1) and (4), which consolidate the superiority of acts of Parliament over international law. In fact, Article 231 (1) of the Interim Constitution provided that:

> All rights and obligations under international agreements which immediately before the commencement of this Constitution were vested in or binding on the Republic within the meaning of the previous Constitution, shall be vested in or binding on the Republic under this Constitution, unless provided otherwise by an Act of Parliament.

Whereas Article 231 (4) read as follows:

> The rules of customary international law binding on the Republic, shall, unless inconsistent with this Constitution or an Act of Parliament, form part of the law of the Republic.

---

70 *Id.* at 570 paras E–F.
71 See Z. Motala, "The Promotion of National Unity and Reconciliation Act, the Constitution and international law" 28 *Comparative and International Law Journal of Southern Africa* (1995) at 338, quoted in *AZAPO 1*, n. 67 at 573 paras E–F.
72 The contours of this term are circumscribed in the next chapter.
73 *AZAPO 1* at 573 paras F–G.

It is clear from these two subsections that acts of Parliament take precedence over treaties and customary international law. The legal consequence that ensues is the subordination of international law to domestic law.

The court further argued that amnesty itself is permitted by international law. For this contention, it relied on Article 6 (5) of Protocol II of 1977 Additional to the Geneva Conventions of 1949, which reads:

> At the end of hostilities, the authorities in power shall endeavour to grant the broadest possible amnesty to persons who have participated in the armed conflict, or those deprived of their liberty for reasons related to the armed conflict, whether they are interned or detained.

In elaborating on the provisions of the Interim Constitution and of Additional Protocol II, Friedman JP and Farlam J came to the conclusion that subsections 231 (1) and (4) of the Constitution enabled parliament to pass laws, which are contrary to *jus cogens*.[74] That Article 6 (5) of Additional Protocol II, to which apartheid South Africa was not party, constituted an exception to the peremptory rule prohibiting amnesty for crimes against humanity, applicable to conflicts of the kind that existed in South Africa. And finally that the *jus cogens* did not constitute a basis for limiting the meaning of the word 'amnesty' as used in the post-amble.[75] Consequently, and on the basis of these findings, the court declined to further consider the applicability of the concept of *jus cogens* in interpreting the Constitution.

The court finally dismissed the application on the grounds that applicants had neither established a clear right entitling them to an interdict, nor established a *prima facie* right, though open to some doubt.[76] As a consequence, the Amnesty Committee was permitted to proceed with its task of granting amnesty.

The Amnesty Law Before the Constitutional Court

In line with the Cape Provincial Division's approach, the Constitutional Court found that the right of access to court provided for in Section 22 of the Interim Constitution could be limited not only by the limitation clause contained in Section 33, but also by another constitutional provision. As a result of this finding, the Court held that the epilogue of the Interim Constitution entitled 'National Unity and Reconciliation', which expressly recommended amnesty constituted a permissible limitation to the Section 22 right. Like the Cape Provincial Division, the Constitutional Court rejected the claim that amnesty in the post-amble of the Interim Constitution was intended to cover criminal liability only and not civil liability also. However, unlike the Cape Provincial Division whose decision on this

---

74 *Id.* at 574 para. B.
75 For the whole argument, see *AZAPO 1* at 574 paras B–J to 575 paras A–D.
76 *Id.* at 576 para. E.

contention was based on controversial grounds,[77] the Constitutional Court took a more cautious approach, based not on legal reasoning, but rather on political justifications, to find that amnesty in the post-amble was capable of being construed so as to protect a wrongdoer from both criminal and civil liabilities. In so doing, the court relied on the argument that the Amnesty Act sought to address the problem of concealed brutality and torture which had occurred during the apartheid era by encouraging:

> [S]urvivors and the dependants of the tortured and the wounded, the maimed and the dead to unburden their grief publicly, to receive the collective recognition of a new nation that they were wronged, and crucially, to help them to discover what did in truth happen to their loved ones, where and under what circumstances it did happen, and who was responsible. That truth, which the victims of repression seek so desperately to know is, in the circumstances, much more likely to be forthcoming if those responsible for such monstrous misdeeds are encouraged to disclose the whole truth with the incentive that they will not receive the punishment which they undoubtedly deserve if they do. Without that incentive there is nothing to encourage such persons to make the disclosures and to reveal the truth which persons in the positions of the applicants so desperately desire. With that incentive, what might unfold are objectives fundamental to the ethos of a new constitutional order.[78]

In considering whether the granting of amnesty in respect of civil liability was in violation of the Interim Constitution, the Court *per* Mahomed DP argued that depending on the context and the circumstances, the word 'amnesty' might be construed in a limited sense to mean immunity from criminal liability as well as in a much broader sense to extend to civil liability.[79] The Court went on to state in this regard that:

> Central to the justification of amnesty in respect of the criminal prosecution for offences committed during the prescribed period with political objectives, is the appreciation that the truth will not effectively be revealed by the wrongdoers if they are to be prosecuted for such acts. That justification must necessarily and unavoidably apply to the need to indemnify such wrongdoers against civil claims for payment of damages. Without that incentive the wrongdoer cannot be encouraged to reveal the whole truth which might inherently be against his or her material or proprietary interests. There is nothing in the language of the epilogue which persuades me that what the makers of the Constitution intended to do was to encourage wrongdoers to reveal the truth by providing for amnesty against criminal prosecution in respect of their acts but simultaneously to discourage them from revealing that truth by keeping intact the threat that such revelations might be visited with what might in many cases be very substantial claims for civil damages. It appears to me to be more reasonable to infer that the legislation

---

[77] As mentioned earlier, such grounds are at least threefold: firstly, the argument that Article 231 (1) and (4) of the Interim Constitution enable Parliament to pass laws that are contrary to *jus cogens*; secondly, the contention that Article 6 (5) of Additional Protocol II of 1977 is an exception to the peremptory rule prohibiting amnesty for crimes against humanity; finally, the statement that *jus cogens* does not constitute a basis for limiting the meaning of the word 'amnesty' in the post-amble.

[78] *AZAPO 2*, at 1027 para. 17 J–1028 para. 17 A–C.

[79] *Id.* at 1035–1036 para. 35.

contemplated in the epilogue would, in the circumstances defined, be wide enough to allow for an amnesty which would protect a wrongdoer who told the truth, from both the criminal and the civil consequences of his or her admissions.[80]

Whether the TRC has succeeded in trading amnesty for truth is hard to tell. However, it is recorded that Desmond Tutu's experience as Chairperson of this Commission led him to remark that most of those that testified before the commission "lied like it was going out of fashion".[81]

Another contention raised by the applicants was that Section 20 (7) of the Amnesty Act was in contradiction with the 1949 Geneva Conventions, which oblige States to prosecute persons responsible for gross human rights violations. They relied on a provision common to the four Geneva Conventions to the effect that:

> The High Contracting Parties undertake to enact any legislation necessary to provide effective penal sanctions for persons committing, or ordering to be committed, any of the grave breaches...
>
> Each High Contracting Party shall be under the obligation to search for persons alleged to have committed, or to have ordered to be committed, such grave breaches, and shall bring such persons, regardless of their nationality, before its own courts. It may also, if it prefers, and in accordance with the provisions of its own legislation, hand such persons over for trial to another High Contracting Party concerned, provided such High Contracting Party has made out a prima facie case.[82]

The expression 'grave breaches' is further defined as:

> [T]hose involving any of the following acts, if committed against persons or property protected by the Convention: wilful killing, torture or inhuman treatment, including biological experiments, wilfully causing great suffering or serious injury to body or health, and extensive destruction and appropriation of property, not justified by military necessity and carried out unlawfully and wantonly.[83]

It is worth mentioning here that the Geneva Conventions of 1949 and their two Additional Protocols of 1977 codify international humanitarian law, which is a set of rules aimed at humanising the conduct of war between belligerents by limiting their choice of weapons as well as the manner in which the hostilities may be conducted. In commenting on States' obligations under the 1949 Geneva Conventions, the International Committee of the Red Cross held the view that such obligations are imperative and that the contracting parties are "more strictly bound to enact the necessary legislation...."[84]

Both the Cape Provincial Division and the Constitutional Court rightly noted that in terms of the South African law an Act of Parliament takes precedence over any

---

80 *Id.* at 1036 para. 36 G–I–1037 para. 36 A–B.
81 See B. Chigara *Amnesty in International Law: The Legality under International Law of National Amnesty* (2002) at 82.
82 Article 49 of Geneva Convention I, Article 50 of Geneva Convention II, Article 129 of Geneva Convention III, and Article 146 of Geneva Convention IV.
83 Article 50 of Geneva Convention I, Article 51 of Geneva Convention II, Article 130 of Geneva Convention III and Article 147 of Geneva Convention IV.
84 See J.S. Pictet (ed.), *Commentary of Geneva Convention I* (1951) at 363.

right or obligations under international law. However, Mahomed DP addressed the international law argument by first rejecting the relevance of international law in the determination of the constitutionality of amnesty and by limiting its application to the interpretation of the Constitution only. In this regard, he noted that:

> The issue which falls to be determined in this Court is whether section 20 (7) of the Act is inconsistent with the Constitution. If it is, the enquiry as to whether or not international law prescribes a different duty is irrelevant to that determination. International law and the content of international treaties to which South Africa might or might not be a party at any particular time are, in my view, relevant only in the interpretation of the Constitution itself, on the grounds that the lawmakers of the Constitution should not lightly be presumed to authorise any law which might constitute a breach of the obligations of the State in terms of international law.[85]

With respect to the possible application of the Geneva Conventions, the learned judge expressed his doubts as to the relevance of these documents to the conflict that took place in South Africa. He wrote:

> In the first place it is doubtful whether the Geneva Conventions of 1949 read with the relevant Protocols thereto apply at all to the situation in which this country found itself during the years of the conflict to which I have referred.[86]

Then he went on to argue that:

> Secondly, whatever be the proper ambit and technical meaning of these Conventions and Protocols, the international literature in any event clearly appreciate the distinction between the position of perpetrators of acts of violence in the course of war (or other conflicts between states or armed conflicts between liberation movements seeking self-determination against colonial and alien domination of their countries), on the one hand, and their position in respect of violent acts perpetrated during other conflicts which take place within the territory of a sovereign state in consequence of a struggle between the armed forces of that state and other dissident armed forces operating under responsible command, within such a state on the other hand. In respect of the latter category, there is no obligation on the part of a contracting state to ensure the prosecution of those who might have performed acts of violence or other acts which would ordinarily be characterised as serious invasions of human rights. On the contrary, Article 6 (5) of Protocol II to the Geneva Conventions of 1949 provides that…[87]

In reality, the Court's distinction between international and non-international armed conflict is in conformity with the provisions of the four Geneva Conventions of 1949 and their two Additional Protocols of 1977. In this regard, Article 2 common to the four Geneva Conventions, defines the field of application of the Conventions in the following manner:

> [T]he Present Convention shall apply to all cases of declared war or of any other armed conflict which may arise between two or more of the High Contracting Parties, even if the state of war is not recognised by one of them.

---

85 *AZAPO 2*, at 1031 para. 26 F–G.
86 *Id.* at 1032 para. 29 H.
87 *Id.* at 1033 para. 30 A–D.

The Convention shall also apply to all cases of partial or total occupation of the territory of a High Contracting Party, even if the said occupation meets with no resistance.

Meanwhile, Additional Protocol I of 1977 relating to the Protection of Victims of International Armed Conflicts extended the field of application of the Geneva Conventions to include:

[A]rmed conflicts in which peoples are fighting against colonial domination and alien occupation and against racist regimes in the exercise of their right of self-determination, as enshrined in the Charter of the United Nations and the Declaration on Principles of International Law concerning Friendly Relations and Co-operation among States in accordance with the Charter of the United Nations.[88]

Therefore, two situations are envisaged for the application of the 1949 Geneva Conventions, namely any situation of armed conflict involving at least one of the contracting parties, and all cases of occupation of the territory of a State party, be it total or partial. Whereas Additional Protocol I applies to situations in which people are fighting for self-determination against colonial domination, alien occupation and racist regimes. The obligation to punish offenders of grave breaches of the Geneva Conventions is extended to situations covered by Additional Protocol I.[89]

Contrary to the 1949 Geneva Conventions and Additional Protocol I, which put great emphasis on the international character of the conflict, Additional Protocol II relating to the Protection of Victims of Non-International Armed Conflicts only applies to:

[A]rmed conflicts [...], which take place in the territory of a High Contracting Party between its armed forces and dissident armed forces or other organised armed groups which, under responsible command, exercise such control over a part of its territory as to enable them to carry out sustained and concerted military operations...[90]

Unlike the four Geneva Conventions and Additional Protocol I, Additional Protocol II does not contain a specific obligation to search for and punish persons guilty of its breach.

Although the Constitutional Court's argument on the non-existence of a specific obligation to prosecute in terms of Additional Protocol II is true, can one then hastily conclude that the commission of war crimes, crimes against humanity, torture or genocide is allowed in the context of non-international wars? Or that individual States are legally justified in shielding the perpetrators of such horrendous crimes by granting them amnesty? What is clear from the Constitutional Court's reasoning in *AZAPO* is that international customary law, the customary nature of the Geneva Conventions and the existing general human rights law treaties were left untouched. A careful consideration of these aspects of international law in light of

---

88 Article 1 (4).
89 See Part V Section II of Protocol I entitled "Repression of breaches of the Conventions and of this Protocol" in JS Pictet (ed.), *Commentary on the Additional Protocols of 8 June 1977 to the Geneva Conventions of 12 August 1949* (1987) at 973.
90 Article 1 (1).

new developments that took place with the end of the Cold War era would have undoubtedly produced a different outcome. Nevertheless, the Constitutional Court followed the example of the Cape Provincial Division in rejecting the application on the grounds that Section 20 (7) of the Amnesty Act was authorised by the Constitution itself, and, as a result, was constitutional.[91]

The decision of the Constitutional Court to uphold the validity of the Amnesty Law left many unsatisfied and established an atmosphere of division among the South African legal opinion. This situation justifies Dugard's declaration with reference to the Amnesty Law that:

> Its opaque origins and the understandable desire for retribution that persists in many quarters, have made it the most controversial legislation of post-apartheid South Africa.[92]

The next section shall attempt to identify and to critically assess some of the most salient points of criticism expressed by amnesty commentators.

Criticism of the South African Amnesty System

Although the South African amnesty policy appeared to be more acceptable by the international community, the courts' ruling on the constitutional validity of the Amnesty Law and the manner in which the amnesty procedure was conducted nevertheless contained some limits.

Limits of the Courts' Decisions on Amnesty

As already mentioned above, among the arguments raised by the applicants in support of their claim were the submissions that the State is obliged by international law to prosecute those responsible for gross human rights violations and that the provisions of Section 20 (7) of the Amnesty Act, which provided for both criminal and civil amnesty, constituted a breach of international law. According to several authors, the judgement of the courts on these two points is disappointing from at least two perspectives. Firstly, from the international law perspective, the courts are criticised for having failed to address adequately the issue of whether conventional and customary international law oblige a successor regime to punish officials of a prior regime for violations of international law.[93] Secondly, from the interpretative perspective, critics believe that the Constitutional Court failed to achieve the harmony between international law and the South African municipal

---

91 *AZAPO 2*, at 1041 para. 50.
92 J. Dugard, n. 44 at 260.
93 See e.g., J. Dugard, n. 44 at 258–268; Z. Motala "The Constitutional Court's approach to international law and its method of interpretation in the 'amnesty decision': intellectual honesty or political expediency?" 21 *South African Yearbook of International Law* (1996) at 29–59; see also A. O'Shea, chap. II, n. 5 at 151–159.

law, thus reverting from the position it held in previous cases, in which a careful analysis of international law has guided its decisions.[94]

Limited Analysis of International Law

The Cape Provincial Division as well as the Constitutional Court analysis of the applicability of international law in the amnesty decision has been incomplete. Only treaty law was heavily relied upon, whereas another important aspect of international law, namely customary international law, was neglected.

As far as treaty law is concerned, some critics agree with the Cape Provincial Division and the Constitutional Court that only the 1949 Geneva Conventions, to which South Africa became a party in 1952, were applicable.[95] However, in their interpretation of these Conventions read together with their two Additional Protocols of 1977, the two courts reached a similar conclusion to the effect that these documents do not prohibit the granting of amnesty for the crimes they proscribe. Critics argue that the courts have erred in their interpretation of the provisions of these instruments as far as their meaning and relevance to the South African constitutional scheme is concerned. Thus, according to Professor Dugard:

> The judgement [of the Cape Provincial Division] contains two unfortunate comments, one of law and the other of history. First, the obiter dictum that the South African interim Constitution would 'enable Parliament to pass a law, even if such law is contrary to the jus cogens' was both unnecessary [...] and unwise as it seriously undermines the Constitution's clear intention of establishing harmony between international law and municipal law. Secondly, the finding that article 1 (4) of Additional Protocol I to the Geneva Conventions, which extends the protection of the Conventions to armed conflicts in which people are fighting against racist regimes in the exercise of their right of self-determination, takes no account of the fact that, historically, the clause was included to deal with apartheid in South Africa. [...] If the court had read the careful judgement of Conradie J in *S v. Petane* and the writings of South African academic lawyers on this subject it might have obtained a clearer understanding of the history, scope and purpose of this clause.[96]

This remark also holds for the Constitutional Court's approach in holding that the 1949 Geneva Conventions and their Additional Protocols were not applicable to the conflict in South Africa and that nothing in Section 20 (7) of the Amnesty Act could be said to be a breach of the obligations of South Africa in terms of public international law.[97] On these two points, Professor Motala observed that the court failed to consider the mention in Protocol I of apartheid as a grave breach of international law, nor did it consider the myriad characterisation by the United Nations and other bodies of the fight against apartheid as an international conflict

---

94 See e.g., the Constitutional Court interpretation of international law in *S.v. Makwanyane and Mchunu*.

95 See J. Dugard, n. 44 at 262.

96 *Id.* at 264–265.

97 *AZAPO 2* at 1034 para. 32 H.

and a struggle for self-determination.[98] In addition, he noted that the court failed to investigate the status of the Geneva Conventions and their Additional Protocols under customary international law or as principles of *jus cogens*.[99]

Concerning the applicability of customary international law in the evaluation of the legal validity of amnesty, Dugard is of the opinion that:

> No mention is made of the possible obligation under customary international law to prosecute crimes against humanity despite the fact that as a customary international law rule it would occupy a higher status under municipal law than the unincorporated Geneva Conventions and the unsigned Protocols I and II.[100]

In addition to these criticisms, one may add the courts' selective reference to foreign amnesty experience. In this respect, the Constitutional Court briefly referred to comparative transitional arrangements in Chile, Argentina and El Salvador,[101] but did not go further so as to mention that in other cases such as in the German Democratic Republic, Romania, Hungary, Colombia or Guatemala persons guilty of gross human rights violations such as torture, forced disappearance, executions and crimes against humanity were excluded from amnesty provisions.[102] The Court also did not consider the Inter-American Commission of Human Rights conclusions to the effect that a successor regime is obliged under the ACHR to investigate international human rights violations and to prosecute the perpetrators thereof. More pertinent in this regard is the 1992 decision of the Inter-American Commission on the Salvadorian amnesty law, which held that:

> The present Amnesty law, as applied in these cases, by foreclosing the possibility of judicial relief in cases of murder, inhumane treatment and absence of judicial guarantees, denies the fundamental nature of the most basic human rights. It eliminates perhaps the single most effective means of enforcing such rights, the trial and punishment of offenders.[103]

It is also worth mentioning that when adopting their amnesty acts, Chile and El Salvador acknowledged their obligations under international law to prosecute persons responsible for gross human rights abuses.[104]

Like South Africa, Uruguay adopted an indemnity act which granted full and total amnesty to gross human rights abusers as part of its politics of reconciliation. However, requested to comment on this case, the Inter-American Commission declared that the Uruguayan amnesty law, the effect of which is to deny the victims

---

98   See n. 93 at 31.
99   *Id.* at 40.
100 J. Dugard, n. 44 at 265.
101 *AZAPO 2* at 1030 paras 22 C–D and 23 E–F.
102 Z. Motala, n. 93 at 49.
103 Report 26/92 case 10.287 El Salvador, quoted by Z. Motala, n. 93 at 51.
104 See N. Roht-Arriaza "State responsibility to investigate and prosecute grave human rights violations in international law" 78 *California Law Review* (1990) at 496–497.

the possibility of participating in the criminal proceedings, violated its obligation in respect of the right of fair trial under the ACHR.[105]

The Court also failed to comment on the Inter-American Court of Human Rights ruling in the *Velasquez Rodriguez* case, which further suggests that persons responsible for gross human rights violations shall be punished.[106] Furthermore, the ruling of the ICTY, which rejects amnesty for gross human rights violations,[107] has not been considered by the Court. This limited inquiry into international practice led Motala to state that the Constitutional Court presented a selective picture which resulted in a distorted view of the use of amnesty under international law.[108]

Nevertheless, Dugard does not disagree with the conclusion reached by the Constitutional Court. However, he expresses his dissatisfaction with the reasoning of the Court and the fact that the "harmony between international law and municipal law that the interim and the final Constitution seek to achieve has not received full judicial recognition."[109] This remark is pertinent in that on other occasions, the Constitutional Court has interpreted the constitutionality of a domestic statute involving rules and principles of international law so as to ascertain the sources and content of such rules in accordance with Article 38 (1) of the ICJ,[110] and to prefer an interpretation that advances international human rights principles.

Departure from the Courts' Previous Interpretation of International Law

In other landmark cases such as the *Makwanyane Case*,[111] which resulted in the abolition of the death penalty in South Africa, serious consideration was given to international law in the interpretation of the right to life contained in Article 9 of the Interim Constitution. Chaskalson DP noted in this case that Section 35 (1) of the Interim Constitution, which dealt with the interpretation of fundamental rights, enables South African courts to consider both binding and non-binding decisions. He further observed that international agreements and customary international law provide a framework within which the chapter on fundamental rights is to be evaluated and understood. Moreover, he stated that the work of other instances such as the United Nations Committee on Human Rights, the Inter-American Commission on Human Rights, the Inter-American Court of Human Rights, and in appropriate

---

105 Report 29/92, cases 10.029, 10.036, 10.145, 10.305, 10.372, 10.373, 10.374 and 10.375 Uruguay, 2 October, 1992, quoted by Z. Motala, n. 93 at 51–52.
106 See Judgment of 21 July, 1989, reprinted in N.J. Kritz, chap. I, n. 3 at 739; see especially the Court's reasoning at paragraphs 32 and 33.
107 See the *Furundzija* Case, chap. IV, n. 80 at 151–157.
108 See n. 93 at 30.
109 See n. 44 at 267–268.
110 *Makwanyane*, chap. III, n. 18 at para. 35; the relevant Article of the Statute of the ICJ provides that the court shall apply international conventions, customs, general principles of law and, as a subsidiary means, judicial decisions and the teachings of the most prominent publicists to determine international law.
111 See n. 110.

instances, the specialised agencies, may provide guidance for the correct interpretation of fundamental rights enshrined in Chapter 3 of the Constitution.[112] In the same ruling, Mokgoro J emphasised that in terms of Section 35 (1) the courts are required to proceed to public international law and foreign case law for guidance in constitutional interpretation, thereby promoting the ideal and internationally accepted values in the cultivation of a human rights jurisprudence for South Africa.[113] A careful look into the treatment of international law in *AZAPO* clearly testifies to the Court's poor reliance on the various sources referred to above.

Furthermore, in *Coetzee and Others v. Government of the Republic of South Africa*,[114] the Constitutional Court *per* Sachs J affirmed South Africa's need to locate itself "in the mainstream of international democratic practice"[115] when determining whether a limitation of rights is justifiable in an open and democratic society based on freedom and equality. Whereas in *S v. Mhlungu and Others*,[116] the Constitutional Court dealt extensively with the conditions under which a fundamental right may be limited. It argued that chapter 3 of the Constitution seeks not to invade but to expand rights. And further that the principle that a Constitution shall be construed generously so as to allow to all persons the full benefit of the rights conferred on them contains certain limits, but that such limits are to be found in the language of the Constitution itself.[117] The Court finally held unanimously that only the most compelling language would justify a departure from the protection afforded by chapter 3 of the Interim Constitution.[118] If one seriously dwells upon the Constitutional Court's approach in *AZAPO* it will appear that although the postscript to the Interim Constitution permits some sort of limitation in the form of amnesty, nothing in its wording can be said to be as compelling as to warrant curtailment of the right of access to court enshrined in Section 22. In this respect, therefore, Motala's argument that the amnesty decision has deviated from the approach laid down by the Court in its previous judgements is very significant.[119]

Unlike Dugard, Motala seems to disagree totally with both the conclusion reached by the court and the line of reasoning which led to such a conclusion. In his words, the Constitutional Court failed in its duty in the amnesty decision to fully canvass international law for guidance when gross violations of human rights have been alleged. It has disregarded the significant volume of international law authority affirming a peremptory duty to prosecute for war crimes and crimes against

---

112 At para. 35.
113 At para. 304.
114 1995 (4) SA 631 (CC).
115 At para. 51.
116 1995 (3) SA 867 (CC).
117 See Kentridge A.J. concurring opinion at paras 76 and 78.
118 See e.g., Sachs J. concurring opinion at para. 110.
119 See n. 93 at 47 and 48.

humanity[120] and has departed from its earlier decisions on the role of international law in the Interim Constitution.[121]

Limits of the Amnesty Process

Due to its political origin, the South African amnesty process was limited in scope and object: that of fulfilling the political goal of reconciliation through truth telling. Such a limitation had a negative impact on the nature of the power of the TRC, as well as on the definition of the crimes in respect of which amnesty was to be granted. This resulted in amnesty being granted for acts which, in normal circumstances, would be qualified as crimes against humanity.

Powers of the Truth and Reconciliation Commission

The TRC consisted of seventeen members, appointed by the President in consultation with the Cabinet. Section 3 of the Amnesty Act sets out the main objectives of the Commission; namely, to establish a complete picture of the gross human rights violations committed between March 1960 and 1993, by means of hearings and investigations, to facilitate the granting of amnesty, to recommend reparation to the victims of human rights abuse, and to prepare a report containing recommendations of measures to prevent future violations of human rights.[122]

As already noted earlier, three Committees were established to achieve the objectives of the Commission.[123] Firstly, the Committee on Human Rights Violations which conducted inquiries pertaining to gross human rights violations, with extensive powers to gather and receive evidence and information. Secondly, the Committee on Reparation and Rehabilitation, which was also given the powers to receive and gather information and evidence for the purpose of recommending to the President suitable reparations for victims of gross human rights abuses. Thirdly, and of utmost relevance for this study is the Committee on Amnesty, which played a pivotal role in the amnesty process. It consisted of three judges and two commissioners entrusted with the task of considering amnesty applications. They could grant amnesty if they were satisfied that the applicant who had committed a gross human rights violation fully disclosed all the relevant facts, that his act was committed in the course of the conflicts of the past and that such act was associated with a political objective.[124] An unusual feature of the process here is that criminal acts committed in furtherance of apartheid as well as those committed in resisting apartheid were to be equally investigated by the Truth Commission.

---

120 *Id.* at 37.
121 *Id.* at 36.
122 Subsections 3 (1), (a), (b), (c) and (d).
123 Section 3 (3).
124 See Sections 17 (3), 19, and 20 (1).

However, it is worth remembering that the TRC was only empowered to investigate acts that constituted crimes under South African law. An inquiry into the system of apartheid itself as a crime against humanity was not contemplated. It had no power to compel an amnesty applicant to tell the truth or to facilitate the gathering of evidence for the purpose thereof. Gross violations of human rights to be investigated by the Commission were confined, amongst others, to the killing, abduction, torture or severe ill-treatment of any person.[125] Under the apartheid legal order, these would amount to murder, culpable homicide, kidnapping and assault.[126] However, some experts believe that "many of these acts at the same time qualify as war crimes, crimes against humanity, torture or cruel, inhuman or degrading treatment—that is, as international crimes."[127]

This remark leads to believe that the South African amnesty process did not differentiate between serious international crimes and common domestic crimes. As a consequence, any crime, be it inhuman acts, crimes against humanity or war crimes, could qualify for amnesty if they were committed in the course of the conflict of the past and could be clearly linked to a political objective. In fact, the essence of the South African amnesty was the connection between the offence for which indemnity was being sought and the political conflict short of apartheid that took place in South Africa. This requirement is contained in the words "act, omission or offence associated with a political objective". Therefore, the concept of 'political offence' or 'political crime' was central to the South African amnesty process. The question whether the torturing, maiming and murdering of anti-apartheid activists were political offences was not sufficiently addressed by the Constitutional Court.

Definitional Limits

The Amnesty Law regretfully failed to appropriately clarify the term 'political offence' for the purposes of granting amnesty. This notion entered international law in the context of political asylum as (an offence constituting) an exception to extradition.[128] In this regard, the Convention Relating to the Status of Refugees of 1951[129] defines a refugee as a person who:

---

125 Article 2 (1) (ix) (a) and (b).
126 J. Dugard, n. 44 at 260.
127 *Id.*
128 See e.g., Article 3 (1) of the 1957 European Convention on Extradition, available at www.conventions.coe.int/treaty/EN/treaties/Html/024.htm; Article 4 (4) of the 1981 Inter-American Convention on Extradition, available at www.oas.org/juridico/english/treaties/b-47(1).html; and Article 4 (1) of the 1994 Economic Community of West African States Convention on Extradition, available at www.iss.co.za/AF/RegOrg/unity_to_union/pdfs/ecowas/4ConExtraditionpdf.
129 Adopted on 28 July, 1951 by the UN Conference of Plenipotentiaries on the Status of Refugees and Stateless Persons convened under General Assembly Resolution 429 (V) of 14 December, 1950 and entered into force on 22 April, 1954, text available at www.unhchr.ch/html/menu3/b/o_c_ref.htm.

[O]wing to well-founded fear of being persecuted for reasons of race, religion, nationality, membership of a particular social group or political opinion, is outside the country of his nationality and is unable or, owing to such fear is unwilling to return to it.[130]

Excluded from this definition is:

[A]ny person with respect to whom there are serious reasons for considering that:

a) he has committed a crime against peace, a war crime, or a crime against humanity, as defined in the international instruments drawn up to make provision in respect of such crimes;

b) he has committed a non-political crime outside the country of refuge prior to his admission to that country as a refugee;

c) he has been guilty of acts contrary to the purposes and Principles of the United Nations.[131]

Political offences as an exception to extradition later evolved as an important clause in almost all extradition treaties and extradition acts. Thus, Article 3 of the 1957 European Convention on Extradition provides for example that:

1. Extradition shall not be granted if the offence in respect of which it is requested is regarded by the requested Party as a political offence or as an offence connected with a political offence.

2. The same rule shall apply if the requested Party has substantial grounds for believing that a request for extradition for an ordinary criminal offence has been made for the purpose of prosecuting or punishing a person on account of his race, religion, nationality, or political opinion, or that that person's position may be prejudiced for any of these reasons.[132]

Whereas Article 1 of the 1975 Additional Protocol to the European Convention on Extradition[133] excludes from 'political offences' the following:

[T]he crimes against humanity specified in the Convention on the Prevention and Punishment of the Crime of Genocide adopted on 9 December 1948 by the General Assembly of the United Nations.

[T]he violations specified in Article 50 of the 1949 Geneva Convention for the Amelioration of the Condition of the Wounded and Sick in Armed Forces in the Field; Article 51 of the 1949 Geneva Convention for the Amelioration of the Condition of the Wounded, Sick and Shipwrecked Members of Armed Forces at Sea; Article 130 of the 1949 Geneva Convention relative to the Treatment of Prisoners of War and Article 147 of the 1949 Geneva Convention relative to the Protection of Civilian Persons in Time of War.

[A]ny comparable violations of the laws of war having effect at the time when this Protocol enters into force and of customs of war existing at that time, which are not already provided for in the above-mentioned provisions of the Geneva Conventions.[134]

---

130 Article 1A2.
131 Article 1F.
132 See also Article 4 (4) of the Inter-American Convention on Extradition; or Article 4 (1) of the Economic Community of West African States Convention on Extradition.
133 Adopted in Strasbourg on 15 October, 1975.
134 In the same manner, Article 7 of the 1948 Genocide Convention and Article 4 of the 1951 Draft Code of Offences against the Peace and Security of Mankind exclude

Of utmost interest for South Africa is Article 11 of the Apartheid Convention of 1973, which excludes apartheid from the definition of 'political offence' for the purposes of extradition.

Although none of the documents referred to above understandably gives a specific definition of the concept of political offence,[135] they all converge in excluding serious international crimes from the scope of what may constitute a political offence. This trend has unfortunately not been followed by the South African amnesty law makers. However, one would hope that a strict application of the criteria adopted by the Amnesty Committee in determining the political character of the perpetrator's crime could by itself have excluded serious crimes from the purview of amnesty. This is because, as stated earlier, gravity and proportionality were retained as criteria against which to measure whether an act, omission or offence is associated with a political objective

Whereas the word 'gravity' connotes the seriousness of an act,[136] the notion of proportionality is used in a number of foreign extradition laws as a criterion to determine whether a particular act amounts to a political offence. For example, in interpreting Article 10 of the Swiss Extradition Act of 1892, which deals with politically motivated crimes, the Swiss Federal Court held in the *Ktir Case* that the murder of a rebel for treason against the Algerian government was not a political offence because there were alternative means of achieving the political purpose in question.[137] Similarly, in the *Della Savia Case*, the Swiss Federal Court held the view that acts of violence are not proportional to their political objective if:

> [They] result in gratuitous acts of violence which—because of their seriousness and their dangerousness—are repugnant to any civilised conscience, and amount to acts of indiscriminate and gratuitous terrorism.[138]

Neither the criterion of gravity nor that of proportionality can be said to have been properly applied by the South African Amnesty Committee. This argument may be evidenced by the verdict reached by the Committee in the case of Mr Benzien's amnesty application.

Mr Jeffrey Theodore Benzien is a former security police officer who appeared before the Amnesty Committee to seek amnesty for the crimes he had committed while employed by the apartheid internal security services. Before the Commission, he admitted of torturing his victims and demonstrated how they would be handcuffed

---

respectively genocide, war crimes, crimes against humanity and aggression from what they consider as political crimes for the purposes of extradition.

135   C. van den Wyngaert points to the elasticity of the concept of political offence, its functional character and its ambiguity which do not facilitate the adoption of a unanimous definition thereof, in *The Political Offence Exception to Extradition: The Delicate Problem of Balancing the Rights of the Individual and the International Public Order* (1980) at 95–159.

136   See the meaning of this word as connected to crimes against humanity in chapter II above.

137   Judgment of 17 May, 1961, 87 ATF I 134.

138   Judgment of 26 November, 1969, 95 ATF I 470.

and made to lie face down. Benzien would then sit on the victim's back, place a wet bag over the victim's head and tighten it around the neck as a method for extracting information. The former police officer also admitted to have shocked his victims with an electric device in the nose, ears, genitals and rectum.[139] After hearing Benzien's arguments, the Committee decided as follows:

> On a consideration of all the evidence, the Committee has come to the conclusion that the offences for which the applicant seeks amnesty were committed during and arose out of the conflicts of the past between the State and Liberation Movements.
>   Benzien is granted amnesty for:
>   Although there was no evidence of ill treatment and assault on Anwar Dramat or Alan Mamba, we are of the view that he should be given amnesty for assault and with intent to do grievous bodily harm on them and on Tony Yengeni, Gary Kruser, Peter Jacobs, Ashley Forbes and Niclo Pedro.[140]

Although some of the decisions reached by the Amnesty Committee are to be praised as being in conformity with the criteria set out in the Amnesty Act, the ruling in the Benzien case is far from conforming to the standards of gravity of the offences and of proportionality between the offence and the political objective pursued. It is doubtful whether Benzien could receive amnesty if the *Della Savia* approach had been adopted in his case. In addition, one can question the relevance of the 1984 Torture Convention to the Amnesty Committee's decision. In fact, Article 2 of the Torture Convention imposes on States the obligation to criminalize the practice of torture. It provides:

> Each State Party shall take effective legislative, administrative, judicial or other measures to prevent acts of torture in any territory under its jurisdiction.
>   No exceptional circumstances whatsoever, whether a state of war or a threat of war, internal political instability or any other public emergency, may be invoked as a justification of torture.
>   An order from a superior officer or a public authority may not be invoked as a justification of torture.

In addition, Article 4 obliges States to impose appropriate penalties on torturers, while Article 7 requires that States extradite or prosecute persons responsible for torture. More relevant to the Benzien case is the Appeals Chamber of the ICTY's interpretation of the Torture Convention which pointed to the fact that the prohibition against torture has reached the status of a *jus cogens* norm.[141] That is, an imperative or peremptory rule of international law for which there can be no derogation except by virtue of another rule of similar status. The Appeals Chamber further evaluated the legal status of an amnesty in respect of a *jus cogens* crime as follows:

> At the inter-State level, it serves to internationally de-legitimise any legislative, administrative or judicial act authorising torture. It would be senseless to argue, on the one

---

139 A. Krog, n. 1 at 76.
140 See Jeffrey T. Benzien Case No. AC/99/0027 (Amnesty Committee).
141 See *Prosecutor v. Furundzija*, chap. IV n. 80; see next chapter on the legal meaning of *jus cogens*.

hand, that on account of the jus cogens value of the prohibition against torture, treaties or customary rules providing for torture would be null and void ab initio, and then be unmindful of a State say, taking national measures authorising or condoning torture or absolving its perpetrators through an amnesty law. If such a situation were to arise, the national measures, violating the general principle and any relevant treaty provision, would produce legal effects discussed above and in addition would not be accorded international legal recognition.[142]

It is therefore clear from the provisions of the Torture Convention as interpreted by the Yugoslavia Tribunal that amnesty for torture would not be accepted. Whether South Africa was or was not a party to the Torture Convention at the time of the commission of the acts of torture for which amnesty was sought is irrelevant. The ICTY approach also contradicts the position held by the Cape Provincial Division in *AZAPO*, to the effect that a *jus cogens* did not constitute a limitation to the word 'amnesty' as contained in the post-amble of the Interim Constitution.

Summary

The South African experience shows how a country can struggle to reconcile political amnesty with its international legal obligations arising out of the prohibition against gross violations of human rights law and humanitarian law. It demonstrates that individual States are easily willing to accommodate amnesty within their national legal system and to prefer an interpretation that will help to achieve their political objectives of national reconciliation. In this sense, the South African amnesty was in conformity with South Africa's domestic law in that it was permitted by the Interim Constitution itself not only as an acceptable limitation to the fundamental rights entrenched in its Chapter 2, but also as a means of establishing a bridge between the past and the present. Similarly, the amnesty law was in conformity with South Africa's conventional obligations as they existed at the time the crimes for which amnesty was sought were committed. This is because, with the exception of the 1949 Geneva Conventions, apartheid South Africa was not Party to any major human rights or humanitarian law conventions. It did not adhere to the UDHR and was not Party to the ICCPR, the Genocide Convention, and the Torture Convention. The only remaining option was therefore customary international law, which the Cape Provincial Division as well as the Constitutional Court failed to adequately address.

Nevertheless, since the new political dispensation in 1994, South African Courts have adopted a line of interpretation which attributes a prominent status to international law, both customary and conventional. The Constitutional Court's interpretation in the *Makwanyane, Coetzee* and *Mhlungu Cases* are of this kind. The Cape Provincial Division's arguments that amnesty constitutes an exception to the peremptory norm of *jus cogens* and that an Act of Parliament can over-

---

142 *Furundzija* chap. IV, n. 80 at para. 155.

ride any *jus cogens* constitute therefore, a blow to the positive stance held in the Constitutional Court's previous rulings. The neglect to further explore the status of customary international law has led the courts to make unsatisfactory conclusions as to the legal relationship between amnesty and the crime against humanity of apartheid. This omission raises a fundamental issue that will constitute the main focus of the next chapter, and the crux of this volume; namely whether and to what extent international law permits amnesty for gross human rights violations in general, and for crimes against humanity in particular.

INTERNATIONAL LAW AND THE REJECTION OF THE AMNESTY EXCEPTION ARGUMENT

Introduction

Present international law provides general protection for certain core values and interests that are common to mankind as a whole. Such values, which form the *raison d'être* of the international community are enshrined in the texts of various international law instruments such as the Charter of the United Nations, the UDHR, the ICCPR, etc. However, certain international values and interests are so fundamental that their effective protection necessitates special arrangements aimed at punishing persons who trample them underfoot. Thus, acts of war crimes, aggression, terrorism, genocide, slavery, torture and crimes against humanity constitute criminal acts punishable under international law. These offences, generally referred to as *delicti jus gentium*, do not only constitute crimes under international law, but their prohibition is believed to have reached the status of *jus cogens* thereby imposing certain imperative obligations upon each State to be exercised in their own interest and in the interest of the international community as a whole.

This chapter examines crimes against humanity as an offence under international law (or as part of *delicti jus gentium*) and as a *jus cogens* crime. The aim here is to demonstrate that the characterisation of crimes against humanity as both an international crime and a peremptory norm produces one fundamental consequence: their prohibition does not permit any form of derogation, thereby constituting a profound limitation to the State's sovereign power to grant amnesty. On the basis of recent developments in international law and practice, it is argued that amnesty for crimes against humanity is legally invalid under international law.

Faustin Z. Ntoubandi, Amnesty for Crimes against Humanity under International Law, pp. 185–226.
© 2007, *Koninklijke Brill NV. Printed in The Netherlands.*

Crimes against Humanity as Delicti Jus Gentium

The very concept of *delicti jus gentium* connotes the existence of certain core values that are common to mankind and that are protected by both customary and conventional international law. Therefore, making crimes against humanity an offence under international law is fundamental for the survival of entire human groups and their prosecution is in the interest of all nations.

The Concept of Delicti Jus Gentium

Delicti jus gentium refers to offences against the law of nations, crimes against the law of mankind, or simply to international crimes.[1] The expression 'international crime' finds its source in the 1996 version of the International Law Commission's (ILC) Draft Articles on State Responsibility,[2] which provides in its Article 19 that:

1. An act of State which constitutes a breach of an international obligation is an internationally wrongful act, regardless of the subject matter of the obligation breached.
2. An internationally wrongful act which results from the breach by a State of an international obligation so essential for the protection of fundamental interests of the international community that its breach is recognised as a crime by the community as a whole constitutes an *international crime*.
3. Subject to paragraph 2, and on the basis of the rules of international law in force, an *international crime* may result, *inter alia*, from:
   (a) a serious breach of an international obligation of essential importance for the maintenance of international peace and security, such as that prohibiting aggression;
   (b) a serious breach of an international obligation of essential importance for safeguarding the right of self-determination of people, such as that prohibiting the establishment or maintenance by force of colonial domination;
   (c) a serious breach on a widespread scale of an international obligation of essential importance for safeguarding the human being, such as those prohibiting slavery, genocide and apartheid;
   (d) a serious breach of an international obligation of essential importance for the safeguarding and preservation of the human environment, such as those prohibiting massive pollution of the atmosphere or of the seas.
4. Any internationally wrongful act which is not an *international crime* in accordance with paragraph 2 constitutes an international delict.

---

1 J.M.C. Divino "Delicti Jus Gentium: A limitation on the State's power to grant amnesty" 40 *Ateneo Law Journal* (1995) at 202–250.
2 See text of the Draft Articles as provisionally adopted by the International Law Commission on first reading, available at www.javier-leon-diaz.com/humanitarianIssues/State_Resp. pdf; the modifications of this provision as introduced by the 2001 final version of the Draft Articles are dealt with in the next sections.

At least twenty-two offences are believed to exist as international crimes. These are: aggression, war crimes, unlawful use of weapons/unlawful emplacement of weapons, crimes against humanity, genocide, racial discrimination and apartheid, slavery and related crimes, torture, unlawful medical experimentation, piracy, aircraft hijacking, threat and use of force against internationally protected persons, taking of civilian hostages, drug offences, international traffic in obscene publications, destruction and/or theft of national treasures, environmental protection, theft of nuclear materials, unlawful use of the mails, interference with submarine cables, falsification and counterfeiting and bribery of foreign officials.[3]

International crimes or *delicti jus gentium* present three distinctive features. Firstly, the objective of prohibiting the commission of international crimes is the protection of human rights.[4] Secondly, international crimes are characterised by the presence of an international or trans-national element in their definition. Thirdly, the aggrieved party in the commission of *delicti jus gentium* is not the only immediate victim, but also the international community in its entirety.[5]

As regards the first feature, it is worth noting that the prohibition of international crimes aims at preventing actions by the State, through its officials, from depriving individuals of their fundamental rights and at requiring States to ensure that such rights are not violated by private individuals.[6] Since the end of World War II the protection of human rights has become a matter of international concern. This is reflected in various international human rights law and humanitarian law instruments adopted under the auspices the United Nations since 1945. Among these are the 1948 UDHR, the 1966 ICCPR, and the 1949 Geneva Conventions and their two Additional Protocols of 1977. The rationale behind the international protection of human rights is that certain forms of depredations become issues of international concern when committed under the aegis of State policies because of the presumed international impact of such behaviour. It is believed, therefore, that collective effort is required to protect against policies that may ultimately affect the entire international community.[7]

The second feature of *delicti jus gentium* requires the presence in their definition of an international or trans-national element. As far as the definition of the international element of international crimes is concerned, Divino argues that:

---

3 J.M.C. Divino, n. 1 at 218–219.
4 *Id.* at 219.
5 *Id.*
6 *Id.*
7 See M.C. Bassiouni and D.H. Derby "An appraisal of torture in international law and practice: the need for an international convention for the protection and suppression of torture" 48 *Revue Internationale de Droit Pénal* 17 (1977); see also J.M.C. Divino, n. 1 at 219, quoting V. Nanda.

> This element can be found in the very nature of the violative conduct, the target-victim, or in the impact. The international element can be defined by virtue of the impact of the conduct, which affects the collective security interests of the world community, or if by reason of the seriousness or and magnitude of the violative conduct, it constitutes a threat to the peace and security of human kind.[8]

On the other hand, the trans-national element only affects the interests of more than one State and is, therefore, more limited in its impact on world order than the international element.[9] Bassiouni is more specific on this question when he describes an international or trans-national element of a crime by mentioning that an international crime is an act which contains not only the elements of a common crime, but also the following five elements: it takes place in more than one State; it takes place where no State has exclusive jurisdiction; it affects internationally protected persons, i.e., diplomats and personnel of international organisations; and it affects internationally protected objects, e.g., international civil aviation and international means of communication.[10] On the other hand, as demonstrated in chapter II above, the definition of crimes against humanity as an international offence displays two fundamental requirements as far as its international element is concerned, namely the requirement of a 'widespread' or that of a 'systematic' attack against a civilian population.

Bassiouni shares the view that the terms 'widespread or systematic' are equivalent to the international element of crimes against humanity. He argues that the purpose of these terms is twofold: firstly, to eliminate spontaneous or uncontrolled group conflict from the scope of the crime; secondly, to reflect the existence of State action or policy by State actors, and the element of policy for non-State actors. He then goes on to explain that the terms 'widespread or systematic' characterise not only the manner in which the victimisation takes place, but also the very nature of the conduct and thus reflects the underlying policy that brought it about.[11] On the basis of their elements of widespreadness and systematicity, crimes against humanity are international crimes *per se* that fall within the ambit of the 1996 version of the ILC Draft Article 19 (3) (c), which includes slavery, genocide and apartheid in its definition of what amounts to an international crime.

However, the final version of the Draft Articles, adopted on second reading by the ILC in November 2001, and entitled Draft Articles on Responsibility of States for Internationally Wrongful Acts,[12] did not contain any mention of the term 'international crime'. It referred instead, only to 'serious breach' by a State of an obligation arising under a peremptory norm of general international law, which

---

8   See n. 1 at 221.
9   *Id.*
10 M.C. Bassiouni, *International Criminal Law: A Draft International Criminal Code* (1980) at 487.
11 M.C. Bassiouni, chap. III, n. 97 at 245.
12 See Official Records of the General Assembly 56th Sess. Supp. No. 10 (A/56/10) chap. IV.E.1.

must involve a gross or systematic failure by the responsible State to fulfil its international obligations.[13]

The third feature of *delicti jus gentium* is that the aggrieved party in the commission of such crimes is the international community as a whole. This consideration is expressed by the very definition of *delicti jus gentium*. These are, as already pointed out above, offences against the law of nations, crimes against the laws of mankind, *crimen contra omnes* as opposed to common offences which merely affect the sovereignty or the security of a particular State in which they have been committed. The commission of international crimes therefore affects the interests of all States. It constitutes an injury to mankind. Since all nations are victims of offences that constitute violations against mankind, all nations are consequently entitled to assume jurisdiction over such offences on behalf of the community of nations. Such jurisdiction is based on the theory of universal jurisdiction.

Delicti Jus Gentium *and Universal Jurisdiction*

In fact, international law recognises five theories of jurisdiction. These are: territorial jurisdiction, which is based on the place where the offence is committed; the active personality or nationality theory, which is linked to the nationality of the offender, the passive personality theory, which is based on the nationality of the victim; the protective theory, which is based on the interest affected; and the universality theory which is based on the international character of the offence.[14]

The theory of universal jurisdiction finds its roots in the 1600's customary international practice according to which pirates and brigands were considered *hostis humani generis* or enemies of all mankind over whom any State could assert jurisdiction.[15] It is generally admitted that the establishment of universal jurisdiction over pirates stemmed from the fact that pirates perpetrated their criminal trade on the high seas, which were outside the territorial jurisdiction of any State. In fact, the high seas were jurisdictionally regarded as a *res omnium communes* belonging to all nations. Judge Moore endorsed this view in his dissenting opinion in the *Lotus Case*[16] when he stated that:

> [A]s the scene of the pirate's operations is the high seas, which is not the right or duty of any nation to police, he is denied the protection of the flag which he may carry, and is treated as an outlaw, as the enemy of all mankind—*hostis humani generis*—whom any nation may in the interest of all capture and punish.[17]

---

13 Article 40 (1) and (2).
14 M.C. Bassiouni, chap. III, n. 97 at 227.
15 *Id.* at 229–233.
16 *The Lotus Case* (*France v. Turkey*) PCIJ 7 September, 1927, Ser A (Judgments) No. 10 (Judgment No. 9) (1927).
17 Text available at www.worldcourts.com/pcij/eng/decisions/1927.09.07_lotus/dissent_more. htm.

However, due to the atrocities committed during World War II, the criterion for the application of universal jurisdiction has shifted from the locality of the commission of the crime (the high seas) to the heinous nature of the crime committed, thus extending this principle in scope. According to Bassiouni the extension of the principle of universal jurisdiction to war crimes and to crimes against humanity was confirmed by the proceedings before the IMT and before the subsequent post-World War II Tribunals. The argument of this author is based on the following comment contained in the IMT judgement:

> The Signatory Powers created this Tribunal, defined the law it was to administer, and made regulations for the proper conduct of the Trial. In doing so, they have done together what any one of them might have done singly; for it is not to be doubted that any nation has the right to set up special courts to administer law.[18]

This author suggests that reference made in this comment that 'any nation' has the right to set up special tribunals to prosecute the Charter's crimes (namely: war crimes, crimes against peace, and crimes against humanity) connotes universal jurisdiction for the said-crimes.[19]

As far as subsequent prosecutions in connection with World War II are concerned, it is remarkable to note that the principle of universality was heavily relied upon by the Allied Powers to prosecute violations of the Charter's crimes. The following pronouncements in various prosecutions pursuant to Control Council Law No. 10 are instructive in this regard.

In *The Hostages Case*,[20] many German officers were charged with the killing of hundreds of thousands of civilian hostages. The tribunal explained the universal character of such crimes in the following terms:

> An international crime is [...] an act universally recognised as criminal, which is considered a grave matter of international concern and for some valid reason cannot be left within the exclusive jurisdiction of the state that would have control over it under ordinary circumstances.[21]

Likewise, *In re Eisenträger and Others*,[22] The United States Military Commission declared that:

> A war crime [...] is not a crime against the law or criminal code of any individual nation, but a crime against the *jus gentium*. The laws and usages of war are of universal application, and do not depend for their existence upon national laws and frontiers. Arguments to the effects that only a sovereign of the *locus criminis* has jurisdiction and that only the *lex loci* can be applied are therefore without foundation.[23]

---

18 See IMT *Reports*, chap. III, n. 50 at 461.
19 M.C. Bassiouni, chap. III, n. 97 at 236.
20 *U.S.A v. Von List and Others* 11 *Trials of War Criminals Before the Nuremberg Military Tribunal Under Control Council Law No. 10, Oct. to Apr. 1949*, 757 (1950).
21 *Id.* at 1241.
22 14 *Law Reports of Trials of War Criminals* 8 (1949), US Military Command, Shanghai (1947).
23 *Id.* at 15.

More pertinent to the application of the theory of universal jurisdiction to war crimes and to crimes against humanity is the argument raised by the Israeli courts in the *Eichmann Case*.[24] The accused in this instance was prosecuted for, among others, war crimes and crimes against humanity. These crimes were all committed during or in connection with World War II, in which Israel was not a belligerent. The State of Israel did not even exist then. However, the Israeli courts declared themselves competent to try the accused for his alleged offences, and examined the basis of the State of Israel's jurisdiction over the alleged offender in the following way. The District Court of Jerusalem:

> The State of Israel's 'right to punish' the accused derives [...] from two cumulative sources: a universal source (pertaining to the whole mankind) which vests the right to prosecute and punish crimes of this order in every State within the family of nations; and a specific national source, which gives the victim nation the right to try any who assault their existence.[25]

Following the same line of argument, the Israeli Supreme Court declared on appeal that:

> [T]here is full justification for applying here the principle of universal jurisdiction since the international character of 'crimes against humanity' [...] dealt with in this instant case is no longer in doubt [...] the basic reason for which international law recognises the right of each State to exercise such jurisdiction in piracy offences—notwithstanding the fact that its own sovereignty does not extend to the scene of the commission of the offence [...] and the offender is a national of another State or is stateless—applies with even greater force to the above mentioned crimes.[26]
>
> Not only do all the crimes attributed to the appellant bear an international character, but their harmful and murderous effects were as embracing and widespread as to shake the international community to its very foundations. The State of Israel therefore was entitled, pursuant to the principle of universal jurisdiction and in the capacity of a guardian of international law and an agent for its enforcement, to try the appellant. That being the case, no importance attaches to the fact that the State of Israel did not exist when the offences were committed.[27]

Meanwhile, in the *Barbie Case*,[28] the accused's claim that he had been victim of disguised extradition was dismissed by the French *Court de Cassation* in the following manner:

> [B]y reason of their nature, the crimes against humanity [...] do not simply fall within the scope of French municipal law but are subject to an international criminal order to which the notions of frontier and extradition rules arising therefrom are completely foreign.[29]

---

24 See chap. I, n. 23.
25 *Id.* at 50.
26 *Id.* at 299.
27 *Id.* at 304.
28 See chap. III, n. 44.
29 *Id.* at 130.

More recently, the ICTY endorsed the theory of universal jurisdiction for crimes against humanity and grave breaches of the Geneva Conventions. A Trial Chamber of the *Tadic Case*[30] remarked that:

> [T]he crimes which the International Tribunal has been called upon to try are not crimes of a purely domestic nature. They are really crimes which are universal in nature, well recognised in international law as serious breaches of international humanitarian law, and transcending the interest of any one State. The Trial Chamber agrees that in such circumstances, the sovereign rights of States cannot and should not take precedence over the right of the international community to act appropriately as they affect the whole of mankind and shock the conscience of all nations in the world. There can therefore be no objections to an international tribunal properly constituted trying these crimes on behalf of the international community.[31]

The Appeals Chamber confirmed this approach in its subsequent decision on the Defence Motion for Interlocutory Appeal on Jurisdiction[32] when it declared that:

> Borders should not be considered as a shield against the reach of the law and as a protection for those who trample underfoot the most elementary rights of humanity.[33]

The Nuremberg Tribunal's interpretation of the provisions of the Charter as well as post-Charter legal documents and interpretations, lead to the conclusion that crimes against humanity as international offences of serious character are subject to universal jurisdiction. Such crimes threaten the social and legal foundation of humanity as a whole. Therefore, like it happened in former times with pirates and brigands, all States are entitled to prosecute criminals against humanity. Since the right to prosecute crimes against humanity is equally vested in all nations, no individual State, which does not want to exercise its jurisdictional rights in respect of such offences, can validly grant an amnesty to the perpetrators thereof. Such an amnesty would only amount to a waiver of that State's rights to prosecute. However, such an abstention from prosecution does not affect other State's rights to exercise jurisdiction, based on universality, in respect of the crimes which have been amnestied.

As mentioned at the outset, there exist at least twenty-two international crimes. Whereas the commission of any of the known international crimes negatively affects the interests of the international community as a whole, one shall bear in mind that there are some crimes whose gravity and seriousness have the potential to shake the conscience of mankind in its very foundation. The prohibition of such crimes stems therefore from the necessity to protect certain higher values and interests, which are fundamental to mankind at large. An outline of such values

---

30 *Prosecutor v. Dusko Tadic*, A/K/A "Dule" Decision on the Defence Motion on Jurisdiction of 10 August, 1995.
31 See para. 42.
32 See *Prosecutor v. Dusko Tadic*, chap. V, n. 37.
33 At para. 58.

and interests is provided by the Charter of the United Nations,[34] the UDHR[35] and the ICCPR.[36]

Values and Interests Protected by the Prohibition of Crimes against Humanity as Delicti Jus Gentium and their Consequences on Amnesty

Divino assumes that the prohibition of *delicti jus gentium* seeks generally to protect human rights, which are embodied in the UDHR and the ICCPR.[37] These two instruments are considered by many commentators as an expression of international custom, and therefore binding on all States.[38] Among the human rights protected by the international proscription of crimes, Bassiouni identifies the following, which are contained in the UDHR and in the ICCPR as well: right to equal treatment; right to life, liberty, and personal security; freedom from slavery and forced labour; right to be free from torture and from cruel, inhuman, or degrading treatment or punishment; recognition as a person before the law; freedom from arbitrary arrest or detention; freedom of opinion, expression and association; right to a fair criminal trial; freedom of movement; right to family; right to property; and freedom of religion.[39] The massive and systematic violations of some of these human rights amount to crimes against humanity under both conventional and customary law.

Crimes against Humanity in Conventional International Law and their Consequences on Amnesty

A substantial number of international instruments regulate conduct that fall within the sphere of crimes against humanity. Among them are: the London Charter of 1946, the Apartheid Convention of 1973, the Genocide Convention of 1948, the Hostages Convention of 1979,[40] the Torture Convention of 1984, the ICTY Statute of 1993, the ICTR Statute of 1994, the Draft Code of Crimes against the Peace and

---

34   Signed at San Francisco on 26 June, 1945, 59 Stat. 1031 TS 993, 3 Bevans 1153.

35   See chap. III, n. 168.

36   See chap. IV, n. 141.

37   See n. 1 at 223.

38   In the *Namibia Case* e.g., Judge Ammoun stated in his separate opinion that: "the provisions of the Universal Declaration of Human Rights [...] can bind States on the basis of custom within the meaning of paragraph 1(b) of [Article 38 of the Statute of the International Court of Justice], whether because they constituted a codification of customary law, as was said in respect of Article 6 of the Vienna Convention of the Law of Treaties, or because they have acquired the force of custom through a general practice of law, in the words of Article 38, paragraph 1 (b), of the Statute." *ICJ Report* (1971) at 16; see also JMC Divino, n. 1 at 225.

39   See n. 10 at 19–24.

40   International Convention against the Taking of Hostages, adopted on 17 December, 1979 by GA Res. 34/146.

Security of Mankind of 1996 and the Rome Statute of the ICC of 1998.[41] These treaties criminalise, under specific context and circumstances, war crimes; crimes against humanity; acts of genocide, conspiracy to commit genocide, attempt to commit genocide and complicity in genocide; murder; extermination; enslavement; deportation; imprisonment; torture; persecutions on political, racial or religious grounds; apartheid; forced disappearances; rape, sexual slavery, enforced prostitution, forced pregnancy, enforced sterilisation, or any other form of sexual violence of comparative gravity.[42]

Of particular significance to crimes against humanity are the values protected by the Genocide Convention, the Torture Convention[43] and the ICC Statute. These documents are significant to crimes against humanity in that, they deal with particularly heinous crimes that can be committed both in time of peace and in time of war; and, depending on the circumstances of their commission, genocide, torture and any other crime within the Rome Statute can become a crime against humanity when the conditions of its existence are met.

The Genocide Convention

The Genocide Convention puts strong emphasis on punishment as the most appropriate deterrent against the commission of acts of genocide. In this regard, Article 4 of this Convention provides that persons who conspire or attempt to commit genocide, together with accomplices or direct perpetrators of genocide, shall be punished irrespective of whether they are constitutionally responsible rulers, public officials or private individuals. In addition, under Article 1, Parties to this Convention confirm the international criminal character of genocide irrespective of the context of its commission and undertake to prevent and punish it. The main value protected by the criminalisation of genocide is that of safeguarding the natural right of existence of particular groups. This rationale was clearly emphasised in a 1946 proclamation by the General Assembly of the United Nations, when it stated that the crime of genocide is:

---

41 See M.C. Bassiouni, chap. III, n. 97 at 177–207; see also B. Chigara, chap. VI, n. 81 at 85.

42 B. Chigara, chap. VI, n. 81 at 86.

43 The Genocide Convention and the Torture Convention are linked to crimes against humanity in one way or another: whereas torture, when perpetrated in a widespread or systematic manner falls within the meaning of the crime against humanity of "inhumane acts", genocide, when committed without the required intent to destroy, in whole or in part, a national, ethnic, racial, or religious group as such, may well amount to a crime against humanity of persecution or extermination; in addition, some commentators argue that genocide is a special kind of crime against humanity, while others hold the view that crimes against humanity was given the name genocide in a post-war treaty, see e.g., B.V.A. Röling, The law of war and the national jurisdiction since 1945, in 100 *Recueil des Cours* (1960 II) at 330.

[A] denial of the right to existence of entire human groups [such denial which] shocks the conscience of mankind, results in great losses to humanity in the form of cultural and other contributions represented by these human groups, and is contrary to moral law and the spirit and aims of the United Nations.[44]

The same principles were later reiterated by the ICJ in its Advisory Opinion on *Reservations to the Genocide Convention*, which, in addition, restated the customary law character of the prohibition of genocide:

> The origins of the Convention show that it was the intention of the United Nations to condemn and punish genocide as 'a crime under international law' involving a denial of the right of existence of entire human groups, a denial which shocks the conscience of mankind and result in great losses to humanity, and which is contrary to moral law and to the spirit and aims of the United Nations. The first consequence arising from this conception is that the principles underlying the Convention are principles which are recognised by civilised nations as binding on States, even without any conventional obligation.[45]

It appears therefore that the Genocide Convention would preclude any form of national amnesty, which is intended to prevent the realisation of the main purpose of the Convention, namely, the prosecution and punishment of perpetrators as the most effective deterrent measures against the commission of acts of genocide. Moreover, any grant of amnesty for acts of genocide would run counter to the binding principles underlying the Convention. However, although the Genocide Convention does not expressly provide for universal jurisdiction[46] it is believed that this may be implied from its nature as a *jus cogens* prohibition.[47]

The Torture Convention

Like the Genocide Convention, the 1984 Torture Convention insists on the legal resolution of cases of torture. As mentioned earlier on in chapter four, Article 1 of this Convention defines torture as any act by which severe pain or suffering, whether physical or mental is intentionally inflicted on a person for such purposes as obtaining from him or a third person information or a confession, punishing him for an act he or a third person has committed or is suspected of having committed, or intimidating or coercing him or a third person, when such pain or suffering is inflicted by or at the instigation of or with the consent or acquiescence of a public official or other person acting in an official capacity.

---

44 GA Res. 96 (1) UN GAOR, 1st Sess. Part II, UN Doc A/64/Add 1 (1947).
45 *ICJ Reports*, chap. V, n. 165 at 14, 23; see also *Case Concerning the Application of the Convention on the Prevention and Punishment of the Crime of Genocide* (*Bosnia and Herzegovina v. Yugoslavia* (Serbia and Montenegro)) ICJ (1993) 1 (8 April).
46 In terms of Article 5 of the Genocide Convention, the jurisdiction over genocide is restricted territorially, except in the case of an international criminal court being established.
47 See J.D. van der Vyver "Prosecution and punishment of the crime of genocide" 23 *Fordham International Law Journal* 2 (1999) at 287.

Article 2 (1) of the Torture Convention directs States Parties to take effective legislative, administrative, judicial or other measures to prevent acts of torture in any territory under their jurisdiction, while Article 2 (2) excludes all forms of derogations from the punishment of torturers either in peace time or in period of war. It stipulates in this respect that:

> No exceptional circumstances whatsoever, whether a state of war or a threat of war, internal political instability or any other public emergency, may be invoked as a justification of torture.

In addition, States Parties to the Torture Convention must ensure that acts of torture are criminalised under their domestic criminal law, and that appropriate penalties are inflicted on torturers.[48] More important is Article 5, which establishes the principle of *aut dedere aut judicare* over the crime of torture. Each State Party to the Convention is thus directed under Article 5 (1) to establish its jurisdiction over offences of torture, whereas Article 5 (2) makes sure that such jurisdiction is exercised over the alleged offender who is present in any territory under the Party's jurisdiction, in case such a Party elects not to extradite him.

The proscription of acts of torture is intended to safeguard certain essential principles, which are already contained in other international documents. In this regard, the Preamble to the Torture Convention refers to the United Nations Charter's principle of equal and inalienable rights of all members of the human family as the foundation of freedom, justice and peace in the world.[49] Such rights, in terms of the Preamble, derive from the inherent dignity of the human person and States are under the obligation to promote universal respect for, and observance of, human rights and fundamental freedoms. The preamble goes on to recall that torture is already condemned under the UDHR, the ICCPR, and under General Assembly Resolution 3452 (XXX) of 9 December, 1975 on the Declaration on the Protection of All Persons from Being Subjected to Torture and Other Cruel, Inhuman or Degrading Treatment. Furthermore, the preamble specifies the purpose of the Convention, which is to make more effective the struggle against torture and other cruel, inhuman or degrading treatment or punishment throughout the world.

Therefore, the Torture Convention seeks to effectively tackle the issue of severe mistreatment of persons by State's authorities throughout the world. The nature of State's obligations in respect of the proscription of torture is so compelling that no exceptional situation can justify recourse to torture. The grave nature of this crime was thoroughly examined in the judgements of the ICTY. For instance, in *Furundzija*,[50] the Tribunal linked torture to other crimes of similar gravity such as violations of common Article 3 of the Geneva Conventions of 1949, and Article 4 of Additional Protocol II of 1977, which both prohibit torture.[51] It went on to explain that depending upon the specific circumstances of each case, torture may

---

48 Articles 4 (1) and (2) of the Torture Convention.
49 Preamble to the UN Draft Convention against Torture, chap. III, n. 201 at 1027.
50 See chap. IV, n. 80.
51 *Id.* at para. 135.

be prosecuted as serious violations of humanitarian law, grave breaches of the Geneva Conventions, crimes against humanity or genocide.[52] Therefore, under current international law, the torturer has become, like the pirate and the slave trader before him, *hostis humani generis*, an enemy of all mankind.[53]

The prohibition of torture as laid down in human rights treaties enshrines an absolute right which can never be derogated from, not even in time of war or public emergency. In this sense, rules prohibiting torture are considered to have reached a particularly higher status in international law, namely that of *jus cogens*,[54] a status similar to the status of those principles that prohibit genocide, slavery, racial discrimination, aggression, the acquisition of territory by force and the forcible suppression of the right of peoples to self-determination.[55] The Trial Chamber in *Furundzija* confirmed this approach when it stated that the prohibition against torture displays three important features: it covers potential breaches, it imposes obligations *erga omnes*, and it has acquired the status of *jus cogens*.[56]

As far as the first feature is concerned States are under the obligation not only to prohibit and punish torture, but also to forestall its occurrence. Consequently, they are bound to put in place all those measures that may pre-empt the perpetration of torture.[57] To reach this conclusion, the Tribunal relied on an authoritative ruling of the European Court of Human Rights in the *Soering Case* where the Court held that international law intends to bar not only actual breaches but also potential breaches of the prohibition against torture. The Tribunal then extended the interpretation of the European Court so as to include within the scope of the prohibition of torture, any failure to adopt the national measures necessary for implementing the prohibition and the maintenance in force or passage of laws which are contrary to the prohibition.[58]

The second feature of the prohibition on torture is that it imposes obligations *erga omnes*.[59] These are obligations owed by each State to all other members of the international community, each of which possesses a correlative right.[60]

As regards the third feature of the prohibition against torture, the Yugoslavia Tribunal stated that the importance of the values protected by the proscription of torture justifies its elevation to the status of peremptory norms or *jus cogens*,[61] that is, norms that enjoy "a higher rank in the international hierarchy than treaty law and even 'ordinary' customary rules."[62] The immediate consequence of a *jus cogens*

---

52 *Id.* at para. 141.
53 See a United States court's statement in *Filartiga v. Pena-Irala*, 630F 2d 876 (2d Cir 1980).
54 See *Furundzija*, chap. IV, n. 80 at para. 153.
55 *Id.* at para. 147.
56 See paras 148–158.
57 *Id.* at para. 148.
58 *Id.* at paras 148–150.
59 This concept is further elaborated in the following section on *jus cogens*.
60 *Furundzija*, chap. IV n. 80 at para. 151.
61 This concept is thoroughly examined below.
62 *Furundzija*, at para. 153.

norm is that it cannot be derogated from by States through international treaties, or local or special customs, or even through general customary rules not endowed with the same normative force.[63] On the basis of the peremptory character of the proscription of torture, the Tribunal went on to make two important pronouncements, which do not only exclude any form of amnesty for acts of torture, but also establish the legal basis for universal jurisdiction for torture. In relation to amnesty the Trial Chamber stated that:

> At the inter-state level, it [the *jus cogens* prohibition on torture] serves to internationally de-legitimise any legislative, administrative or judicial act authorising torture. It would be senseless to argue, on the one hand, that on account of the *jus cogens* value of the prohibition against torture, treaties or customary rules providing for torture would be null and void *ab initio*, and then be unmindful of a State say, taking national measures authorising or condoning torture or absolving its perpetrators through an amnesty law. If such a situation were to arise, the national measures, violating the general principle and any relevant treaty provision, would produce the legal effects discussed above and in addition would not be accorded international legal recognition.[64]

The Trial Chamber went on to address the issue of universal jurisdiction for torture in the following way:

> [E]very State is entitled to investigate, prosecute and punish or extradite individuals accused of torture, who are present in a territory under its jurisdiction. Indeed, it would be inconsistent on the one hand to prohibit torture to such an extent as to restrict the normally unfettered treaty-making power of sovereign States, and on the other hand bar States from prosecuting and punishing those torturers who have engaged in this odious practice abroad. This legal basis for State's universal jurisdiction over torture bears out and strengthens the legal foundation for such jurisdiction found by other courts in the inherently universal character of the crime.[65]

Other consequences that flow from the Trial Chamber's findings are that, like crimes against humanity and war crimes,[66] torture may not be covered by a statute of limitations and may not constitute a political offence exception for the purpose of extradition.[67]

The latter consequence of torture was extensively dealt with by the House of Lords in the *Pinochet Case*.[68] This case started with the arrest and detention of Senator Pinochet by the English authorities pursuant to an extradition warrant issued by a Spanish judge. In fact, Senator Pinochet, President of Chile between September 1973 and March 1990, stepped down from power after having granted a sweeping amnesty to himself and to other members of his military regime. While in the United Kingdom in 1998 for medical treatment, a Spanish court issued a

---

63 *Id.*
64 *Id.* at para. 155.
65 *Id.* at para. 156.
66 See Convention on the Non-Applicability of Statutory Limitations to War Crimes and Crimes against Humanity, chap. I, n. 17.
67 *Furundzija*, at para. 157.
68 See chap. III, n. 173.

provisional arrest warrant seeking his extradition to Spain in order to be prosecuted there for certain crimes allegedly committed in Chile under his dictatorship. He was accused, among other things, of genocide, murder on a large scale, torture, and the taking of hostages.[69] The fundamental issue to determine in this case was whether, as a former Head of State, Pinochet was entitled to immunity from arrest and extradition proceedings in the United Kingdom in respect of the crimes alleged to have been committed whilst he was head of State. The High Court before which the question of State immunity was first raised held that Senator Pinochet, in his capacity as former Head of State, was entitled to immunity from the criminal process. Consequently, he could not be extradited to Spain. Spain challenged this decision before the British Appellate Committee and on 24 March, 1999 the Appellate Committee, by a majority of six to one, handed down its decision in favour of Spain.[70] This decision allowed the extradition proceedings against Pinochet to proceed on allegations of acts of torture and conspiracy of torture. In so deciding, the Lords of Appeal established a principle of international law according to which former Heads of State are not immune from criminal process for the international crime of torture. This principle was based on the rationale that by signing the Torture Convention, States Parties have agreed from the time of signing, that immunity no longer applied in respect of the official acts of a former Head of State that amounted to an international crime.[71]

What is remarkable in the *Pinochet Case* is the fact that the majority law Lords did not even find it necessary to deal with amnesty which Pinochet granted to himself. Only Lord Browne-Wilkinson of the Appellate Committee slightly referred to it when he wrote that:

> For example, in this case it is alleged that during the Pinochet regime torture was an official, although unacknowledged, weapon of government and that, when the regime was about to end, it passed legislation designed to afford an amnesty to those who had engaged in institutionalised torture. If these allegations are true, the fact that the local court had jurisdiction to deal with the international crime of torture was nothing to the point so long as the totalitarian regime remained in power: a totalitarian regime will not permit adjudication by its own courts on its own shortcomings. Hence the demand for some international machinery to repress state torture which is not dependent upon the local courts where the torture was committed.[72]

This comment tends not only to reject the validity of amnesty for torture granted under Pinochet, but also to point out the inability of domestic courts to deal effectively with cases of torture when the perpetrators thereof still hold powerful positions in governmental institutions. This remark is important in that torture is

---

69 *Regina v. Bartle and the Commissioner of Police for the Metropolis and Others Ex Parte Pinochet* 37 *ILM* 1302 (1998).
70 See chap. III, n. 173 at 595, 609, 627, 641, 643, 652, and 663.
71 See C. Nicholls "Reflections on Pinochet" 41 *Virginia Journal of International Law* (2000) at 145; see also the opinion of Lord Browne-Wilkinson in *Pinochet*, chap. III, n. 173 at 595.
72 See chap. III, n. 173 at 590.

itself an act usually perpetrated under the colour of official authority, hence the urgency of the establishment of international mechanisms of repression as the most appropriate means to respond to this crime.

The Rome Statute of the International Criminal Court

Adopted on 17 December, 1998 the Rome Statute is the most recent international document outlawing the commission of the most serious crimes in international law. It entered into force on 1 July, 2002 after the 60th instrument of ratification was deposited.[73] The Rome Statute establishes the first permanent international judicial system designed to complement national judicial systems in the prosecution of the offences of genocide, crimes against humanity, war crimes and aggression when national judicial systems are unable or unwilling to do so.[74] It is worth mentioning at this point that the Rome Statute provides the most complete definition to date of crimes against humanity and of genocide.

The notion of crimes against humanity as crystallised in Article 7 of the Statute takes into account the developments that started during the proceedings before the Nuremberg tribunals and that culminated in the deliberations before the *ad hoc* tribunals of the former Yugoslavia and of Rwanda. A few new crimes have been added to the traditionally known acts of crimes against humanity. Among the added new crimes, are rape and forced pregnancy as developed by the ICTY. On the other hand, sexual slavery and enforced prostitution, which were not punished under both the Nuremberg and the Tokyo Charters, have become crimes against humanity in their own right. According to Robertson Q.C., the inclusion of these two crimes within the jurisdiction of the ICC is a belated recognition of the Japanese army's enslavement of 'comfort women' from Taiwan and Korea to service its soldiers during World War II.[75] The status of apartheid as a crime against humanity is confirmed in Article 7 (1) (j). Maybe the only alarming provision relating to crimes against humanity is Article 7 (3). In fact Article 7 (1) (h) introduces the crime of persecution on grounds of gender, whereas Article 7 (3) defines gender in the following manner:

> For the purpose of this Statute, it is understood that the term 'gender' refers to the two sexes, male and female, within the context of society. The term 'gender' does not indicate any meaning different from above.

---

73 In terms of Article 126 of the Rome Statute, the Statute shall enter into force on the first day of the month after the 60th day following the date of the deposit of the 60th instrument of ratification, acceptance, approval or accession with the Secretary-General of the United Nations; in accordance with this Article, the 60th instrument of ratification was deposited on 11 April, 2002.

74 See Article 17 of the Rome Statute.

75 G. Robertson Q.C. *Crimes against Humanity: The Struggle for Global Justice* (1999) at 313.

Commentators are preoccupied that this clause provides a leeway to discriminate against lesbians, homosexuals and transsexuals and does not afford protection to these groups in case of large scale persecution.[76]

Nevertheless, crimes against humanity are defined in the Rome Statute as any of the following acts when committed as part of a widespread or systematic attack directed against any civilian population, with the knowledge of the attack: murder; extermination; enslavement; deportation or forcible transfer of population; imprisonment or other severe deprivation of physical liberty in violation of fundamental rules of international law; torture; rape, sexual slavery, enforced prostitution, forced pregnancy, enforced sterilization, or any other form of sexual violence of comparable gravity; persecution against any identifiable group or collectivity on political, racial, national, ethnic, cultural, religious, gender, or other grounds that are universally recognised as impermissible under international law, in connection with any act referred to in this paragraph or any crime within the jurisdiction of the Court; enforced disappearance of persons; the crime of apartheid; other inhumane acts of a similar character intentionally causing great suffering, or serious injury to body or to mental or physical health.[77]

The definition of genocide, which is also a manifestation of crimes against humanity,[78] is taken verbatim from the Genocide Convention of 1948. That is, any of the following acts committed with intent to destroy, in whole or in part, a national, ethnical, racial or religious group, as such: killing members of the group; causing serious bodily or mental harm to members of the group; deliberately inflicting on the group conditions of life calculated to bring about its physical destruction in whole or in part; imposing measures intended to prevent births within the group; forcibly transferring children of the group to another group.[79] Like the Genocide Convention, the Rome Statute did not find it necessary to include political and social groups within the meaning of 'group' for the purpose of genocide.

As far as the guiding values of the Rome Statute are concerned, the Preamble provides, among other things, as follows:

> Recognising that such grave crimes threaten the peace, security and well-being of the world,
>
> Affirming that the most serious crimes of concern to the international community as a whole must not go unpunished and that their effective prosecution must be ensured by taking measures at the national level and by enhancing international cooperation,
>
> Determined to put an end to impunity for the perpetrators of these crimes and thus to contribute to the prevention of such crimes,
>
> Recalling that it is the duty of every State to exercise its criminal jurisdiction over those responsible for international crimes,

---

76   *Id.* at 314.
77   See Article 7 of the Rome Statute and Article II of the Genocide Convention of 1948.
78   See M.C. Bassiouni, chap. III, n. 97 at 203.
79   See Article 6 of the Rome Statute.

> Emphasising that the International Criminal Court established under this Statute shall be complementary to national criminal jurisdictions,
>
> [....]

The words used in the preambular statements make it conspicuous that the main objects and goals of the Rome Statute are to put an end to the culture of impunity[80] for serious violations of human rights, through criminal prosecution of the most serious crimes of international concern. In this way, the Preamble stands as a reliable source for the interpretation of the provisions of the Statute. The question that comes to mind is whether such an imperative of punishment makes room for any sort of derogation in the form of amnesty, in respect to the crimes listed in the Statute.

Any attempt to address this issue invites to look into certain provisions of the Rome Statute that might be interpreted as either allowing the Court, under certain specific circumstances, to accept national amnesties, or as totally forbidding any recognition of amnesty. Such provisions are linked to the exercise of jurisdiction by both the ICC and national criminal jurisdictions. Among them are Article 16 dealing with deference of investigation or prosecution by the Security Council, Article 17 dealing with the issue of complementarity, and Article 53 relating to the matter of prosecutorial discretion.

The jurisdiction of the ICC is narrow in scope and is based on the express acceptance of States.[81] Articles 12 and 13 of the Rome Statute envisage three situations in which the ICC may exercise its jurisdiction with respect to a crime. Firstly, the matter may be referred to it by a State Party. Such a State Party must either be the one on the territory of which the conduct in question occurred, or the one of which the accused is a national. The jurisdiction of the ICC may also, in terms of Article 12 (3), extend to non-Parties to the Rome Statute which have accepted its jurisdiction. Secondly, a matter may be referred to the ICC by the Security Council acting under Chapter VII of the United Nations Charter. In this case, special deference to the national choices of the State concerned is not necessary, since a Security Council decision under Chapter VII of the Charter entails that

---

80 Many notorious criminals who have committed some of the most serious atrocities in the last two decades have still never been punished; these include alleged human rights offenders such as Pinochet, Hissen Habre, Charles Taylor (his trial began on 4 June, 2007 before the Special Court for Sierra Leone, which has been relocated in The Hague for this specific case), those who founded and implemented apartheid in Southern Africa, as well as members of the Indonesian Army Militia which systematically organized the killings of East Timorese in 1999 for rejecting unity with Indonesia. On impunity for gross human rights violations, see e.g., C. Bongiorno "A culture of impunity" 33 *Columbia Human Rights Law Review* 3 (2002), pp. 623–692; C.C. Joyner (ed.), *Reining in Impunity for International Crimes and Serious Violations of Fundamental Human Rights* (1998); E. Popoff "Inconsistency and impunity in international human rights law" 33 *George Washington International Law Review* 2 (2001), pp. 363–395.

81 See D. Robinson "Serving the interests of justice: amnesties, truth commissions and the International Criminal Court" 14 *European Journal of International Law* 3 (2003) at 485.

the situation is a threat to international peace and security, and makes compliance by all States mandatory under the United Nations Charter.[82] Finally, the ICC may exercise jurisdiction if the Prosecutor has initiated an investigation in respect of the crimes concerned.

The relationship between the ICC and national criminal jurisdictions is governed by paragraph 10 of the Preamble, Article 1 and Article 17 of the Rome Statute. These provisions define a relationship between the ICC and national criminal courts based on the principle of complementarity. The Preamble and Article 1 give priority of jurisdiction to national criminal courts in that the exercise of the ICC jurisdiction is only complementary to that of national courts. However, Article 17 which deals with issues of admissibility introduces a limit on the ICC as well as on States' freedom to deal with criminal cases under the Rome Statute. In terms of Article 17 (1) the jurisdiction of the ICC is excluded in the following situations: a) where the case is being investigated or prosecuted by a State which has jurisdiction over it; b) if after investigation, the State concerned elects not to prosecute the person concerned; c) where the person concerned has already been properly tried for conduct which is the subject of the complaint; and d) where the case is not of sufficient gravity to justify further action by the Court. Nevertheless, if it is clear from situations (a) and (b) that the competent State is unwilling or unable genuinely to carry out investigation or prosecution, the ICC shall exercise its jurisdiction.

Article 17 (2) introduces certain criteria that will help the ICC to determine a State's unwillingness to prosecute. In so doing, the Court shall consider whether one or more of the following exist:

(a) The proceedings were or are being undertaken or the national decision was made for the purpose of shielding the person concerned from criminal responsibility for crimes within the jurisdiction of the Court referred to in article 5;
(b) There has been an unjustified delay in the proceedings which in the circumstances is inconsistent with intent to bring the person concerned to justice;
(c) The proceedings were not or are not being conducted independently or impartially, and they were or are being conducted in a manner which, in the circumstances, is inconsistent with intent to bring the person concerned to justice.

The definition of amnesty as given in the preceding chapters of this book demonstrates that the very essence of amnesty is oblivion or forgetfulness, while its main consequence is to prevent, or to discontinue any proceedings against the beneficiaries thereof. If one holds this assumption to be true, it is therefore undeniably plain that if a State were to grant amnesty for cases of crimes against humanity, genocide, war crimes or aggression, the perpetrators thereof would never have to answer for their horrible deeds. Such a course of event would be inconsistent with the State's main goals under the Preamble to bring the perpetrators to justice and would amount to the State's unwillingness under Article 17 (a), (b) and (c)

---

82 *Id.* at 485; see also Article 13 (b) of the Rome Statute and Articles 25, 48 and 103 of the United Nations Charter.

to prosecute. Although the Rome Statute does not specifically exclude recourse to amnesty, an interpretation (in good faith in accordance with the ordinary meaning to be given to the terms of the treaty in their context and in light of its object and purpose) of the imperative of prosecution contained in its Preamble may also lead to conclude that in all circumstances, amnesty for acts it criminalizes cannot be condoned. This argument is based on the 1969 Vienna Convention on the Law of Treaties,[83] Articles 26 and 31 of which suggest that a treaty must be performed and interpreted in good faith in light of its object and purpose. For the purpose of interpretation, Article 31 (2) of this instrument suggests that the text of a treaty includes its preamble which, in the case of the ICC Statute, provides that the most serious crimes of concern to the international community must not go unpunished and that the Statute is determined to put an end to impunity.[84] However, in order to combat impunity, certain behaviour have to be condemned as criminal and have to give rise not to amnesty, but rather to criminal investigations and prosecutions.[85] Therefore, granting amnesty to any of the ICC Statute crimes would contradict the purpose of the International Criminal Court.[86]

Moreover, various provisions of the Rome Statute may also be interpreted as rejecting amnesty in respect of the Rome Statute's crimes. In effect, Article 27 (2) stipulates for example that:

> Immunities or special procedural rules which may attach to the official capacity of a person, whether under national or international law, shall not bar the Court from exercising its jurisdiction over such a person.

It has been demonstrated earlier on that a decision to grant amnesty is a special act of sovereign power designed to deal with special situations, such as the consolidation of the termination of an international war and the establishment of a lasting peace, or the achievement of national reconciliation and restoration within a divided State. As recent cases demonstrate, special measures of amnesty grants mainly aimed at those who committed crimes while acting in the interest of the State, meaning in their official capacity as representatives of the State. Consequently, Article 27 (2) may well be interpreted so as to include national amnesty within the meaning of the words 'special procedural rules', which in fact cannot constitute an obstacle to the Court's exercise of its jurisdiction.

On the other hand, although the main mandate of the ICC remains, *a priory*, the prosecution of the most serious crimes of international concern, there may exist exceptional circumstances in which the objectives of the Rome Statute can only be

---

83   Text available at www.unorg/law/ilc/texts/treaties.htm, hereinafter VCLT.
84   Preambular paragraphs 4 and 5.
85   See Human Rights Committee Report on Question of Impunity of Perpetrators of Human Rights Violations, Civil and Political, UN Doc E/CN.4/Sub.2/1997/20 (1997) at Annex II, definition A states that 'criminal proceedings' are the most appropriate response to atrocities.
86   See El Zeidy "The principle of complementarity: A new machinery to implement international criminal law" 23 *Michigan Journal of International Law* 869 (2002) at 942.

achieved through non-prosecutorial proceedings. This opens a limited possibility for the Court to defer to national measures of amnesty, especially when the latter is used as a bargaining chip available to mediators attempting to bring an end to an international or internal conflict.[87] There exist at least three mechanisms by which deference to national amnesty measures of amnesty may be possible. First, where the Security Council determines that investigation or prosecution would interfere with efforts to maintain or restore international peace and security, it may require the Court to suspend action (Article 16). Secondly, deference is possible under the complementarity regime where the alternative mechanisms being employed so closely meet the goals of accountability that they can be considered 'genuine' proceedings (Article 17). Thirdly, the prosecutor may in some circumstances decline to prosecute on the grounds that criminal prosecution may not serve the interests of justice (Article 53).[88]

The first mechanism of deference is provided for in Article 16 of the Rome Statute. This provision deals with an action by the Security Council, which under certain exceptional circumstances may realise that a national amnesty is more suitable to maintain or restore international peace and security than criminal investigation or prosecution by the ICC. In this case, it may adopt a resolution, acting under Chapter VII of the United Nations Charter, requesting the Court not to commence an investigation or to defer to any prosecution already commenced. In this case the Council's arguments may constitute a legal ground to validate national amnesty. It is not quite explicit whether the ICC has any authority to review the legality of the Security Council's action under Article 16 of the Rome Statute. However, it is suggested that the ICC could grant itself such an authority on the basis of a decision of the Appeals Chamber of the Yugoslavia Tribunal in *Tadic*, in which it was held that the Tribunal has the authority to independently assess whether a decision by the Security Council to defer a case meets the requirements of the existence of a threat to international peace and security.[89] If this position also holds true as far as the ICC is concerned, then it would be difficult to contemplate how this Court will condone amnesties for the perpetrators of genocide, war crimes, or crimes against humanity, which are generally believed to constitute serious threats to international peace and security, and for the prosecution of which the Court was created. As Scharf puts it:

> While an amnesty accompanied by the establishment of a truth commission, victim compensation, and lustration might be in the interests of justice in the broad sense, it would nonetheless be in contravention of international law where the grave breaches provisions of the 1949 Geneva Conventions or the Genocide Convention are applicable. It is especially noteworthy that the Geneva Conventions requires parties 'to provide effective penal sanctions for persons committing, or ordering to be committed, any of the grave breaches of the Convention,' and that the Genocide Convention requires parties 'to provide effective penalties for persons guilty of genocide.' This would suggest

---

87   See M.P. Scharf, chap. II, n. 117 at 508.
88   See D. Robinson, n. 81 at 486.
89   See M.P. Scharf, chap. II, n. 117 at 523; also *Tadic*, n. 30 at para. 6.

that the International Criminal Court might not defer to the Security Council under
Article 16 of the Rome Statute where the accused is charged with grave breaches of
the Geneva Conventions or the Genocide Convention.[90]

Nevertheless, in case of a disagreement between the ICC and the Security Council
as to the existence or not of a threat to international peace and security, the ICJ
shall be competent, under Article 36 of its Statute, to decide upon the matter.
A decision of the Court certifying the non-existence of a threat to international
peace and security may serve as a legal basis for the ICC to refuse to defer to
the Security Council action under Article 16 of the Rome Statute.

The second mechanism of deference is based on the principle of complementarity
in terms of Article 17. This principle may be read as permitting national amnesties in exceptional situations, if anything close to genuineness of investigation or
prosecution by national authorities can be established by the ICC. For example,
a State may claim recognition of its amnesty measures if the mechanism of truth
commission is supplemented with genuine investigations, genuine criminal prosecutions of certain categories of offenders (especially the most responsible or the most
cruel ones) by the competent courts, and substantial compensation of the victims of
the atrocities that have been committed. Such a situation may present itself when
the commission of crimes has occurred in such a large scale and has involved so
many perpetrators that prosecution of all offenders would be practically, financially
and logistically impossible. For instance, the extent of the Rwandan population's
participation in the perpetration of genocide in 1994 made it quite impossible to
prosecute all alleged criminals before the ICTR.[91] Robinson states in this regard
that to deal with a significant portion of the population through criminal proceedings and incarceration may not be the best approach to rebuilding a traumatized
society.[92] Therefore, it may be useful to draw a distinction between the persons
most responsible for international crimes and lesser offenders. The former i.e.,
planners, leaders, and those committing the most notorious crimes should be
criminally prosecuted and punished, whereas the latter offenders can be dealt with
through truth commissions and conditional amnesties.[93] This position accords with
Orentlicher's arguments that:

> [C]ustomary law would [...] not require prosecution of every person. [...] Prosecu-
> tion of those who were most responsible for designing and implementing a system
> of human rights atrocities or for especially notorious crimes that were emblematic of
> past violations would seemingly discharge governments' customary law obligation [...]

---

90 See chap. II, n. 117 at 523–524.
91 In 2003, 120000 persons were detained in Rwandan prisons in connection with geno-
    cide, and were awaiting judgment; moreover, a law of March 2001 established 8000
    traditional jurisdictions, called *gacaca*, throughout the country to deal with these cases,
    see J. Kagabo "Le sens d'une commemoration" *Le Monde Diplomatique* (March 2004)
    at 20.
92 See n. 81 at 494.
93 *Id.* at 493–494.

provided the criteria used to select potential defendants did not appear to condone or tolerate a past abuse.[94]

The indictment by the ICTY of offenders of the kind of Slobodan Milosevic, Radovan Karadjic, Radko Mladic, and Dusko Tadic, or the indictment by the ICTR of influential members of the Hutu-led former regime points to the fact that international criminal liability for the commission of serious international crimes weighs more on the most notorious perpetrators. Therefore, within the context examined above, namely that of a widespread commission of the Rome Statute crimes involving a huge portion of the population of a given State, the ICC may well defer to genuine prosecution of the most responsible perpetrators, while endorsing amnesty accorded to lesser offenders.

The third mechanism of deference under Article 53 of the Rome Statute grants discretionary powers to the prosecutor to decline to initiate an investigation where, in the absence of an action by the Security Council, he determines that there is no reasonable basis under the Statute to proceed. A decision of the prosecutor not to prosecute shall be based at least on one or more of the following: that there is not a sufficient legal or factual basis to seek a warrant or summons; that the case is inadmissible under Article 17; or that a prosecution will not serve the interests of justice, taking into account all the circumstances, including the gravity of the crime, the interests of victims and the age or infirmity of the alleged perpetrator, and his or her role in the alleged crimes. This latter ground may open a possibility of validating an amnesty for the Rome Statute's crimes. In fact, if amnesty, supplemented with compensation to victims, is granted to an alleged perpetrator of crimes against humanity, war crimes, or genocide on the basis, for example, of his impaired mental capacity or his minor age, it would be doubtful whether the prosecutor's decision to prosecute such cases would serve the interests of justice. In this exceptional situation, amnesty may well be accommodated. The question of children involved in the commission of brutal crimes was crucial in the context of the horrors of the Sierra Leonean civil war, where children where abducted, injected with drugs and forced to carry out the rebel's gruesome campaign.[95] Called to address this question, the Security Council recommended that those who bear the greatest responsibility for the crimes committed should be prosecuted,[96] thus foreseeing, as it appears in Article 7 of the Statute of the SCSL as referred to in Chapter 4, a possibility of guaranteeing a special treatment for minor criminals.

However, the prosecutor's decision not to initiate an investigation is subject, under Article 53 (3), to review by the Pre-Trial Chamber of the ICC. According

---

94 See chap. V, n. 85 at 2599.
95 See D.J. Macaluso "Absolute and free pardon: the effect of the amnesty provision in the Lome Peace Agreement on the jurisdiction of the Special Court for Sierra Leone" 27 *Brooklyn Journal of International Law* (2001–2002) at 354, quoting a BBC News Online article entitled *Brutal Child Army Grows Up* (June 1, 2000), available at http://www.news.bbc.co.uk/hi/english/world/africa/newsid_743000/743684.stm.
96 *Id.* at 356.

to Scharf, in reviewing whether respecting an amnesty would better serve the interests of justice, the Pre-Trial Chamber would have to evaluate the benefits of a particular amnesty and consider whether there is an international legal obligation to prosecute the offence.[97]

In sum, the legal status of national amnesties in the Rome Statute still remains ambiguous. Although the *travaux préparatoires* tend to show that States purposefully excluded from the Rome Statute provisions allowing for amnesty,[98] many commentators believe that such an omission was deliberate. Thus, according to Philippe Kirsch, the Chairman of the Rome Diplomatic Conference, the provisions of the Rome Statute reflect 'creative ambiguity' which could potentially allow the prosecutor and judges of the ICC to interpret the Statute as permitting recognition of an amnesty exception to the jurisdiction of the Court.[99] Moreover Robinson reports that during the ICC negotiations many negotiators had misgivings about laying down an iron rule for all time mandating prosecution as the only acceptable response in all situations. On the other hand, creating an explicit exception allowing for amnesties was equally untenable. Some delegations opposed any exceptions in principle, whereas others were concerned that any exception would be immediately exploited and abused.[100] He concludes that the drafters of the Rome Statute finally turned to the faithful and familiar friend of diplomats, namely ambiguity, thus leaving a few small avenues open to the Court and allowing the Court to develop an appropriate approach when faced with concrete situations.[101]

The development of such an approach is still to come. What is clear is that no matter what direction such a course of development will take, it will not negate or empty the Rome Statute of its substance, which is clear and compelling, namely:

> [T]o ensure the investigation and punishment of serious international crimes, and to prompt States to overcome the considerations of expedience and realpolitik that had so often led them to trade away justice in the past.[102]

It appears therefore that international conventions such as the Genocide Convention, the Torture Convention, the Hostages Convention, or the Rome Statute, which may apply to circumstances covered by national amnesties, put great emphasis on legal resolution of cases of crimes against humanity. The nature of the values they seek to promote and the phraseology of their provisions are so compelling that no political arrangement to the contrary is permitted. Consequently, amnesty in respect of the most serious crimes of international concern shall be declared invalid as being inconsistent with international aspirations of a universal culture

---

97 See chap. II, n. 117 at 524.
98 See Report of the Preparatory Committee on the Establishment of an ICC, UN GAOR 51st Sess. Vol. 1 Supp. No. 22, UN Doc A/51/22 (1996) at 37.
99 See M.P. Scharf, chap. II, n. 117 at 521–522.
100 See n. 81 at 483.
101 *Id.*
102 *Id.*

of human rights and human dignity, unless very narrow exceptional circumstances as explained above justify its grant.

Crimes against Humanity Under Customary International Law and Amnesty

Crimes against humanity are customary international law offences par excellence. For this reason, they are not contained in any specific treaty mandating their prosecution.[103] Consequently, any prosecution of crimes against humanity shall be based either on custom, or on treaties dealing with specific aspects of such crimes, following the example of the Torture Convention, the Genocide Convention or the Slavery Convention. As stated earlier, criminals against humanity were treated as *hostis humani generis*. Consequently, any State, including their own, could set up national courts to prosecute them. This principle of universal jurisdiction is thought to be permissive under international law in respect of the crimes that exist by virtue of international custom (including slavery, torture, piracy, war crimes and crimes against humanity) and to require prosecution, but not amnesty for such crimes.[104]

It was demonstrated above that the values protected by both the Genocide and the Torture Conventions are widely held to be of customary law origin. The House of Lords meant this when it stated in *Pinochet* that the systematic use of torture was an international crime for which there could be no immunity even before the Torture Convention came into effect. The House of Lords generally held the view that murder, torture, disappearances, and grave violations of basic human rights, were not official duties of the State which qualified for immunity from prosecution under international law.[105] It appears therefore that customary international law insists on the criminal prosecution of these crimes against humanity and rejects the granting of State's privileges, such as immunity and amnesty, to State officials involved in their commission.

However, the two important elements of custom, namely uniform State practice and *opinio juris* do not co-exist as far as prosecuting crimes against humanity is concerned. Whereas the element of *opinio juris* appears to reject amnesty and to promote prosecution for acts of crime against humanity, State practice, on the contrary, tends to privilege *de facto* impunity or the granting of amnesty to the perpetrators thereof.[106] This dichotomy is a source of controversy as to the position of customary international law in respect to the relationship between crimes against humanity and amnesty. What is fundamental to note here is the fact that

---

103 See M.P. Scharf, chap. II, n. 117 at 519; also M.C. Bassiouni, chap. III, n. 65 at 463.

104 See e.g., C. Edelenbos, chap. I, n. 24 at 15; see also D. Orentlicher, chap. V, n. 85 at 2540; or in general S.R. Ratner and J.S. Abrams, chap. III, n. 118.

105 See in general the law Lords opinions in the third *Pinochet* hearing, chap. III, n. 173.

106 See Chapter 4 above; see also M.P. Scharf, chap. II, n. 117 at 521; or else A. O'Shea, chap. II, n. 5 at 251; as far as State practice of granting amnesty is concerned see in general N.J. Kritz, chap. I, n. 3.

an *opinio juris* expressed by a State may be viewed, in certain circumstances, not only as an official position of such a State in respect of a specific rule, but also as its acceptance of the validity of such a rule. The International Court of Justice adopted this position when it declared in the *Nicaragua Case* that:

> [An] *opinio juris* may though in all due caution, be deduced from, *inter alia*, the attitude of the Parties and the attitude of States towards certain General Assembly resolutions, and particularly resolution 2526 (XXV) entitled "Declaration on Principles of International Law Concerning Friendly Relations and Co-operation among States in Accordance with the Charter of the United Nations". The effect of consent to the text of such resolutions cannot be understood as merely that of a "reiteration or elucidation" of the treaty commitment undertaken in the Charter. On the contrary, it may be understood as an acceptance of the validity of the rule or set of rules declared by the resolution by themselves.[107]

On the basis of the ICJ's opinion as expressed above, one can argue that certain General Assembly resolutions relating to grave crimes are believed to have been accepted as expressing *ipinio juris* of the signatory States as to their duty to prosecute and punish such crimes. These are, for example, the United Nations Declaration on Territorial Asylum,[108] which is usually cited as the earliest international recognition of a legal obligation to prosecute perpetrators of crimes against humanity.[109] This instrument provides, among other things, that States shall refrain from granting asylum to any person in respect to whom there are serious reasons for considering that he has committed a war crime, a crime against peace and a crime against humanity.[110] In addition, General Assembly Resolution 2840 (XXVI) of 18 December, 1971 on the Question of the Punishment of War Criminals and of Persons who have Committed Crimes against Humanity[111] stipulates that refusal by States to cooperate in the arrest, extradition, trial and punishment of persons guilty of war crimes and crimes against humanity is contrary to the purposes and principles of the Charter of the United Nations and to generally recognised norms of international law.[112] Likewise, the Principles of International Cooperation in the Detection, Arrest, Extradition and Punishment of Persons Guilty of War Crimes and Crimes against Humanity[113] provides in Principle 1 that war crimes and crimes against humanity, wherever they are committed, shall be subject to investigation and the persons against whom there is evidence that they have committed such crimes shall be subject to tracing, arrest, trial and, if found guilty, to punishment. Moreover, the 1968 Convention on the Non-Applicability of Statutory Limitations to War Crimes and Crimes against Humanity and the 1974 European Convention

---

107 See chap. V, n. 189 at para. 188.
108 GA Res. 2312 (XXII) of 14 Dec. 1967, UN GAOR 22nd Sess. Supp. No. 16 at 81, UN Doc A/6716 (1967).
109 See M.P. Scharf, chap. II, n. 117 at 521.
110 Article 1 (2).
111 Text available at www.unorg/documents/ga/res/26/ares26.htm.
112 Article 4.
113 See chap. V, n. 183.

on the Non-Applicability of Statutory Limitations to Crimes against Humanity and War Crimes prescribe that States Parties shall not apply any statutory limitation to war crimes and to crimes against humanity. Whereas these instruments do not contain an express obligation to prosecute alleged offenders of crimes against humanity, they nevertheless provide States Parties with a reliable legal ground for the punishment of alleged perpetrators of such crimes.

Yet, as already stated in Chapter 5, the problem inherent in General Assembly resolutions is that they are not generally binding to support an existing State duty to prosecute crimes against humanity. Even the two Conventions on statutory limitations referred to above do not contain strong language that may be interpreted as mandating prosecution. However, as it is demonstrated in the *Nuclear Weapons Case*,[114] a General Assembly resolution may indicate the existence of an *opinio juris* on a duty to prosecute crimes against humanity, depending on its content and the conditions of its adoption, its normative values or the repetition of the condemnation contained therein.[115]

As regards the element of uniform State practice in respect of crimes against humanity, Robinson notes a shift from history's tacit endorsement of amnesties to today's consistent rejection of them for serious international crimes.[116] Irrespective of the accuracy of Robinson's views, what is certain today is that there is a crystallizing norm in States' behaviour, which consists of excluding serious international offences from the purview of their amnesty laws. Three recent cases may illustrate this assertion. The first one relates to the Statute for the Special Court for Sierra Leone as amended on 16 January 2002,[117] the second case is connected with Regulation No. 2001/10 on the Establishment of a Commission for Reception, Truth and Reconciliation in East Timor,[118] whereas the third case is that of the Liberian TRC Act of 2005.[119]

As regards the first case, the Statute of the SCSL which was annexed to the agreement establishing that court[120] states in its Article 10 as follows:

---

114 See chap. V, n. 186.
115 At para. 70 and 71.
116 See n. 81 at 491.
117 Security Council Resolution 1315 of 2000 authorized the setting up of the Special Court to prosecute charges of crimes against humanity, war crimes, other serious breaches of international humanitarian law, and other crimes committed in violation of the Sierra Leonean domestic criminal law; text of the resolution available at http://www.special-court.org/documents/Statute.html.
118 UNTAET/REG/2001/10 of 13 July, 2001, available at http://www.unorg/peace/etimor/untaetR/Reg10e.pdf.
119 Enacted by the National Transitional Legislative Assembly on 12 May, 2005, and which became operational on 12 February, 2006 when the nine members of the TRC took their oaths of office at a ceremony presided over by the newly-elected Liberian President, Ellen Johnson Sirleaf.
120 Agreement between the United Nations and the Government of Sierra Leone establishing the SCSL for the prosecution of persons who bear the greatest responsibility for serious violations of international humanitarian law and Sierra Leonean law committed in the territory of Sierra Leone since 30 November, 1996.

An amnesty granted to any person falling within the jurisdiction of the Special Court in respect of the crimes referred to in Articles 2 to 4 [crimes against humanity, serious violations of article 3 common to the Geneva Conventions, and other serious violations of international humanitarian law] of the present Statute shall not be a bar to prosecution.

The SCSL interpreted this provision to the effect that it constitutes an express limitation on an exercise of the discretion of the Court to bar proceedings solely on the strength of such amnesty.[121] More important is the Court's argument that a State cannot bring into oblivion and forgetfulness a crime against international law, which other States are entitled to keep alive and remember.[122] In the opinion of the Court, whatever effect the amnesty granted under the Lomé Accord may have on the prosecution of the most serious offences in the national courts of Sierra Leone, it is ineffective in removing the universal jurisdiction to prosecute persons accused of such crimes that other States have by reason of the nature of the crimes. It is also ineffective in depriving an international court such as the Special Court of jurisdiction.[123]

As far as the East Timorese case is concerned, serious criminal offences are excluded from the competence of the Community Reconciliation Process set up to facilitate national reconciliation among the Timorese people. In this regard, Schedule 1 (4) to Regulation No. 2001/10 on the Establishment of a Commission for Reception, Truth and Reconciliation in East Timor specifies that: "in no circumstances shall a serious criminal offence be dealt with in a Community Reconciliation Process." Meanwhile, Section 1.3 of Regulation No. 2000/15 on the Establishment of Panels with Exclusive Jurisdiction over Serious Criminal Offences[124] defines the expression 'serious criminal offences' as to include genocide, crimes against humanity, war crimes, murder, sexual offences and torture.

Similarly, the Liberian TRC Act which establishes a Commission to promote national peace, unity, security, reconciliation, and to investigate and document human rights violations that occurred in Liberia between 1979 and 2003 provides for amnesty, to the extent that:

[A]mnesty or exoneration shall not apply to violations of international humanitarian law and crimes against humanity in conformity with international laws and standards.[125]

To sum up this section, one may argue that the prohibition of *delicti jus gentium*, or international crimes, is aimed at preserving internationally shared values and

---

121 See *Prosecutor v. Morris Kallon, Brima Bazzy Kamara*, Case No. SCSL-04-15-PT-060-II, Appeals Chamber Decision of 13 March, 2004 on Challenge to Jurisdiction: Lomé Accord Amnesty, para. 80.

122 See para. 67.

123 See para. 88; see further pronouncements in C. Laucci *Digest of Jurisprudence of the Special Court for Sierra Leone* (2007), pp. 82–88.

124 UNTAET/REG/2000/15 of 6 June 2000, available at http://www.unorg/peace/etimor/untaetR/Reg0015E.pdf.

125 See Article VII, Section 26 (g) of the Act.

principles. Such values and principles are protected by both conventional international law and customary international law. However, certain crimes are so appalling and destructive to humankind that their proscription assumes a special character. Among these are war crimes, aggression, genocide and crimes against humanity. In the words of Bassiouni, crime against humanity is not only an international crime; it is also "an international category of crime that has risen to the level of *jus cogens*".[126]

Crimes against Humanity as Jus Cogens Offences

Doctrine of Jus Cogens

Jus cogens or peremptory norm[127] of international law is referred to in the 1969 VCLT in the following manner:

> A treaty is void if, at the time of its conclusion, it conflicts with a peremptory norm of general international law. For the purposes of the present Convention, a peremptory norm of general international law is a norm accepted and recognised by the international community of States as a whole as a norm from which no derogation is permitted and which can be modified only by a subsequent norm of general international law having the same character.[128]

In light of the above-mentioned definition, Suy insists on the legal consequences of peremptory norms by specifying that they are general rules of law whose non-observance may affect the very essence of the legal system to which they belong to such an extent that the subjects of law may not, under pain of absolute nullity, depart from them in virtue of particular agreements.[129] By the same token, Bassiouni qualifies *jus cogens* as 'the compelling law' that holds the highest hierarchical position among all other norms and principles.[130] As a consequence of that standing, *jus cogens* norms are deemed to be peremptory, non-derogable, absolutely binding and restrictive of the Parties freedom.[131]

---

126 M.C. Bassiouni, chap. III, n. 97 at 245.

127 For a comprehensive analysis of this concept, see L. Hannikainen *Peremptory Norms in International Law* (1988); see also J.A. Frowein Jus cogens in R. Bernhardt (ed.), *Encyclopedia of Public International Law* (1984), Instalment 7, pp. 327–330.

128 Article 53.

129 E. Suy, The concept of *jus cogens* in public international law, in Carnegie Endowment for International Peace *Papers and Proceedings II: The Concept of Jus Cogens in International Law* (1967) at 18, 3rd Conference on International Law held in Lagonisi (Greece) between 3–8 April 1966.

130 M.C. Bassiouni "International crimes: *Jus cogens* and *obligatio erga omnes*" 59 *Law and Contemporary Problems* 4 (1996) at 67.

131 *Id.* See also E. Suy, n. 129 at 18.

The origin of the notion of *jus cogens* is not known with certainty[132] and there seems to be no scholarly consensus as to the content of a peremptory norm and to how a specific rule rises to that level.[133] The ILC endorsed this view when it admitted that there is not yet any generally recognised criterion by which to identify a general rule of international law as having the character of *jus cogens*.[134] However, it added that to constitute an international *jus cogens*, a rule of international law must have attained at least relative universality, i.e., form part of general international law.[135] In light of this argument, legal literature has developed some elements on the basis of which a *jus cogens* rule may be defined. Among these are: (1) international pronouncements, or what can be called international *opinio juris*, reflecting the recognition that certain crimes are deemed part of general customary law; (2) language in preambles or other provisions of treaties applicable to certain crimes which indicates such crimes' higher status in international law; (3) the large number of States which have ratified treaties relating to certain crimes; and (4) the *ad hoc* international investigations and prosecutions of perpetrators of such crimes.[136] Taking into consideration all of these elements, the following crimes are believed to have risen to the status of *jus cogens* crimes: aggression, genocide, crimes against humanity, war crimes, piracy, slavery and slave-related practices, and torture.

Many commentators argue that all these crimes contain at least one of the two essential factors which establish the *jus cogens* status of a particular crime, namely a threat to the peace and security of mankind and the capacity of a specific conduct to shock the conscience of humanity.[137] The values and principles protected through the promotion of peace, security and dignity of humankind are shared by all States and are universally accepted. This is evidenced by the overwhelming recognition of the United Nations Charter principles as binding on all members of the international community. In this sense, the principles contained in the Charter are *jus cogens* principles. The ICJ has recognised the *jus cogens* character of the Charter principles in at least two cases.

In the *Corfu Channel Case*,[138] the Court held that Albania was under the obligations to notify, for the benefit of shipping in general, the existence of a minefield and to warn the approaching British warships of the imminent danger. In the opinion of the Court, such obligations were founded on:

---

132 E. Suy, n. 129 at 18–19.
133 M.C. Bassiouni, n. 130 at 67.
134 The International Law Commission's Draft Articles on the Law of Treaties (1964) Article 37, available at 58 *The American Journal of International Law* 264 (1964).
135 *Id.*
136 See M.C. Bassiouni, n. 130 at 68.
137 *Id.* at 69; see also G. Abi-Saab, Definition of *jus cogens*, in Carnegie Endowment for International Peace *Papers and Proceedings II: The Concept of Jus Cogens in International Law* (1967) at 13.
138 See *United Kingdom v. Albania*, judgment of 9 April, 1949, *ICJ Reports* (1949) 1.

[C]ertain general and well recognised principles, namely: elementary considerations of humanity, even more exacting in peace than in war, the principle of the freedom of maritime communication; and every State's obligation not to allow knowingly its territory to be used for acts contrary to the rights of other States.[139]

More relevant to crimes against humanity is the ICJ Advisory Opinion in the *Case Concerning Reservations to the Genocide Convention*. As already stated earlier on, the Court considered genocide to be a denial of the right of existence of entire human groups; a denial which shocks the conscience of mankind and results in great losses to humanity, and which is contrary to moral law and to the spirit and aims of the United Nations. The Court then specified that the principles underlying the Convention are principles which are recognised by civilised nations as binding on States, even without any conventional obligation.

It is without doubt that the commission of crimes against humanity violates elementary considerations of humanity and undermines the principles of both the United Nations Charter and the Genocide Convention. The massacres of the Armenian population by the Turks during World War I, the extermination of the Jewish population in Nazi Germany during World War II, the Cambodian and Rwandan genocides, the policy of ethnic cleansing in former Yugoslavia or the apartheid system in South Africa, have shaken the international community from its very foundation. These events have given rise to fierce protests and condemnations throughout the world, and have prompted the establishment of global legal mechanisms designed to prevent their occurrence in the future. The most recent global legal response to serious crimes is the establishment of the ICC Statute, the preamble of which refers to the two essential factors that confirm the *jus cogens* status of crimes against humanity.[140]

In addition to the above-mentioned four elements on the basis of which a *jus cogens* offence may be defined, Bassiouni proposes three other considerations that must be taken into account in determining whether a given international crime has reached the status of *jus cogens*. He explains that:

> The first has to do with the historical legal evolution of the crime. Clearly, the more legal instruments that exist to evidence the condemnation and prohibition of a particular crime, the better founded the proposition that the crime has risen to the level of *jus cogens*. The second consideration is the number of states that have incorporated the given proscription in their national laws. The third consideration is the number of international and national prosecutions for the given crime and how they have been characterised. Additional supporting sources that can be relied upon in determining whether a particular crime is a part of *jus cogens* is other evidence of general principles of law and the writings of the most distinguished publicists.[141]

---

139   *Id.* at 22.
140   Paragraphs 2 and 3 of the Preamble to the Rome Statute reiterate the potential of the Statute crimes to shock the conscience of humanity and to threaten the peace, security and well-being of the world.
141   See n. 130 at 70–71.

It is clear that crimes against humanity followed a constant and steady evolution through international legal instruments such as the Versailles Treaty of 28 June, 1919, the Charter of IMT of Nuremberg of 1945 as well as the Charter of the IMT for the Far East and Control Council Law No. 10. Post-World War II was characterised by the refinement of the definition of the offence of crimes against humanity through instruments such as the 1948 Genocide Convention, the 1973 Apartheid Convention, the 1984 Torture Convention, the 1993 Statute of the ICTY, the 1994 Statute of the ICTR and the recent Statute of the SCSL. This process of evolution culminated with the adoption in 1998 of the Statute of the ICC, which provides the most complete definition to date of what would amount to crimes against humanity. This process of evolution of crimes against humanity to the category of *jus cogens* crimes has been supplemented by domestic prosecutions as is evidenced in the *Eichmann*, and the *Klaus Barbie Cases*. Today, more and more nations have incorporated the proscription of genocide, torture, slavery and other crimes against humanity in their national laws. Among these nations are Israel, France, Canada, Germany, Belgium and South Africa.

It seems therefore that a norm rises to the level of *jus cogens* when the values or principles it embodies or protects are universally or quasi-universally accepted. The prohibition of crimes against humanity is aimed at protecting the universally shared and accepted values of peace among nations and dignity among human beings. Consequently it is without doubt that the proscription of such crimes has achieved the status of *jus cogens* prohibition the legal implications of which are embodied in the expression *obligatio erga omnes*.

Consequences of Jus Cogens Norms

Obligatio erga omnes is a consequence, or as Frowein clearly specified, one of the consequences of a given international crime having risen to the level of *jus cogens*.[142] It means flowing to all.[143] This expression connotes a sense of legal obligation incumbent on all States and that each State can exercise in the protection of its own interests and in the interests of the international community in general. The ICJ meant this when it stated in the *Barcelona Traction* case[144] that:

> [A]n essential distinction should be drawn between the obligations of a State towards the international community as a whole, and those arising *vis-à-vis* another State in the field of diplomatic protection. By their very nature the former are the concern of

---

142 Die Verpflichtungen erga omnes im Völkerrecht und ihre Durchsetzung in R. Bernhardt etc. (ed.), *Völkerrecht als Rechtsordnung, internationale Gerichtsbarkeit, Menschenrechte*: Festschrift für Hermann Mosler (1983), West Berlin, pp. 241–263.
143 See Bassiouni, n. 130 at 63, 72 and 73.
144 *Barcelona Traction, Light and Power Co. Ltd.* (Belgium v. Spain), *ICJ Reports* (1970) at 1.

all States. In view of the importance of the rights involved, all States can be held to have a legal interest in their protection; they are obligations *erga omnes*.[145]

The ICJ went on to enumerate examples of *erga omnes* obligations in the following manner:

> Such obligations derive, for example, in contemporary international law, from the outlawing of acts of aggression and of genocide, as also from the principles and rules concerning the basic rights of the human person, including protection from slavery and racial discrimination. Some of the corresponding rights of protection have entered into the body of general international law (*Reservations to the Convention on the Prevention and Punishment of the Crime of Genocide, Advisory Opinion, I.C.J. Reports* 1951, p. 23); others are conferred by international instruments of a universal or quasi-universal character.[146]

It appears from this pronouncement that the commission of acts such as genocide, slavery and racial discrimination may give rise to an obligation *erga omnes* to punish the perpetrators thereof. Whereas, as demonstrated above, genocide is viewed as a special form of crimes against humanity; the Rome Statute lists slavery and racial discrimination as acts of crime against humanity and prohibits them under the headings 'enslavement' and 'apartheid' respectively. Consequently, and despite the fact that the Court did not specifically identify these crimes as *jus cogens*, commentators have indicated that genocide, slavery, racial discrimination, crimes against humanity and gross violations of human rights have achieved the status of *jus cogens*, thus creating the corresponding obligations *erga omnes* to prosecute the perpetrators thereof.[147]

It is not yet quite clearly established whether *obligatio erga omnes* arising out of the violation of a *jus cogens* prohibition is mandatory upon States or whether it simply grants them a right to prosecute alleged perpetrators of the norm violated. However, according to Bassiouni, the implications of *jus cogens* are those of a duty and not of optional rights. Consequently, such obligations are non-derogable in times of war as well as in times of peace. Thus, recognising a crime as *jus cogens* carries with it the duty to prosecute or extradite, the non-applicability of statutes of limitation to such crimes, and universality of jurisdiction over such crimes.[148] If one subscribes to this approach, it becomes evident that a *jus cogens* prohibition establishes a strong basis for the limitation of States' sovereign discretion to grant amnesty.

---

145   *Id.*, second Phase of the Judgment 5 February, 1970, *ICJ Reports* 3 (1970) at 32.
146   *Id.*
147   See e.g., M.C. Bassiouni, chap. III, n. 97 at 210–217.
148   See n. 130 at 65–66.

Jus Cogens *Offences and their Implications on States' Sovereign Discretion to Grant Amnesty*

According to Chigara, sovereignty is juridically a tripartite idea comprising the external, internal and territorial dimensions.[149] External sovereignty refers to States' authority to determine their relations with other subjects of international law without prior authorisation or control of another State; internal sovereignty implies the State's exclusive right or competence to determine the character of its own institutions, to ensure and provide for their operation, to enact laws of its own choice, and to ensure their respect; and territorial sovereignty of a State refers to the State's exclusive authority over all persons and objects existing on, under or above its territory.[150] Sovereignty is therefore one of the fundamental principles of international law based on the idea that:

> All members [of the United Nations] shall refrain in their international relations from the threat or use of force against the territorial integrity or political independence of any State, or in any other manner inconsistent with the purposes of the United Nations.[151]

One of the many consequences of sovereignty is the possibility for each State to exercise its sovereign powers within the limits of its territory as it deems fit. Granting amnesty is therefore considered as a manifestation of the State's sovereign power of clemency. In this sense, amnesty finds its foundation in sovereignty itself. This argument is supported by jurists such as José María Rodríguez Devesa who wrote that the right of clemency is the right of the State as the sole guardian of the right to punish, to renounce the imposition of penalty, or to demand fulfilment if already imposed by tribunals.[152] Likewise, Story declared in his *Commentary on the Federal Constitution of the United States* that the power of pardon is an indispensable consequence of the power of punishment itself, upholding both figures of sovereignty itself. Passina, in his *Elements of Penal Law* wrote that the faculty of clemency, whatever the form it adopts, is an attribute of sovereignty.[153] These views undoubtedly influenced recent decisions of various courts which decided either to uphold the validity of amnesty laws,[154] or to declare themselves incompetent to rule on the legality of such laws on the grounds that the faculty of granting amnesty or clemency is a manifestation of sovereignty and, consequently, a purely political act they are not entitled to hear.[155] Whereas this approach may conform to the juridical definition of sovereignty as given above, it nevertheless

---

149 B. Chigara, chap. VI, n. 81 at 28.
150 *Id.* at 28–29.
151 Article 2 (4) of the United Nations Charter of 1945.
152 See the Supreme Court of El Salvador in its decision on the *Amnesty Law* Proceedings No. 10–93 of May 1993, reproduced in N.J. Kritz, chap. I, n. 3 at 553.
153 *Id.*
154 See the *AZAPO Cases* for example.
155 See El Salvador Supreme Court of justice decision on amnesty, in N.J. Kritz, chap. I, n. 3 at 553–554.

ignores fundamental developments in the field of human rights that took place in the aftermath of World War II and whose effect is to limit the exclusive exercise of sovereignty by States in respect of human rights issues. The Charter of the United Nations, the Genocide Convention, the Torture Convention, the UDHR and the ICCPR, together with international mechanisms established to enforce them, make it clear that the treatment by States of its own citizens is subject to the scrutiny of international human rights law. Therefore, the sovereign will of the State is not uncapped, but very much under supervision of international law, international institutions and organisations.[156]

The limitation of State sovereignty in respect of the most serious crimes under international law was addressed in 1946 at the Nuremberg proceedings when the Nuremberg Tribunal stated that:

> It was submitted that international law is concerned with the actions of sovereign states and provides no punishment for individuals; and further, that where the act in question is an act of state, those who carry it out are not personally responsible, but are protected by the doctrine of the sovereignty of the state. In the opinion of the Tribunal, both these submissions must be rejected.[157]

The Tribunal went on to state that:

> He who violates the laws of war cannot obtain immunity while acting in pursuance of the authority of the state, if the state, in authorising action moves outside its competence under international law.[158]

A German court echoed the idea of State's limited sovereignty in its 1991 judgment on the *Trial of Border Guards*.[159] In this case, the Berlin State Court was called to determine whether it might be permissible for a State (in this case, the former German Democratic Republic) to threaten with death, or even to kill a person who does not want to abide by the exit prohibition, or a person who violates it. The Court held that it has been recognised in Supreme Court jurisprudence that there is a certain core area of law which no law and no sovereign act may touch according to the legal consciousness of the general public.[160] More important, the Court quoted the following piece of judgment handed down by the German Federal Court in 1952:

> The freedom of a State to determine, for its area what is lawful and what is unlawful, no matter how widely it is determined, however, is not unlimited. In the consciousness of all civilised nations, with all of their differences revealed by the various national bodies of law, there is a certain nucleus of the law which, according to general legal concepts, must not be violated by any law and by any other sovereign State measure. It encompasses certain basic principles of human behaviour that are considered untouch-

---

156 See B. Chigara, chap. VI, n. 81 at 34.
157 IMT *Reports*, chap. III, n. 50 at 465.
158 *Id.* at 466.
159 Berlin State Court Docket No. (523) 2 Js 48/90 (9/91) reprinted in N.J. Kritz, Chap. I, n. 3 at 576.
160 *Id.* at 578.

able and that have taken shape with the passage of time among all cultured nations on the fertile ground of coincident basic moral views and which are considered to be legally binding, regardless of whether individual regulations in national bodies of law seem to allow that they be disregarded.[161]

Those 'general legal concepts' that "must not be violated by any law and by any other sovereign State measures" are norms that belong to the category of peremptory general international rules, otherwise known as *jus cogens*, that all nations have agreed to condemn. Such rules include those outlawing, genocide, torture, war crimes and crimes against humanity. In the words of Chigara, peremptory norms or *jus cogens* overarch national constitutions, denying States the defence of national sovereignty for breaches of international law.[162] This author went on to state that:

> Norms of *peremptory* general international law sometimes referred to as norms *jus cogens* are of such importance to the international legal system that even in the exercise of their sovereign right to enter treaties one with another, States may not breach norms of this category. The Vienna Convention on the Law of Treaties states in Article 53 that: 'A treaty is void, if, at the time of its conclusion, it conflicts with a peremptory norm of general international law. For the purposes of the present Convention, a peremptory norm of general international law is a norm accepted and recognised by the international community of States as a whole as a norm from which no derogation is permitted and which can be modified only by a subsequent norm of general international law having the same character.'[163]

Likewise Abi-Saab notes that *Jus cogens* rules are those from which States cannot violate or contract out by unilateral acts or omission, rules from which they cannot derogate by agreement even in their mutual *inter se* relations.[164] As to the legal consequences of acts contravening *jus cogens* rule, he adds that:

> [A]n act or omission which is contrary to a *jus cogens* rule is devoid of any legal effect. It cannot give place through recognition, acquiescence or prescription, to a new legal regime, as would violations of other rules of international law.
>
> In case of treaties, the sanction is always an absolute nullity, even in the *inter se* relations of the parties. A treaty contravening a *jus cogens* rule would be void *ab initio* and not simply voidable, inoperative or inopposable.[165]

As *jus cogens*, crimes against humanity are international crimes in the highest sense. They permit universal jurisdiction for their breach and are subjected to the principle of *aut dedere aut judicare*, either you extradite or you prosecute.[166] States

---

161 See *Case BGH St* 2, 234, 237, reprinted in N.J. Kritz, chap. I, n. 3 at 579.
162 See chap. VI, n. 81 at 36.
163 *Id.*
164 See G. Abi-Saab, n. 131 at 10.
165 *Id.* at 10–11.
166 See e.g., Article IV of the 1973 Apartheid Convention; Article 8.1 of the 1979 Hostages Convention; Common Articles of the Four Geneva Conventions of 12 August 1949 on repression of grave breaches; or N. Boister and R. Burchill "The implications of the Pinochet Decision for the extradition of former South African Heads of States for crimes

cannot therefore validly enter into bilateral agreements to commit or condone the commission of crimes against humanity, nor can they unilaterally rely on the exercise of their sovereign powers to pardon the perpetrators of crimes that have offended all of humanity.[167] Such amnesty would legally be invalid, as implied by the example of Pinochet, whose domestic amnesty and immunity did not prevent the British courts to start legal proceedings against him.

Crimes against humanity appear therefore to limit the State's sovereign power to grant amnesty. This argument is in sharp contradiction with the South African Cape Provincial Division's approach in *AZAPO* to the effect that the South African Parliament is competent to pass an amnesty legislation that is contrary to international *jus cogens* norms.[168]

The present volume has so far established that amnesty for the most serious crimes of international concern cannot be valid under international law. Nevertheless, international law permits derogations in certain specific situations of urgency. It might be asked, then, whether amnesty may validly be invoked by national authorities as a form of derogation from their obligations in respect of gross human rights violations. In other words, does international law recognise amnesty as an exception to the *erga omnes* obligations arising out of the proscription of crimes against humanity?

International Crimes and Permissible Derogations Under International Law

Two forms of derogation are fundamental as far as States' obligations in respect of the most serious crimes under international law are concerned: derogation in time of public emergency and derogation under Article 6 (5) of Additional Protocol II to the Geneva Conventions of 12 August, 1949.

Derogations Based on 'Public Emergency'

Public emergency represents the most common context under which human rights obligations may be derogated from. In this regard, Article 4 (1) of the ICCPR provides that:

> In time of public emergency which threatens the life of the nation and the existence of which is officially proclaimed, the States Parties to the present Covenant may take measures derogating from their obligations under the present Convention to the extent strictly required by the exigencies of the situation, provided that such measures are not inconsistent with their other obligations under international law and do not involve

---

committed under apartheid" 11 *The African Journal of International and Comparative Law* (1999) at 631.

167 B. Chigara, chap. VI, n. 81 at 39.

168 See the previous chapter, or *AZAPO I*, chap. VI, n. 67 at 574 B–C.

discrimination solely on the ground of race, colour, sex, language, religion or social origin.

Both the ECHR of 1950 and the ACHR of 1969 contain similar derogative provisions.[169] According to a European Court of Human Rights' interpretation of these provisions, a danger, in order to qualify as a public emergency, must be actual or imminent; its effects must involve the whole nation; and the continuance of the organised life of the community must be threatened. In addition, the danger or crisis must be exceptional in that normal measures or restrictions permitted by the Convention for the maintenance of public safety, health and order, are plainly inadequate.[170]

It can be argued that the risks of disruption, implosion, political upheaval or civil wars that recently threatened transitional societies such as Argentina, El Salvador, Chile or South Africa could be qualified as public emergency requiring the adoption of special derogative measures to restore peace. Amnesty laws could therefore be justified as part of such measures.

However, the public emergency exception under the ICCPR is not unlimited. It is made subject to the observance by States Parties of their other obligations under international law. Three provisions of this instrument are fundamental as far as crimes against humanity are concerned. Firstly, Article 6 (1) and (2) prohibits derogations from the right to life, except in terms of pre-existing law of general application and not contrary to the obligations under the Covenant and under the Genocide Convention. This provision is consistent with Article 1 of the Genocide Convention which prohibits derogation in all circumstances by making genocide, whether committed in time of peace or in time of war, a punishable crime under international law. Secondly, Article 7 does not extend the emergency exception to cover cases of torture, cruel, inhuman or degrading treatment or punishment. This provision echoes the strong language of Article 2 (2) of the Torture Convention which expressly stipulates that no exceptional circumstances whatsoever, whether a state of war, internal political instability or any other public emergency, may be invoked as a justification of torture. War, which is the most extreme form of public emergency is also excluded by the Geneva Conventions of 1949 as a situation justifying derogations from the obligations to punish persons alleged to have committed grave breaches of the Conventions.[171] Finally, Article 8 (1) and (2) exclude the crimes against humanity, of slavery, slave-trade and servitude from the ambit of Article 4 (1). In addition, the proscription in Article 4 (1) of the ICCPR of derogative measures based on discriminatory grounds would mean that no exceptional circumstance may justify the crime of apartheid.

---

169 See Articles 15 and 36, as well as Article 27 (1) respectively.
170 See *The Greek Case*, 12 *Yearbook of the European Convention on Human Rights* (Suppl.) (1969) at 511; see also the European Court of Human Rights decision in *Ireland v. The United Kingdom* (Appl. No. 00005310 of 18–01–78), available at www.echr.coe. int, at paras 203–224.
171 See e.g., Article 2 (1) of Geneva Convention I.

It can therefore be concluded that the emergency exception under the ICCPR is limited as far as the prosecution of crimes against humanity is concerned. The obligations arising out of the proscription of such crimes are non-derogable. No situation of public emergency—be it a state of war or any other armed conflict, internal political instability or disturbance—may justify the commission of crimes against humanity.

Derogations Based on Additional Protocol II

Many recent decisions on amnesty have relied on Article 6 (5) of Additional Protocol II of 8 June, 1977 as a support for their decisions that amnesties for serious human rights violations are permitted under international law.[172] This provision provides that:

> At the end of hostilities, the authorities in power shall endeavour to grant the broadest possible amnesty to persons who have participated in the armed conflict, or those deprived of their liberty for reasons related to the armed conflict, whether they are interned or detained.

The South African Constitutional Court referred to Article 6 (5) to find that amnesty as an instrument of peace, reconciliation and reconstruction was justified;[173] while the Supreme Court interpreted this provision as establishing a form of derogation to the *erga omnes* obligation of *jus cogens* norms prohibiting the commission of crimes against humanity. This court held that:

> [T]here is an exception to the peremptory rule prohibiting an amnesty in relation to crimes against humanity contained in Additional Protocol II to the Geneva Conventions.[174]

And further that:

> In our judgment this sub-article indicates that there is no peremptory rule of international law which prohibits the granting of the broadest possible amnesty in the case of conflicts of the kind which existed in South Africa.[175]

Likewise, the Salvadorian Supreme Court emphasised the validity of amnesty by pointing to the provisions of Article 6 (5) of Additional Protocol II;[176] whereas the Chilean Supreme Court stated that amnesty under Article 6 (5) of Additional Protocol II was necessary in order to relieve grave political tension and to restore social tranquillity.[177]

---

172 See e.g., El Salvador Supreme Court's Decision on Amnesty, in N.J. Kritz, chap. I, n. 3 at 555; see also *AZAPO I*, chap. VI, n. 67 at 575 A–B and *AZAPO II*, chap. I, n. 31 at 1033 D.
173 *AZAPO II*, at 1033 D.
174 See the Cape Provincial Division of the Supreme Court in *AZAPO I*, at 574 D–E.
175 *Id.* at 575 B–C.
176 N.J. Kritz, chap. I, n. 3 at 555.
177 See *Romo Mena Case* Corte Suprema de Chile, 26 October, 1995.

However, it is not clearly established whether amnesty under Article 6 (5) of Additional Protocol II was meant to constitute a form of derogation to the *jus cogens* prohibition of crimes against humanity. Yet, what is fundamental is that this clause can only be understood within the general framework of the Geneva Conventions of 1949 requiring prosecution for grave breaches of the Conventions. In this regard, Domb suggests that any international agreement purporting to establish amnesty for war crimes would be null and void under Article 53 of the VCLT because of its derogation from the international peremptory norms requiring prosecution and punishment of war criminals.[178] Similar reasoning may well be valid in respect of domestic measures designed to indemnify perpetrators of crimes against humanity. This is because, as explained above, the crimes outlawed by the Geneva Conventions, the Genocide Convention, the Torture Convention and the Statute of the ICC are all *jus cogens* crimes requiring a positive action from all States even in the absence of a domestic law requiring it. Therefore, any attempt to interpret Article 6 (5) in relation to crimes against humanity must take into account the peremptory nature of the prohibition of such crimes.

As to the field of application of Article 6 (5), it is important to note that various arguments point to its limited scope. Cassel argues for example that citing Article 6 (5) of Protocol II to the Geneva Conventions as an international legal justification of amnesties for gross violations of human rights is misplaced. According to this author, this provision merely sought to encourage amnesty for combat activities otherwise subject to prosecution as violations of the criminal laws of the State in which they take place. It was not meant to support amnesties for violations of international humanitarian law.[179] This argument is pertinent in that it echoes a line of interpretation of Article 6 (5) adopted in a communication addressed in 1995 to the ICTY by the ICRC. This document states that:

> Article 6 (5) of Protocol II is the only and very limited equivalent in the law of non-international armed conflict of what is known in the law of international armed conflict as "combatant immunity", *i.e.*, the fact that a combatant may not be punished for acts of hostility, including killing enemy combatants, as long as he respected international humanitarian law, and that he has to be repatriated at the end of active hostilities. In non-international armed conflicts, no such principle exists, and those who fight may be punished, under national legislation, for the mere fact of having fought, even if they respected international humanitarian law. The "travaux préparatoires" of [Article] 6 (5) indicate that this provision aims at encouraging amnesty, *i.e.*, a sort of release at the end of hostilities, for those detained or punished for the mere fact of having participated in hostilities. It does not aim at an amnesty for those having violated international humanitarian law.[180]

Of fundamental relevance to the intended meaning of Article 6 (5) of Additional Protocol II is a statement made by the Soviet delegate at the Diplomatic Conference

---

178 See chap. II, n. 115 at 311.
179 See chap. I, n. 32 at 218.
180 *Id.* at 218.

at which Protocol II was negotiated, that Draft Article 10, which later became Article 6 (5):

> [C]ould not be construed as enabling war criminals or those guilty of crimes against peace and humanity, to evade severe punishment in any circumstances whatsoever.[181]

Moreover, it is suggested that the intent behind the Geneva Conventions of 1949 and Protocol II indicates a desire to limit the reach of Article 6 (5). These instruments were in fact designed to protect victims of armed conflicts.[182] Article 3 of the Geneva Conventions of 1949 deals with non-international armed conflict and prohibits torture, cruel treatment, outrages on personal dignity, the taking of hostages, and extrajudicial killings of persons not actively involved in the hostilities. However, since no requirement of penal sanctions is made in respect of these acts, it is believed that Protocol II is intended to fill this gap by ensuring more protection for victims.[183]

Finally, it would be very difficult to accept the proposition that amnesty under Article 6 (5) of Additional Protocol II was intended to apply to cases of crimes against humanity. This is illustrated by the fact that Additional Protocol II itself covers acts committed in the context of armed conflicts of a non-international character in contrast to the original four Geneva Conventions which apply to situations of international armed conflicts. On the other hand, crimes against humanity are capable of being committed not only in the context of armed conflicts—either international or non-international—but also in peace times. The definition, nature, and content of crimes against humanity whether committed in times of international war, non-international war or in times of peace remain unchanged. Therefore, if the Geneva Conventions make crimes against humanity punishable in situations of international war, it would be contradictory to subscribe to the proposition that amnesty under Article 6 (5) of Additional Protocol II was meant to be granted with respect to the same offence when committed in the context of non-international armed conflicts. This is simply because the context (i.e., international armed conflict, non-international armed conflict, and peace times) of the commission of crimes against humanity does not in itself change anything in the gravity of such crimes.

Therefore, both policy reasons (torture for example, is proscribed as a non-derogable right because it is so repugnant to the international community that no exceptional circumstance can justify it) and legal arguments support the conclusion that while a State may permissibly pass amnesties in response to a perceived emergency, or in order to re-establish peace within the nation, no amnesty may preclude investigation and prosecution of those responsible for offences that violate non-derogable rights. Such rights include freedom from torture, the right to be protected from genocide, war crimes or crimes against humanity.

---

181 *Id.* footnote 28.
182 N. Roht-Arriaza and L. Gibson, chap. II, n. 97 at 865.
183 *Id.*

Summary

In sum, international law appears unequivocal in rejecting amnesty for crimes against humanity irrespective of whether or not national legislatures adopt laws designed to indemnify the perpetrators thereof. This argument is strengthened by a 1985 report on amnesty laws by a United Nations Special *Rapporteur* which suggests that international crimes or crimes against humanity should not be subject to possible amnesty to avoid a situation in which "the infringement of the human condition is such that the right of oblivion may become a right to impunity."[184] The trend in international law is therefore to favour legal resolution of cases of crimes against humanity. This trend can be traced back to the first recorded trial of crimes against humanity in the fifteenth century at Bresach of a war criminal accused of trampling underfoot the laws of God and of humanity. Then followed the Nuremberg and Tokyo trials in 1945 and 1946 of persons accused of committing war crimes, crimes against humanity and crimes against peace during World War II. The ongoing proceedings before the *ad hoc* international criminal tribunals established under the auspices of the United Nations Security Council to prosecute persons alleged to have committed crimes against humanity in the former Yugoslavia, in Rwanda and in Sierra Leone also point to the fact that amnesty for these crimes cannot receive legal validation. To these jurisdictions, can be added, the establishment of a permanent ICC to try cases of Crimes against humanity, war crimes, genocide and aggression, or the proposed tribunal to prosecute members of the Khmer Rouges responsible of committing crimes against humanity and other atrocities in Cambodia.[185] The exclusion of amnesty for serious violations of international law by the Liberian amnesty Act is the most recent example that crystallizes the emerging trend as regards grant of amnesty. Because crimes against humanity are international offences and *jus cogens* crimes par excellence, their prosecution is a matter of international public policy and a matter of *erga omnes* obligations. Consequently, no State can claim the right individually to absolve the perpetrators of these crimes by granting them amnesty. In the eyes of current international law applicable to crimes against humanity, as the SCSL has correctly demonstrated in the *Kallon, Kamara Cases*, such an amnesty would be null and void and should not receive foreign or international validation.

---

184 "Study on Amnesty Laws and their Role in the Safeguard and Promotion of Human Rights" Preliminary Report by L. Joinet, Special *Rapporteur* of the United Nations Commission on Human Rights UN Doc E/CN.4/Sub.2/1985/16 (1985).

185 On Tuesday 13 May, 2003 the UN General Assembly approved an accord creating a war crime tribunal for Cambodia, see http://fr.news.yahoo.com/030514/5/370cz.html, consulted on 14 May, 2003.

GENERAL CONCLUDING ASSESSMENT AND SUGGESTIONS

Concluding Assessment

Synopsis

The main issue to determine in this study was, as set out in Chapter 1, whether amnesty for crimes against humanity can be legally valid under international law. In an attempt to answer this question, Chapter 2 has defined amnesty as an act of sovereign power designed not only to forgive persons who have committed certain specific offences (e.g., treason, sedition, rebellion, draft evasion) against the State, but also to help such persons lose memory of the existence of such offences. It has demonstrated that historically, the practice of granting amnesty developed in the context of war as an exception to the right of the victor to punish the vanquished. Usually provided for in peace treaties, amnesty has been granted consistently both in international and in non-international wars. In international wars, amnesty aims at consolidating the termination of the war and of establishing lasting peace, whereas in non-international wars its main purpose is to create conditions for peace, national reconciliation, rehabilitation and restoration within a divided State. It has also been shown that the legal effects of amnesty are mainly to discharge the offender from personal liability, to discontinue any court proceedings pending against him or to nullify any sentence already imposed on him.

However, the international criminalisation of crimes against peace, war crimes and crimes against humanity in 1945 and the codification of the principles of individual liability in respect thereof have had a deep impact on the institution of amnesty. In this regard, Chapter 3 has studied the concept of crimes against humanity as an extremely grave offence the commission of which affects humanity in its entirety. These crimes have been examined with reference to their foundations, meaning, nature, evolution, scope and content, and have been defined as any of the specific acts (of murder or persecution) committed as part of a widespread or systematic attack directed against a civilian population, in execution of a group, State or organisational policy, and with knowledge of the attack.

Chapter 4 has introduced the principle of individual criminal responsibility for crimes against humanity and has shown that such a principle calls for the individual liability of criminals against humanity and, consequently, does not favour the granting of amnesty. This Chapter has traced the legal sources of individual criminal liability for crimes against humanity back to the Versailles Treaty of 1919 and has examined participation as the main basis of liability for these crimes. It has finally identified different grounds for excluding criminal liability with the view to show that amnesty does not form part of such excluding grounds.

On the other hand, Chapter 5 has attempted to underscore the extent of State duties with respect to crimes against humanity. This chapter has presented different sources of State obligations to prosecute crimes against humanity and has shown that existing international criminal law treaties such as the four Geneva Conventions of 1949, the Genocide Convention of 1948, the Torture Convention of 1984, all of which impose a mandatory duty on States to prosecute define certain aspects of crimes against humanity. On the other hand, other documents such as general human rights instruments and certain United Nations resolutions have been examined as either not being explicit on the nature of States duties in respect of crimes against humanity, or as not carrying any binding legal force. Finally, it has been demonstrated with respect to the customary law duty to prosecute criminals against humanity that the difference between an *opinio juris* that strongly advocates criminal prosecution and the lack of a settled State practice in this regard has led to conclude to the existence of only a permissible jurisdiction to prosecute.

Chapter 6 has studied the South African case as an example of the application of the concept of amnesty to crimes that may otherwise be qualified as crimes against humanity. This case has shown how Section 20 of the South African amnesty law has extended the traditional scope of amnesty (namely, the crimes committed against the State) to include the criminal acts committed by the State itself. It has also demonstrated how the imperatives of national reconciliation have led the Cape Provincial Division of the Supreme Court to consider amnesty as an exception to international *jus cogens* rules. Such imperatives have also prevented the Constitutional Court from making a thorough inquiry into international law in order to determine the international legal validity of a domestic amnesty law. All these shortcomings have resulted in an unsatisfactory decision on the international lawfulness of the South African amnesty law.

Chapter 7 has attempted to establish the international legal status of amnesty in respect of crimes against humanity. It has demonstrated that amnesties for such crimes would be fundamentally illegal and invalid because they are in direct violation of international law. Consequently, States should refrain from granting such amnesties. In order to reach this conclusion, crimes against humanity have been presented as serious offences under international law the commission of which shocks the conscience of mankind and threatens the internationally shared values of dignity, peace and security. The force of the *jus cogens* status of crimes against humanity has proved to constitute a limitation on the object of a domestic amnesty law, whereas recent developments in international law and practice have highlighted a complete rejection of amnesty for these crimes.

In general, it can be concluded that the obligation not to grant amnesty for certain crimes against humanity is clear under treaty law (e.g., Genocide, Torture or the Geneva Conventions), whereas Article 27 of the VCLT bars States from unilaterally invoking their national laws as justification for not complying with international treaty obligations. Consequently there is no doubt that amnesty for acts of torture, genocide and war crimes are unlawful under international law.

However, the legal position of amnesty under customary international law is still uncertain, but not impossible to determine. This may be inferred from the obligations attached to specific aspects of crimes against humanity (such as torture, genocide, slavery, apartheid, piracy, etc.) that are contained in specialised conventions. Such conventions insist on prosecutions and punishments when the crimes they defined have been committed. In addition, crimes against humanity are universally rejected and their capacity to threaten international peace and security and to shock the conscience of mankind is no more in doubt, hence their elevation to the status of *jus cogens* crimes which impose obligations *erga omnes*. Moreover, recent international pronouncements and international practice on amnesty tend to demonstrate that amnesty cannot be legally valid for the customary law offence of crimes against humanity. It would be, for example, contradictory to outlaw the application of statutory limitations to crimes against humanity and, at the same time, permit amnesty to stand as a *de facto* limitation to the punishment of the perpetrators thereof.

Comments

Three important observations have been made throughout this study. The first relates to the basic meaning of amnesty. In this regard, amnesty has been defined in chapter 2 as oblivion, forgetfulness, losing memory or a sovereign act designed to apply the principle of *tabula rasa* to past crimes. In this context (i.e., that of war), grants of amnesty are not subject to any further investigation. However, the South African conditional amnesty which was made subject to full disclosure of past crimes supplemented with serious investigations by a truth commission, witness hearing, confrontation between the victims or their family and their torturers, and the instruction to keep full record of all what happened, has added another dimension to the original definition of amnesty. Amnesty is no more an act of forgetfulness only; it has also become, at least in the context of political crisis or public emergency, a means of exorcising the past, a means of remembrance.

Secondly, it shall be noted that a purposive and value-laden interpretation of international instruments dealing with crimes against humanity coupled with the pronouncements of certain international human rights institutions such as the

United Nations Commission on Human Rights or the ICRC, and the judgments of international and national tribunals (e.g., in *Pinochet* and *Furundzija*) could strictly limit the application of Article 6 (5) of Additional Protocol II to crimes against humanity. This argument is strengthened by the imperative of punishment contained in the ICC statute and by Article 10 of the Statute of the SCSL, which suggests that amnesty for crimes against humanity is not a bar to prosecution.

The final finding is that amnesty granted to criminals against humanity is inherently and fundamentally invalid under international law. The only exceptions being, in addition to the traditional grounds for excluding criminal responsibility in international law, the narrow circumstance in which a huge proportion of a population would be involved in the perpetration of these crimes. In this case, the prosecution of all offenders may prove logistically, financially and humanely impossible. Therefore, criminal prosecution for the most responsible offenders and conditional amnesty for lesser offenders could be an acceptable option, unless such an option is a threat to international peace and security. It is also worth mentioning here that in international law, amnesty is neither a bar to criminal prosecution, nor a ground for excluding criminal liability.

Suggestions

The approach adopted in this book does not advocate a total rejection of the institution of amnesty. It is rather a claim for its limitation where it aims at indemnifying persons who have committed serious crimes under international law. Therefore, whenever domestic authorities are called to grant amnesty for serious violations of human rights, it is suggested that they apply, as far as possible, international standards of human rights in evaluating the lawfulness of such an amnesty. In this regard, Cassel has developed certain guidelines that may strengthen the international legal force of a domestic amnesty decree. Among these are the following:

(1) Democratic adoption, in terms of which amnesties must be adopted by democratic bodies, such as the legislature. In this regard, self-amnesties by lawless regimes cannot be valid.

(2) Investigations: amnesties must be followed by serious investigations of the violations allegedly committed, in order to vindicate both society's right to know the truth and survivors' right to know what happened to their relatives. Those responsible for the atrocities must be identified and their names must be made public.

(3) Compensation: Amnesties may not foreclose or limit the right of victims or survivors to obtain adequate compensation for violations.

(4) Crimes against humanity: amnesties must not apply to crimes against humanity, including forced disappearances.

(5) Prosecution and Punishment: States must prosecute and effectively punish perpetrators of serious human rights violations. Such perpetrators may not be amnestied.[1]

To these guidelines, the following recommendations could be added:

To States

Treaty Law Crimes: States parties to treaty crimes, such as the Torture Convention, the Genocide Convention, the Slavery or the Geneva Conventions, etc, shall refrain from granting amnesties for such crimes.

Customary Law Crimes: States must not grant amnesties for any customary international law crime when it has reached the status of *jus cogens*. Many argue that States are not obliged to prosecute crimes against humanity because no law exists that clearly establishes a duty to prosecute such crimes. This argument shall be rejected for the following reason: given the fact that crimes against humanity are an offence whose commission is not generalised (i.e., which are committed only from time to time) the evaluation of the existence or not of a State duty to prosecute the perpetrators thereof shall not be based on a strict requirement of a uniform State practice, or strict universality. Moderate State or international practice supplemented with the already existing strong *opinio juris* condemning the commission of crimes against humanity, together with the importance of the values protected by the prohibition of such crimes shall be sufficient to establish such a duty.

Minor Children: total amnesty shall always be granted to minor children who have committed crimes against humanity. This shall, at all times, be supplemented with a programme to rehabilitate and reintegrate them within the society, as well as an action by State authorities to alleviate the plight of the victims or of the victims' families.

Post-Conviction Amnesties: amnesty for crimes against humanity may well be valid if it takes place long after the perpetrator has been prosecuted, convicted and has spent a substantial amount of time in jail. He may, for example, be amnestied on medical grounds. However, pre-conviction amnesties must be avoided.

To the United Nations

It is suggested that a multilateral treaty be adopted prohibiting the grant of amnesty in respect of war crimes and crimes against humanity. This may take the form of an Additional Protocol to the Convention on the Non-Applicability of Statutory Limitations to War Crimes and Crimes against Humanity of 1968, which

---

1   See n. 32 at 228–229.

would contain a provision expressly excluding amnesty for war crimes, genocide, and crimes against humanity.

The United Nations Security Council may be permitted, at all time, to declare any domestic amnesty for crimes against humanity unlawful as in contradiction with Chapter VII of the United Nations Charter. This will only give more sense to States' rejection of these crimes as they usually express it in their deliberations within the United Nations General Assembly.

To the International Criminal Court

When amnesty has been granted to lesser perpetrators of crimes against humanity in the context of a widespread perpetration involving an important proportion of a population, a specialised *ad hoc* committee within the ICC shall be able to investigate the genuineness of the process of selecting those eligible for such amnesty and to ensure that the most responsible perpetrators are brought before the courts.

The newly established ICC should develop its jurisprudence on amnesty in respect of the Statute's crimes, which could serve as a yardstick on the basis of which the international lawfulness of domestic amnesties may be measured. Such jurisprudence may follow, for example, the same line as that of the ICTY in the *Furundzija* case, that of the ICJ Advisory Opinion on the Genocide Convention, or that of the interpretation line adopted by the SCSL in the *Kallon, Kamara Cases*.

BIBLIOGRAPHY

The following bibliography lists the works and names of the principal authors cited in this volume. It also contains a list of international and national legal documents, as well as internet links that appear throughout the book. The most relevant cases for the topic discussed in the text are listed in the index, whereas the complete case law of the entire volume is included in the present bibliography.

Books and Collected Works

Abi-Saab, G. Definition of *jus cogens*, in *Papers and Proceedings II: The Concept of Jus Cogens in International Law* (3rd Conference on International Law held in Lagonisi, Greece, between 3–8 April 1966) (1967), Geneva, Carnegie Endowment for International Peace, pp. 7–15

Axelrod, Alan and Phillips Charles L. *Encyclopedia of Historical Treaties and Alliances* Volume I, *From Ancient Times to World War I* (2001), Chicago, Fitzroy Dearborn Publishers

Bass, Gary Jonathan *Stay the Hands of Vengeance: The Politics of War Crimes Tribunals* (2000), New Jersey, Princetown University Press

Bassiouni, M. Cherif *Crimes against Humanity in International Criminal Law* (1992), The Hague, Kluwer Law International;
Crimes against Humanity in International Criminal Law (1999), The Hague, Kluwer Law International;
Crimes against Humanity in International Criminal Law (2000), The Hague, Kluwer Law International;
International Criminal Law: Crimes 2nd ed. (1999), New York, Transnational Publishers Inc.;
International Protection of Victims (1988), Toulouse, Eres;
International Criminal Law: A Draft International Criminal Code (1980), Sijthoff and Noordhoff, Alphen aan den Rijn;
——, and Wise, Edward M. *Aut dedere, Aut Judicare: The Duty to Extradite or Prosecute in International Law* (1995), Dordrecht, Martinus Nijhoff Publishers

Basson, Dion *South Africa's Interim Constitution* (1994), Kenwyn, Juta and Co., Ltd

Bettati, Mario, Le crime contre l'humanité, in Herve Ascensio, Emmanuel Decaux and Alain Pellet (ed.), *Droit International Pénal* (2000), Paris, Éditions A. Pedone, pp. 293–317

Black-Branch, Jonathan L, Sovereign immunity under international law: the case of Pinochet, in D. Woodhouse *The Pinochet Case: A Legal and Constitutional Analysis* (2000)
Oxford-Portland, Oregon, Hart Publishing, pp. 93–113

Black, H.C. *Black's Law Dictionary* 6th ed. (1992), St. Paul MN, West Publishing Co.

Brownlie, Ian *Principles of Public International Law* 4th ed. (1990), New York, Oxford
University Press Inc.;
  Principles of Public International Law 5th ed. (1998), New York, Oxford University
  Press Inc.

Burgers, J. Herman and Hans Danelius *The United Nations Convention Against Torture: A
Handbook on the Convention Against Torture and Other Cruel, Inhuman or Degrading
Treatment or Punishment* (1988), Dordrecht, Martinus Nijhoff Publishers

Cassese, Antonio *International Criminal Law* (2003), New York, Oxford University Press
Inc

Chigara, Ben *Amnesty in International Law: The Legality under International Law of National
Amnesty* (2002), Harlow, Longman

Concise Oxford Dictionary, 9th ed. (1995), Oxford, Oxford University Press

Dalloz *Nouveau Code Pénal Français* (1992), Paris, Éditions Dalloz

de Villiers, Bertus (ed.), *Birth of a Constitution* (1994), Kenwyn, Juta & Co., Ltd

de Villiers, Susan *Truth and Reconciliation Commission of South Africa Report* Volume I
(1998), Cape Town, Juta & Co., Ltd

De Zayas, Alfred-Maurice, Amnesty clause, in R. Bernhardt (ed.), *Encyclopaedia of Public
International Law*, Volume I, (1992), Amsterdam, Elsevier Science Publishers B.V., pp.
148–151

Dixon, Martin and Robert McCorquodale *Cases and Materials on International Law*
3rd ed. (2000), London, Blackstone Press Ltd

Domb, Fania, Treatment of war crimes in peace settlements—prosecution or amnesty?, in
Yoram Dinstein and Mala Tabory (ed.), *War Crimes in International Law* (1996), The
Hague, Kluwer Law International, pp. 305–320

Du Plessis, Lourens, Amnesty and transition in South Africa, in Alex Boraine, Janet Levy
and Ronel Scheffer (eds.), *Dealing with the Past: Truth and Reconciliation in South Africa*
(1994), Cape Town, IDASA, pp. 107–116

Ferencz, Benjamin B. *An International Criminal Court, a Step toward World Peace—A
Documentary History and Analysis: Half a Century of Hope* Volume 1, (1980), New
York, Oceana Publications, Inc.;
  Crimes against humanity, in: R. Bernhardt (ed.), *Encyclopedia of Public International Law*
  Volume 1, (1992), Amsterdam, Elsevier Science Publishers B.v., pp. 869–871

Frowein, Jochen Abr. *Das de-facto Regime im Völkerrecht—eine Untersuchung zur Rechtsstel-
lung "nichtanerkannter Staaten" und ähnlicher Gebilde* (1968), Köln, Heyman;
  Jus cogens, in R. Bernhardt (ed.), *Encyclopedia of Public International Law*, Instalment
  7 (1984), Amsterdam, Elsevier Science Publishers B.v., pp. 327–330;
  Die Verpflichtungen erga omnes im Völkerrecht und ihre Durchsetzung in R. Bernhardt etc.
  (ed.), *Völkerrecht als Rechtsordnung—internationale Gerichtsbarkeit—Menschenrechte*:
  Festschrift für Hermann Mosler, (1983), West Berlin, Springer, pp. 241–263

Greig, D.W. *International Law* 2nd ed. (1976), London, Butterworth & Co., Ltd

Hartigan, Richard Shelly *Lieber's Code and the Law of War* (1983), Chicago, Precedent
Publishing, Inc.

Hannikainen, Lauri *Peremptory Norms (Jus Cogens) in International Law* (1988), Helsinki,
Finnish Lawyers' Publishing Company

Institute for Human Rights and Development *Compilation of Decisions on Communications
of the African Commission on Human and Peoples' Rights: Extracts from the Commission's
Activity Reports 1994–2001* (2002), Dakar, Les Presses de L'Imprimerie Saint-Paul

International Committee of the Red Cross (ed.), *Basic Rules of the Geneva Conventions and
their Additional Protocols* (1983), Geneva, International Committee of the Red Cross

International Military Trials: Nazi Conspiracy and Aggression Volume II, (1946), Washington D.C., US Government Printing Office

International Military Tribunal *Trial of the Major War Criminals before the International Military Tribunal*: 14 November 1945–1 October 1946 volumes I and 22 (1947), Buffalo, New York, Hein

Israel, Fred L. (ed.), *Major Peace Treaties of Modern History 1648–1967* volumes I and II (1967), New York, Chelsea House Publishers;
Major Peace Treaties of Modern History: 1648–2000 vol. IV (2002), Philadelphia, Chelsea House Publishers

Jackson, Robert Houghwout, Report to the President, in *Trial of War Criminals* (1945), Washington D.C., US Department of State Publication, pp. 1–12

Jennings, Robert and Arthur Watts, (eds.), *Oppenheim's International Law* 9th ed., Volume I, (1992), London, Longman

Joyner, Christopher C. (ed.), *Reining in Impunity for International Crimes and Serious Violations of Fundamental Human Rights* (1998), Toulouse, Ed. Érès

Kershaw, Ian *Hitler 1889–1936, Hubris* (1999), New York, WW Norton & Company, Inc.

Kritz, Neil J. (ed.), *Transitional Justice: How Emerging Democracies Reckon with Former Regimes* Part III (1995), Washington, US Institute of Peace Press

Krog, Antjie *Country of my Skull* (1998), Johannesburg, Random House

Larousse, Pierre *Grand Dictionnaire Encyclopédique Larousse* Volume I, (1982), Paris, Publications Larousse

Lattanzi, Flavia The International Criminal Court and national jurisdictions, in M. Politi and G. Nesi *The Rome Statute of the International Criminal Court: A Challenge to Impunity* (2001), Hants, Ashgate Publishing Ltd., pp. 177–196

Laucci, Cyril *Digest of Jurisprudence of the Special Court for Sierra Leone* (2007), Leiden, Martinus Nijhoff Publishers

Law Report of the Trial of the Major War Criminals Before the International Military Tribunal (1947), London, His Majesty's Stationary Office

McDonald, Gabrielle Kirk and Swaak-Goldman, Olivia (ed.), *Substantive and Procedural Aspects of International Criminal Law: The Experience of International and National Courts*, Volume I, Part I, and Volume II, Part I, *Documents and Cases* (2000), The Hague, Kluwer Law International

Mendelson, Maurice H., The formation of customary international law, in 272 *Recueil des Cours: Collected Courses of the Hague Academy of International Law* (1998), The Hague, Martinus Nijhoff Publishers, pp. 155–410

Meredith, Martin *Nelson Mandela: A Biography* (1997), London, Penguin Group Ltd

Meron, Theodor, The Humanization of the Law of War, in 301 *Recueil des Cours: Collected Courses of the Hague Academy of International Law* (2003), The Hague, Martinus Nijhoff Publishers, pp. 24–111

Nesi, Giuseppe, The obligation to co-operate with the International Criminal Court and States not Party to the Statute, in M. Politi, M. and N. Nesi, *The Rome Statute of the International Criminal Court: A Challenge to Impunity* (2001), Hants, Ashgate Publishing Ltd., pp. 221–223

O'Shea, Andreas *Amnesty for Crime in International Law and Practice* (2002), The Hague, Kluwer Law International

Palmer, HA and Henry Palmer *Harris Criminal Law*, 19th ed. (1954), London, Sweet and Maxwell Ltd

Paust, Jordan J., Content and contours of genocide, crimes against humanity, and war crimes, in Sienho Yee and Tieya Wang (eds.), *International Law in the Post-Cold War World, Essays in Memory of Li Haopei* (2001), London, Routledge, pp. 289–306

Pictet, Jean S. (ed.), *Commentary on the Additional Protocols of 8 June 1977 to the Geneva Conventions of 12 August 1949* (1987), Geneva, Martinus Nijhoff Publishers;
Commentary of Geneva Convention I (1951), Geneva, The International Committee of the Red Cross Publication

Pilloud, Claude *Commentary on the Additional Protocols of 8 June 1977 to the Geneva Conventions of 12 August 1949* (1987), (The International Committee of the Red Cross), Geneva, Martinus Nijhoff Publishers

Politi, Mauro and Giuseppe Nesi *The Rome Statute of the International Criminal Court: A Challenge to Impunity* (2001), Hants, Ashgate Publishing Ltd.

Ratner, Steven R. and Abrams Jason S. *Accountability for Human Rights Atrocities in International Law: Beyond the Nuremberg Legacy* (1997), New York, Oxford University Press Inc.

Robertson, Geoffrey Q.C. *Crimes against Humanity: The Struggle for Global Justice* (1999), London, Penguin Press

Roht-Arriaza, Naomi, Non-treaty sources of the obligation to investigate and prosecute, in Naomi Roht-Arriaza (ed.), *Impunity and Human Rights in International Law and Practice* (1995), New York, Oxford University Press, Inc.

Röling, B.V.A., The law of war and the national jurisdiction since 1945, in 100 *Recueil des Cours* (1960 II), The Hague, Martinus Nijhoff Publishers, pp. 325–456

Rwelamira, M.R. and G. Merle *Confronting Past Injustices: Approaches to Amnesty, Punishment, Reparation and Restitution in South Africa and Germany* (1996), Durban, Butterworths

Schlunck, Angelika *Amnesty versus Accountability: Third Party Intervention Dealing with Gross Human Rights Violations in Internal and International Conflicts* (2000), Berlin, Verlag Arno Spitz GmbH

Schwarzenberger, Georg and E.D. Brown *The Manual of International Law* 6th ed. (1976), Oxon, Professional Books Ltd

Shabas, William A., The Crime of Genocide in the Jurisprudence of the International Criminal Tribunal, in Horst Fisher, Knut Ipsen and Joachim Wolf, *Bochumer Schriften zur Friedenssicherung und zum Humanitären Völkerrecht*, Band 38 (2000), Berlin, Berlin Verlag Arno Spitz GmbH

Scott, James Brown *The Hague Conventions and Declarations of 1899 and 1907* (1915), New York, Oxford University Press

Simma, Bruno (ed.) *The Charter of the United Nations: A Commentary* (2nd ed.), vol. I and II (2002), New York, Oxford University Press

Sloan, Blaine *United Nations General Assembly Resolutions in our Changing World* (1991), New York, Transnational Publishers

Sunga, Lyal S. *Individual Responsibility in International Law for Serious Human Rights Violations* (1992), Dordrecht, Nijhoff

Suy, Erik, The concept of *jus cogens* in public international law, in *Papers and Proceedings II: The Concept of Jus Cogens in International Law* (3rd Conference on International Law held in Lagonisi, Greece, between 3–8 April 1966) (1967), Geneva, Carnegie Endowment for International Peace, pp. 17–69

Triffterer, Otto (ed.), *Commentary on the Rome Statute of the International Criminal Court* (1999), Baden-Baden, Nomos

Van den Wyngaert, Christine *International Criminal Law: a Collection of International and European Instruments* (1996), The Hague, Kluwer Law International; *The Political Offence Exception to Extradition: The Delicate Problem of Balancing the Rights of the Individual and the International Public Order* (1980), Deventer, Kluwer

Viljoen, Frans, Overview of the African regional human rights system, in Christof Heyns (ed.), *Human Rights Law in Africa* (1998), The Hague, Kluwer Law International, pp. 128–199

Villiger, Mark E. *Customary International Law and Treaties: A Manual on the Theory and Practice of the Interrelation of Sources* Revised 2nd ed. (1997), The Hague, Kluwer Law International

Walter, Yust *Encyclopaedia Britannica*, Volume I, (1960), London, Encyclopaedia Britannica

Watts, Sir Arthur *1994–III Recueil des Cours: Collected Courses of the Hague Academy of International Law*, Volume 247 of the Collection, (1995), Dordrecht, Martinus Nijhoff Publishers

Woodhouse, Diana *The Pinochet Case: A Legal and Constitutional Analysis* (2000), Oxford-Portland, Oregon, Hart Publishing

Articles

Arsanjani, M.H. "The international criminal court and national amnesty laws" 93 *The American Society of International Law Proceedings of the 93rd Annual Meeting of March 24–27 1999* (2000), Washington D.C., The American Society of International Law, pp. 65–68

Bassiouni, M. Cherif and Daniel H. Derby "Final report on the establishment of an international criminal court for the implementation of the Apartheid Convention and other relevant international instruments" 9 *Hofstra Law Review* (1981), Hempstead, Hofstra Law Review Association, pp. 523–592;

"Crimes against humanity: The need for a specialised convention" 31 *Columbia Journal of Transnational Law* (1994), New York, Oceana Publications, pp. 457–494;

"Searching for peace and achieving justice: the need for accountability" 59 *Law and Contemporary Problems* 4 (1996), Durham, The Duke University School of Law, pp. 9–28;

"International crimes: *Jus cogens* and *obligatio erga omnes*" 59 *Law and Contemporary Problems* 4 (1996), Durham, Duke University School of Law, pp. 64–74;

———, and Daniel H. Derby "An appraisal of torture in international law and practice: the need for an international convention for the protection and suppression of torture" 48 *Revue International de Droit Penal* 17 (1977), Toulouse, ed. Erès

BBC News Online "*Brutal Child Army Grows Up*" (June 1, 2000), available at http://www.news.bbc.co.uk/hi/english/world/africa/newsid_743000/743684.stm

Boister, Neil and Richard Burchill "The implications of the Pinochet Decision for the extradition of former South African Heads of States for crimes committed under apartheid" 11 *The African Journal of International and Comparative Law* (1999), London, The African Society for International and Comparative Law, pp. 619–637

Bongiorno, Carla "A culture of impunity: applying international human rights law to the United Nations in East Timor" 33 *Columbia Human Rights Law Review* 3 (2002), pp. 623–692

Cassel, Douglass "Lessons from the Americas: Guidelines for international responses to amnesties for atrocities" 59 *Law and Contemporary Problems* 4 (1996), Durham, The Duke University School of Law, pp. 196–230

Cassese, Antonio "Reflections on international criminal justice" 61 *The Modern Law Review* 1 (1998), London, Blackwell Publishers, pp. 1–10;

"The Martens Clause: half a loaf or simply pie in the sky?" 11 *European Journal of International Law* 1 (2000), Oxford, Oxford University Press, pp. 187–216

D'Amato, Anthony A. "The concept of Special custom in international law" 63 *American Journal of International Law* (1969), Washington D.C., The American Society of International Law, pp. 211–223

de Hemptinne, Jerôme "La définition du crime contre l'humanité par le TPIY" 9 *Revue Trimestrielle des Droits de l'Homme* 36 (1st October 1998), Bruxelles, Bruylant, pp. 763–779

Divino, Jacob Milton C. "*Delicti Jus Gentium*: A limitation on the State's power to grant amnesty" 40 *Ateneo Law Journal* (1995), Manila, The Ateneo de Manila University School of Law, pp. 202–250

Dugard, John "Is the truth and reconciliation process compatible with international law? An unanswered question" 13 *The South African Journal on Human Rights* (1997), Kenwyn, Juta & Co. Ltd., pp. 258–268

Edelenbos, Carla "Human rights violations: a duty to prosecute?" 7 *Leiden Journal of International Law* 14 (1994), Leiden, Faculty of Law Leiden University, pp. 5–21

Glaser, Stefan "Le principe de la légalité des délits et des peines et les procès de criminels de guerre" 28 *Revue de Droit Pénal et de Criminologie* (1947–8), Paris, Dalloz, pp. 230–238;
"Le principe de la légalité en matière pénale, notamment en droit codifié et en droit coutumier" 46 *Revue de Droit Pénal et de Criminologie* (1966), Paris, Dalloz, p. 899

Green, L.C. "Command responsibility in international humanitarian law" 5 *Transnational Law and Contemporary Problems* 2 (1995), Iowa City, The University of Iowa College of Law, pp. 319–371

Jackson, Robert H. "Report to the President" 39 *American Journal of International Law* (1945), Washington D.C., The American Society of International Law p. 180

Jankelevitch, Vladimir "Opinion libre", *Le Monde* (3 January 1965), Paris, Publications du Groupe Le Monde, p. 3;
"L'imprescriptible" *La Revue Administrative* No. 103 (January-February 1965), Paris, Montchrestien, pp. 37–42

Kagabo, José "Le sens d'une commémoration" *Le Monde Diplomatique* (March 2004), Paris, S.A. Le Monde Diplomatique, p. 20

Levy, Albert G.D. "Criminal Responsibility of individuals and international law" 12 *The University of Chicago Law Revue* 4 (1945), Chicago, The University of Chicago Law School, pp. 313–332

Macaluso, Daniel J. "Absolute and free pardon: the effect of the amnesty provision in the Lome Peace Agreement on the jurisdiction of the Special Court for Sierra Leone" 27 *Brooklyn Journal of International Law* (2001–2002), New York, The Brooklyn Law School, pp. 347–380

Mansfield, Leslie "Crimes against humanity: Reflections on the Fiftieth Anniversary of Nuremberg and a forgotten legacy" 64 *Nordic Journal of International Law* (1995), Dordrecht, Nijhoff, pp. 293–341

Menon, PK "Primary, subsidiary and other possible sources of international law" 1 *Sri Lanka Journal of International Law* (1989), Colombo, Faculty of Law and the Department of International Relations, University of Colombo, pp. 113–149

Meron, Theodor "International criminalization of internal atrocities" 89 *The American Journal of International Law* (1993), Washington D.C., The American Society of International Law, pp. 554–577;
"Rape as a crime under international humanitarian law" 87 *The American Journal of International Law* (1993), Washington D.C., The American Society of International Law, pp. 424–428;
"The Martens Clause, principles of humanity, and dictates of public conscience" 94 *American Journal of International Law* 1 (2000), Washington D.C., The American Society of International Law, pp. 78–89

Moellendorf, Darrel "Amnesty, truth and Justice: AZAPO" 13 *South African Journal on Human Rights* (1997), Cape Town, Juta & Co., Ltd., pp. 283–291

Motala, Ziyad "The Constitutional Court's approach to international law and its method of interpretation in the 'amnesty decision': intellectual honesty or political expediency?" 21 *South African Yearbook of International Law* (1996), Pretoria, Verloren van Themaat Centre for Public Law Studies, pp. 29–59

Nicholls, Clive "Reflections on Pinochet" 41 *Virginia Journal of International Law* (2000), Charlottesville, Virginia Journal of International Law Association, pp. 140–151

Orentlicher, Dianne "Settling accounts: the duty to prosecute human rights violations of a prior regime" 100 *The Yale Law Journal* 8 (1991), Connecticut, The Yale Law Journal Company Inc., pp. 2537–2615

Parker, Peter "The politics of indemnities, truth telling and reconciliation in South Africa" 17 *Human Rights Law Journal* No. 1–2, (1996), Kehl am Rhein, N.P. Engel, pp. 1–13

Popoff, Evo "Inconsistency and impunity in international human rights law: can the International Criminal Court solve the problems raised by the Rwanda and Augusto Pinochet cases?" 33 *George Washington International Law Review* 33 (2001), pp. 363–395

Puurunen, Tapio "The committee on amnesty of the South African truth and reconciliation commission—a new model of conflict resolution" 9 *The Finnish Yearbook of International Law* (1998), The Hague, Kluwer Law International, pp. 297–348

Rikhof, Joseph "Crimes against humanity, customary international law and the international tribunals for Bosnia and Rwanda" 6 *National Journal of Constitutional Law* (1996), Toronto, Carswell Thomson Professional Publishing, pp. 233–268

Robinson, Darryl "Serving the interests of justice: amnesties, truth commissions and the International Criminal Court" 14 *European Journal of International Law* 3 (2003), Munich, Law Books in Europe P.A. Beck, pp. 481–505

Roht-Arriaza, Naomi "State responsibility to investigate and prosecute grave human rights violations in international law" 78 *California Law Review* (1990), Berkeley, The University of California Press, pp. 451–513;

——, and Lauren Gibson "The developing jurisprudence on amnesty" 20 *Human Rights Quarterly* 1 (1998), Cincinnati, The John Hopkins University Press, pp. 843–885

Scharf, Michael P. "The amnesty exception to the jurisdiction of the International Criminal Court" 32 *Cornell International Law Journal* 3 (1999), Ithaca NY, SOC, pp. 507–527;
"The letter of the law: the scope of the international legal obligation to prosecute human rights crimes" 59 *Law and Contemporary Problems* No. 4 (1996), Duke Durham, University School of Law, pp. 41–61

Schwelb, Egon "Crimes against humanity" 23 *British Yearbook of International Law* (1946), London, Oxford University Press, pp. 178–226

Schoiswohl, Michael "De facto regimes and human rights obligations—the twilight zone of public international law?" 6 *Austrian Review of International and European Law* (2001), Leiden, Martinus Nijhoff Publishers, pp. 45–90

Simma, Bruno and Andreas L. Paulus "The responsibility of individuals for human rights abuses in internal conflicts: A positivistic view" (Symposium on Method in International Law) 93 *American Journal of International Law* 2 (1999), Washington D.C., The American Society of International Law, pp. 302–316

Simon, Pierre F. "La clause d'amnistie dans les traités de paix" 26 *Revue Générale de Droit International Public* (1919), Paris, Pedone, pp. 245–261

Slye, Ronald C. "Apartheid as a crime against humanity: A submission to the South African Truth and Reconciliation Commission" 20 *Michigan Journal of International Law* (1998), Ann Arbor, University of Michigan Law School, pp. 267–300

Stirling-Zanda, Simonetta "The individual criminal responsibility of judicial organs in international law in the lights of international practice" 48 *The Netherlands International Law Review* 1 (2001), Dordrecht, Kluwer Law International, pp. 67–100

Van der Vyver, Johan D. "Prosecution and punishment of the crime of genocide" 23 *Fordham International Law Journal* 2 (1999), New York, Fordham University School of Law, pp. 286–356

Van-Schaack, Beth "The definition of crimes against humanity: Resolving the incoherence" 37 *Columbia Journal of Transnational Law* 3 (1999), New York, Oceana Publications, pp. 787–850

Weisman, Norman "A history and discussion of amnesty" 4 *Columbia Human Rights Law Review* 1 (1972), New York, The Columbia University School of Law, pp. 529–540

Zeidy, El "The principle of complementarity: A new machinery to implement international criminal law" 23 *Michigan Journal of International Law* 869 (2002), Ann Arbor, University of Michigan Press

International Legal Instruments

Additional Protocol to the European Convention on Extradition, 1975
African Charter on Human and Peoples' Rights, OAU Doc. CAB/LEG/67/3 rev.5, 21 *I.L.M.*
58 (1982)
American Convention on Human Rights, O.A.S.T.S. 1, OEA/ser.L./V/II.23, doc.21 of
1979
Charter of the International Military Tribunal for the Far East, 1946
Charter of the International Military Tribunal for the Trial of the Major War Criminals of
the European Axis, 8 August 1945, 82 UNTS, 279, 288
Charter of the Organisation of the African Unity, 1963
Charter of the United Nations (1945), 59 Stat. 1031, TS 993, 3 Bevans 1153
Control Council Law No. 10, Punishment of Persons Guilty of War Crimes, Crimes against
Peace and Crimes against Humanity, 1945
Control Council for Germany, 3 *Official Gazette*, Control Council for Germany 50–55
(1946)
Convention against Torture and Other Cruel, Inhuman or Degrading Treatment or Punish-
ment, 1984, G.A. Res. 39/46, U.N. Doc. A/39/51 (1984)
Convention on the Non-Applicability of Statutory Limitations to War Crimes and Crimes
against Humanity, 1968, G.A. Res. 2391 (XXIII), U.N. Doc. A/RES/2391 (XXIII) of 9
December 1968
Convention on the Prevention and Punishment of the Crime of Genocide, 1948, GA Res.
260 A (II), 78 UNTS 227
Convention on the Rights of the Child, 1989, GA Res. 44/25 of 20 November 1989
Convention Relating to the Status of Refugees, 1951
Declaration on Basic Principles of Justice for Victims of Crimes and Abuse of Power, 1985,
GA Res. 40/34, 40 UN. GAOR Supp. No. 53, at 213, UN Doc. A/40/53 (1985)
Draft Code of Crimes against the Peace and Security of Mankind, ILC 43rd Session, UN
Doc. A/CN.4/L.459 (1991)
Draft Code of Crimes against the Peace and Security of Mankind, ILC 51st Session, UN
Doc. A/51/10 (1996)
Draft Code of Offence against the Peace and Security of Mankind, 1951
Draft Convention against Torture and Other Cruel, Inhuman or Degrading Treatment or
Punishment, 23 *ILM* 5, 1027 (1984)
Economic Community of West African States Convention on Extradition, 1994
European Convention for the Protection of Human Rights and Fundamental Freedoms,
1950, 213 U.N.T.S. 222
European Convention on Extradition, 1957
European Convention on the Non-Applicability of Statutory Limitations to Crimes against
Humanity and War Crimes, 1974, *European Treaty Series* No. 82
Final Declaration and Programme of Action, 1993 World Conference on Human Rights,
Part II, 60, UN Doc. A/Conf/57/24, reprinted in 32 *ILM*, 166 (1993)
General Assembly Proclamation on Genocide (1946), G. A. Res. 96 (1), U. N. GAOR, 1st
Sess., Part II, U. N. Doc. A/64/Add. 1 (1947)
Geneva Conventions (I) of 12 August 1949 for the Amelioration of the Condition of the
Wounded and Sick in the Armed Forces in the Field, 6 U.S.T. 311, T.I.A.S. No. 3362,
75 UNTS. 31
Geneva Convention (II) for the Amelioration of the Condition of the Wounded, Sick and
Shipwrecked Members of the Armed Forces at Sea, 6 U.S.T. 3217, T.I.A.S. No. 3363,
75 UNTS. 85
Geneva Convention (III) Relative to the Treatment of Prisoners of War, 6 U.S.T. 3316,
T.I.A.S. No. 3364, 75 UNTS. 135
Geneva Convention (IV) Relating to the Protection of Civilian Persons in Time of War, 6
U.S.T. 3516, T.I.A.S No. 3365, 75 UNTS. 287

Hague Convention for the Protection of Cultural Property in the Event of Armed Conflict, 1954

Hague Convention II, Respecting the Laws and Customs of War on Land, 1899

Hague Convention IV, Respecting the Laws and Customs of War on Land, 1907

Human Rights Committee Report on Question of Impunity of Perpetrators of Human Rights Violations, Civil and Political, U.N. Doc. E/CN.4/Sub.2/1997/20 (1997)

Inter-American Commission on Human Rights Report No. 28/92 of 2 October 1992 on Argentina's Full Stop and Due Obedience Laws

Inter-American Commission on Human Rights Report No. 29/92 of 2 October 1992 on the Uruguayan *Ley de Caducidad*

Inter-American Convention on Extradition, 1981

Inter-American Convention on the Forced Disappearance of Persons, 1994, 33 *ILM* 1429 (1994)

International Convention against the Taking of Hostages (1979), G.A. Res. 34/146, of 17 December 1979

International Convention on the Elimination of All Forms of Racial Discrimination, 1966

International Convention on the Suppression and Punishment of the Crime of Apartheid, 30 November, 1973 GA Res. 3068, UN GAOR, 28th Session, Supp. No. 30, UN Doc. A/9030 (1974)

International Covenant on Civil and Political Rights, 1966, G.A. Res. 2200A (XXI), 21 UN GAOR Supp. No. 16 at 52, UN Doc. A/6316 (1966)

International Covenant on Economic, Social and Cultural Rights, 1966, G.A. Res. 2200A (XXI)

International Law Commission Commentary of the Draft Code of Crimes against the Peace and Security of Mankind, 1996

International Law Commission Draft Articles on Responsibility of States for Internationally Wrongful Acts (2001), Off. Rec. GA 56th Session Supp. No. 10 (A/56/10), chp.IV.E.1

International Law Commission Draft Articles on State Responsibility (1996)

International Law Commission Draft Articles on the Law of Treaties (1964), 264 *AJIL* (1964)

International Law Commission Draft Code of Crimes against the Peace and Security of Mankind, 1996

International Law Commission Finalised Draft Text on the Elements of Crime, Doc. PCNICC/2000/1/Add.2, of 2 November 2000

International Law Commission 13th Report on the Draft Code of Crimes against the Peace and Security of Mankind, 1995

International Law Commission Report on the Draft Code of Crimes against the Peace and Security of Mankind, 1996

Preliminary Report (Louis Joinet) on the "Study on Amnesty Laws and their Role in the Safeguard and Promotion of Human Rights", Special *Rapporteur*, United Nations Commission on Human Rights, U.N. Doc. E/CN.4/Sub.2/1985/16 (1985)

Principles of International Cooperation in the Detection, Arrest, Extradition and Punishment of Persons Guilty of War Crimes and Crimes against Humanity (1973), G.A. Res. 3074 (XXVIII) of 3 December 1973, 28 UN GAOR Supp. No. 30, at 79, UN Doc. A/9030 (1973)

Principles of International Law Recognised in the Charter of the Nuremberg Tribunal and in the Judgement of the Tribunal, 1950, UNGAOR, 5th Session, Supp. No. 12, UN Doc. A/1316 (1950)

Principles on the Effective Prevention and Investigation of Extra-Legal, Arbitrary, and Summary Executions, ECOSOC Res. 1989/65 of 24 May 1989, Annex ECOSOC Off. Rec. 1989, Supp. No. 1, p. 5 (1990), endorsed by GA Res. 44/162 of Dec. 15 1989, GAOR, 44th Sess., Supp. No. 49, p. 235 (1990)

Protocol Additional to the Geneva Conventions of 12 August 1949, and Relating to the Protection of Victims of International Armed Conflicts, 1977

Protocol Additional to the Geneva Conventions of 12 August 1949, and Relating to the Protection of Victims of Non-International Armed Conflicts, 1977

Protocol to the African Charter on Human and Peoples' Rights on the Establishment of an African Court on Human and Peoples' Rights, 1998, OAU Doc., OAU/LEG/EXP/AFCHPR/PROT (III) of 9 June 1998

Question of the Punishment of War Criminals and of Persons who have Committed Crimes against Humanity, G.A. Res. 2840 (XXVI) of 18 December 1971, available at www.un.org/documents/ga/res/26/ares26.htm.

Report of the Inter-American Commission on Human Rights on the Situation of Human Rights in El Salvador, OEA/ser.L/V/II.85 Doc. 28 rev. of 11 February 1994 at 11 & 69–77

Report of the International Law Commission on the Work of its 43rd Session, (1991) G.A.O.R., 46th Sess. Supp. No. 10, U.N. Doc. A/46/10

Report of the Preparatory Committee on the Establishment of an ICC, U.N. GAOR, 51st Sess., vol. 1 Supp. No. 22, U.N. Doc. A/51/22 (1996)

Report of the Secretary-General Pursuant to Paragraph 2 of Security Council Resolution 808 of 3 May 1993, recommending the establishment of the Yugoslavia Tribunal

Rome Statute for the International Criminal Court, UN Doc. A/CONF. 183/9 (17 July, 1998)

Security Council Resolution 748, SCOR, 1992, for the Extradition of Libyan Suspects in the Lockerbie Bombing, 1992

Security Council Resolution 948, 1994, on the return to Haiti of President Aristide, 1994

Security Council Resolution 837, SCOR, 1993, for the Arrest and Prosecution of the Somali Warlord Mohamed Aidid, 1993

Security Council Resolution 827, SCOR, 25 May 1993, Establishing the International Tribunal for the Prosecution of Persons Responsible for Serious Violations of International Humanitarian Law Committed in the Territory of Former Yugoslavia Since 1991

Security Council Resolution 955, SCOR, 8 November 1994, Establishing the International Criminal Tribunal for the Prosecution of Persons Responsible for Genocide and Other Serious Violations of International Humanitarian Law Committed in the Territory of Rwanda and of Neighbouring States between 1 January and 31 December

Security Council Resolution 1315 of 14 August 2000 establishing the Special Court for Sierra Leone, available at http://www.specialcourt.org/documents/Statute.html

Security Council Resolution 1593 of 31 March 2005 referring the situation in Darfur/Sudan since 1 July 2002 to the Prosecutor of the International Criminal Court

Slavery Convention of 1926 as amended on 7 December, 1953 by the Supplementary Convention on the Abolition of Slavery, the Slave Trade, and Institutions and Practices Similar to Slavery; Adopted by Economic and Social Council Resolution 608 (XXI) of 30 April 1956; entered into force on 30 April 1957

Statute of the International Criminal Tribunal for the former Yugoslavia, S/RES/808 (1993)

Statute of the International Criminal Tribunal for Rwanda, S/RES/935 (1994)

Statute of the International Court of Justice, 1946

Statute of the Special Court for Sierra Leone, annexed to the Agreement between the United Nations and the Government of Sierra Leone pursuant to Security Council Resolution 1315 of 14 August 2000 (as amended on 16 January 2002)

United Nations Secretary-General Report on the Salvadorian amnesty laws of 1992 and 1993, UN Doc. S/25812 of 21 May 1993

United Nations Commission on Human Rights Report on the Consequences of Impunity U.N. Doc. E/CN.4/1990/13 (1990)

United Nations Declaration on Territorial Asylum, G.A. Res. 2312 (XXII) of 14 Dec, 1967, U.N. GAOR, 22nd Sess., Supp. No. 16, U.N. Doc. A/6716 1967

United Nations Human Rights Committee Comment on the Situation of Human Rights in Uruguay, UN Doc CCPR/C/79/Add. 19 (1993)

United Nations Human Rights Committee General Comment No. 20 (44), UN Doc CCPR/ C21/Rev.1/Add.3, (April 1992)
Uniting for Peace Resolution, GA Res. 377 (V) of 3 November 1950, GAOR (V) Supp. No. 20, (1950)
Universal Declaration of Human Rights, GA Res. 217 A (III) of 10 December 1948, UN Doc. A/810 (1948)
Vienna Convention on the Law of Treaties, 1969

National Legal Instruments

Argentina

Argentina Amnesty Nullification Law No. 23.040 of 27 December 1983
Argentina Due Obedience Law No. 23521 of 4 June 1987
Argentina Full Stop Law No. 23492 of 23 December 1986
Argentina Law of National Pacification, Law No. 22.924 of 22 September 1983
Argentina Presidential Decree No. 1002/89 of 6 October 1989 and Decree No. 2741/90 of 29 December 1990

Chile

Chilean Amnesty Decree Law No. 2.191 of 18 April 1978

East Timor

Regulation No. 2001/10 on the Establishment of a Commission of Reception, Truth and Reconciliation in East Timor, UNTAET/REG/2001/10 of 13 July 2001, available at http:// www.un.org/peace/etimor/untaetR/Reg10e.pdf.
Regulation No. 2000/15 on the Establishment of Panels with Exclusive Jurisdiction Over Serious Criminal Offences, East Timor UNTAET/REG/2000/15 of 6 June 2000, available at http://www.un.org/peace/etimor/untaetR/Reg0015E.pdf.

El Salvador

Law on General Amnesty for the Consolidation of Peace, Decree No. 486 of 20 March 1993

Haiti

Pact of New York of 16 July 1993 providing for amnesty to human rights offenders in Haiti (Doc. S/26297)

Israel

Isreali Nazi and Nazi Collaborators Act of 1950

Liberia

Truth and Reconciliation Commission Act of Liberia, 2005

Sierra Leone

Statute of the Special Court for Sierra Leone, 2002

South Africa

Constitution of the Republic of South Africa Act 200 of 1993
Further Indemnity Act 151 of 1992
Government Gazette No. 12470, 17 May 1990
Government Gazette No. 12834, 7 November 1990
Government Gazette No. 12838, 9 November 1990
Government Gazette No. 14401, 9 November 1992
Government Gazette No. 16774, 16 October 1995
Groote Schuur Minute (the), 4 May 1990, reprinted in 6 *SAJHR* (1990), pp. 318–324
Indemnity Act 35 of 1990
Pretoria Minute (the), of 6 August 1990, reprinted in 6 *SAJHR* (1990), pp. 318–324
Promotion of National Unity and Reconciliation Act 34 of 1995
Promotion of National Unity and Reconciliation Amendment, Act 87 of 1995
Separate Registration of Voters Bill, 1951

Case Law

Amnesty Case in El Salvador, Supreme Court Decision of 20 May 1993, Proceedings No. 10–93
Attorney-General of the Government of Israel v. Eichmann, District Court of Jerusalem 1961, 36 *ILR* (1962)
Azanian Peoples Organisation (AZAPO) and Others v. President of the Republic of South Africa, 1996 (8) BCLR 1015 (CC); 1996 (4) SA 671 (CC)
Azanian Peoples Organisation (AZAPO) and Others v. Truth and Reconciliation Commission 1996 (4) SA 562
Barcelona Traction, Light and Power Co. Ltd. (Belgium v. Spain), Second Phase of the Judgment, ICJ, 5 February 1970, *ICJ Reports* (1970)
Boaboeram v. Surinam, Comm. No. 146/1983 and No. 148–154/1983, 40 UN GAOR, Supp. No. 40, Annex X, UN Doc A/40/40 (1985)
Case BGH St 2, German Federal Court Decision
Case Concerning Military and Paramilitary Activities in and against Nicaragua (Nicaragua v. United States of America), ICJ Judgment, 27 June 1986, available at www.icj-cij. org/icjwww/icases/inus/inus_ijudgment/inus_ijudgment_19860627.pdf.
Case Concerning the Application of the Convention on the Prevention and Punishment of the Crime of Genocide (Bosnia and Herzegovina v. Yugoslavia (Serbia and Montenegro)), ICJ, Advisory Opinion of 8 April 1993, *ICJ Reports* (1993)
Coetzee and Others v. Government of the Republic of South Africa (Case No. CCT 19/94) 1995 (4) SA 631 (CC)
Corfu Channel Case (United Kingdom v. Albania), ICJ, Judgment of 9 April 1949, *ICJ Reports* (1949)
Dagli v. Togo, African Commission on Human Rights, Communication No. 83/92, available at www.achpr.org
Danube Case, PCIJ Series B, No. 14 (1927)
Fédération Nationale des Déportés et Internés Résistants et Patriotes and Others v. Klaus Barbie, 78 *ILR* (1988)
Filartiga v. Pena-Irala, U.S. 630F. 2d 876 (2d Cir. 1980)
Fisheries Case, (Norway/United Kingdom) ICJ Judgment, *ICJ Reports* (1951)

Greek Case, (European Court of Human Rights), 12 *YECHR* 511 (Suppl.) (1969)

Hostages Case (The), *U.S.A v. Von List and Others*, 11 *Trials of War Criminals Before the Nuremberg Military Tribunal Under Control Council Law No. 10, Oct. to Apr. 1949* (1950)

In re Eisenträger and Others, U.S. Military Command, Shanghai (1947), 14 *IMT Reports* (1949)

Ireland v. The United Kingdom (European Court of Human Rights), Appl. No. 00005310 of 18–01–78), available at http://www.echr.coe.int; 25 *ECHR* (Ser. A) (1978)

Leander v. Sweden, Application No. 9248/81, European Court of Human Rights, (1987), 9 *EHRR* 433

Legal Consequences for States of the Continued Presence of South Africa in Namibia (South West Africa) Notwithstanding Security Council Resolution 276 (1970), ICJ Advisory Opinion of 21 June 1971, *ICJ Reports* (1971)

Legality of the Threat or Use of Nuclear Weapons, ICJ Advisory Opinion of 8 July 1996, reprinted in 17 *HRLJ* No. 7–10 (1996)

Lorsé v. Netherlands, Application No. 52750/99, European Court of Human Rights, reprinted in 37 *EHRR* 3 (2003)

Lotus Case (France v. Turkey), 1927, Judgment of the PCIJ, Ser. A. (Judgments), No. 10 (Judgment No. 9) (1927)

Lotus Case (France v. Turkey), 1927), Dissenting Opinion of Judge Moore, text available at www.worldcourts.com/pcij/eng/decisions/1927.09.07_lotus/dissent_more.htm.

Mekongo v. Cameroon, African Commission on Human Rights Communication No. 59/91

Muteba v. Zaire, Comm. No. 124/1982, 39 UN GAOR, Supp. No. 40, Annex XIII, UN Doc A/39/39/40 (1984)

North Sea Continental Shelf Cases, (Federal Republic of Germany/Denmark; Federal Republic of Germany/The Netherlands, ICJ, Judgement of 20 February, 1969), *ICJ Reports* 3 (1969)

Prosecutor v. Anto Furundzija, ICTY, Case No. IT-95-17/1-T *"Lasva Valley"*, TC, 10 December 1998

Prosecutor v. Clement Kayishema and Obed Ruzindana, Case No. ICTR-95-1-T, 21 May 1999

Prosecutor v. Dragoljub Kunarac, Radomir Kovac and Zoran Vukovic, ICTY, Cases No. IT-96-23 and No. IT-96-23/1, *"Foca"*, 22 February 2001

Prosecutor v. Drazen Erdemovic, ICTY, Case No. IT-96-22-T, (TC. I, 29 November, 1996), (Appeal Chamber, 7 October 1997), (TC II, 5 March 1998)

Prosecutor v. Dusko Tadic, ICTY Case No. IT-94-1-AR72, Appeals Chamber, Decision on the Defense Motion for Interlocutory Appeal on Jurisdiction, 2 October 1995

Prosecutor v. Dusko Tadic, ICTY, Case No. IT-94-1-T, TC II, 7 May 1997

Prosecutor v. Dusko Tadic, ICTY, Case No. IT-94-1-A, Appeals Chamber, 15 July 1999

Prosecutor v. Dusko Tadic A/K/A "Dule", ICTY, T. C. Decision on the Defence Motion on Jurisdiction, 10 August 1995

Prosecutor v. Ferninand Nahimana, Jean-Bosco Barayagwisa, Hassan Ngeze, Case No. ICTR-99-52-T, 3 December 2003

Prosecutor v. Jean Paul Akayesu, Case No. ICTR-96-4-T, T C I, 2 September 1998

Prosecutor v. Kupreskic et al., ICTY, Case No. IT-95-16-T, T C II, 14 January 2000

Prosecutor v. Morris Kallon; Brima Bazzy Kamara, Case No. SCSR-04-15-PT-060-II, Appeals Chamber Decision on Challenge to Jurisdiction: Lomé Accord Agreement, 13 March 2004

Prosecutor v. Radovan Karadzic and Ratko Mladic, ICTY Cases No. IT-95-5-R 61 and No. IT-95-18-R 61

Prosecutor v. Tihomir Blaskic, ICTY, Case No. IT-95-14, T C, 3 March 2000

Prosecutor v. Zdravko Mucic et al., ICTY, Case No. IT-96-21 *"Celebici Camp"*, 9 October 2001

Prosecutor v. Zlatka Aleksovsky, ICTY, Case No. IT-95-14-1, "*Lasva Valley*", TC I, 25 June, 1999

Quinteros v. Uruguay, Comm. No. 107/1981, 38 UN GAOR, Supp. No. 40, Annex XXII, UN Doc A/38/40 (1983)

Ramirez v. Canada: Minister of Employment and Immigration, 1992, 2 Federal Court 306, 89 DLR (4th) 173, 135 NR 390 (CA)

Re Krupp and Ten Others, US Military Tribunal at Nuremberg, reprinted in 15 *ILR* (1948)

Re Ohlendorf and Others, US Military Tribunal at Nuremberg, reprinted in 15 *ILR* (1948)

Regina v. Bartle and the Commissioner of Police for the Metropolis and Others Ex Parte Pinochet 38 *ILM* 581 (1999)

Regina v. Bartle and the Commissioner of Police for the Metropolis and Others Ex Parte Pinochet 37 *ILM* 1302 (1998)

Regina v. Imre Finta, (1994) 1 Supreme Court of Canada (SCR), 701 1994

Republic of Ireland v. The United Kingdom, Series A, No. 25 (January 1978), 2 *EHRR* 25 (1978)

Reservations to the Genocide Convention, ICJ Advisory Opinion of 28 May 1951, *ICJ Reports* (1951)

Right of Passage Case, ICJ Reports (1960)

Romo Mena Case, Corte Suprema de Chile, 26 October 1995

S. v. Makwanyane and Mchunu 1995 (6) BCLR 665 (CC), 1995 (3) SA 391 (CC)

S. v. Mhlungu and Others 1995 (3) SA 867 (CC)

Soering v. United Kingdom, Series A, No. 161, Application No. 14038/88 (7 July 1989), 11 *EHRR* 439 (1989), London, Sweet & Maxwell Ltd.

Trial of Border Guards, Berlin State Court, Docket No. (523) 2 Js 48/90 (9/91)

USA v. Flick et al, Law Reports of the Trial of the Major War Criminals before the IMT (1947), 171

Velasquez Rodriguez Case, 4 Inter-American Court of Human Rights (Ser C) No. 4 (1988), at 174

Vukovar Hospital Case (*Mile Mrksic, Miroslav Radic, Veselin Sljivancanin*), ICTY, Case No IT-95-13-R 61, 3 April 1996

Websites

http://www.el-mouradia.dz/français/algerie/histoire/accord%20evian.htm
http://www.yale.edu/lawweb/avalon/westphal.htm (Westphalia Peace Treaty of 1648)
http://www.historicaldocuments.com/TreatyofParis1763.htm
http://www.napoleon-series.org
http://www.napoleon-series.org/research/government/diplomatic/c_amiens.html
http://www.napoleon-series.org/research/government/diplomatic/c_luneville.html
http://www.zum.de/psm/div/ostsee/mowat24.php3
http://www.firstworldwar.com/source/armisticeterms.htm
http://www.lib.byu.edu/~rdh/wwi/1918p/lausanne.html
http://www.yale.edu/lawweb/avalon/imtfech.htm
http://www.courttv.com/archive/casefiles/nuremberg/jackson.html
http://www.deoxy.org/wc/wc-nurem.htm
http://www.google.com (The Dayton Peace Accords)
http://www.org.za/back/justice.htm (Memorandum annexed to the South African Promotion of National Unity and Reconciliation Bill available)
http://www.yahoo.fr/actualités (Argentina new Nullification Law of 2003); consulted on 17 August 2003 at 21:05)

http://www.un.org/icc (Status of the ratification of the Rome Statute for an International
Criminal Court as of 29 March, 2003)

http://www1.umn.edu/humanrts/instree/z1afchar.htm (Text of the African Charter on Human
and Peoples' Rights

http://www.un.org/Overview/rights.html (Text of the Universal Declaration of Human Rights,
1948)

http://www.unhchr.ch/html/menu3/b/treaty1gen.htm (Status of the ratification of the Genocide
Convention)

http://www.polity.org/govdocs/legislation.za (Text of the South African Amnesty Act)

http://www.iss.co.za/AF/RegOrg/unity_to_union/pdfs/ecowas/4ConExtradition.pdf (Text of the
Economic Community of West African States Convention on Extradition, 1994)

http://www.conventions.coe.int/treaty/EN/treaties/Html/024.htm (Text of the European Convention on Extradition, 1957)

http://www.oas.org/juridico/english/treaties/b-47(1).html (Text of the Inter-American Convention on Extradition, 1981)

http://www.unhchr.ch/html/menu3/b/o_c_ref.htm (Text of the Convention Relating to the
Status of Refugees, 1951)

http://www.conventions.coe.int/treaty/en/treaties/Html/086.htm (Text of the Additional Protocol to the European Convention on Extradition, 1975)

http://www.javier-leon-diaz.com/humanitarianIssues/State_Resp.pdf (Text of the International
Law Commission Draft Articles on State Responsibility, 1996)

http://www.un.org/law/ilc/texts/treaties.htm (Text of the Vienna Convention on the Law of
Treaties, 1969)

http://www.fr.news.yahoo.com/030514/5/370cz.html (Text of the UN General Assembly accord
approving the creation of a war crime tribunal for Cambodia)

INDEX

Faustin Z. Ntoubandi, Amnesty for Crimes against Humanity under International Law, pp. 249–252.
© 2007, *Koninklijke Brill NV. Printed in The Netherlands.*